Children of the Silent Majority

Children of the Silent Majority

Young Voters and the Rise of the
Republican Party, 1968–1980

Seth Blumenthal

 University Press of Kansas

© 2018 by the University Press of Kansas
All rights reserved

Published by the University Press of Kansas (Lawrence, Kansas 66045), which was
organized by the Kansas Board of Regents and is operated and funded by Emporia
State University, Fort Hays State University, Kansas State University, Pittsburg State
University, the University of Kansas, and Wichita State University.

Library of Congress Cataloging-in-Publication Data is available.
ISBN 978-0-7006-2701-1 (cloth : alk. paper)
ISBN 978-0-7006-2702-8 (ebook)

British Library Cataloguing-in-Publication Data is available.

Printed in the United States of America

10 9 8 7 6 5 4 3 2 1

The paper used in this publication is recycled and contains 30 percent
postconsumer waste. It is acid free and meets the minimum requirements of
the American National Standard for Permanence of Paper for Printed Library
Materials Z39.48-1992.

Dedicated to Mom, Penelope, and Reese

Contents

Acknowledgments

I owe so many thanks for the support I received even before this project's start. First, David Dowdy awakened my passion for writing, and I will always remember his caring and rigorous ability to promote the humanity this skill requires. The professors I met at Colby College introduced me to the controversies and debates that deepened my curiosity in American history. Special thanks to the legend Charlie Bassett, who helped set my career path as a teacher and scholar.

Vincent Cannato played an instrumental role in this endeavor, and I am truly in debt to the model he provided as a caring and trusted mentor. This project originated as a research paper in Brooke Blower's provocative course, and her role continued throughout the dissertation process. In addition, Jonathan Zatlin and Sarah Phillips always offered helpful, thoughtful, and considerate suggestions. I also thank Jon Roberts and the graduate student dissertation workshop for valuable insight and feedback. In addition, my colleagues in the Boston University (BU) Writing Program have continually been supportive and provided welcomed camaraderie. Of course, Bruce Schulman deserves my deepest gratitude for his friendship as well as his caring and wise guidance.

This research process took me from Boston to Los Angeles; Washington, DC; Tennessee; Ann Arbor; and Princeton; and then back to LA. Along the way, I relied on staff in several archives at the John F. Kennedy Presidential Library, the National Archives, the Richard Nixon Presidential Library, the Ronald Reagan Presidential Library, the Gerald Ford Presidential Library, the Modern Political Archives in the Howard H. Baker Center, and Special Collections at Princeton University and Lipscomb University. In addition, Rick Perlstein and Maurice Immerman graciously shared personal papers. Last, I thank the former members of Nixon's campaign and leaders of the Young Voters for the President for agreeing to interviews about their experience in 1972. This was an amazing opportunity, and I wrote this book with their perspective in mind. I received generous funding for this research from the Ford Library, BU's Metcalfe Dissertation Fellowship, and the Engelbourg Travel Grant as well as generous contributions for publication production from the Boston University College of Arts and Sciences and the Boston University Center for the Humanities. Thank you to friends who gave me shelter during my travels, including Dewitt Hobart Antik and Randy and Nancy Berry. I appreciate the time and energy Charles Myers put into acquiring the manuscript, and David Congdon and the editing team for taking on the project and managing the production process for the University Press of Kansas.

Of course, none of this would be possible without family. First, I am grateful to the Cavallo family and for the Venetian Moon Writing Fellowship. Thanks to Richard Blumenthal and Julie Weiman for their support and encouragement, which has always been a source of comfort for me. Peter Blumenthal, my father, thank you for keeping faith despite all the evidence. Renee, this is as much your accomplishment as it is mine. Throughout this process, your patience and love always kept me moving forward.

Introduction

On January 20, 1973, Richard Nixon celebrated his inauguration with the silent majority's loudest, youngest supporters. After his landslide victory, Nixon tapped the 1972 campaign's Young Voters for the President director, Ken Rietz, to organize the inaugural events that one journalist described as "colossal," with an impressive $4 million price tag, while White House aide Jeb Magruder vowed to bring the "best inauguration ever."[1] Since Nixon requested this "heavy accent on youth," his inauguration planners acceded, as one explained, "after all, it's his party. President Nixon is pretty dedicated to these youngsters who confounded the experts."[2]

Specifically, the celebration focused on young supporters with the slogan, "the Spirit of '76." First, the Inaugural Committee planned an unprecedented youth concert at the Kennedy Center as the Mike Curb Congregation entertained thousands of the twelve thousand invited young campaign workers.[3] On the formal side, while Nixon attended five elegant black-tie events that night, the first-ever Youth Ball served as the perfect setting for Nixon's most lively appearance of the evening. Si Zentner's orchestra sounded so good to the president, he decided to invite any "girls" at the event to dance with him after the first song with his wife. After cutting in on the first couple, one young Nixonette blushed when recalling her presidential moment, joking that she "could have danced all night." However, Nixon let her go after just one song with a hug and a kiss as he had to make time for nine other young women.[4] An exuberant Nixon then climbed on stage in his tux and told his Young Voters for the President, "I see you so young and so virtuous with all your hopes . . . I want to make the next four years the best that can happen."[5] In the wake of Nixon's reelection, before the chaos of Watergate, these young supporters inspired Nixon's vision for his second term and the GOP's future. This moment represented both the height of Richard Nixon's political career and the beginning of young voters' prominent role in the Republican Party.

In 1971, the ratification of the Twenty-Sixth Amendment guaranteed eleven million Americans between the ages of eighteen and twenty the right to vote, contributing to an unprecedented explosion of young voters. This development caused concern in Nixon's administration when experts identified the youth vote as antiwar and left leaning, arguing that the voting booth offered "a fresh sense of power and identity to a generation that until now could test its muscles only in the politics of street protest."[6] After all, a *Life* magazine article in 1972 claimed "the margin of new Democrats over Republicans is roughly 5–2, even in GOP strongholds."[7]

Two obvious factors—the 1960s youth revolt and Nixon's tough stance on the Vietnam War—motivated Democrats' confidence with young voters. Furthermore, Nixon's advisers feared that his "law and order" image personified the gap between the generations and fueled young voters' reluctance to support the president. Additionally, in a time when young Americans warned each other never to trust anyone over thirty, one of Nixon's critics mused that he "seems the kind of kid who [must have] always carried a bookbag. Who was 42 years old the day he was born."[8] Pictures of Nixon dodging the surf while wearing a suit and wingtips further cemented his square reputation. In 1971, before Nixon's campaign managers knew their opponent, pundits, political scientists, and even Nixon's personal pollster, Robert Teeter, predicted potent youth support for the Democratic challenger.[9]

His sights set on a landslide victory, however, Nixon proclaimed that "there can be no generation gap in America" and resolved to fold young people into his constituency.[10] Despite the widespread assumption that the vast segment of young voters casting ballots for the first time would tilt the electorate to the Democratic Party, this book reveals how Republicans recruited young Americans not aligned with the left—people Nixon's staff called the "sons and daughters of the silent majority." After the nation ratified the Twenty-Sixth Amendment in record time, the Committee to Re-elect the President (CRP) promptly established Young Voters for the President (YVP), which included over four hundred thousand members and received unequaled funding and autonomy within the Nixon campaign. Surprisingly, Nixon earned youth's trust and split the youth vote, as one Gallup poll even showed 57 percent of the voters under thirty years old found the president "more sincere and believable" than his antiwar opponent, Senator George McGovern (D-South Dakota).[11]

Children of the Silent Majority investigates the emergence of young Americans as a major force in national politics, arguing that while the

1968 generation initially threatened the conservative realignment that Republican leaders envisioned, it eventually fortified the GOP with a cadre of new voters and party leaders after the voting age fell to eighteen. Recent scholarship on this generation has explored an international cohort that shared a lasting and influential radical political sensibility.[12] While this historiography on the American 1968 generation looks almost exclusively at radicals and long-hairs as part of a transnational movement, most young people did not fit that mold. The 1968 generation in America, however, had unique characteristics that drove the country's political direction both toward and away from liberal policies.

This focus on youth politics within the context of the Republican Party's rise to power after 1968 provides a corrective to the narrative that emphasizes Nixon's antagonistic relationship and conflict with the generation gap.[13] While some of these interpretations show Nixon had a draconian and authoritarian side, others point out that the youth revolt also confused and "discombobulated" Nixon. According to Rick Perlstein, campus turmoil and the generation gap had Nixon "politically on the run."[14] Complicating this approach, scholars have added that Nixon stemmed domestic unrest with youth and African Americans through nuanced, even "Machiavellian" counterintuitive political concessions. Although Nixon's "Black Capitalism" initiative fell short of expectations, Robert Weems and Lewis Randolph argue, it "did help Nixon achieve his larger ideological goal of domestic 'détente' by 'containing' potential domestic black radicalism."[15] In addition, Jeremi Suri points to Kent State as a key factor in motivating Nixon's foreign policy of détente to marginalize radicals on the left. However, while Nixon succeeded in "isolating domestic opponents," Suri argues, "many protesters turned away from politics entirely in the next decade."[16]

For moderate youth, however, Nixon's generational détente included a youth-focused policy agenda, campaign organization, and image that supported Nixon's massive effort to include these young voters into his "silent majority." The YVP established a constituency and leadership cohort for the party's future while it opened the Republican Party to new methods that facilitated the GOP's shift away from both its "backlash" reputation and "country club–big business image."[17] This outreach to young voters signaled the underappreciated history of youth politics and reveals that the press, pundits, Democrats, student radicals, and even some Republicans were wrong about the youth vote.

Research on the 1960s "nonshouters," such as Wayne Thorburn's

A Generation Awakes and John Andrew's *The Other Side of the Sixties*, documents the rise of the devout conservative group Young Americans for Freedom (YAF) to debunk the 1960s mythology that emphasizes "the causes on the New Left to the exclusion of almost anything else."[18] That emphasis, however, develops a counternarrative of the Right to the exclusion of Nixon's less dogmatic young supporters. While YAF activists carried Republican youth politics in the 1960s, the Nixon administration asserted its chances with a wider section of youth: as Charles Colson wrote H. R. Haldeman, "it is very difficult to draw conclusions on last year's experience and even riskier to project what may lie ahead a year hence."[19] With a targeted approach, Nixon's advisers hoped, the youth vote could even become Republican!

At first, Nixon and his advisers took caution and acted defensively to blunt the youth vote's challenge to Nixon's conservative policy agenda. Young voters' increasing influence after 1968 played an important role in determining Nixon's positions on the environment, the Vietnam War, the military draft, and other controversial topics. An examination of the Republican Party's presidential youth efforts during this period shows that young Americans' increasing political roles influenced issues. During Nixon's first term, this generation's independence pushed the GOP and Nixon to moderate the party platform.

Thirty-two percent of twenty-one-to-twenty-four-year-old voters registered as independent in 1964; 52 percent did so in 1972.[20] In an odd twist, the process of declaring themselves as independent linked young voters to a larger, shared political sensibility. Three developments created this rising independence. First, more educated young Americans challenged their parents' politics and developed their own political views, as high school graduation rates rose from 63 to over 80 percent during the 1960s and college enrollment doubled. Second, young voters from traditionally Democratic strongholds such as urban, ethnic, white, and working-class enclaves in the North also broke away from party loyalties. Last, as the political scientist Louis M. Seagull claimed in 1971, party identification and party machines lost the "glue-giving function" because of "mass media and communication."[21] The politics of image also eroded political loyalties that had determined older Americans' votes. Thus, the GOP stood poised to challenge the Democratic Party's claim to the political future.

In the wake of Watergate, this opportunity seemed squandered as the conservative columnist Robert Novak called the Republican Party "a laughing stock among young voters."[22] Yet, young Republicans in the late 1970s revived Nixon's youth constituency and organizational approach to rebuild the GOP. In 1977, Senator Bill Brock (R-Tennessee) became the Republican Party's chairman and utilized the grassroots strategy that he oversaw as the YVP chairman in 1972. Young voters and youth issues have played a central role in the Republican Party's transition from the minority to the majority party after 1968, as Nixon's youth campaign also encouraged the organization and strategy for Ronald Reagan's victories during the 1980s. Youth for Reagan, boasting one hundred thousand members, provided the votes, volunteers, and organizational strategy to build the GOP into a majority party during the 1980s. This book evaluates that long-term influence but also explains that the GOP in the 1980s honed a youth strategy that started during the Nixon era.

Over the past twenty-five years, three problems have dominated historical scholarship on the political history of the postwar United States. First, historians have focused on the rise and fall of the so-called New Deal order. In particular, they have offered rival explanations for the collapse of the liberal electoral coalition that had prevailed since the 1930s. The turmoil of the late 1960s—conflicts over war, race, campus radicalism, and law-and-order issues—detached reliably Democratic voters from their previous allegiances.[23] If many historians focused on the defection of the "silent majority," voters who had supported Kennedy, Johnson, and other Democrats, a second line of analysis has focused on the rise of the Right. This literature examines the development of the conservative movement—the mobilization and maturation of a New Right in precincts (like burgeoning Sunbelt suburbs) and among constituencies (like previously quiescent evangelical Protestants) that exerted little influence on national politics before the 1960s.[24] Finally, scholars across many disciplines have analyzed the period's tectonic shifts in the structure and style of political competition as well as its content. Over the course of the 1960s and 1970s, mass media became the central means of political communication and mobilization, convincing participants and observers of the political potency of carefully crafted images.[25] Specifically, scholars credit or blame Nixon for the dominance of symbolic campaign efforts to define a candidate's image.[26] According to David Greenberg, "Americans came to believe that politics revolves around the construction and manipulation of images—a shadow that Nixon still casts upon our age."[27]

Children of the Silent Majority makes important contributions to these ongoing debates; indeed, this study reveals the centrality of youth politics to all three of these scholarly controversies. First, as the South no longer provided the Democratic Party a dependable electoral region to maintain the New Deal order after 1964, young voters became a central target in liberals' attempt to form a new constituency that would replace the traditionally reliable voters from the Sunbelt. Young people during and after the 1960s, however, carried an independent political position that made this youth realignment difficult and opened a political generation to choosing the GOP. Not only did the Democrats' youth campaign fall short; it also created a devastating cleavage between the party establishment, such as labor leaders, and party reformers like McGovern. Second, while campus protesters and young radicals dominated public perceptions of young people in the 1960s, Republicans rallied a burgeoning evangelical youth population from the South, campus conservatives, and young urban ethnics who found the GOP an attractive alternative to the Democratic Party.[28] Simplistic and derisive interpretations of these young voters have overlooked their significance. As Samuel Freedman wrote in his book about young conservative party switchers after the 1960s, "For all their importance, few groups of voters have been so stripped of depth and complexity."[29] This book shows that shrewd Republican leaders utilized this growing segment to build an infrastructure for training and leadership that fostered the party's future successes. Finally, the 1968 generation, raised in the era of television and carrying an independent sensibility that rejected party affiliation, encouraged new forms of media and targeted campaign methods that pushed politicians to adapt to the realities of a more fluid electorate after the 1960s. *Children of the Silent Majority* also explores how youth politics fueled the politics of image in presidential campaigns between 1968 and 1980, compelling candidates to embrace the visual turn that emphasized their personal characteristics over party loyalty.

This book pursues a narrative that both examines political elites' organization around youth politics from the top down and shows how movement politics intersects with party politics from the bottom up. While historians and contemporary pundits alike question the role young Americans play in the political process, the YVP in fact required massive resources that Nixon's campaign dedicated to the youth vote and also forced significant political change in policy, organization, and style.[30] By showing this relationship, I argue that the youth vote emerged in the 1960s and 1970s as an essential component to the rise of the Right and enabled Reagan's electoral victories that marked the GOP's apex in recent electoral politics.

The first two chapters examine Nixon's law-and-order approach, which attacked American youth's permissive culture to attract older voters during 1968—as Democratic candidates such as Robert Kennedy and Eugene McCarthy had mobilized young voters. Agreeing with the political consultants who defined "middle-America" as "the un-black, the un-poor and the un-young,"[31] in addition, Nixon struggled to find young voters, as ideological purists in Young Americans for Freedom preferred more convincing conservatives such as Ronald Reagan while moderate and independent youth proved elusive.

Thus, Nixon rallied social conservatives in urban ethnic enclaves, in the Sunbelt, and in the suburbs against rebellious young people. Still, Nixon implemented and adapted this hard approach to the politics of youth after winning the White House. Nixon's tough stance on controversial youth issues such as marijuana use and campus unrest underlined his constituency's exasperation with young Americans' permissive protest culture. Even though law and order had fueled Nixon's 1968 campaign, he realized that stance created a structural barrier in his project to usher in a conservative era in American politics. As Nixon's chief of staff H. R. Haldeman characterized a polling report, "Harris believes that all kids tend to identify with each other, they stick together. More than any other generation, they resent being talked down to by their elders" and "it is almost impossible to attack one without attacking all."[32] "They discovered," as Michael Flamm argues, "that controlling crime was more difficult than they had led the American people to believe."[33] A tough law-and-order position on marijuana and campus unrest suited Nixon as a campaigner, but this approach proved more difficult to maintain as president. Still, Nixon's law-and-order issues and policies highlighted the square culture he could wield to segment both his student and nonstudent voters.

Chapters 3 and 4 explain that during Nixon's first term, especially after the tragedy at Kent State in 1970, the administration had to find new ways to appear youth friendly. This effort became more important when the voting age dropped to eighteen. Youth issues—the voting age, the environment, and the draft—pushed Nixon to react defensively, owing to his concerns over young Americans' mounting influence and the wider public relations problem this created. The president, though reluctantly, supported policies that one former YVP organizer called "counterintuitive" to soften the "old Nixon" law-and-order reputation.[34]

Searching for a way to reach young voters in 1972, Nixon found a New Republican, Bill Brock, who rejected the GOP's reputation as the same old party of the "tired and dreary." Several young Republicans joined Brock; as one journalist noted, "Until 1966 . . . Democrats seemed to have a monopoly of political sex appeal."[35] In 1970, Brock's successful campaign to unseat Senator Albert Gore (D-Tennessee) proved the perfect model as he established a Youth for Brock campaign that attracted more young voters than the liberal, antiwar incumbent. In addition to his conservative base, Brock attracted moderates with television- and media-based strategies to circumvent the existing party structure that favored Democrats. While Nixon's Southern Strategy to end the Democratic Party's dominance below the Mason-Dixon line failed (at least in 1970), he eagerly eyed Brock's neatly packaged, youth-focused campaign—and Brock's campaign manager, former public relations executive Kenneth Rietz. In 1971, Nixon hired Brock and Rietz to organize the autonomous, heavily funded youth campaign for his own reelection.

Chapters 5 and 6 show that young voters offered a tantalizing yet problematic segment for Democrats and Republicans. Challenging President Richard Nixon in 1972, Senator George McGovern encouraged Democratic Party reforms that expanded the influence of youth and tied his electoral hopes to young voters. However, McGovern's attempt to ride a youth organization branded his campaign with the radical reputation as the candidate for "Acid, Amnesty and Abortion." McGovern's campaign manager, Robert Kennedy holdover Frank Mankiewicz, tried in vain to counter the senator's "three A's" stigma. His attempt after the convention to shift back to traditional Democratic voters lacked the necessary organization. The results proved disastrous, as Nixon lost only Massachusetts and the District of Columbia in the general election. Despite its liberal reputation, the youth vote also represented an opportunity for New Republicans.

A focus on youth politics from 1968 to 1972 explains that even though Nixon fell short of the electoral realignment he desired, the Republican Party cultivated a youth cohort that strengthened the GOP for decades.[36] YVP's leaders united conservatives on campuses, brought young southern independents into the GOP, and fortified training networks for young Republicans to fine-tune their ability to "Get Out the Vote." Young leaders in the Republican Party welcomed this opportunity, as organizers such as Karl Rove made important contributions to the Fieldman training schools that attracted a new cadre of young voters to the GOP. In addition, Nixon's youth campaign tested the Republicans' new methods and strategies to develop a carefully structured, though autonomous, branch of the CRP.

Chapter 7 explores how youth politics integrated the politics of image into campaigns, organization, and policy. Young voters' independence privileged image over party loyalty, encouraging politicians to appeal directly to voters through media. Nixon's youth campaign in 1972 focused his campaign's appeal to the rising role of image politics. Tom Wicker of the *New York Times* agreed, as he pointed out that television "allows candidates to go over the heads of organizations and delegates" and "focuses on personality rather than record of party service."[37] The youth vote forced an emphasis on new forms of image politics that undermined traditional party affiliations, attracted young voters, and targeted groups with more segmented efforts. Whether during the convention, at rallies, or in television commercials, Nixon's YVP always had a presence in the campaign. This effort sharpened the targeted and sophisticated campaign methods that would enable the GOP to continue to build a new Republican majority while the Democrats struggled to command the image-focused environment of politics after 1972.

Last, chapter 8 examines youth politics' transition after Watergate, allowing for new, more institutionalized, and less moderate youth politics. In addition, although GOP youth leaders and prominent YVP leaders from 1972 became central, youth outreach became an old man's game. Young voters' turnout fell dramatically from 1972 to 1984, allowing the GOP's highly sophisticated youth organization to win a larger percentage of the youth vote on election day.

While Ford lost young voters to Carter in 1976, 54–46 percent, Ronald Reagan increased his success with the youth vote from 44 percent in 1980 to 61 percent in 1984—two percentage points above the 59 percent of the popular vote that Reagan won in his landslide reelection. After Watergate, young conservatives began the rebuilding process within the GOP that ended with a Republican majority in the 1980s. This version of youth politics, however, became more beholden to special interests and ideological commitments on the right. Motivated by the College Republican Fieldman School model for training young leaders, Morton Blackwell founded the Committee for Responsible Youth Politics in 1972 and oversaw the Reagan-Bush campaign's outreach to youth in

1980 that utilized former YVP leaders and its emphasis on organization and "peer group pressure."

This organization's precedent-setting youth campaign remains obscured for two reasons. First, Watergate tarnished the YVP leaders' standing in politics. After YVP director Ken Rietz testified during the Watergate hearings, admitting that he paid a student to infiltrate a peace vigil, Nixon's downfall stigmatized the YVP. Journalist Jack Anderson called the YVP "a network of young spies and dirty tricksters who came to be called the 'Kiddie Corps.'"[38] While Nixon's demise stunted the career of many YVP leaders, Watergate also distracted political observers from the YVP's strategic innovations.[39] Second, the standard narrative exaggerates this generation's rebellious reputation and dismisses the YVP as a contrived oddity. In his book *Richard Nixon and the Quest for a New Majority*, Robert Mason affirms conventional wisdom, claiming: "An appeal to youth was a notable element in the McGovern campaign. In contrast, Nixon and the Republicans made few overtures to young people."[40] By focusing on this overlooked effort, I argue that the Republican Party in 1972 honed a targeted youth strategy to develop the new majority Nixon envisioned.

1 | New Nixon and the Youth Problem, 1968

Running for president in 1968, Richard Nixon offered a flattering view of the nation's youth, those Americans born during or after World War II. "They are more socially conscious, more politically aware, and much better educated than their parents were at age 18," he gushed in an eighteen-minute October 1968 speech on NBC radio. "Youth today is just not as young as it used to be."[1] Playing to this increasingly influential segment in American politics, Nixon encouraged a mature, independent young cohort to participate in the political process.

Still, even as the candidate painted a sanguine portrait of young Americans and downplayed their challenge to authority, his campaign denounced hippies and protesters to restore "law and order." While Nixon allowed for "socially conscious," "politically aware," and "better educated" young people to participate, he laid down the law against the protest culture. "When they engage in conduct which, in effect, denies to others their rights to listen . . . and occupy buildings and insist on their demands with illegal means," Nixon warned, "then out. . . . They should be out of the universities and colleges."[2] Nixon emphasized his own version of "law and order," explaining it as a reaction against the antiwar, permissive, and extremist image many associated with youth. After all, concerns about the home front no longer revolved around the traditional bread-and-butter issues that favored Democrats while the New Deal coalition reigned. As one union member claimed, "the problem in the streets is more important."[3] Thus, young radicals became a convenient foil for Nixon to prove his conservative credibility with voters from the South and ethnic, white urban enclaves.[4] While the growing role of youth politics and image initiated a new emphasis on young voters in both parties, Nixon's 1968 youth campaign exposed the political contradictions and organizational obstacles he eventually navigated to court the youth vote during his first term.

In 1968, this previously superficial outreach to young supporters took on new complexities when Nixon's campaign began to carve out a segment within this voting bloc that would identify with his silent majority. The 1968 campaign taught Nixon's administration tough and important lessons about organizing young people. Specifically, conservative youth politics, including organizations such as the Young Americans for Freedom and the College Republicans, could not provide substantial, reliable, or loyal support. As the 1968 election showed Democrats the urgent need to include young voters, Nixon's struggle to separate his own young supporters from those on the left and the right confirmed his suspicious, cautious, and even reluctant approach.

New Politics

In the 1968 election, young people contributed to the Democrats' confidence that the party could realign with a new approach, New Politics, that targeted a constituency of young voters, women, and minorities. The New Left's emphasis on transparency and young people's efforts to end the war and racism inspired New Politics' practitioners. Cementing this influence, a group of activists gathered to form the National Conference for New Politics in 1966, seeking a 1968 presidential candidate "committed to peace in Vietnam." Led by civil rights activist Julian Bond, the meeting at the luxurious Berkshire Hotel on New York's Madison Avenue assembled fifty people who represented leadership from the civil rights and antiwar movements. The conference set out to raise a $500,000 fund to support like-minded candidates. Although they could not settle on one for the presidential race, many claimed that Senator Robert Kennedy's interests ran "parallel" to their own.[5] Riding the growing wave of antiwar sentiment, these leaders of American grassroots movements envisioned New Politics as a vehicle for entry into the conventional political system.

For Eugene McCarthy, the antiwar senator from Minnesota, this development offered an unprecedented opportunity to change American politics and include young people's voices. One amused critic claimed that McCarthy sold himself as "the biggest thing that has happened to American youth since marijuana."[6] Working out of their own storefront headquarters, McCarthy's youth cadre of mostly graduate students began to organize six weeks before the first primary in New Hampshire.

This effort relied on carefully planned canvassing efforts and mass mailings but ran on sheer enthusiasm and numbers. Days before the New Hampshire primary, despite the campaign's attempt to cancel eighteen buses of students from across the Eastern Seaboard, over one thousand young volunteers arrived to help the senator's challenge to President Lyndon B. Johnson for the Democratic nomination. McCarthy's young male supporters, hoping to attract the "middle-of-the-road" students that made up the bulk of the young population, made a spectacle of their refined appearance when they publicly shaved their hair to shed the hippie stigma and went "Clean for Gene."[7] One Republican family that took in two student McCarthyites from New Jersey marveled at their devotion: "They get out at 8 o'clock in the morning and don't get home from their headquarters until 2 or 3 in the morning. I don't know where they get the strength."[8] Though they could vote only in the GOP primary, the adoptive parents found McCarthy's volunteers persuasive and pledged to write his name on their Republican ballots. While McCarthy did not win in New Hampshire, he won over 40 percent of the Democratic Party's support. This made LBJ's victory pyrrhic, and vindicated New Politics. Most importantly, as Dump Johnson movement leader Allard Lowenstein planned, antiwar voters in New Hampshire forced LBJ to end his campaign for reelection, promising instead to devote the remainder of his term to peace negotiations.

Bringing "street" politics into the system required some finesse, as the more strident, less compliant volunteers found themselves working behind closed doors. One McCarthy organizer joked, "In the last weekend, we had some large telephone banks and if the newspapers had ever gotten pictures of the telephone banks 'the clean for Gene' myth would have gone right out the window."[9] Despite McCarthy's effort to make New Politics respectable, many antiwar voters worried that he could not win the nomination over the party favorite, Hubert Humphrey. It would take a Kennedy to do that.

Senator Robert Kennedy offered a more viable candidacy for young voters who challenged the party leaders. Before announcing his candidacy in March 1968, Kennedy proclaimed his hope that young Americans would bring about a more active, socially concerned electorate.[10] Kennedy admitted that the South and unions could not provide a reliable constituency for the party, and his book *To Seek a Newer World* explained his plan to recruit "kids" as a vital segment to complement the black and poor white voters that he targeted. As a senator, Kennedy fought against the draft while supporting lowering the voting age. In addition, his law-and-order credentials as the former attorney general and his family's popularity among traditional Democratic constituencies made Kennedy a better choice than McCarthy (who also lacked the charismatic personality necessary to bypass the "smoke-filled room").[11] In February 1968, 38 percent of young voters in a New York State poll supported Kennedy's campaign before it even began. By May, a National Student Presidential Poll showed that Kennedy drew 42 percent of students' support, three times more than McCarthy received.[12] With this momentum, Kennedy's supporters hoped that if Kennedy could win enough delegates through primary victories, he could capture the nomination at the convention.

Robert Kennedy's New Politics built on Democrats' previous dominance with young voters. While John Kennedy's appeal to the New Frontier and his Peace Corps symbolically captured the youthful vision of a new decade, Bobby Kennedy maintained the family's aura of celebrity. Wherever Kennedy went, youngsters ranging from sixteen to twenty-six years old formed "a cheering honor guard" to greet him with the star treatment. The Kennedy Girls, "trim and cute in their blue outfits," which included hats and sashes, served partly as loyal cheerleaders and partly as the adoring, fawning harem one would associate with a rock star. Kennedy's handlers chose the Kennedy Girls based on two criteria: attractiveness and enthusiasm. "Wherever the action is," explained one Kennedy press release for tabloids, "that's where you will find the real live wires of this campaign—the Kennedy Girls."[13] This served Kennedy's first goal—looking good.

Robert Kennedy inherited his older brother's youthful image and used media to build his own brand of New Politics. In California, the Kennedy Girls' numbers reached only 250, but the campaign placed them prominently to energize Kennedy's brand. At one major gala in a southern California arena, Kennedy's Hollywood supporters promoted the Standing Room Only show for RFK with headliners that included popular rock bands such as the Byrds and other celebrities such as Sonny and Cher, actor Jack Lemmon, and Hall of Fame football player Roosevelt Grier.[14] Billed as the "biggest, brightest and swingingest show of this or any other season," advertising for the show conspicuously promoted the event's ushers, the Kennedy Girls.

Hundreds of celebrities immediately volunteered for his campaign, as Sammy Davis Jr. performed on college campuses to rally students for

Figure 1. Kennedy Girls: Supporters cheer Senator Robert F. Kennedy's speech at the TRW Plant in Redondo Beach, California, May 16, 1968. (Courtesy Sven Walnum, JFK Library)

Kennedy. Lesley Gore, the teen sensation who sang "It's My Party" and a member of Sarah Lawrence College's graduating class of 1968, headed the First Time Voters for Kennedy, who targeted the thirteen million new voters. Still, Kennedy understood how to utilize the youth vote, rather than rely on it. The Kennedy Girls also fulfilled less glamorous jobs such as distributing literature at shopping centers, and their more mundane responsibilities at the campaign's headquarters equaled their time at appearances. Kennedy's cautious youth plan found criticism from young voters as well.

In addition, politicians feared a backlash to their campaign if they seemed too enthralled with that image. Critics of this youthful, image-focused politics feared that elections had been handed over to slick ad-men who espoused a superficial youth appeal, as journalist Russell Baker suggested: "Packaging is not good enough. . . . Let's bring back old age. And dignity. And grace."[15] This complaint marked only the beginning of the new political environment that "preferred the beautified candidate to the grizzled."[16] Thus, Kennedy, just as most other politicians did in 1968, maintained his youth cadre's mostly symbolic role.

While young voters became more valuable in his campaign, Kennedy quickly learned of complications. Kennedy's slick political campaign (they called it "cornball exhibitionism") did not always sit well with young voters. After surveying hundreds of campuses, one eminent researcher determined that Kennedy soon became "archaic." Students, increasingly sensitive to distortion and public relations manipulation, found Bobby less sincere, as the report observed that "Senator Kennedy's credibility gap makes President Johnson's look like a crack in the sidewalk."[17] Amid the Vietnam War's assault on American trust, or the credibility gap, these were fighting words. Print journalists also objected. "Even on family raft trips," one joked, "he takes publicists along to aid his self-aggrandizement."[18] Another editorial claimed: "Yes, we believe Bobby is well off . . . casting away the 'new youth' look."[19]

Concerning more substantive positions, the Kennedy campaign initially hesitated to involve young people in its central operations, as one memo to the Washington, DC, office dictated, "*No* college students from the area are to be used to fill *any* volunteer needs at National Headquarters."[20] While this concern spoke to the traditionally limited roles Kennedy's campaign offered to young supporters, the 1968 generation became skeptical of Kennedy's appeal to youthful packaging while young voters desired more authenticity and inclusion. Even student leaders shared their fears about the rise of cynicism when the National Student Association president addressed the nine hundred attendees at the yearly convention by claiming that the "unabashed optimism" young people emitted in 1964 and 1965 had disappeared.[21]

Kennedy's experience on the campaign trail confirmed this cause for concern. In one gathering of sixty-five hundred young people just blocks from the hippie epicenter of Haight-Ashbury in San Francisco, Kennedy defended himself against a barrage of hecklers who chanted "Victory for Vietcong." The senator shouted back, "You should do the

Figure 2. Antiwar students gather for a Robert F. Kennedy campaign speech on the campus of San Fernando Valley State College, California. (Courtesy Sven Walnum, JFK Library)

same thing I did and get a haircut" and turned attention to the "problem of the ghetto or the Negroes" in San Francisco.[22] Building a campaign on more than one issue, Kennedy blunted the radical thrust of young liberals and channeled youth politics into less divisive issues. Racial equality offered New Politics a cause that could rally young liberals rather than the divisive politics of Vietnam. As the campaign progressed and Kennedy gained momentum, young voters quickly earned a more considerable role.

According to Kennedy's campaign coordinator in Indianapolis, Walter Sheridan, the difference between John Kennedy's campaign in 1960 and Robert Kennedy's in 1968 was "not the fact of kid volunteers, but the fact of organized kid volunteers." Sheridan recalled that young white volunteers were "willing to go anyplace and went into the black neighborhoods."[23] Sheridan claimed that Mike Riley, the head of the Young Democrats, "was probably more help than any one person in the city of Indianapolis," noting that "the kids' approach was canvassing, and they felt that by going to a person as a representative of the candidate and as a good-looking representative of the candidate and as a person with a mind of their own, that they could . . . convert them."[24] This approach to politics gained attention within the Kennedy organization, as the candidate "appreciated what they were all about more than most of the pols around him anyway" and "was very interested in gradually working this thing into his idea of the campaign." Kennedy eventually offered students the unprecedented opportunity to serve as "full-fledged members of a presidential delegation to a national convention." This move, gloated a Students for Kennedy release, created the chance for young voters to "become involved in the political process at a meaningful level" and "contribute our ideas as well as our manpower and time."[25] As predicted, Democrats stood poised to capture the 1968 generation.

This version of New Politics did not survive, as an assassin ended Kennedy's bid for president only hours after his hard-fought win in the California primary on June 6. The antiwar senator, George McGovern, accepted Kennedy insiders' requests to pick up the pieces after this tragedy and inherited the decimated organization Kennedy had developed. While McGovern's candidacy lacked recognition and viability, he would turn this short-lived run into a more successful campaign for New Politics in 1972.

After Kennedy's death, a successful youth campaign for Democrats seemed a distant prospect. The 1968 generation's rebellious cohort, despite the "Clean for Gene" effort, did its share in provoking New Politics' critics. Yippies, the New Left's radical wing led by irreverent countercultural heroes such as Abbie Hoffman and Rennie Davis, organized a demonstration outside the Democratic National Convention in Chicago that stirred the backlash to youth politics. Competing with other elements of the New Left such as the National Mobilization Committee to End the War in Vietnam (MOBE), Abbie Hoffman organized Yippie "happenings" in Chicago's Grant Park as they held a ceremony to nominate "Pigasus the Pig" for president. Meanwhile the young throngs in the streets quickly realized their limits when Chicago's police arrested and beat protesters outside the convention as the vice president and establishment candidate Hubert Humphrey won the nomination. While the antiwar demonstrators' politics inspired their protest, their countercultural stigma motivated the police's brutal reaction. Speaking about the protesters, one police officer in Chicago explained, "You can't tell the boys from the girls. They wear their hair alike, and they both cuss the same." The demonstrators' appearance offended this officer's gendered sensibility, accentuating the cultural stakes in the application of "law and order" that emerged in the late 1960s. Mayor Daley dismissed demonstrators as the fringe, claiming they "aren't the youth of this country."[26] Youth politics had fallen victim to the rising role of law and order and the backlash against the generation gap's threatening image. Still, the DNC's 1968 debacle proved to Democrats that they would have to do much more to include young people if they wanted to develop a reliable youth constituency. Richard Nixon concentrated on a more focused goal with youth politics: as Democrats looked to young voters as a voting bloc, Nixon's campaign began the important step of identifying and promoting a silent majority among youth.

New Nixon and Youth Politics, 1968

Nixon's reach for young voters had a history. When Nixon first campaigned for Congress in 1946 as a thirty-three-year-old attorney, his ability to satisfy party regulars and extend his appeal to "new blood" secured his nomination and eventual victory over the Democratic incumbent Jerry Voorhis in California's twelfth district.[27] As vice president in the Eisenhower administration, a robust Youth for Ike-Nixon campaign increased its share of the youth vote from 49 percent in 1952 to 57 percent in 1956.[28] After accepting the Republican nomination in 1956, Eisenhower spoke: "Now, of special relevance, and to me particularly gratifying, is the fact that the country's young people show a consistent preference for this Administration," adding, "I shall never cease to hope that the several states will give them the voting privilege at a somewhat earlier age than is now generally the case."[29] While Nixon may have shared Eisenhower's enthusiasm for an expanded youth vote in 1956, the GOP struggled with young voters during the 1960s especially after John F. Kennedy's youthful image made Nixon's reach for younger voters a challenge in 1960. Still, conservative youth had developed an ardent and influential movement after the formation of Young Americans for Freedom. YAF, established at William F. Buckley Jr.'s home in Sharon, Connecticut, gathered America's young conservatives to counter "liberal educationism" on campuses, which turned "the college into an impersonal daycare for the offspring of all carnivorous animals . . . which primarily serve ideological purposes."[30]

In 1964, the YAF played a crucial role in drafting the ideological purist Barry Goldwater as the Republican candidate for president. By 1970, the YAF included over twenty thousand members, as YAF chairman Ronald Docksai explained in 1971: "YAF is a young people's corporation and leadership is our most important product."[31] Barry Goldwater, the YAF dream candidate, owed his campaign to this cadre of conservatives as Youth for Goldwater for Vice-President unsuccessfully tried to get the senator on the ticket with Nixon in 1960.

Then, in 1964, uniformed in white blouses, blue skirts, cowboy boots, and hats with "Goldwater for President" sashes, the Goldwater Girls established themselves as a fixture at his rallies during the presidential campaign. Youth for Goldwater organized independently to promote and beg his candidacy, as its devoted young members greeted the senator at airports and conducted door-to-door volunteering that convinced him to run for president. And while the four well-manicured, guitar strumming "troubadours" known as the Goldwaters hardly rivaled 1960s liberal folk music stars, the bikini-clad "YAFettes" provided a surprisingly risqué element to the campaign's outreach for young voters at the beach. Gregory Schneider argues in his study of the YAF that while young conservatives held the generation gap and the youth culture at a distance, they recognized the need to "respond to the cultural changes that were occurring throughout the decade."[32] After 1960, politicians' decision to include young people in campaigns now carried a symbolic significance—it made candidates cooler. In Goldwater's case, not cool enough. Although the campaign organized and inspired many future conservative leaders, it could not reach mainstream youth, as only 36 percent of Americans under thirty voted for Goldwater. In the 1968 election, Youth for Goldwater's disappointing performance reinforced popular perceptions about young people in the 1960s generation that presupposed they carried a liberal political outlook.

Several factors motivated Nixon's outreach to young voters in 1968. To be sure, measurable gains with student voters in mock elections helped feed the campaign's "win psychology."[33] Still, as New Politics became central to the image-focused political environment, Richard Nixon's campaign needed young supporters to counter popular perceptions that he stood on the wrong side of the generation gap. Nixon's aides wanted "maximum visible support" to overturn his dated reputation and "demonstrate to the public that the student generation wants the Republican ticket." As he became the party's frontrunner, Nixon convened his top aides in his Florida home to discuss his "'new' New Nixon" during the campaign's next phase. They decided in Key Biscayne that Nixon would emphasize his "statesmanlike image" while his campaign projected him as "a 'swinger' with youth appeal."[34] As Nixon's campaign manager, former adman H. R. Haldeman suggested, "The time has come for political campaigning—its techniques and strategies—to move out of the dark ages and into the brave new world of the omnipresent eye."[35] In this media-focused environment, Nixon introduced himself as a "cooler," more image-savvy "New Nixon" who journalists described as a "milder and wiser" presidential candidate than he had been in his unsuccessful 1960 run for the White House.[36] As one political pundit observed, the Republican Party had surprisingly emerged more youthful during the mid-1960s: "Until 1966, Republicans had an abundance of tired dreary politicians, whereas Democrats seemed to have a monopoly of political sex appeal."[37]

Thus, Nixon had reason to be skeptical of youth politics. In the GOP, co-opting youth came across as pandering. In addition, Nixon as hip struck many pundits as laughable. Walking this line, Nixon could not dodge the same old criticism, as one *Rolling Stone* critic considered the New Nixon a sham, contending that "Nixon's presidency will be a collection of those things that can be salvaged from the past."[38] One *Life* magazine interview explored the "New Nixon," now "mellower and wiser" than earlier in his political career.[39] While Nixon downplayed the change, claiming his credentials as a "straightshooter," the interviewer wondered in the article: "Is he going to be capable of reaching the imaginations of those young voters to whom he is largely a dim figure out of some bygone era?"[40] Despite, or because of, these accusations, Nixon stayed clear of any risks as he lacked both the will and ability to emphasize his YVN (Young Voters for Nixon) during the convention.

Though Nixon maintained an ambivalent stance toward a young

campaign image, he still courted young conservatives to establish his opposition to the liberal GOP wing. As Gregory Schneider explains, when Nelson Rockefeller attempted to persuade the incipient YAF's leadership to support him in 1961, one leader revealed the effort's futility: "We hated Rockefeller the way we hated any Communist."[41] Rockefeller intensified this tension throughout the 1960s as he attempted unsuccessfully to prevent groups such as the John Birch Society, what he called the "radical right lunatic fringe" and "vociferous and well-drilled elements," from infiltrating the Young Republicans.[42] More encouraging, YAF president Tom Huston admitted to *Esquire Magazine* that only Nixon offered a candidacy acceptable to all Republicans in 1968.[43] In addition, the YAF's support for Nixon would provide the boots on the ground, or the "militant corps," that Nixon lacked. Still, as the YAF leaders' hatred toward Rocky created an opening for Nixon, they proved more work than they were worth.

When Nixon began his own reach for young supporters, his initial effort looked to a reliably conservative YAFer. After meeting with YAF leader Pat Buchanan in 1966, Nixon brought the young "thorough-going conservative" into his camp as a "research assistant" to bolster his credibility and network with young political activists on the right. Buchanan's role in Nixon's campaign, however, proved the exception as many conservative ideologues preferred Ronald Reagan's ardent stand on the right over Nixon's moderate positions. As one journalist observed, this wooing process proved "how gossamer are the threads binding Nixon with the Republican right."[44]

Buchanan set up meetings between Nixon and YAF leaders in Washington and Newport, Rhode Island, to smooth over the differences.[45] In addition, Nixon's campaign stocked its personnel with conservative "Young Turks" such as Buchanan, Kevin Phillips, and Richard Whalen, who wrote speeches and formulated tactics. Still, Nixon's moderate position did not inspire YAF members. "Richard Nixon may not be *the* conservative candidate in the sense that Senator Goldwater was," admitted one YAF leader, "but he is certainly *a* candidate that we can and should support."[46] Considering this hesitation among young purists, the YAF indicated conservatives' difficult transition to more moderate candidates after 1964. In many ways, Nixon welcomed a loose relationship with YAF.

Rallying GOP youth auxiliaries—the Young Republicans (YR) and College Republicans—also challenged Nixon's youth campaign. Unfortu-

nately for Nixon, the YR's internal divisions hampered its ability to mobilize young voters. In 1967 YR chairman Jack McDonald's leadership
represented the culmination of ultraconservative's ascendancy in the
Young Republican National Federation. Considered a "Goldwaterite,"
McDonald belonged to a group known as "the Syndicate." Under the
tutelage of former Goldwater insider F. Clifton White, this group maintained a tight alliance with the Right and influenced Young Republicans
on the state and local levels. Under the YR constitution, the organization's president appointed thirty-four of the executive committee's
sixty-seven members and established "the Syndicate" as the majority.[47]
Moderate College Republicans complained that "intra-party warfare"
divided YR clubs, as one Massachusetts YR delegate protested: "Their
horse-nonsense drives workers out of the organization . . . and then conservatives can win by default."[48] While Republican candidates shared the
GOP's move back to the middle after 1964, grassroots youth had not.

Making matters worse for the GOP youth drive in 1968, McDonald
ran his victorious campaign for president against "the servant-boss relationship with the National Committee." When the RNC's chairman,
Roy Bliss, attempted to bring the YR under the RNC's umbrella, YR
convention delegates rejected all the proposals except a stipulation
that allowed two nonvoting Republican representatives to sit on the YR
executive board. This arrangement left Nixon, the party favorite, with
limited sway over the GOP's major junior organization.[49] Once their
autonomy had been established, McDonald saw the YR leadership's opportunity to build a more conservative Republican Party. "The center of
our political stage is now being taken over by a new voter group," Mc-
Donald wrote, "—the young voter." As traditional and family loyalties to
political parties waned, McDonald emphasized that "party identification
is at its weakest among voters in their early and middle 20's." This gave
the Republican Party an "excellent opportunity to establish itself once
again as the majority party in the United States."[50] Nixon shared this
goal, but his own campaign struggled to harness this movement. The
autonomy among these conservative youth organizations highlighted
Nixon's reliance on these groups and the necessity for campaigns to
develop a separate, candidate-focused youth effort.

As a first step, McDonald planned to build an "image of the Young
Republicans as a vital part of Young America."[51] McDonald argued that
"Republicans must develop a 'fresh' approach. We must appeal to young
voters on terms of their own problems, their own issues, their own needs

and hopes."[52] To do so, McDonald recommended a series of "America Tomorrow" seminars to discuss conservative alternatives to American youth's problems concerning the draft, the role of the federal government, education, and the environment. "Our nation is placing an ever increasing emphasis on young leadership in business and education," argued McDonald. "Why not expand this emphasis into the realm of political policy making?"[53] Rather than lessons in campaign organization, this training focused on gaining access to political machinery.

In addition to controlling the training, national YR leaders aimed to control the structure as they sponsored a National Leadership Training School in 1968 to recruit members and create future Republican organizers. Pointing out the success of the National Leadership Training School in Washington, DC, for seven hundred students, McDonald called for similar schools overseen by the YR Leadership Development Team in each of the YR's eleven regions and eventually within each state.[54] This plan intended to motivate its members through competition. Using a national publication, YR leaders published each club's progress quantitatively, including totals for club membership, registrants, fundraising, and solicitation of absentee ballots.[55] Still, this effort focused mainly on a vision of a new, autonomous conservative youth movement and did not provide the loyal rank-and-file young volunteers Nixon's campaigners hoped to gather.

Eyeing the growing role that young people played in the Kennedy and McCarthy campaigns, Nixon's aides recommended he position himself to capture "non-partisan youth" who would lack a "hero-leader" once Humphrey became the Democratic nominee. Even though the College Republicans out-organized their Democratic counterparts on campuses across the country, over 60 percent of student voters identified themselves as independent.[56] Expecting that independent young voters would likely support an image-savvy, youth-friendly "hero-leader," Nixon's hopes for the youth vote rested on the fate of his more charismatic counterparts in the Democratic Party. If organized, the Nixon campaign could capture young voters who lacked political loyalties and would not vote for LBJ.

In an effort to regain the reigns of the GOP youth effort, RNC chairman Roy Bliss initiated a new recruitment program for young people, "Opportunities Unlimited." This program, half political conference and half job fair, included seminars titled "Opportunity in Communication," "Opportunities in Business, the Professions and Social Service," and

"Opportunities in Government and Politics." Describing the program's goals to show young people different careers in public service or within the Republican Party, Bliss claimed, "It is a matter of plain hard fact, that we must sharply increase support of the Republican Party among young people."[57] Despite the RNC's efforts, this tall task fell to Nixon's experienced and trusted advisers such as Len Garment and Bill Gavin, who developed Young Voters for Nixon. Predictably, the YVN did not go over well with Young Republicans, who "saw no need for a campaign group separate from theirs."[58] However, the turf fights and demands for a more influential role that defined these groups convinced Nixon's campaign in 1968 to take no risks, and the YVN assumed complete control of Nixon's youth campaign.

Youth for Nixon

As Nixon's point man on the youth vote, Len Garment suggested that Nixon should emphasize his authenticity in contrast to Bobby Kennedy's image-conscious campaign. "Dick Nixon is not going to gain adherents among the under 30 generation by insulting their intelligence," quipped Garment, "as Bobby does when he tries so desperately to be the teen-age 43 year-old father of twelve (or whatever)."[59] Rather than fashion himself as a kindred spirit of all youth, Nixon instead shaped a more focused, selective youth campaign. Nixon's campaign researchers identified the key elements of the "Now Generation." Describing young adults in 1968, one report described them as "anxious," "idealistic," "sensitive," and "mobile." This meant Nixon had to convince young voters "they could be participants."[60] Access became the new focus for youth politics after 1968—the pros called it "participation" and "inclusion." Participation alleviated youth's "anxious" and "sensitive" elements while channeling the "idealistic" and "mobile" young voters into concrete political roles. Though intended in many ways to control youth politics and avoid its push for inclusion, YVN also meant to create an image of young participants.

Initial efforts missed the mark, as a campaign film intended to show Nixon to college audiences in a "friendly, human vein" that came across as "not oriented enough toward issues."[61] Nixon's youth effort required more substance. Thus, Nixon proposed establishing an independent Youth Services Agency while promising to end the draft and lower the voting age. The Young Voters for Nixon campaign poster, considered the Youth Division's "most famous contribution," proclaimed "Nixon is the One," depicting the candidate surrounded by Republican Party leaders, Nixon's children, and Wilt Chamberlain.[62] In the background, the image shows clean-cut young people happily carrying signs that read "18 Year Old Vote," "Student Coalition," and "Dick Wants Volunteer Army" while the poster's border blends a strange mixture of patriotic images such as the White House, the bald eagle, and the stars and stripes, with a "neo-psychedelic" style. According to one aide, "because it was 'in,' the poster 'attracted several major press stories, managed an appearance on a top rated television program and has found a place in the Smithsonian Institute.'"[63] The poster used youth issues to frame Nixon's image as the two became less distinguishable. This tinkering with the politics of youth helped Nixon's reputation, but the rise of young voters required more from Nixon's campaign. Specifically, college students preferred a more direct role.

Focusing on campus politics, Nixon's campaign managers poached two of Rockefeller's "New Majority" leaders to organize the Student Coalition. This group developed ways for student campaign workers to get involved in urban problems while still attending school. Though similar to Kennedy's focus on young people's overwhelming priority, poverty, this effort served to cultivate Nixon's own young supporters. At twenty-eight years old, only four years before his own gubernatorial campaign in Tennessee, Lamar Alexander of United Citizens for Nixon and Agnew sold the Student Coalition's potential, claiming, "If you want to film Nixon in a give and take with students, why not do it with this group of outstanding students and upon this subject?" (He promised, "The students will not embarrass R.N.").[64] Rather than perform to popular expectations of alienated young voters, Republicans countered this image with different youth.

Nixon's campaign managers also sent surrogates to lead seminars for a select group of politically active conservative students on campus. Stating its goals to "take this dissident group . . . and convince it that its best interest lies in voting against Johnson," the program's organizers hoped, "If good, it will reach the media."[65] Concerning these meetings with small groups of students, one Youth for Nixon field representative commented, "those voters annoyed with young and college aged 'rebellion' will like to see the candidate 'stand up' to the 'kids,'" while offering something for those voters "favorably impressed with a man who has a rapport with youth."[66] As Nixon's personal public relations man, for-mer advertising executive Harry Treleavan summed up Nixon's appeal: "Not always loved, he is universally respected. Not glamorous, he does have a certain star quality going for him."[67] Along these lines, Treleavan came up with the campaign slogan "Nixon's the One!" Speaking with young people would underline Nixon's particular brand of charisma. Even these small efforts at more meaningful youth organization served the primary purpose of building Nixon's image. Nixon in command, leading youth, sent the desired message.

Mock elections on campuses also helped Nixon's argument that his youth was the majority. The most prestigious and respected college poll conducted at Washington and Lee had become well known for its ac-curate predictions, and Nixon's campaign funneled funds into secur-ing his victory and high standing with student voters.[68] To help recruit students, Nixon's state campaign managers formed Student Leadership Committees to organize his outreach to young voters. Developing a cam-pus newspaper advertising campaign and planning "giant" youth rallies, the student leaders who joined the Leadership Committees contested the prevailing perceptions of both parties; as one student complained, "The hippies, yippies and war protesters may make the news. But make no mistake about it! They are not representative of the overwhelming majority of young Americans who still believe that free men working together can achieve miracles." If you considered yourself one of "Amer-ica's thinking young adults" who searched for "a national spokesmen with whom they have confidence," they argued, "Nixon's the one."[69] On April 24, thirteen hundred campuses participated in a mock elec-tion entitled "Choice '68." Despite a late start, Nixon's campaign dis-seminated five hundred thousand "Nixon and the Issues" brochures, fourteen thousand "relatively ugly psychedelic posters," one hundred thousand buttons, and one hundred screenings of a Nixon film. Against the odds and a crowded field that included New York mayor John V. Lindsay, Senator Charles Percy (R-Illinois), California governor Ronald Reagan, New York governor Nelson A. Rockefeller, and former gover-nor of Alabama George C. Wallace, Nixon finished third to New Politics' practitioners McCarthy and Kennedy—but first in the GOP.[70]

At first, Nixon hesitated to speak to any students, as his Youth for Nixon director pleaded, "I can understand that he doesn't want to play the Bobby circuit, but a speech or two on the theme, 'You have been promised candor but have been given cant' can help things."[71] As

Nixon's campaign reduced the "Bobby circuit" to a celebrity-focused form of entertainment, Nixon sought to establish himself to youth as a trustworthy leader. When Nixon finally did address a crowd at Syracuse University, he invited several students to voice their concerns through song. When they finished their a cappella that listed their fears about the war, the environment, and student rights, Nixon regained control, stating, "We have allowed them to talk, now we are going to talk and they are going to listen for a while." Comparing this subdued and harmless voice of dissent to the violent Columbia University uprising, Nixon claimed that "these students have set an example" while suggesting student protesters at Columbia should be expelled.[72] Nixon's campaign publicized this effort by disseminating recordings of this speech to radio stations, bolstering his claim that he could unite America and end the divisive 1960s. He could even make students sing. In addition to Nixon's outreach to students, his campaign carefully positioned Youth for Nixon's female contingent of ebullient, well-mannered Nixonettes at rallies and campaign events while they held signs that read "Apple Pie, Mother and Nixon," "Nixon Is Groovy," and "Bring Us Together."[73] This balanced approach sought inclusivity while maintaining loyalty to the parents' politics that called for discipline through law and order.[74] As the Kennedy Girls made Bobby Kennedy's SRO rally the "swingingest show," Nixonettes offered a more wholesome vision of young women.

The Republican National Convention in Miami would put Nixon's image to the test. The most notable confrontation came between the YR conservatives and the young Rockefeller liberals who came from the northeastern liberal establishment.[75] While Rocky's youth cadre fought for his nomination to no avail, they prompted Republican brass to take note of young voters' importance in 1968 politics. Balancing the convention's "conservative, suburban-oriented, law and order tone" with "coolness" that the New Nixon image projected, Nixon had the moderate and youth-friendly New York mayor John Lindsay second the vice presidential nomination for the "short-fused" Spiro Agnew.[76] As for the GOP platform, the preamble began, "Today, we are in turmoil. . . . Many young people are losing faith in our society." The platform first made clear, "We will not tolerate violence," but then recommended lowering the voting age and shortening the period for draft eligibility, claiming: "Their [young people's] political restlessness reflects their urgent hope to achieve a meaningful participation in public affairs."[77] Nixon's critics

Figure 3. The "New Nixon" campaign combined timeless and traditional election imagery with an appeal to young people. (Nixon Library)

took notice and exaggerated the contradiction between the GOP and the New Left movement.

Governor Ronald Reagan, vying to challenge Nixon for the nomination, sported a youthful image as critics accused him of "trying to sway the teenie-bop vote" with his "two toned saddle shoes."[78] Republican appeals to the wider youth vote had limits. Even if Nixon had tried, it would have looked bad. "Never before have the boys in the backroom of American politics paid such obeisance at the altar of youth," cried one reporter. "A tongue-and-cheek-report that Nixon has been fitted with a Nehru Jacket is circulating at the Republican National Committee."[79]

Young observers found the RNC disappointing. Calling the convention's decision makers "party machine regulars" and "aristocratic bigots," one nineteen-year-old from Chicago found the event "tawdry" and "boring." Even worse, another youth complained that image had become central: "Now it's getting so that even the wives are getting looked at, the way they dress . . . their hairstyles." Hoping for a more meaningful convention, a young voter ironically hoped, "Maybe the Democratic Convention will be more exciting."[80] Even his choice for the vice president indicated Nixon's distance from youth politics, as one congressman complained: "The selection ignored the youth movement." Choosing Agnew, who one delegate described as a "shoot-the-looters boy," Nixon appealed to the South and passed over New York City's mayor John Lindsay, a moderate who attracted young supporters.[81]

The DNC simplified Nixon's youth problem, as he stuck to his law-and-order position on youth issues. In one interview while on the campaign trail, Nixon espoused a no-nonsense approach on campuses, as he advised college and university leaders "to get the spine and the backbone" to expel any student or faculty member who "breaks the law and engages in violence." Nixon took an uncompromising line against protesters, arguing, "This idea of sitting down and negotiating with the leaders of a mob . . . all that does is encourage this kind of stuff." While Nixon offered little in terms of policy to suppress campus unrest, he promised, "That would be the national tone I would set."[82]

Nixon's campaign ads relayed his outward stance on the generation gap. To define his approach to youth through "law-and-order" politics, he hired filmmaker Eugene Jones, who centered on hippies and young radicals as a source of anxiety rather than a rejuvenation of the American spirit. One controversial ad, titled *Contravention*, juxtaposed still shots of wounded GIs in combat, poor in Appalachia, and bleeding protesters outside the DNC in Chicago to enhance the chaotic effect while pulsating psychedelic sounds played over the Dixieland song "Hot Time in the Old Town Tonight." In another ad, *The First Civil Right*, Nixon's law-and-order stance comes through loud and clear, and youth are the primary target as the candidate speaks over quickly shifting still shots of shouting youth and burning buildings, "the first civil right of every American is to be free of domestic violence." Rather than racial disturbances and street crime, Nixon's brand of law-and-order politics focused primarily on the youth rebellion. While he bypassed youth politics in favor of his law-and-order position, Nixon could ignore the threat young voters posed to the conservative realignment he envisioned. As Nixon's first term unfolded, however, the youth problem emerged as a central issue in the Nixon administration.

The Lessons of 1968

After the Democratic National Convention, Humphrey tried to pick up on any residual youth power he could muster. Trading the "smoke-filled rooms" of the old politics for the "smoke-filled discotheque" in New York City, Humphrey visited a dance club and took a "fling at 'new politics,'" seeking identification with youth and the artistic community."[83] An awkward photo of Humphrey discussing politics with young people captured the sad state of New Politics in the 1968 campaign after Chicago. Despite this attempt, young liberal voters found little motivation to head to the voting booths. On the University of Missouri campus, the Committee of Concerned Students, originally a coalition of Kennedy and McCarthy supporters, voted in October to not endorse Humphrey.[84] Young Americans across the country led anti-election demonstrations, as one protester in Washington, DC, carried a poster of Nixon, Humphrey, and Wallace that read, "Are you kidding me?"[85]

Although Nixon's youth campaign attempt stirred the political pot, it lacked emphasis. For many observers, outreach to young voters and minorities meant little; as one journalist described the Republican National Convention's 1 percent of delegates under thirty, "The few blacks and young people here in 1968 had less influence on party policy than did the harassed waitresses at these overcrowded hotels. At least the bigwigs talked to the waitress."[86] In total, the YVN gained twelve thousand dues-paying members.[87] Nixon's campaign spent $80,000 on the YVN, a pittance considering he raised over \$20 million for his election.[88] In addition, the YVN suffered from poor leadership. "The job often went to the person who asked for it," Mort Allin's review of the organization joked, "or Charley GOP's nephew."[89] In the end, only half of the youth vote showed up at the polls while 61 percent of eligible Americans voted. Humphrey won 47 percent of voters under thirty while Nixon won 38 percent. Worse, Nixon could not nail down the noncollege youth, which went to Wallace, who won disproportionate support from young voters, mostly in the South.[90] Intensifying Democrats' disappointment with the liberal youth's poor turnout, Humphrey lost the popular vote by less than one percentage point.[91]

As for Nixon, adapting to youth issues came slow, as he pressed on with his law-and-order image when addressing the politics of youth to reach parents' concerns. Many scholars and pundits have mistakenly located the New Nixon in the 1968 campaign. While his modern advertising techniques and moderate political positions did reveal a shift in Nixon's campaign strategy from 1960, his adherence to law and order along with his underwhelming youth effort did little to distinguish himself from the "old Nixon." Campaigning against young people proved a winning approach to the youth problem for the election. Governing, however, called this tough stance on the generation gap into question as Nixon reconsidered youth politics' emerging political influence during his first term. But Nixon's campaign did show that the young voters' rebellious reputation could be countered with an alternative. As youth became more influential, this need to challenge popular perceptions of young voters as antiestablishment increased. The GOP rejected the "star" appeal that Kennedy offered, requiring a more carefully targeted and structured youth campaign.

2 | Law and Order

At first, the Nixon White House's politics of youth continued the law-and-order approach that had shaped the campaign in 1968. In an internal memo titled "The President and Youth," Nixon's aide William Gavin suggested that the president tone down "references to the glories of youth" and the "generation gap," as that would "move the President into an area now dominated by others (the Kennedy Group and its creatures)." Nixon's advisers on the youth problem initially cautioned him to avoid the "middle class, college attending section" that had become synonymous with "youth."[1] This apprehension relied on the media-generated image of "wild in the streets" youth. One editorial claimed: "Semantically the word student has come to mean violence, long hair, LSD, dirt, and sexual freedom to many adults whose major contact with youth has come through mass media."[2]

Rather than embrace the rise of youth politics, Nixon's administration used the "youth problem" to tap into Middle America's ("the forgotten Americans'") anxieties and resentments after 1968. Invoking law and order to confront the threat of rebellious youth, Nixon appealed to Middle America, or the forty-seven-year-old, white woman from Ohio as described in Richard Scammon and Ben J. Wattenberg's influential study *The Real Majority*.[3] Scammon and Wattenberg noted that cultural issues had dethroned the economy's primacy among the concerns of ordinary voters, defining the dominant source of American anxiety as the "social issue" of "crime, violence, drugs, disruption, riot, out-of-wedlock birth, promiscuity, that whole panoply of issues."[4] After all, nearly three-quarters of Americans, including half of the Americans who called the Vietnam War a mistake, saw protesters in a negative light.[5]

Thus, the president used his call for law and order to focus on the image-oriented modern social issues that families confronted in the living room, while Democrats stubbornly clung to the bread-and-butter issues that dominated the kitchen table.[6] As a twenty-something up-and-coming political operative from the Bronx, Nixon's adviser Kevin Phillips explained the previously labeled Southern Strategy that exploited racial fears and resentment to rally voters in the South, in suburbs, and in white urban, ethnic enclaves.[7] "Phillips' analysis," argues Geoffrey Kabaservice, "presented the most direct threat to the moderate worldview and hopes for the future direction of the Republican party."[8] While the Southern Strategy rallied conservatives across the nation against student protesters and marijuana as well, this strategy had to contend with the moderate youth's response.

This chapter explores two important and related law-and-order issues for youth, marijuana use and campus unrest. In both cases, the widespread youth problem required the president to moderate his approach. The 1968 generation could not simply serve as cannon fodder, as one aide reminded the president that this generation's young men and women, many of its campus protesters, and even some of the pot smokers, also included the "the sons and daughters of the 'silent majority.'"[9] Nixon also had to consider his own "square" youth support. "Even though they don't approve of the antics of the 'weirdos' and 'hippies,'" one Minnesota Republican warned the president, "they resent [attacks] and stick up for their generation." Directly referencing Spiro Agnew, Nixon's attack dog vice president, the warning continued: "This language risks alienating the kids who are with us."[10] As youth politics became more influential, however, Nixon's struggle to separate "bad kids" from his own young supporters forced the administration to carefully define who his "silent majority" included.[11]

Campus disorder laws required some leniency, especially after Kent State, when the Ohio State National Guard shot at protesters and killed four students. In 1969, Nixon enjoyed a 57 percent approval rating on campuses, and polls showed a 68 percent approval among all Americans between twenty-one and twenty-nine years old.[12] After Kent State, some polls showed Nixon's approval rating as low as 31 percent on campuses.[13] While many conservative Americans criminalized and in many cases racialized student protesters, Kent State touched a chord in the heightened political discourse over the "generation gap." This problem became even more pressing as hearings on lowering the voting age began that summer.

The other controversy driving the politics of youth, marijuana, also confused the president. Nixon talked tough in public, but his administration's internal dialogue revealed cracks in his antidrug stance. While law and order appealed to the Southern Strategy advocates, marijuana pushed young whites into the law's crosshairs. When Nixon learned that 75 percent of marijuana users were white and under twenty-five years old, he worried about this trend's political significance for his conservative voting base, pointing out, "It's now becoming a white problem."[14] While Nixon restrained his conservative impulses with student unrest, and despite the moderate reforms he conceded to protect victims of drug abuse, predators still faced the full, brutal force of law-and-order policies. Matt Lassiter points out the racial consequences of the gateway theory that distinguished between pushers and white, young users: "Starting in the late 1960s, when generational revolt rather than external villains explained the dramatic increase in illegal drug use in affluent suburbs and on college campuses, similar forces promoted a selective marijuana decriminalization policy to keep 'otherwise law-abiding' youth out of jail."[15] Furthermore, recent scholarship such as Khalil Muhammad's prove that marijuana laws became a tool of the carceral state and intensified painful racial disparities in the justice system, as the modern War on Drugs created "the reciprocal criminalization of blackness and decriminalization of whiteness."[16] This bifurcated drug policy reform, acceptable to even the young white liberals it protected, allowed Nixon to cling to his antidrug stance.

Nixon's policies revealed a flexibility that belied the administration's tough image, often decreasing states' marijuana penalties and matching the enforcement approach with a focus on treatment. The president's own commission on marijuana, the Shafer Commission, recommended decriminalization, while Nixon's proposals allowed judges discretion when penalizing first-time violators. Dealing with campus unrest and marijuana, Nixon protected his voters' children from his tough-on-crime approach.

Finally, Nixon offered an alternative political culture that journalist John Chamberlain called "square power," defined as "the fall in a community's tolerance of moral looseness."[17] This emphasis had a regional origin: as northern and coastal campuses became hotbeds of student activism during the 1960s, schools in the South more often held to more traditional fraternity and football culture. Bruce Schulman argues the nation was "southernized" after 1968, as Nixon spread southern attitudes into the North—distrust of government, anti-elitism, racial resentment, and a "highly personal religiosity."[18] And while those same concerns fueled conservatives in the North and in the suburbs, examining Nixon's reaction to the politics of youth shows the challenges of separating a youth segment as part of the "silent majority." Confronting the youth problem, though Nixon struggled to implement the law-and-order politics he rode to the White House, this lesson informed the culturally square but politically moderate appeal his youth campaign would perfect in 1972.

"It's Getting Freaky": Nixon versus the Students

In 1969, Nixon's meeting with three hundred delegates for a conference to improve communication among student, academic, business, and government leaders focused specifically on campus disorders. Addressing this audience, and alluding to his own days as a college card-sharp, Nixon dismissed rebellious students, arguing that "it is like a poker game. You can be sure that whoever is talking the loudest is sure to be bluffing."[19] While he belittled the protesters' hand, the president's conciliatory gesture concealed his own. Nixon soon after called for one thousand extra FBI agents for "keeping order" on American campuses.[20] From 1968 to 1970, the number of students arrested increased from four thousand to seventy-two hundred.[21]

In addition, Nixon ordered his secretary of health, education, and welfare to send a letter to universities across the country reminding them of their prerogative to revoke federal funding for any student found guilty of a crime. Referring to this letter, Nixon reminded university presidents that "expulsion has been the primary instrument of university discipline," a punishment with added consequences considering the ongoing military draft system.[22] As campus unrest became a central concern, it motivated the president's law-and-order approach to the politics of youth that focused on student demonstrators.

Nixon targeted campus unrest as the youth revolt's most dangerous facet. His hard approach to campus protest followed California governor Ronald Reagan's tried and tested position, about which "polls" exclaimed, "Rarely has one single issue given a state political leader so much public support for his actions."[23] Student protest had become "the meat on which mini-Caesars feed."[24] Because of this approach Reagan became so popular, especially with conservative youth, that he represented an alternative to Nixon for Sunbelt conservatives who had opposed the moderate, liberal Rockefeller Republicans for the nomination in 1968. Though Nixon attempted to stay above the fray, his hard-line position on campus protest increasingly frightened activists: as one campus leader claimed, "Friendly reporters pass on word of calls from the FBI to campus Security Offices, inquiring after me. It's getting freaky."[25]

While liberals appreciated the campus as a bastion of the protest politics that had energized the 1960s political environment, more conservative students and noncollege youth saw campus disorder as a danger to American society. Conservative campuses across the country fumed at the excesses of the student left after the 1960s. For example, Lipscomb University, a Baptist institution smack in the buckle of the Bible belt, offered an alternative to the widely publicized chaotic campus culture. This small Tennessee, Christian college exemplified the oasis of tranquility and tradition that many educational institutions of all levels could only hope to protect amid the era's tumultuous environment. One article in the campus newspaper, the *Babbler*, berated the small group of ten or fifteen students who turned a study break into "a mess of intentionally spilled cake" but also complained that the "mature majority remains silent." Making an eloquent defense of Nixon's campaign for "law and order," the student continued that "rules that seem petty have to be made since the 'silent majority' of students lack the intestinal fortitude to stand up to the few who make them necessary, and let them know they won't stand for such childishness."[26] These students sided with their parents when it came to the resentment and anger at youth's rebelliousness known as "kidlash."

As the *Babbler* editor bragged about his fellow students, "we believe people show their individuality through their actions, not by the kind of clothes they wear or by the length of their hair."[27] Rejecting the notion that students could either be "rabble rousers" or "do nothings," one Lipscomb student argued that his cohort simply offered a moderate balance between "complete power" and "complete apathy."[28] While one liberal student feared that "Nixon will use repressive measures to put down protest," a campus conservative hoped the president would: "I think he'll adopt a tough line of not tolerating rioting and he'll probably favor cutting off aid to rioters."[29]

Lipscomb's students who sought a more traditional, conservative campus environment did not question the radicals' right to dissent but asked about their methods, wondering, "What is violence accomplishing to make learning more effective?"[30] These conservative students feared that the minority had stigmatized the majority. Another editorial in the *Babbler* wondered: "Could it be that the prosperity of the United States has bred its own generation of spoiled brats?" The article continued, "student extremists making all the noise care very little about progressing toward reasonable solutions," but they simply called "attention to itself and giving a false image of Americans students on the whole."[31] Even students themselves found campus unrest as a rallying point for contradictory visions of America's future. One protest flyer railed against protestors: "These are the ones that hate Jesus Christ."[32] In Nixon's effort to divide and conquer the youth vote, attacking student protest became especially popular with his intended constituency from square America that included suburban whites, blue-collar urban ethnics, and southern and religious social conservatives.

The shocking violence at Kent State brought antiwar youth politics into the national spotlight, shedding doubt on Nixon's claim to a young majority. The nation reacted in horror as images relayed the bloody confrontation to Americans. Most famously, John Paul Filo's Pulitzer Prize–winning photograph captured Mary Ann Vecchio's anguish as she knelt over a dying student and cried for help. The antiwar movement reenergized around this tragedy as protests mounted against Nixon's policies on youth issues; both his decision to expand the conflict into Cambodia that sparked the Kent Sate protest and his callous approach to student demonstrators fueled the tensions between an increasingly defiant student power movement and an increasingly troubled "Middle America." The majority of Americans did not observe these images sympathetically; nearly 60 percent supported the National Guard's use of violence.[33] However Americans felt about it, Kent State challenged popular perceptions of an elite, radical-liberal youth culture that inflamed the campus unrest problem.

The Nixon administration's reaction continued previous efforts to marginalize student protesters. Attorney General John Mitchell announced that the FBI could investigate and prosecute students suspected of using explosives with or without consent from local police or college presidents. Law and order prevailed at first. While students opposed any FBI role on campus by an overwhelming 90 percent, local police supported the administration's aggressive use of federal agents by 80 percent.[34] Kent State's aftermath also pronounced the divide between young Americans themselves.

In the days following Kent State, protestors flooded the streets outside the New York Stock Exchange to demonstrate against the relationship between corporations and the war, sparking a violent confrontation with pro-Nixon "Hard Hats." This confrontation brought together the divergent elements of the 1968 generation and even strengthened Nixon's hand. Defending patriotism and Wall Street, proestablishment Hard Hats in New York publicized young, ethnic blue-collar workers' shift from the Democrats to the Republican Party. One adviser on the ethnic vote pointed out that "it is needless to emphasize the ethnic composition of the hard hats" and "the conspicuous absence of youth of the so called 'working families'" during "youth disorders."[35] Ken Jurewicz, a twenty-seven-year-old Polish American factory worker in Detroit, summed up this tension, claiming that students think "they're better than you and you're nobody." While Jurewicz voted for Humphrey in 1968, the youth revolt inspired him to support Nixon, as one observer argued that "the young guys in the auto plant are pi——ed off at the liberals."[36] As nonstudent youth rallied against long-haired protestors, Kent State also blurred these divisions on campus.

The national student strike following Nixon's Cambodia announcement and Kent State presented an obvious geographic difference. In the North, while liberal student bodies such as Boston University's held huge marches that forced "Berkeley East" to cancel its commencement, and almost 100 percent of Massachusetts's colleges participated, only 25 percent of southern schools joined the nationwide demonstrations. Still, conservative universities also felt this student power effect more than they had in 1969.[37] Even docile southern students sympathized with protesters. If Kent State, a "Middle America" campus, could suffer such violence, students imagined that it could happen anywhere. Describing the students in the crowd that the National Guard targeted that day, a twenty-three-year-old sophomore and Vietnam veteran at Kent explained: "Most of them (students) were clean-cut fraternity kids."[38] As one University of Tennessee student wrote, "We could easily identify with Ohio—Ohio is not unlike Tennessee."[39] The University of Tennessee's campus, a calm exception amid the growing "student power" movement that disrupted universities and colleges across the nation, joined the fight after Kent State. The student leadership called for its own three-day student strike as 65 percent of the students did not attend class for several days.[40] While Nixon maintained distance from the national uproar, Kent State intensified the pressure on his administration to act.

Fortune magazine commissioned a Yankelovitch survey of 250 chief executive officers to record their opinion of the White House that revealed growing sentiment for bridging the generation gap. "Most strikingly,"

Yankelovich observed after examining the negative responses, "the Administration's lack of communication with the nation's youth has come from nowhere to rank right up with Vietnam. The President's failure to unite the country also was mentioned for the first time."[41] Soon it became clear to Nixon and the White House that the youth revolt would not go away, and memos began to fly about the "youth problem."

In late May, Attorney General John Mitchell continued to play the "strong man" on campus unrest. Concerning the attorney general's call for more enforcement, a concerned reader of the *Modesto Bee* protested this authoritarian approach, pointing out that "tough laws" do not always work. Instead, the letter suggested "perhaps, by working hand in hand with our youth we can discover together the real underlying causes. Who knows, maybe we can even get to know and like one another."[42] This event heightened Americans' fears that the nation's young people had lost faith in the system. A journalist from *Christian Century* editorialized that the best way to respond to the youth problem is "by planting, cultivating, pruning and then harvesting."[43] This moderate position influenced Nixon's cabinet, as Secretary of the Interior Walter Hickel admitted: "There is a concern in America, that if 'law and order' stretches too far, it finally becomes hate and order." Hickel asked Nixon to "welcome the questioning of the young," because, "perhaps youth does have part of the solution."[44] In building Nixon's image as a unifier, he conceded the "problems of the generation gap" existed but assured one youth group representing student governments that "those of us in this administration . . . are concerned about the problems you are concerned about."[45]

The White House could not continue to "repress and isolate" as the tense political environment during the hot summer of 1970 forced a more youth-friendly image to establish the differences between protesting youth and "the moderate majority." As one of Haldeman's young aides, Tom Davis, argued, "The sons and daughters of the 'silent majority,' who were lost on Cambodia, are yet saveable."[46] The administration needed to act but drew the line between openness and acquiescence. Thus, Nixon's aides attempted to distinguish moderate youth's desire to participate from the rabblerousing Left's more ambitious reputation.

The administration's approach to student protestors began to divide Nixon's cabinet. Nixon's researchers concluded that the youth revolt could help him exploit divisions in the New Deal coalition and proposed a speech "after some particularly outrageous campus incident" to denounce "those who have attempted to politicize and destroy the great American universities."[47] Nixon's secretary of the interior, Walter Hickel, disagreed when he wrote a letter to the White House protesting that the administration "is turning its back on the great mass of American youth and thereby contributing to anarchy and revolt." That same day, a White House director of students and youth, Toby Moffett, resigned along with several other members of his staff. In leaving, Moffett criticized Nixon's handling of Kent State and charged the president with using the "most vicious tactics" against dissenters.[48] As one young Nixon adviser observed, "When Secretary Hickel admonished Nixon about student discontent, he was instantly transformed, in the eyes of many, from a polluting profiteer to a knowledgeable and objective government official."[49] Nixon's tough approach landed him on the wrong side of the generation gap.

In response to Kent State, White House aide Jeb Magruder, only thirty-two himself, produced a memo recommending the president send his staff out to better communicate the White House's positions to students, or else "we can expect trouble on the campuses similar in nature [to Kent State]." Magruder's memo pointed out the practical benefits of having a wider presence in the student community, as it would "diffuse the activities of the moderates and push the radical fringe as far left as possible."[50] Furthermore, Magruder framed this suggestion within Nixon's "silent majority" of southern conservatives, blue-collar laborers, and suburban whites. Magruder understood how to present issues in terms that Nixon understood, pointing out that "the Dayton housewife won't be upset if her president sends out his staffers to talk things over with students." Magruder made clear that this strategy would "create no new enemies."[51] Shifting its approach, the White House grappled with the youth problem, forcing it to reconsider its law-and-order stance. As Kent State compelled Nixon to cultivate a more receptive young constituency, his administration looked beyond the radical students who had become synonymous with youth.

After eight junior staff members conducted campus visits during the student moratorium protesting Kent State's tragic outcome, they reported to the president, White House aide Jeb Magruder, and Haldeman about possible responses to the "youth phenomenon." While they left the previous effort to "repress and isolate the militant students so as to gain political mileage" on the table, the entire group chose the alternative option to "create a conciliatory mood between the administration and youth."[52] Signaling the new direction, Magruder and Haldeman supported "the eight." With this strategy, Magruder felt, "We should not lose, by default, the allegiance of the vast middle segment of collegiate youth."[53] As one journalist explained: "The disastrous combination of the Cambodian adventure and the tragedies at Kent and Jackson—and not the hallucinations of a fringe of extremist students—has aroused hitherto moderate students to a new level of anger and frustration."[54] Thus, out of this necessity, Nixon began the painstaking process of culling out a square, white, and moderate youth bloc to marginalize his most vocal and radical opponents on the left. This reach out to youth started selectively.

Nixon's first public appearance after Kent State, Billy Graham's one-hundred-thousand-person youth rally at the University of Tennessee's (UT) sacred building, Neyland Stadium, made perfect sense. Nixon invited himself to the sold-out event on May 28 for several reasons. A recent article on UT had claimed that "football, fraternities and fundamentalism controlled the campus," and a poll of the attendees showed that 71 percent had voted for Nixon in 1968.[55] With this turnout—the silent majority's children as a witness—Nixon's voters on campus could find comfort in numbers. Speaking about campus unrest, Graham argued, "this nation could not withstand another depression because of its lack of moral fiber." Still, Graham offered a solution, predicting that the 1968 generation's questioning sensibility would lead to a more religious life—"curiosity leads to Christ."[56]

Nixon's speech at the Youth Rally signaled the president's deliberate identification with religious Christians to cultivate a conservative campus culture. "Government can provide peace, clean water, clean air, clean streets and all the rest," he clarified, but "that quality of spirit . . . that each one of us hungers for must come from him [Graham]." While he may not have been known for his religious convictions, Nixon argued that every president left office "more dedicated and more dependent on his religious faith than when he entered it."[57] Beyond this consideration, Nixon spent the speech focused on the business at hand: student protest. Pointing out the crowd's loyalty, Nixon claimed, "I am just glad that there seems to be a rather solid majority on one side rather than the other side." Nixon promised "the great majority of our young people who go to colleges and universities" do so for the noble "purpose of getting an education."[58] Contrasting this gathering with the bloody confrontations on campuses that spring, Nixon continued, "I am proud to say that the great majority of America's young people do not approve of violence." This mixture of southern football and religion made a welcomed elixir for Nixon's youth problem.

This event addressed Nixon's silent majority in religious terms. For parents, religious students, and the adherents to UT's traditional football culture, Graham's rally countered the youth problem on campuses with Nixon's "square power." After the protest, one UT flyer claimed, "the good citizens of this community are beginning to see a climate of concern growing and are anxious to see Christian Leadership take control of the University of Tennessee and use of the strictest discipline against this minority element of evil and demonstrate to our nation we have courage to handle these law violators."[59] On a theological level, defining antiwar protesters on campus as immoral provided Nixon with a spiritual superiority to students on the left. Campus protesters defended themselves at the Youth Rally with their own, antiwar morality.

Nixon's appearance provoked the University of Tennessee's diminutive protest movement to action. Hundreds of demonstrators sat together amid Graham and Nixon supporters, standing and shouting with signs that read "Thou Shalt Not Kill." Though the police arrested only a handful of students, they did photograph protesters who they later arrested for "disrupting a religious service." The courts eventually dismissed most of the charges after a lengthy battle over whether or not the president's presence made the event something other than religious. In addition, Graham's presence riled some campus religious leaders. A local university chaplain complained that Graham refused to meet with students, instead limiting his engagement to his "skillfully controlled Crusade meeting where the audience is barraged with attractions, revival music, personalities and a promise of deliverance from their deepest anxieties and fears." Furthermore, the chaplain observed, Graham's audience included only the white middle class who shared his concerns.[60] While campus unrest and antiwar protest challenged Nixon's appeals to religious conservatives, the political causes and solutions for student violence caused restraint.

On June 13, Nixon agreed to one moderate request and ordered former governor William Scranton (R-Pennsylvania) to head the President's Commission on Campus Unrest. Under these polarized circumstances, the commission conducted open hearings in Washington, DC; Jackson, Mississippi; Kent, Ohio; and Los Angeles over the summer, and Scranton submitted the 358-page report to the president in October.

The study, completed in the mandated three months, made up in length what it lacked in specifics. The commission decided not to name names and instead claimed the cause for student unrest "is not a single or uniform thing. Rather it is the aggregate result, or sum, of hundreds and thousands of individual beliefs and discontents, each of them as unique as the individuals who feel them." Calling attention to the generational crisis, the commission spread blame and warned that "a nation driven to use the weapons of war upon its youth is a nation on the edge of chaos. A nation that has lost the allegiance of part of its youth is a nation that has lost part of its future."[61] As for the commission's proposed solutions, ending the Vietnam War assumed a more urgent emphasis to solve the ongoing distrust. The commission also connected the unrest to the president, claiming that "only the President can offer the compassionate, reconciling moral leadership that can bring the country together again." Hardly the ivory tower Nixon and Agnew attacked before the shootings, Kent State pushed the president to question his ability to marginalize campus protesters.

After all, Scranton reported about Kent State's student body, "They are predominantly the children of middle class families, both white collar and blue collar, and in the main go on to careers as teachers and as middle-level management in industry."[62] These students belied the notion that all protesters were radicals. One Kent State undergrad, a self-described "straight" who stood only three feet from Allison Krause when she was killed, recalled that she intended to attend class when the National Guard prevented students from crossing campus, prompting her to join only her second rally.[63] These were Nixon voters' kids. Still, the president maintained his political emphasis on law and order and the Southern Strategy to win over Sunbelt conservatives on social issues such as campus unrest.

In addition, Scranton's report included an overview of the less publicized murder of two student demonstrators only two weeks after Kent State at Jackson State, a black college in Mississippi. This tragedy differed from Kent State in several ways. First, Phillip Lafayette Gibbs and Alexander Hall were killed by police during a protest that revolved around racial tensions with the local town's people. As one expert testified for the commission about black student unrest: "The main target of those protests—nearly always precise and concrete in objective contrast to the cosmic scope of white radical protest—is our persistently racist society." Scranton's report, and Americans in general, framed Jackson State as a separate issue and emphasized Kent State as a result of a "new culture of the young" and Vietnam War protests on campuses across the nation. As the report admitted, "Our subject is primarily the protest of white students."[64] Second, Kent State received more press. As one University of California, San Diego, student complained, even the commission report's chapter on "black student movements shrinks from a complete discussion."[65] While Filo's infamous photo of dead white students splashed across newspapers captured the moment of terror and grabbed Americans' attention, the obvious racial distinction contributed to this uneven concern. As Mark Giles argues about these different responses, "Racism is normal, not aberrant in American society. Because racism is an ingrained feature of our landscape, it looks ordinary and natural to persons in the culture."[66] This disproportionate coverage also influenced political reactions.

Even though a US court of appeals ruled in 1974 that the Jackson State killings were an overreaction, police officers who participated in that shooting avoided civil or criminal punishment. During Scranton's interviews, when his commission asked one local Jackson law enforcement leader if he planned any corrective steps in the future to prevent this violence, he responded, "Not that I know of."[67] Yet, Joseph Rhodes Jr., the only black member of the commission, explained that systemic racism, not student unrest or the Vietnam War, motivated Jackson State's violence, clarifying: "Mississippi lawmen fired a 400 round volley . . . because of the racial hatred that has characterized lawmen of the south and increasingly across the nation." Rhodes concluded, "The president has clearly written off the black community."[68] As one Jackson State student recalled, "It was just another day of business as usual, racist law enforcement officials victimizing black people in Mississippi."[69] While Rhodes saw Jackson State as a continuation of racist police brutality, black protesters also attributed their concerns to inequalities, as one wrote Scranton, "We as blacks are unrested in Detroit because Wayne State University is only 10% black while the city public school system is 65–75% black."[70] Black students' concerns lost out to the factors motivating the majority of white students' protests, as Kent State provoked years of litigation and eventually a significant reform in the way officers and the National Guard used force on campuses. Thus, although the police response to containing black youth gained little attention, larger demonstrations on white campuses called for new practices. While Scranton at least acknowledged the racial differences in campus unrest, many Americans confused the nuance to simplify the crisis.

Social conservatives such as Senator Robert Byrd (D-West Virginia) encouraged a monolithic version of student protests, as his response to the Scranton report separated the "mini-mini minority" he called "hoodlums, negro and white" from the overwhelming majority "who wish to dissent from dissenters."[71] Byrd claimed that the major flaw in Scranton's analysis was its exaggeration, as he underlines the fact that students made up only 4 percent of the country. Small as it was, as Byrd explains, this student minority existed because of the very college admission quotas and financial aid programs that Scranton's report suggested to cure the problem. For Byrd, this solution only opened campuses to less "scholarly qualified" students who caused more disturbances. Thus, cutting financial aid for these students, Byrd argued, could punish them, protect taxpayers from supporting "lawbreakers," and also solve the problem of unqualified, unruly students.

Byrd took direct aim at black students benefiting from quotas and financial aid, as the former KKK leader quoted a report about violence at Cornell University: "As soon as there are 50 black students on campus, they organize and rebel."[72] In another report, Byrd recalled a story about the University of Illinois, Urbana, where "more than 200 entering black students and outside supporters went ape" in the student union and scrawled "black power" over mutilated portraits of the university's past presidents.[73] In the fast-moving sixties, however, Byrd's analysis quickly became outdated as a congressional report on black colleges showed an increase in quiet campuses in 1970 that school presidents attributed to improved communication, student representation, and new programs in community involvement and black studies. As one Howard student claimed, black students entered "a period of quiet self-awareness and development." "They have gone on," he added, "unswayed by young, white America."[74]

Still, while racism explains the uneven treatment in national media and history toward the Kent State and Jackson State tragedies, the racialized depiction of student protesters explains why conservatives saw little distinction between the two events. After all, a flyer distributed during the University of Tennessee's strike connected white and black student activists when it asked, "Who helped these long haired, unintelligent, dark skinned, poorly dressed . . . protesters?"[75] Nixon's silent majority racialized student protesters, marginalizing them and blurring the distinctions between Jackson State and Kent State to mobilize both class and racial resentment against campus unrest.

In the president's letter responding to the report, despite his moderate tone, Nixon took exception with the liberal characterizations of students and the generation gap, claiming he met "tens of thousands of young people who do not in the slightest conform to the predominant description of students and young people in this report."[76] As for Jackson State and the racial violence that caused that tragedy, Nixon dedicated one paragraph toward the end of his seven-and-a-half-page response. Rather than address African American students' specific concerns about inclusion on white campuses and resources on black ones, Nixon offered a race-blind solution to increase student aid and create more access to higher education for all Americans.

In the end, Nixon chose restraint on campus unrest. On one hand, Nixon refrained from intervening to defend protesters' rights or release federal funds to train police and administrations to protect campus demonstrations. Nixon declined to intervene after he determined that campus unrest must be left up to the individual institutions and the states in which they reside. While seemingly a diplomatic approach, California's state legislature alone introduced over seventy bills in 1969 to "put down students," and one representative declared they would rid the state campuses of the "typhoid Mary's" of student rebellion. On the other hand, Nixon avoided the punitive approach that would refuse aid to offending students and punish universities that tolerated disturbances. Blacks, radical students, liberal professors, and outside agitators could be blamed for campus protest. Most Americans, however, saw Kent State differently. Mort Allin laid out the problem: "The hippies can be roundly criticized if need be, but we can't allow parents to think the administration is against *their* children."[77] Explaining that many parents "look with disfavor on the youth culture, they look with familial pride on their individual sons and daughters." Besides, "many of their kids have long hair."[78]

Nixon struggled to split the difference during a speech at the University of Nebraska when he promoted an "alliance of generations" that differed from his law-and-order image before the summer of 1970. Reviewing the media reaction to this more moderate tone, however, he took issue with journalists' omission of his "determination not to tolerate violence on the part of the minority of the young."[79] Nixon wanted to defuse the youth revolt through leadership, not as a conciliator. After 1971, however, campus protest subsided with the American withdrawal from and peace talks in Vietnam. In 1970, almost 40 percent of the colleges and universities in the US reported a large demonstration on campus. In 1978, only 13 percent reported campus unrest.[80]

Nixon's attempt to foster a conservative campus culture had help as the students cooperated. In journalist David Broder's distressed plea for responsible party politics, *The Party's Over*, he observed the change even in America's most liberal academic enclaves. Walking through Harvard's famed courtyards and out into the notoriously bohemian urban environs, Broder noted "the startling return of squareness to Harvard Square" and that "campus bulletin boards advertise more concerts and poetry readings than political meetings."[81] *SQUARE Magazine* even hoped to capitalize on the new "square chic": under the headline "Students Quietly Undertaking American Revolutionary Endeavors," it attempted to boost its readership with spokeswoman Nancy Jones as "the first *SQUARE* Cher."[82] While Nixon struggled to divide young voters on the issue of campus unrest, young Americans' response to laws concerning marijuana created an even foggier picture.

Many social conservatives connected the permissive counterculture to student power. "Habitual users of marijuana," one columnist argued, "tend to go along when the excitement of a demonstration begins."[83] Despite Kent State, Nixon maintained his cynical assumption about student unrest. While many conservative and nonstudent youth could support Nixon's tough approach to campus unrest, his stance on marijuana struggled to attract his own youth segment. Criminalizing white middle-class kids on campuses became problematic, but Nixon's War on Drugs exaggerated this dilemma. Even though the politics of youth concerning marijuana hindered Nixon's law-and-order agenda, he used this issue as well to define his youth campaign's square political culture.

War on Marijuana

Spelling out marijuana's gateway potential to Chicago mayor Richard Daley, President Richard Nixon explained: "Once you cross that line, from the straight society to the drug society—marijuana, then speed, then it's LSD, then it's heroin, etc. then you're done."[84] Nixon, the first president to declare a "War on Drugs," railed against marijuana's role in the youth revolt and drug culture as he cheered his aides to "hit it hard," opting to "enforce the law . . . you've got to scare them."[85] Still, Nixon conceded the problems with a law-and-order solution to drug abuse: "You know, when people think about drugs, they're just disgusted by it. They just want to lock them up, and throw away the key. But it's more complex than that."[86] Recent scholarship on drug policy and carceral studies has focused on marijuana politics to examine these complexities, as youth's increasing marijuana use on campuses and in America's suburbs inspired middle-class white parents to fear their children could get caught in the War on Drugs.[87] After all, even conservative leaders such as William F. Buckley Jr. argued, "*But* at the same time, American parents . . . did not desire *their* 18-year-old boys and girls to be sent to jail for smoking pot."[88]

Thus, Nixon's approach to the marijuana problem balanced these conflicting interests to negotiate the shifting political terrain. His signature contribution to the War on Drugs, the Controlled Substances Act of 1970, maintained the Justice Department's central role and harsh penalties for drug dealers but also lowered penalties for marijuana users, appointed a presidential commission to "to see things as youth sees them," and split the funding allocation with other agencies such as the Department of Health, Education, and Welfare (HEW) that emphasized harm reduction through prevention and treatment.[89] Marijuana's growing popularity with young Americans confused the president's effort to separate "hard core dissidents" from youth that Nixon could target for his own constituency.

The war on marijuana had begun well before Nixon took office.[90] From the 1930s through 1962, Federal Bureau of Narcotics director Harry Anslinger criminalized marijuana users through an antiviolence lens. In keeping with the antimarijuana message from the infamous 1936 film *Reefer Madness*, Anslinger affirmed the drug's reputation as a rage-inducing "evil weed" while he presumed most users to be Mexican immigrants or jazz culture's urban blacks. By the late 1960s, after the baby boomers got a hold of marijuana, those assumptions had become untenable. Estimates for Americans who had tried marijuana in 1968 ranged from eight to twelve million, including one-third of college students.[91]

Still, marijuana's spread into mainstream culture exaggerated fears that youth's permissive attitudes and the creep of urban crime had taken over America's most sacred spaces. "Marijuana is no longer a ghetto drug" one expert pointed out; "it has entered the suburbs, the board rooms, the colleges and even . . . the sanctity of the family living room."[92] Nixon rallied white southerners, the Sunbelt's suburbanites, and former Democrats who he defined as "working class white ethnics" under the "silent majority" label. For these voters, this danger underlined their concerns about race, especially for the Sunbelt suburbians in places such as Orange County, California. As Lisa McGirr explains, they "had moved from Los Angeles to escape the congestion, crime and diversity of the city."[93] The predatory reputation behind marijuana challenged suburban parents' grasp for that peace and security.

Fears about marijuana as a gateway to the drug culture inspired this crackdown. In addition, LSD cast a dark light on both pot and the drug culture that linked the two. John E. Ingersoll responded to the growing protest against the severity of penalties for use of marijuana, stating that "people who use marijuana extensively also have a tendency to branch out into more damaging drugs."[94] The issue resonated too much with the "silent majority" for Nixon to ignore, as one disgruntled *Spokane Daily* reader asked, "How can you be of greater service to your city than by helping to finance an all-out war on drugs?" Urging Spokane's entire citizenry, from the American Red Cross to the business community, to participate in this effort, the letter makes one last request, "How about some drug laws with teeth in them?"[95] In one typical city hearing to acquire funds, a community cynic argued, "the youth should be in jail if they have problems" and "you should build brick walls around them so they can't cause problems."[96]

Middle America's opposition to marijuana sharpened when the crime rate for young Americans rose dramatically throughout the 1960s, as it became twice as high among youths between fifteen and twenty-five than among older Americans.[97] Nixon blamed the drug culture—"the worst sickness in American history"—for "riots in cities, disturbances in colleges and the upsurge in crime."[98] In addition, Nixon saw the War on Drugs as a way to target his enemies. Years later, John Ehrlichman admitted, "We knew we couldn't make it illegal to be either against the war or black," but busting pushers meant "we could arrest their leaders, raid their homes, break up their meetings, and vilify them night after night on the evening news."[99] Thus, as with campus protesters, the young targets in Nixon's initial law-and-order effort against marijuana were criminalized for the interchangeable offense of protesting or not being white.

Marijuana had also taken on a political dimension. Popular books such as Theodore Roszak's *The Making of a Counter Culture*, Charles A. Reich's best seller *The Greening of America*, and Democratic adviser Frederick Dutton's *Changing Sources of Power* defined the youth revolt's Consciousness III as a permissive, communal sensibility. Arguing for the connection between marijuana and youth politics, Roszak explained: "It [marijuana] is not simply an excrescence that can be surgically removed from our culture by indignant rejection. [Timothy] Leary and his followers have succeeded in endowing it with such a mystique that it now seems the very essence of that politics of the nervous system in which the young are so deeply involved."[100] This literature predicted that the 1968 generation's rebellion, intrinsically intertwined with the psychedelic drug culture, would drive youth to the Democratic Party's New Politics that targeted young voters, women, and blacks.

Common perceptions about marijuana's negative health and habitual effects on the user caused concern for Americans on both sides of the aisle. In addition, social conservatives feared pot's new role in society as one young antimarijuana journalist in the *National Review* admitted, "I care not a fig for its physical effects." Rather, the article continued, the problem with pot was that it initiated "a lifestyle that generally rejects or seeks to bring down 'ordered life as we know it.'" According to this framework, more political antimarijuana laws meant "to lean on, to penalize the Counterculture."[101] The stakes could not have been higher, as marijuana became a lightning rod for the culture wars fueling American politics during Nixon's era. While Nixon struggled to provide moral leadership on the campus unrest controversy, he could take a more austere position on marijuana. In expanding his reach to "square" Americans, this issue took on more political significance with the evangelical movement in the Sunbelt that Nixon sought to include in his New Majority.

The political role for youth in this religious appeal became clear when Billy Graham organized an "Honor America Day" at the Lincoln Memorial on the Fourth of July. This event, endorsed by Nixon, meant to exhibit the young Americans who fit into the silent majority. Before the scheduled flag procession to the White House Ellipse, Graham addressed ten thousand people at the Capitol steps for the morning's religious service to warn about the "rising sea of permissiveness," urging young people in the audience to "pursue the vision, reach toward the goal, fulfill the dream—and as you move to do it, never give in."[102]

Graham stood directly in contrast to the drug culture; as one young banker explained during Honor America Day, "It's nice to get away from the problems of the cities. . . . Instead of smoking pot, you go hear Billy Graham."[103] Graham shared this view, as he even grew his hair long, and would wander in disguise through protest marches, demonstrations, or rock concerts to engage young people in conversation. When one young man recognized Graham at a show, he asked the evangelical leader to "pray for good weed," to which Graham responded, "You can also get high on Jesus."[104] Here, Graham's spiritual revival, steeped in the anxieties of a shifting, more suburban demographic in the Sunbelt, overlapped neatly with Nixon's appeal to an American "renewal of spirit."

Young people had flocked to Christianity during this period, creating a Jesus movement, complete with its signature hand signal. A slight adaptation of the 1960s peace symbol, Graham described the "One Way" gesture as simply a "raised index finger pointing upwards." While Graham welcomed traditionally "straight," middle-class youth groups such as Intervarsity Christian Fellowship members, a religious revival within the counterculture resonated with Graham's quest to bring America back from the 1960s through a spiritual awakening. Co-opting the counterculture's language during one speech to the Kansas City Youth Crusade in 1967, Graham asked the audience to "Tune into God, then turn on . . . drop out—of the materialistic world. The experience of Jesus Christ is the greatest trip you can take."[105]

Young conservatives linked their politics with the self-described Jesus Freaks around a common foe—the counterculture. One columnist for the YAF's *New Guard* explained that though Jesus Freaks lived in communes while they dressed and talked like hippies, "they break sharply with the hippie subculture at crucial points—at the points of morality and religion." In turn, conservative politicians resonated with these "hip" evangelicals who "campaign actively against the moral laxity and putrid permissiveness that have gone so far in corrupting American middle class, especially suburban middle-class, society."[106]

Despite the backlash that motivated Nixon's hard stance on pot, the various disparities in penalties for marijuana possession in different states pushed Nixon's drug law reforms. Under the larger project of curtailing young Americans' narcotics abuse during the 1960s, local enforcement efforts disproportionately punished marijuana users. One opportunistic state attorney in Florida's Twelfth Judicial Circuit,

Frank Schaub, proudly announced in 1968 that his own "war on narcotics" had yielded "32 charges for possession . . . mostly marijuana." With harsh penalties, including a minimum sentence of one year of probation for possession and some sentences reaching five years in prison for selling, Schaub proclaimed, "we are dealing with young people. I hope that our progress in this area will make other young people think before becoming involved in drug abuse."[107] The punishments State Attorney Schaub handed out paled in comparison to the thirty-year sentence one man received for crossing the border into Texas with a matchbox full of marijuana cigarettes or the ninety-nine-year sentence on the books in North Dakota for selling pot.[108]

Many young Americans, right and left, agreed that draconian marijuana laws deserved rethinking. In 1968, the voice of American conservatism, the *National Review*, published an issue dedicated to the marijuana controversy. One article arguing for its legalization interviewed James White III, legal counsel for the Committee to Legalize Marijuana (LeMar). Surprisingly, White was no hippie. "At least, he voted for Goldwater in '64." According to White, conservatives and liberals agreed that the marijuana laws were "reducing respect for law enforcement—just as prohibition did."[109] The uneven and severe punishments for marijuana in different states undermined law enforcement's credibility. Even the mainstream youth groups on the right agreed, as the platform adopted at the 1972 College Republican Convention in Virginia said that "there was no evidence the use of marijuana leads to experimenting with hard drugs nor does its use play a part in the commission of crimes."[110] While youth's concern about harsh marijuana laws crossed the political divide, politicians' support for the War on Drugs was equally bipartisan.

Perhaps the most prominent advocate for reform in Congress, Senator Thomas Dodd (D-Connecticut) proposed a bill that would codify his own voters' suburban, white, middle-class kids' safety from the punitive laws against weed.[111] First, his reforms restored "judicial discretion" and eliminated minimum sentences for first-time offenders. While this effort met parents' concerns about their kids getting caught up in the War on Drugs, it also hoped to regain young Americans' confidence in the system. Testifying in Dodd's hearings on drugs, the National Student Association's director of drug studies, Bard Grosse, explained the marijuana controversy as a youth issue. Here, Dodd's policies fit students' interests, as Grosse explained: "Because of these changes and the revised penalty structure contained in Senator Dodd's legislation, we endorse this bill rather than the administration's bill." In another hearing, Grosse argued that overly punitive marijuana laws undermined youth's faith in the system—"as long as you are lying about pot, and as long as you have these laws on pot, the kids are not going to listen to you."[112] A twenty-something lawyer wrote Dodd, "you will be the first one to scream for 'law and order' and wonder why young people have no respect for law. . . . To them it is not a participatory democracy, but rather an illusory democracy."[113] The credibility gap that had poisoned this generation's perception of the Vietnam War also influenced young Americans' cynical attitudes toward the war on pot.

Mental health officials agreed. When he testified to Congress, the president of the National Association of Mental Health complained that Nixon's proposals pushed the law-and-order approach too hard, warning the punitive approach "will result in bitterness, cynicism, hostility and widespread disrespect for the law, all will deprive the government and society of the allegiance and goodwill of much of its youth and of much of value that they might otherwise have contributed."[114]

Dodd also emphasized treatment and prevention, or harm reduction, which critics preferred over a punitive approach. When he asked Grosse about conducting the antidrug efforts through agencies such as HEW and the Institute of Mental Health, the National Student Association (NSA) representative responded: "I think it will make a tremendous difference to young people, and I think it will make a tremendous difference in actuality."[115] This made a law-and-order approach to marijuana acceptable to parents, and to young people. Dodd claimed, as recent scholarship has shown, that the laws punished the wrong people—white, middle-class young people on track to fill the future managerial and white-collar positions so revered in the American economy. Dodd held out hope for these low-level drug users as he claimed, "They are college students, often children of parents who suffer from no lack of opportunity in the economic and educational sense."[116] Still, Dodd pressed that these reforms, more than calming parents' anxieties, could assuage young people's concerns, conceding: "They have been alienated from their parents, from their Government and from their universities and schools." Until Congress replaced these laws with more proportionate punishments, Dodd argued, "drug abuse is one way the 'alienated' will thumb their noses at organized society."[117] While Dodd's approach allowed room for nuance, the Nixon administration held its more strident pose.

For example, H. R. Haldeman, Nixon's chief of staff, disputed the wording of an administration report on Nixon's marijuana policy that promised to fight drugs in a "variety of ways." This language did not work with Nixon's tough talk, as Haldeman admitted, "but 'handl[ing] it in a variety of ways' really says we don't know how to handle it. Which may be the truth. But it sure isn't the thing to say."[118] Still, Nixon negotiated with Dodd on reforms. After all, Dodd's approach appeared moderate compared to that of his peers on the Senate juvenile delinquency subcommittee who proposed failed amendments to lower sentences for marijuana offenders even further, strip the "no-knock" provision for drugs busts, and give HEW the ability to reschedule drugs rather than the Justice Department.[119] Dodd's bill, the Comprehensive Drug Abuse Prevention and Control Act, passed overwhelmingly with the administration's support, 82–0. The new law created five schedules to categorize "controlled substances" and determine each drug's controls, placing marijuana in Schedule I, with the most dangerous drugs that lacked any medical use but were highly addictive. Title II of the bill, the Controlled Substances Act (CSA), established the process for the legal War on Drugs, maintaining the Justice Department's role atop the departmental hierarchy to decide on any changes to scheduling and penalties. This federal law eliminated mandatory minimum sentences for first-time offenders and allowed for judicial discretion to sentence users to probation but established minimum sentencing for repeaters and "peddlers." As for funding, the CSA created an impressive budget that allocated over $40 million to each the Justice Department and HEW in the first year and then quadrupled that amount by 1972. In this political climate, Dodd told critics of "law and order" that the Senate reforms "were going as far as we can go."[120]

Many young Americans disagreed. Across the political spectrum, youth looked cynically at the new marijuana law as they criticized the gateway theory, the subtle racism in the laws' enforcement, hawks' attempts to blame the failed war in Vietnam on stoned American soldiers, and an attempt to shift Americans' attention to a new, internal war.[121] While young Americans on the left and right questioned this rationale, the war on marijuana's execution confirmed their concerns. Although the bill dedicated over two million dollars to rehabilitation, the proposal's teeth gained more attention as it contained a "no-knock" provision that allowed federal narcotics agents to enter a house without a warrant or warning. Nixon signed the Comprehensive Drug Abuse Prevention and Control Act of 1970 on national television, only weeks before the 1970 midterm elections, just as the Southern Strategy entered its final, fateful stretch.

Nixon's approach to marijuana adhered to his tough stance despite the pushback from his opponents. In 1969, police arrested over 250,000 Americans for marijuana possession, mostly below the age of thirty. Nixon expanded this effort yearly, arguing in 1972 that "there isn't a penalty too great for drug traffickers who prey upon youth" as he requested $600 million from Congress to support his newly established Office of Drug Abuse Law Enforcement. Nixon called for "strong, tough prosecution" to combat what he termed "the number one domestic problem that concerns the American people."[122] During Nixon's presidency, spending on criminal justice as a percentage of US GNP increased from 1.0 percent ($10.5 billion) to 1.4 percent ($15 billion) from 1971 to 1974 alone. Over the same short period, federal spending on the judicial system grew by 62 percent and on policing by 52 percent, while the number of police nationally grew 13.6 percent, from 575,000 to 653,000 personnel.[123] Buttressed by the formation of the Drug Enforcement Agency, marijuana arrests jumped from 292,179 to 420,700 from 1972 to 1973.[124] The racial disparities in these arrests quickly became evident. In an interview with Dan Baum, Ehrlichman explained the motives: "We knew we couldn't make it illegal to be either against the war or black, but by getting the public to associate the hippies with marijuana and blacks with heroin, and then criminalizing both heavily, we could disrupt those communities. We could arrest their leaders, raid their homes, break up their meetings, and vilify them night after night on the evening news. Did we know we were lying about the drugs? Of course we did."[125]

Marijuana arrests became an effective way to silence young activists who opposed Nixon. Even in the most conservative bastion of Nixon supporters, such as the University of Tennessee, more police meant an attack on the antiwar student counterculture. For example, federal drug enforcement agencies funded and organized drug sweeps in Knoxville with handles such as "Project Aquarius" that revealed their targets. Confirming its focus on students, the Knoxville police arrested twenty-two UT undergrads for marijuana possession in one day. Randy Tyree, Knoxville's safety director who UT students dubbed the city's "number one narc," explained the motivation for the crackdown: "Young people have always experimented . . . and to this generation the experimentation is with drugs." Indicating the futility of such efforts, according to the UT's yearbook that year, students still found drugs readily available on campus.[126]

Marijuana versus Square Culture

Nixon maintained his tough position on pot, though it proved problematic with young Americans. After meeting with twelve young White House staffers, HEW secretary Robert Finch appreciated the generation gap's political influence and sought to diminish Nixon's role in the war on marijuana by using HEW's agencies that emphasized a preventative rather than punitive approach. First, Finch explained one problem with "law and order" in a memo warning Nixon to stay out of the pot issue as it "accentuates any generation gap there may be."[127] Even Nixon admitted that while a substantial rise in young voters forced political elites to listen to them, the stakes were higher as the administration opened its communication with young people to solve the "credibility problem on social issues" such as marijuana: "It's not just the 18 year old vote" Nixon explained; "it's the contractual obligation that goes with it."[128] Nixon understood that the arguments he made to win in 1968 had to change.

Marijuana, the symbolic drug of the counterculture, quickly became a political football in the increasingly heated dialogue surrounding the generation gap. Hoping to diffuse this tension, President Nixon appointed Governor Raymond Shafer of Pennsylvania, a former prosecutor, as head of the National Commission on Marijuana and Drug Abuse to develop guidelines for prevention and law enforcement. Shafer, along with White House liaison Geoff Shepard, inherited the commission's impetus to make Nixon's law and order more credible with young Americans. As one supporter explained, "Presidential commissions seem to be the one group which tend to think as youth thinks—to see things as youth sees them."[129] The committee's personnel exemplified the White House's intention to legitimate the study as an indication of Nixon's sensitivity to youth but also showed the problems the commission faced in translating this issue into legislation and action.

The Shafer Commission conducted the most extensive and comprehensive examination of marijuana ever performed by the US government. They recorded thousands of pages of transcripts of formal and informal hearings, solicited all points of view, including those of public officials, community leaders, professional experts, and students. They also organized a nationwide survey of public beliefs, information, and experience with drugs. In addition, they conducted separate surveys of opinion among district attorneys, judges, probation officers, clinicians, university health officials, and "free clinic" personnel. In total, they commissioned more than fifty projects to survey enforcement of the marijuana laws in six metropolitan jurisdictions.

The final report supported Nixon's racialized distinction between dealers and young users, offering a complicated solution that decriminalized marijuana use but maintained the tough laws for selling cannabis. As historian Matt Lassiter points out, "The marijuana-as-gateway mystique . . . helped institutionalize two interlinked but spatially distinct approaches: public health campaigns in white middle-class neighborhoods and militarized interdiction in urban minority areas."[130] Thus, the war on pot after World War II involved a racist, punitive "New Jim Crow" emphasis on enforcement.[131] Nixon agreed with the commission's suggestion to level heftier sentences for those selling marijuana, as he claimed "everyone knows a kid next door who is smoking dope, but not everyone knows a pusher."[132] Nixon's voters smoked pot too. Even when he utilized the Advertising Council to produce antidrug pop songs, "Help a Junkie, Bust a Pusher" promoted this distinction between victim and predator.[133] This meant Nixon could rationalize more lenient penalties for marijuana use while increasing his emphasis on the supply side.

While Nixon could agree with the commission's supply-side focus, he found himself in the familiar position of opposing his own study as the report claimed that marijuana was not harmful and did not cause hallucinations and that there was no evidence pot itself caused "crime, sexual immorality or addiction to hard drugs." Thus, the commission recommended that private use be legalized, and other penalties lessened.[134] As Congressman James Scheuer (D-New York) observed, the commission's recommendation to decriminalize marijuana represented a "great step forward in regaining the credibility of the youth in our country."[135] The Shafer Commission had some detractors among young Americans. One high school senior from Oklahoma feared that if the government legalized private consumption, "we're going to have a lot of freak kids running around." More common, college students mostly embraced its findings as the managing editor of the University of Missouri student newspaper claimed: "I definitely think they are on the right track. . . . From what I've read and seen the only thing wrong with it [marijuana] is that it's illegal."[136]

Considering the commission's unprecedented price tag, Nixon maintained a conspicuous distance from the study. In one memo revealing Nixon's position on the commission, Geoff Shepard wrote, "I cannot see any presidential meeting, except for him to use as a forum to blast marihuana again!!!" Instead, Shepard hoped to placate the commission with certificates, "because they think they are doing a good job for the President—misguided though they be."[137] Nixon never wanted the commission, and his relationship with its ongoing study confirms that he supported it only out of necessity. The Shafer Commission maintained felony penalties for drug dealers, but Nixon refused to accept a proposal that would contradict the gateway theory.

Politicians' reactions to his commission on marijuana confirmed Nixon's belief in this issue's ability to tie together his "silent majority." James "Curley" Walsh, an Indiana state representative, asked the president to "purge the report" and start a new one that included "parents of son and/or daughter who are addicts." Revealing its religious sensibility, the letter concludes, "Why give god's blessing to the devil?"[138]

A crucial component of the silent majority, Sunbelt suburban parents, used the Shafer Commission to support the gateway theory. Specifically, mothers pushed for a solution to the drug problem that protected their kids from drugs and harsh laws. A Harris poll in 1970 showed the "difficulty to raise children, drugs, generation gap" as the greatest problems in being a woman.[139] In a letter to the president, the president of the Del Rosa Federated Junior Women's Club in San Bernardino underlined that "a serious drug abuse problem existed not only among the minority community" as she spelled out the role marijuana played in spreading drugs to the youth "who were supposed to come from backgrounds immune to drug related problems." Confirming Nixon's understanding of marijuana as an entry drug, the letter argued that of the 75 percent of the youth in San Bernardino who had tried drugs, almost all of them began with marijuana. Speaking as mothers, the women wrote, "If a youth is brave enough to experiment with marijuana in the house, then he would be brave enough to experiment with hard narcotics."[140]

This club had firsthand experience after it funded and organized the conversion of an old bank into the Christian, faith-based Agape House for young people. However, these women agreed with the commission's emphasis on treatment over punishment. Nixon also agreed with Agape's religious version of prevention and treatment, as the president told Haldeman, "In my opinion, there are some [psychiatrists] that are important and necessary, but most, most people would do a hell of a lot better with a preacher than a psychiatrist."[141] At the heart of the problem, the Department of Health, Education, and Welfare's secretary, Robert Finch, pointed out, was the "unknown facts about marijuana make it difficult to talk about except in the moral context—where the greatest controversy lies."[142] Still, Nixon ignored Finch's warning to avoid the marijuana issue's "moral context," and in fact replaced the secretary of HEW with Elliot Richardson after one year. To the contrary, the president's reach for religious voters demanded a tough stance as he told Haldeman that this was an area to assume the role of a "moral force."[143] Revealing this problem's spiritual threat, Nixon asked Congress to increase funding to the CSA, comparing drug use to "a tide which has swept this country in the last decade and which afflicts both the body and soul of America."[144] Nixon noted in his address that "it comes quietly into our homes, and destroys children, it moves into neighborhoods and breaks the fiber of community."[145]

This reaction to the Shafer Commission underlined the approach Nixon took on marijuana decriminalization.[146] The politics made sense here; no matter what the commission said, Nixon later admitted, he would not legalize marijuana.[147] In the end, his approach proved well calculated, as the 1972 referendum on legalizing marijuana in California, Proposition 19, could muster only 34 percent of the voters' support. While medical researchers and lawmakers agreed that one should not get "ten for two" (ten years for two joints), Nixon established a federal emphasis on law enforcement. Early in the commission's effort, Shafer learned how inconsequential Nixon intended to make its call for less federal enforcement. In reality, the Shafer report's fate was sealed well before it even started. After all, Dodd negotiated with the administration that only the Justice Department could change marijuana's scheduling, an unlikely prospect no matter what the commission argued. Even with this control, Nixon bemoaned the law and attempted to shift funding into law enforcement, explaining, "Get it out of HEW, we had the right people on the bill and we screwed it up." "I don't want psychiatrists," the president grumbled; "I want to smash the dope peddlers."[148] Thus, while Nixon's position on marijuana struggled with the youth problem as well, the religious and racial context bolstered the moral stance in the War on Drugs that he avoided with campus unrest. During Nixon's presidency, even though his law-and-order policies struggled with the politics of youth, his effort to southernize youth culture made progress.

In 1972, an *Esquire* article on campus life told students that Nixon had won, reporting, "Your pot parties have turned into beer busts," sarcastically lamenting that "we never thought to see Consciousness III awash in the suds of the hard hats."[149] Here, the drug (or drink) of choice symbolized the politics. Nixon's tough stance on marijuana also placed his cultural politics firmly in step with the blue-collar, working-class beer guzzlers he hoped to peel away from the Democratic Party.

Nixon's ambiguous relationship with young Americans became even more obvious as the youth vote gained political momentum and Nixon's liberal opponents in Congress threatened an alliance with their young counterparts. The youth problem ostensibly presented a barrier to Nixon's conservative agenda, as he admitted in 1970, "On the issue side, we still haven't gotten through the strong position on law and order." The president realized the limitations of this project, as he bemoaned his administration's inability to pass tough laws "despite our leadership in this field, all of the public relations devices we use to get it across and my hitting it hard in the campaign."[150]

As he was campaigning for president in 1968, Nixon's ads conflated the student and youth problem with civil rights violence to portray a combined danger to America's future. As middle-class white protesters and suburban kids emerged as the largest threat in 1970, Nixon's approach to marijuana and student unrest adapted and encouraged the racially separated application of law and order. However, as Nixon continued his politics of youth to court his middle-aged silent majority with cultural and religious appeals on these issues, moderate young Americans demanded further concessions on their own issues such as the environment, the draft, and of course the right to vote.

3 | "The Orderly Process of Change"
Nixon and Youth Issues

Even as Congress moved with historical haste to lower the voting age in 1971, the prospect of twenty-seven million first-time voters frightened the president. "Give someone direct orders and responsibility to stop this: Highest Priority," Nixon wrote White House aide John Ehrlichman.[1] The president's concern about the lower voting age for the 1972 election crystallized two of his most notable political problems. First, it signaled the generation gap that separated Nixon from young Americans born after World War II. Second, the youth vote heightened the structural obstacles to Nixon's turn to the right, as many of his liberal opponents in Congress embraced the youth movement by supporting lowering the voting age and advocating on behalf of issues near and dear to young people. The prospect of a lower voting age forced Nixon to show young Americans that his administration could respond to their two central issues: the draft and the environment.

Youth politics, with its increasing demands on political elites, gave liberals in Congress the impetus to push through legislation that they hoped would both motivate the 1968 generation's transition into "the system" and corral young people as a constituency. Nixon aide Mort Allin accused the White House of "sticking our head in the sand and ignoring the reality after the 18-year old vote decision was handed down while the Dems jumped on the bandwagon."[2] Internally, the Nixon administration began to reconsider their uncompromising stance on the politics of youth. According to Nixon's early point man on the youth problem, secretary of HEW Robert Finch, "most people do not object to youth participation in 'legitimate' activities," and "want to feel they are 'coming into the establishment.'"[3] Perhaps, critics such as Allin suggested, policy decisions could channel youth's protest politics into traditional mechanisms such as the vote and congressional hearings—or as the kids called it, "the system," while providing a steam valve to relieve young Americans' anti-Nixon sentiment.

Despite the youth vote's liberal potential, optimistic conservative young people interpreted the amendment as the end of the 1960s, when students "marched with a bomb in one hand and a desecrated flag in the other." In one article, a Lipscomb University student editorialized that after Kent State, "The 1970s foreboded a continuation of these practices." After the vote, however, young people learned that "rose bushes will not grow from thorns," bringing in a new era where young people worked "within the established system in a decent, orderly manner."[4] These terms, "within the system" and "orderly," became staples in each debate on the different youth issues. In this context, bridging the widely perceived generation gap motivated Nixon's concessions.

This chapter first analyzes the contradictory reasons behind lowering the voting age. While liberals thought this could bring in a new constituency, all lawmakers used this maneuver to mollify campus youth who had gained unprecedented attention after Kent State. The year 1970 marked the emergence of youth politics on a new scale, and a poll taken in December of that year showed potential Democratic opponents for the 1972 election trouncing the president with this segment. The environmentalist from Maine, Senator Ed Muskie, gained 49 percent of young voters' support with only 22 percent going to Nixon.[5] The growing relationship between youth organizations such as the Youth Franchise Coalition and liberal Democrats in Congress who came into office during the Kennedy era embraced a sympathetic approach to youth concerns that positioned itself to attract young voters. Thus, youth politics prevented the law-and-order campaign that many in the GOP had wanted to initiate. Moderate Republican groups such as the Ripon Society reacted defensively, as their polling showed over one-third of the sons and daughters of Republicans did not support Nixon and defected to the Democratic Party. Suggesting bold moves such as endorsing the legalization of marijuana, the Ripon Society hoped to counter this hemorrhaging by publishing a new book, *Instead of Revolution*.[6] While Geoffrey Kabaservice examines the fall of moderates and the Ripon Society within the GOP, he contradicts scholarship that "emphasized that the administration's incipient Southern strategy and the continuation of the war in Vietnam had turned the President toward conservatives," arguing: "in fact Nixon continued to try to keep the moderates on board."[7]

In fact, after the voting age fell to eighteen, Nixon acquiesced on youth issues. On the environment, young people from across the political spectrum shared ecological concerns. Nixon's administration could not resist demands for new regulations when an equally diverse cross-section of congressional members advanced laws that protected air and water from pollution. Finally, Nixon's move to end the draft served as the pièce de résistance in his administration's effort to control the generation gap's political damage. Contrary to interpretations that view Nixon's policies as liberal or conservative, this chapter argues that Nixon's concessions on youth issues cut across the political spectrum and were meant to defuse anti-Nixon youth politics but also to build trust with moderate and conservative young voters.[8] This problem divided Nixon's focus between his short-term focus on reelection and his conservative political agenda. This opening produced lasting and influential changes. Young Americans did not win these policy victories on their own, as the 1968 generation's demonstrable frustration with politics emboldened opportunistic Democrats in Congress and prompted the president's acquiescence on key issues. Hardly the "evil genius" in this realm, the president acted defensively. Many historians magnify Nixon's Machiavellian leadership and overlook the pall of confusion that youth politics cast over his administration. Nixon's tempered approach earned him faint praise, as one student explained his verdict on the president's early policy efforts, "I'll wait and see." A former McCarthyite admitted Nixon's image favorably impressed her but questioned his credibility: "His public relations man probably deserves more credit than Nixon for that."[9] While good press helped, the youth problem forced Nixon to produce substantial action.

The Vote

In 1970, all signs indicated that the youth vote could offer the Democratic Party a new and desperately needed constituency. After polls showed Humphrey gaining ground among young people, Charles Colson wrote that this "underscores its [youth] volatility" as "Humphrey did very badly in this group" during the 1968 election.[10] A Gallup poll of college students in that same year showed they declared themselves as liberals at a ratio of two to one, as they ranked Spiro Agnew last among seventeen government officials with an 87 percent negative—putting his renomination as the vice presidential candidate for the 1972 election into question. "Republican-Liberal" mayor of New York City John Lindsay scored the highest, followed by Muskie, as Nixon placed ninth.[11] While Kent State inspired Nixon to reach out across the generation gap, the specter of eleven million new voters intensified his resolve to "bridge the gap" or at least appear to try.

Young people played an important role in organizing the youth vote movement. One group, Project 18, combined the National Education Association (NEA) educators most committed to expanding citizenship. Project 18 formed when the NEA's 1968 National Representative Assembly voted overwhelmingly to make the youth vote its major objective. This leadership then founded the Youth Franchise Coalition, which included members from groups such as the NAACP and the AFL-CIO.

As young Americans lobbied for the vote, political elites called the most loudly for lowering the voting age. As youth politics became known for its protest politics during the late 1960s and early 1970s, antiwar and liberal congressional members embraced the effort to expand the youth vote. Democratic senators Ted Kennedy (D-Massachusetts) and Mike Mansfield (D-Montana) attached a rider to the 1970 extension of the Voting Rights Act that included lowering the voting age. Although this bill focused on ending the literacy tests that prevented blacks from voting, the ongoing attempt to lower the voting age since 1943 had reached its moment. That this legislation combined the voting age and black voting rights represented a historical relationship; as Rebecca de Schweinitz explains, the first calls for a lower voting age came from young black civil rights activists in the 1960s.[12] While many historians attribute this change to the "old enough to fight, old enough to vote" argument, the debate after Kent State focused on how best to control the youth problem and channel it into the political system. Before this, especially during the 1960s, politicians who tried to lower the voting age faced stiff opposition.

In 1969, Warren D. Chamberlain, a conservative state representative in Minnesota, spoke to the League of Women Voters against the eighteen-year-old vote. Chamberlain linked the problems back to Dr. Spock. "The same loving permissiveness that allows unlimited candy and pop to decay their children's teeth," he lamented, "begets the permissiveness that decays morals, life and all sense of responsibility."[13] Pointedly, Chamberlain asked Minnesotan mothers, "Would you turn the most important decisions of your family over to your 19 year old child?" For conservatives, this moral problem did not require an accommodating political solution. After 1968 referenda to lower the voting age failed in Ohio and New Jersey, politicians attributed their defeat to this "backlash." One concerned citizen from Connecticut asked Nixon to oppose the Twenty-Sixth Amendment because "the young are fanatics," "immature," and "incapable of reasoning." To solve the youth problem, this letter instead called "for law and order and logical reasoning which can solve all the problems and the one way to effect this is to deny the vote to the 'mentally ill generation.'"[14] Thus, Nixon's tough stance on youth issues came into direct conflict with the mounting support for lowering the voting age.

Before Kent State, in congressional debates over lowering the youth vote, Louisiana Democratic representative John Rarick, a hawk on Vietnam policy (and the 1980 nominee of George C. Wallace's American Independent Party), pointed out the limits of connecting the war with young voters' rights. "The screaming mob espousing ['old enough to fight, old enough to vote'] are not veterans nor fighting men but rather draft dodgers, draft card burners, and revolutionary vandals who have no intention whatsoever of fighting—at least not for the United States."[15] Rarick rejected the notion that contemporary youth were more intelligent and better informed than previous generations. Unimpressed, Rarick found that "records in our public schools, the Selective Service System, and our Armed Forces show a constant decline in both intelligence and aptitude averages." Anecdotally, Rarick also observed, "The common experience of adults—especially employers—is that today's young people cannot spell, cannot read, and cannot reason."[16] Rarick's dismissive tone resonated in the halls of Congress as many politicians and voters saw more discipline as the solution to the youth problem.

Advocates for the vote, such as the Youth Franchise Coalition's Clark Wideman, hoped the image of "radical campus protesters" would not sway anyone's opinion on lowering the youth vote either way. Claiming that the national focus on "the militant 1 percent" distorted youth's reputation, Wideman explained that the politics of parenthood shaped how "the average voter identifies with basically three different young people—his son, his neighbor's son, and what we call the 'media kid.'" According to Wideman, "the media kid" gained the most visibility because of the "breakdown in family structure." Thus, alienation due to inadequate nurturing in the home, not young peoples' naked antipathy, could be blamed for popular fears about marauding students. This

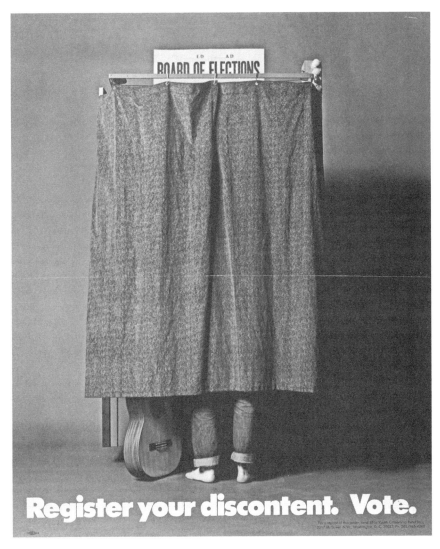

Figure 4. A poster for the Youth Citizenship Fund tells students to channel their protest politics into the system for the first youth vote in 1972. (Courtesy Wisconsin Historical Society, WHS-56754)

shifted responsibility for youth's radical image away from the young and emphasized the structural causes for the youth problem.[17] Still, the idea that young people stood out as the most educated and civically minded generation in American history dominated the dialogue.

Liberal Democrats in particular appealed to the promises of citizenship instead of stoking the fears of a revolution when they advocated for the youth vote. These leaders emphasized young people's higher levels of education, making them ready for higher responsibility and even capable of improving the political system. While only 14 percent of young people graduated high school in 1940, 1970s graduation rates topped 78 percent.[18] Representative Herbert Tenzer (D-New York) agreed: "In these troubled times, [lowering the voting age] will give us the opportunity to bridge the 'generation gap' by reaching out to the youth of the Nation and not merely allowing them—but asking them to join hands in the process of self-government and share in the establishment of the goals necessary for the improvement of society."[19] For voting rights advocates, the system relied on a lower voting age.

Despite conservatives' opposition, many in the GOP appreciated the defusing, steam-valve effect of lowering the voting age. In 1970 Representative James Cleveland (R-New Hampshire) warned: "A consequence of not lowering the voting age seems to be that young people who are interested and involved in public issues tend to become frustrated, thus providing a ready audience for the small number of radical disrupters who are always looking for a confrontation."[20] Those harboring this rationale hoped that opening the system would contain the problems.

While some Republicans supported the youth vote for these defensive purposes, others believed that it offered an opportunity to build their own youth constituency. As Barry Goldwater spoke for lowering the voting age, he gushed that youth's idealism "is exactly what we need in this country . . . more citizens who are concerned enough to post high social and moral goals for the nation."[21] This change also appealed to a common desire for a spiritual renewal through a youth vote. Expanding the vote became the patriotic thing to do. After Goldwater witnessed the way conservative youth organized when he ran for president with the support of the YAF, he understood before Nixon that not all youth leaned left. Setting the stage for Nixon's own youth campaign in 1972, Sunbelt Republicans like Goldwater and Bill Brock (R-Tennessee) disputed the youth vote's characterization as a monolithic bloc. Nixon's administration did not share this optimistic survey of the GOP's chances with youth politics.

Even as politicians of all stripes soon found common cause in lowering the voting age, Nixon remained halfhearted. While his deputy attorney general, Richard Kleindienst, supported lowering the voting age for federal elections, he advised restraint and argued that individual states should decide voting ages for local or state elections. This "compromise" made sense as a federal statute would face legal challenges concerning local and state elections, and Kleindienst made clear that the White House wanted an amendment that still left the voting age up to states despite its constitutional authority over all voting procedures.[22]

When Senators Kennedy and Mansfield set off a campaign to convince their cohorts to lower the voting age, they hardly needed to do much. In 1970, one month after Kent State, the vote won approval in both houses. Even though Nixon's advisers suggested a veto, fearing he would enfranchise "voters who would defeat him in 1972," Nixon signed the bill.[23] While this did acquiesce to public sentiment, the change had other implications that made it more palatable for Nixon. As Rick Perlstein explains, "As usual, Nixon saw subterranean fissures rumbling beneath the surface" as Old Politics' Democrats feared the advent of New Politics in the upcoming primaries. Arguing that Nixon recognized this change would "harden the split," Perlstein contends that eventually, "Nixon *did* favor the measure. It would help him wedge the Democrats."[24]

As predicted, the law immediately ran into problems as the Supreme Court ruled in *Oregon v. Mitchell* that Congress could not extend the vote to eighteen-year-olds for state and local elections. That required a constitutional amendment. Faced with the dizzying and costly prospect of dual voting, or two ballots, the consensus easily built around the amendment. During the 1960s, twenty states had defeated efforts to lower the voting age. The results changed in 1971 for two reasons. First, Americans had developed a more sympathetic approach to youth issues after the Kent State "massacre." Second, as the ratification process concentrated votes in state legislatures that also dictated election rules, these politicians understood the need to act swiftly and avoid a bureaucratic nightmare. Only hours after Congress voted overwhelmingly for the amendment on March 23, 1971, both Minnesota and Delaware's legislatures raced to become the first to ratify. On July 1, Ohio's state representatives voted 81–9 to become the thirty-eighth state in favor of the amendment, making it law.[25]

Ken Rietz, the director of Nixon's incipient Young Voters for the President (YVP), prodded the White House to embrace the amendment through a signing ceremony. "Some will call it a political move," Rietz predicted, "but in the long run there will be more of a negative reaction to no action."[26] Nixon's aides went to great lengths to control the situation. They scrambled to find the perfect backdrop for the ceremony. A local musical orchestra, the Young Americans, happened to be in town on July 2 before they headed to Europe for a two-month tour. This five-hundred-member ensemble included an orchestra, a choir, and a concert band. Ranging from fifteen to twenty years old, this group represented the exact effect Nixon desired. Nixon staffer Ron Walker went to New York only three days before the ceremony to "get backstage so as to obtain a good reading on the caliber and character of these kids." They passed the sniff test. In their matching blue blazers with grey pants or skirts, "they are all races, all colors and I would imagine all creeds . . . and they are very beautiful children." "There are only a couple of long hairs," noted Walker, "and I talked to both."[27] As for the music, Walker recommended one of their numbers, "We're Going to That Ball": "It's a knee slapper and lots of clapping."[28]

On July 5, Nixon joined the Young Americans in the East Room. As they sang their "knee slapper," Nixon signed a certificate with three members from the group, and the photo op had been achieved. Though, hardly the maestro here, Nixon's smile concealed the concerns he held about the youth vote. Nixon then spoke to the audience and praised young people's role in politics: "You will infuse into this nation some idealism, some courage, some stamina, some high moral purpose that this country always needs."[29] Emphasizing the unprecedented speed and efficiency with which the government extended the vote, Nixon offered an olive branch, announcing: "Let this historic amendment, then, be a sign and pledge of solidarity of our land." Nixon hoped the amendment process testified to "the trust of the older generation in the younger, and the younger in the older."[30]

Despite Nixon's attempt to eliminate the generation gap, his opponents attempted to revive it. Dwayne Draper, the president of the left-leaning Association of Student Governments, scoffed at the idea that new voters would follow their elders: "It's the silliest thing in the world to say that they will vote like their parents."[31] Anticipating that the sons and daughters of the silent majority would break from their elders' politics, Democrats hoped to enlist as many young people as possible.

This sanguine hope did not hold up as young Americans still found obstacles in the registration process. Only six months away from the primary season, regulations required voters to register fifty-four days prior to the election, before interest peaked, and before college freshman got settled on campus in the fall of 1972. Anecdotal evidence began to creep in about students getting "hassled" by officials in Alabama when they tried to register.[32] In addition, the cumbersome absentee registration process still threatened the campus vote, and students studying far from their parents' homes found many obstacles in exercising their new voting rights. A Harris survey in June 1972 showed that "the feeling of alienation" rose from 40 to 47 percent over the previous year. Rather than the cause for apathy, the argument shifted blame from the youth to the unique responsibilities young Americans face when reaching voting age. As Michael McDonald and Samuel Popkin explain, "An explanation for lower turnout in America than in most other industrial democracies, we suggest, must begin with the institutional structure of the political system, not the psychology of the voters or the tactics of the parties and candidates."[33] Testifying to Congress, Common Cause's director of the Voting Rights Project argued that "a very important way to reduce these unacceptable high levels of alienation is to remove any barriers which may block the ballot box."[34] In response, groups like Common Cause and the National Movement for the Student Vote put their efforts toward registration.

One branch of Common Cause, the National Student Lobby (NSL), formed to publish how politicians voted on youth issues, including registration reform that allowed students to register where they attended school. NSL also convinced Congress and Nixon to declare September "National Voter Registration Month" and keep registration open until October 7 for students returning to campus in the fall.[35] Anne Wexler of Common Cause, and Senator George McGovern's future campaign aide, led a series of lawsuits to allow students to vote in their college towns. Thus, Common Cause and other groups such as Student Vote and the ACLU developed a legal strategy to expose discrimination. As one youth vote advocate in New York wrote, resistance to student registration undermined "whatever confidence the state's young men and women may have had in the willingness of society to open its orderly processes of change to them."[36] Proving discrimination came easy, as students from out of state first fulfilled their requirements by registering their cars and acquiring drivers' licenses in states where they attended college. Once enough students had been denied, they filed lawsuits throughout the nation that earned victories that relaxed residential requirements, though local registrars continued to resist. As young people secured the vote, other youth issues also surfaced amid this wider effort to bring young people into the orderly system. While Nixon struggled to balance his political interests with youth issues, he met young Americans' demands on environmental policy with similar reluctance.

The Environment, Industry, and the Youth Problem

In 1970, during a lull in antiwar protest, youth protest politics turned toward ecological concerns. On the first Earth Day in April 1970, thousands of people joined Phil Ochs in singing, in his popular adaptation of the antiwar song, "All we are saying, is give earth a chance."[37] This movement, similar to its antiwar predecessor, allowed antiestablishment liberal youth to continue their critique of American society and capitalism. One environmentalist speech, published in the University of Texas's underground paper the *Rag*, argued that "there will be no clean air in this society" unless America changed "the values of overconsumption, growth for its own sake, profit and competition."[38]

As did the antiwar movement, the environmental movement helped transition the counterculture into politics. Hippies clearly understood the environment's significance as the alternative to the consumer-driven world from which they escaped. Describing the initial Earth Day, a *New York Times* article reported a "block long polyethylene bubble on 17th Street where crowds could breathe pure, filtered air that reeked of marijuana after only half an hour." Guerrilla theater, the entertaining version of the 1960s youths' street politics, also worked on Earth Day when University of Minnesota students interrupted the General Electric stockholders' meeting with a mock funeral for a coffin filled with appliances.[39] The environment cannot entirely be pigeonholed as a youth issue. A study of mainstream magazines such as *Readers Digest* shows a spike in environmental stories that Americans of all ages read during the 1969–1971 period.[40] Still, most Americans understood the focus on environmental protection as a result of young Americans' growing concerns. One White House memo suggesting a "Youth Strategy" to

Charles Colson pinpointed the policy initiatives that held "special appeal to Young Voters." The list included a "youth ecology corps" and "strong Presidential emphasis on pollution free automobiles by 1975."[41] The environment also presented a youth issue that Nixon would have to concede.

Liberal Democrats certainly appreciated the political benefits here. "The environment movement, as it has emerged this spring for the environmental teach-in," Congressman Stewart Udall (D-Arizona) stated, "is a movement of the youth."[42] In his testimony on the issue during Udall's hearing on environmental education, the artist Robert Motherwell put it more bluntly. "We talk about a generation gap," Motherwell opined; "I prefer to call it a 'sanity gap,' of a young generation saying to their elders, 'The way you go on covering our natural parks with filth, waste, and vomit, for the sake of monetary gain and monetary economy is insane.'" For Motherwell, environmental pollution explained the youth problem: "Millions of young people now seem only happy when drugged" as they confront the depressing "waste of modern civilization, covering the landscape like a slimy coating of vomit."[43] While Udall had supported environmental protection for a decade, the youth movement provided him and other liberals with the impetus to push the administration harder for immediate change.

As America celebrated the first national Earth Day in April 1970, however, Nixon made himself conspicuously absent from the day's festivities. After all, Republicans such as Senator Gordon Allott of Colorado complained that "some extremists want to use the environment issue as one more club with which to beat America."[44] Still, his ambivalence toward the first Earth Day betrayed the White House's environmental staff's advice. Secretary of the Interior Walter Hickel urged Nixon to embrace the opportunity and issue an executive order that declared Earth Day a national holiday. Pointing out the political benefits, Hickel claimed this more assertive role in the environmental movement would "involve young people in national concerns." Hickel had reason to believe this possible, as he had held nine regional seminars for a student advisory board named Student Council on Pollution and the Environment (SCOPE) with all positive responses toward the administration.[45] Instead, portending Nixon's 1972 surrogate election strategy, Nixon's aides sent representatives across the country to speak on behalf of the president and show his environmental concerns. Walter Cronkite affirmed the political consequences, as he described the Earth Day crowd as "predominantly white, predominantly young and predominantly anti-Nixon."[46] However, the media portrayal misrepresented the environmental movement's wider, generational appeal.

While Nixon dismissed young liberals' environmentalism, conservative youth groups shared a concern about the degradation of the environment. The YAF newsletter the *New Guard* explained the environmental quality program within its mostly anticommunist and antigovernment Young Americans' Freedom Offensive. In the May 1970 environmental edition, the *New Guard* published YAF executive director Randall Cornell Teague's memo to the YAF's board of directors before the vote during its conference in Washington, DC, earlier that year. Teague asked the board to look past the environment's political implications, and instead consider the environmental agenda because "it is our air, water and land that we will have to be a part of for a longer period of time than many of those who will do the proclaiming about it." In the same edition, a Missouri college student wrote, "Environmental control is not something we can allow to become the monopoly of the liberal and radical left." If this happened, he warned, "pollution might well be what finally radicalizes the 'silent majority' of young people."[47] As a result, these young Americans would lose faith in the system and turn to "advocates of sabotage." Hoping to prevent this disorder, young Americans across the political spectrum asked for tighter environmental control. That the YAF's libertarian, free-market-defending, conservative ideologues would support any political interference seems contradictory. Pragmatic YAFers realized the inevitable compromise with the growing environmental movement by the early 1970s.

After all, even some captains of industry acknowledged the need for environmental protection and government regulation to bring youth back into the system. In 1970, *Fortune* magazine published an edited compilation of articles titled *The Environment: The Mission for the Seventies*. One entry pointed to the way the environment filled the activist vacuum in the 1970s after the civil rights movement and antiwar protest petered out. "Environmental groups are sprouting on campus just as S.D.S. chapters did a while back," explained one corporate insider. The environment assumed a new political significance, as students replaced 1960s politics by "parading, picketing, threatening boycotts of polluters and turning up at conservation conferences to pepper the speakers with difficult questions." This did not follow partisan political lines, though as the commentator claimed "even members of the John Birch Society and the S.D.S. can agree that clean air and water are desirable."[48]

Corporations feared that young Americans' emphasis on environmental issues hurt their image. In 1970, the international pulp and paper company Boise Cascade attempted to soften its reputation as an environmental enemy. Picturing two young people planting trees, one ad included the caption, "Opportunity: We think youth can be shown that business also shares their reasoned concerns."[49] In one attempt to "welcome the questioning of the young," Nixon's former ad agency that created the Pepsi Generation—Batten, Barton, Durstine and Osborn (BBDO)—invited eight student leaders into their new "'ad lab' for a rap session." While the students initially believed that "capitalism is, in reality, socialism for the few," they learned about "the genuinely good things businessmen are doing in the area of ecology," citing the paper industry for "going all out to make their products bio-degradable." In radio coverage of the meeting, the announcer commented, "They [young people] are not always right, but it would be healthy for the country if the business community started listening to them."[50] This could easily pass for political advice as well, and Nixon's youth campaign quickly obtained BBDO's videotape of the session for research.

In his introduction to *Fortune*'s environmental issue, Richard Nixon connected three post-1960s areas of crisis: environment, industry, and youth rebellion. In his effort to transition the 1960s into a more conservative decade, Nixon compromised his economic dogma to negotiate a series of reforms between the growing environmental movement and the corporations that they targeted. The results, a series of acts that regulated aspects of environmental concern ranging from reform in energy production, pesticides, and water pollution to the formation of the Environmental Protection Agency, met the growing disillusionment with business on terms acceptable to business. As Nixon's environmental adviser John Whitaker argued, Nixon conceded only what he had to and carefully considered the corporate and industrial leaders' input when he made his decisions on environmental policy.[51] This context clearly frames Nixon's environmental position—willing, but not eager. This shifting political terrain produced a Janus-faced politics that historians struggle to explain. Despite the rise of conservatism in the 1970s, the politics of youth continued the 1960s liberal political sensibility during the Nixon era.

By 1971, Nixon utilized his environmental program to improve his image. Returning to the University of Nebraska in January 1971, Nixon encouraged a receptive audience to work within the establishment: "If we suffer a setback or if we lose on an issue, the answer is not to blame the system but to look within ourselves to see how we can strengthen our resolve and intensify our effort." Nixon asked the crowd to "consider the environment" as a problem "we must face together. There can be no generation gap."[52] The YVP brochure to attract Nixon voters bragged, "The President's environmental package was drafted by a 23-year-old."[53] Though Nixon could not embrace the environmental movement, he could not deny its political influence as the 1968 generation gained the vote and established its influence in the system.

The Draft

Concern over Kent State created a more concerted effort to alleviate young Americans' frustration. Considering the role of the Vietnam War and the draft in feeding into the youth's antiestablishment sentiment, Nixon accelerated his efforts to make American military service purely voluntary. One concerned citizen wrote Nixon, "Young people in this country are close to revolution against what they justifiably feel is a society operating against their interest." Pointing out that young people felt excluded, the letter continues, "Selective Service Boards represent clearly vested interests . . . heavily weighted toward white, aging, conservative, ex-military men."[54] Critics of the draft also felt that selective service remained a relic of the past that denied this generation's focus on individuality, as one female freshman from the University of Tennessee editorialized in the school's paper that "these laws should be changed; not only in this matter, but in all situations where sex, race, age or origin pigeonhole an individual into a stereotyped role."[55] Nixon-friendly campuses such as Lipscomb University saw the draft as a "specter" that "haunts every college campus in America."[56] When Milton S. Eisenhower led a National Commission on the Causes and Prevention of Violence, his twelve-page report emphasized lowering the voting age and ending the draft as two crucial steam valves.[57]

Nixon agreed that America would need to modernize the system and move toward a voluntary military in 1970, and he moved the draft to a lottery system that included only nineteen-year-old men rather than the nine-year draft eligibility.[58] In addition, the minimum age for draft board membership dropped from thirty to eighteen years old. Conventional interpretations of Nixon's motivations to end selective service often promote this move as a political maneuver that allowed the executive power to maintain control over the military and the national security state.[59] The draft had given Americans too much stake in its foreign policy as it stirred popular resentment and restricted the president during Vietnam. Young Americans' new voting rights also motivated this reform, as the politics of youth brought added attention to the draft controversy.

Congress saw the draft as another way to expose Nixon's youth problem. Liberal Democrats such as Congressman Frank Thompson Jr. (D-Maryland) called the draft "indefensible" and refused to testify during a hearing on draft reform because the subcommittee had not opened it to the public.[60] Congressman Ed Koch (D-New York), younger blood, held an even more sympathetic view, claiming that young men "are forced into the heartrending dilemma of service in a war they deeply oppose or prison or flight from the country. . . . We have an obligation to free decent and ethical young men from this terrible choice." The first-term New Yorker even extended the agenda to develop leniency for conscientious objectors and "draft dodgers."[61]

Republicans also found the draft troublesome. At the same hearing, the moderate Republican congressman Fred Schwengel (R-Iowa) made sure to denounce student protesters and reminded them "they are not emulating the early revolutionaries if they have not exhausted every remedy under the law." Still, he agreed that should the government end the draft, "we would be very close to doing away with one of the most undemocratic institutions in the United States, one of the aspects of American life which has been the most responsible for the disillusionment of America's youth."[62] Ending the draft gained wider momentum, as building young Americans' trust focused politicians on youth issues.

Central to Nixon's attempt to end the draft was the requirement that he replace the aged, cantankerous head of Selective Service, General Lewis Hershey. Hershey had become a symbol of the Vietnam War, as the draft itself inspired much of the youth rebellion. As one internal memo admitted, this image matched reality, claiming: "The Organization set up by General Hershey is inadequate for the management of a modern draft system." In addition, "the personnel are old and of generally limited ability."[63] Thus, the transition to new leadership had been part of the White House's larger, careful attempt to reform the draft.

Events conspired to accelerate this plan, as the Vietnam moratorium in 1969 landed just as Nixon announced Hershey had been awarded a fourth star—promoted out of the job.

Dan Rather from CBS jumped on the story, as it seemed Nixon had "acted hastily to take the steam out of the Moratorium." Suddenly, Nixon's critics thought he caved in. Denying this, Nixon's aide Ken Cole told the staffers to refute this accusation. "You should work together to get out a story on your outrage that the Hershey event had anything to with the Moratorium," Cole forcefully suggested. "The fact is that it has been in the works for quite a long time."[64] Whatever motivated Nixon to replace Hershey, his successor, Curtis Tarr, helped resolve the draft controversy. While Hershey cared little for image and youth issues, Nixon's aides wrote that Tarr's "campaign for Congress in California gives him some political awareness and his having been a university president should enable him to relate to youth."[65] Presiding over Lawrence University throughout the 1960s, Tarr sustained a strong rapport between the administration, faculty, and students with the Lawrence University Community Council, which he established in 1968.

Nixon envisioned draft reform as a way to preserve America's ability to maintain national security. This effort also carefully considered the youth problem. Replacing Hershey with Tarr portended a wider change in the Selective Service Administration's leadership. When Tarr immediately requested retirements from two officers from state offices in Tennessee, Mississippi, and North Carolina, Bill Nichols (D-Alabama) questioned his motives. "I think they were doing a good job," Nichols protested; "perhaps you as a new Director wanted to present maybe a more youthful image."[66] While Nichols emphasized the change's symbolic significance, young Americans demanded a more substantial effort.

Continuing this youth-friendly direction, Nixon had formulated a Youth Advisory Commission that would recruit young volunteers from each state to advise local draft boards on decisions around exemptions, ensuring equity and to determine larger reforms to the system. Meeting with its pilot group, Nixon spoke to the press and claimed, "It will provide a way in which young people can help to shape government policies in which they have very special stake."[67] The president warned, "Established institutions of all varieties are under attack today, especially from youth, for being distant and unresponsive. . . . The Selective Service

System has been a major target for such criticism."[68] As Nixon attempted to bring young people into the system, it was not always orderly.

Even after Nixon unveiled his Youth Advisory Commission, Nixon's critics questioned his sincerity. A twenty-year-old college junior wrote the president with a skeptical tone. After observing a photo of the ten-member pilot group, the architecture major complained, "They all look like young Republicans—light ties, black laced shoes, short hair, etc." "May I remind you," the letter continues, "only 23% of college students considered themselves Republicans to the 33% Democrats and 44% Independents?"[69] Another letter accused the Youth Advisory Boards of serving as "public relations fronts to legitimate illegitimate policy decisions." Denying the group's lack of representation, assistant to the president Peter Flanigan explained, "it included three blacks and one of Chinese extraction." In addition, four were Democrats and "one of the blacks was a ghetto youth worker from Harlem."[70] The inclusive approach Nixon tested here taught his aides about the accompanying controversy over representation.

While the Youth Advisory Committee played a central role in Nixon's public relations attempts to deal with the draft, it also created an opportunity for young people to play a role in the reform. By March 1970, more than six hundred young men and women combined to make up fifty-six Youth Advisory Committees.[71] Along with this effort, the Selective Service System sent speakers to meet with high schools. Celebrating their momentum, the youth advisory groups held a national conference that included 109 delegates from across the country to announce their progress in June 1970. In clear terms, the commission recommended an end to the student deferments and the establishment of an all-volunteer armed forces, as "compulsory military service creates the feeling that military service is a punishment which the nation inflicts upon the citizen, not an honorable occupation." Furthermore, Tarr agreed with the youth delegates' recommendation to provide a "draft education and information program directed at high school seniors."[72] Reflecting on the conference, Tarr boasted that the recommendations "appear to me to be the responsible suggestions made by youth who are working within the system to effect positive change."[73] While Nixon distanced himself from other youth issues, the draft and the youth advisory had modeled an inclusive approach to attract the sons and daughters of the silent majority.

Introducing its changes, the Selective Service System's headquarters issued a report bragging that in one year it "came under new leadership, changed the selection process, introduced a new 'image,' and instituted new policies that spread the obligation to serve more equally among the nation's young men."[74] After Tarr took over, and in the din of the post–Kent State youth crisis, the White House invited fifteen representatives of the Youth Advisory Commission to a conference in July 1970 to meet White House staffers.[75]

The meeting came across so well that a White House aide asked Tarr and his staff if they could make some suggestions for the upcoming decennial White House Conference on Youth and Children so it "can be carried off in a similarly successful manner."[76] While White House youth coordinators such as Nixon staffer Jon Rose claimed these programs "aimed at getting new ideas into the system," they also provided "an important means of making youth aware that their problems are being considered sympathetically and that they are being listened to."[77] Clearly, image mattered here, as the Selective Service System's public information officer doubled as the point man on these youth programs. Nixon's effort to moderate his image required substantive changes as well. The lines between image and policy blurred as young voters became increasingly significant to political elites.

While Nixon struggled to contain the antiwar youths' political power, his quest for an all-volunteer military also signaled his new reach out to young voters who would support him. One evening, Nixon's chief of staff, H. R. Haldeman, had Young Voters for the President director Ken Rietz and other organizers over for dinner to discuss the president and young voters. When Haldeman asked what Nixon could do, they responded emphatically and in unanimity that he could end the draft. "And I know that had an influence," Rietz recalled, as three weeks later Haldeman called and said, "you are going to really like the announcement this afternoon."[78] Later that day, on July 28, 1972, Nixon announced that the draft would officially end the following July.

In 1980, Nixon characterized his decision to eliminate the draft as a miscalculation, one that limited rather than strengthened the national security strategy.[79] Long before this confession, however, Nixon had expressed regret over this decision for other reasons. In hindsight, Nixon saw 1970 as a period of weakness. The tumultuous political environment had put the White House on its heels. Referring to the move to dump General Hershey from the Selective Service System, and symbolically remove a relic of the draft era, Nixon barked in 1971 after meeting with students that his staff had to toughen up on youth issues. Telling Haldeman to never "act under duress," Nixon explained that they should avoid throwing "pearls before swine." As Haldeman recalled, Nixon blamed that mentality for "the same kind of thinking that got him to fire Hershey."[80] Nixon questioned these moves retrospectively, perhaps forgetting that the political elite's anxiety over the youth problem during his first term gave him few options.

Making concessions on the environment, the voting age, and the draft made political sense as these issues resonated with young people across the political spectrum. While this approach made Nixon's politics of youth defensive, GOP members such as Tennessee senator Bill Brock would provide Republicans, and the president, with a more creative and proactive model to reach young voters. With these issues resolved, Nixon could now pursue his political realignment by separating the sons and daughters of the silent majority from the 1968 generation.

4 | Nixon and New Republicans

Despite the president's defensive measures on youth issues, Nixon's problems with young voters continued. After his summer internship under Secretary Finch, Princeton University student Harding Jones published a memoir disputing Nixon's continually negative reputation among young people. Blaming colleges' "brainwashing," and the news media's "lack of sophistication" for young people's attitudes, Jones noted that White House staff "are more than willing to hear from young people," though interns "did not return the enthusiasm." Criticizing his young cohorts' immaturity, Jones claimed that "most had abysmal misconceptions about how government works" as "they still hold the childlike attitude that money is produced by the government, failing to recognize that it comes from their own parents."[1] Facing this new constituency, Nixon struggled for an answer to critics who took great pleasure in describing young Americans' lackluster support for his administration. However tough Nixon wanted to appear through his law-and-order policy, the president also had to reach out to a youth segment that held a more mature perspective on politics and the economy. Following Secretary Finch's suggestion to "increase presidential exposure to youths," which defined Nixon's previous contact with youth as "cosmetic," the White House shifted to include young people.[2]

During his first term, Nixon responded defensively to youth politics. In policy, public relations, political organization, and image, Nixon mined whatever political capital he could from criticizing antiwar youth and the permissive counterculture without appearing too hostile to the "sons and daughters of the silent majority." He also neutralized the possibility of a mass mobilization of young voters against him in 1972 through concessions on significant youth issues. Searching for an aggressive approach on youth politics, Nixon looked south, to Tennessee. Here, Senator Bill Brock (R-Tennessee) opened up the Republican Party to a new sensibility that cultivated the GOP's own brand of youth-friendly politics. Brock pioneered a New Republican approach to the politics of youth that built the GOP's popularity with young voters through grassroots organization and mass media efforts. This approach provided Nixon with a way to turn a negative into a positive, proving that Republicans could mobilize youth politics—widely considered a liberal reconstruction of American politics—and energize the Right.

After Kent State, Nixon and Billy Graham claimed the youth rally they headed at the University of Tennessee's Neyland Stadium, attracting over one hundred thousand, transcended politics. On the stage, however, Bill Brock, Nixon's favorite senatorial candidate for that year's campaign, sat next to the president. Nixon liked Brock's chances and saw the opportunity to defeat the longtime incumbent, Albert Gore Sr. A prominent Tennessee businessman from the predominantly Democratic city of Chattanooga, Bill Brock made his way into influence as the owner of a major candy-manufacturing company. Perhaps selling a product to young people gave Brock experience with the youth segment, but his political approach appealed to young voters as he built a formidable Young Volunteers for Brock campaign in 1970, and he eventually headed the youth campaign for Richard Nixon's reelection in 1972.[3]

Nixon's support for Brock in 1970 went further than an invitation to sit next to him at the Billy Graham Youth Night. As the campaign heated up through the Tennessee summer, two professional admen from DC arrived and pushed the Brock campaign into overdrive. Nixon's infamous media guru, Harry Treleavan, and a young partner in his public relations firm, Ken Rietz, helped produce a campaign to build on Brock's youthful persona and capitalize on the Republican Party's potential with young voters who did not attend college—Brock won the youth vote two to one, to defeat the longtime incumbent Al Gore Sr. in 1970.

Brock's victory in 1970 marked his transition from a local phenomenon to a national youth politics expert, as he shaped a conservative vision of an American future that included conservative, moderate, or "square" students and working youth.[4] Nixon appreciated young candidates like Brock who understood the GOP brand's problems, as the president complained, "It [the Republican Party] has the sound of big business, minority party, elitist old farts."[5] The youth-oriented political culture demanded attention. Early in his first term, when Nixon looked for White House staff who "looked hippie" to join his meeting with "a bunch of long-haired college newspaper editors," the best he could find was John W. Dean III, hardly Woodstock material.[6] Unlike other

Republicans, Nixon told Haldeman, "Brock gets it."[7] Especially after Nixon's law-and-order-focused Southern Strategy suffered a setback in the 1970 election, he noticed Brock's victorious strategy as a potential blueprint for a Republican majority. Nixon formed his own youth initiative—labeled the "open door policy"—which included the White House Youth Conference and policies, ranging from lowering the age of majority to diplomacy with China, that gained young voters' praise. This New Republican approach emboldened the president and provided his youth outreach the public relations opportunities to attract moderate young voters.

As Nixon's administration scrambled to solve the youth problem before it hurt the president's reelection campaign, Brock's inclusive approach provided a model to win young voters. Thus, Nixon tapped Brock to head his youth campaign early in 1971. Brock's enlistment marked a turn for the Nixon administration on the youth problem, as it moved to transform the president's biggest weakness into a political strength. This shift mapped out Nixon's youth campaign but also motivated his administration and other New Republicans to reach new voter groups such as women and ethnic voters. Republican National Committee (RNC) cochair Anne Armstrong admitted: "If the youth vote depends solely on party images, the Republican Party comes out second best."[8] Shedding the GOP's image as the "tired" and "dreary" party, the politics of youth became a vehicle with which Republicans could reassert their role in modern politics.

Bill Brock

Bill Brock had established his bona fides with students and Young Republicans well before his 1970 senate campaign. During his own youth, Brock served as the National Teen Age Republicans' (TAR) chairman, when he published the TAR manual. During his 1962 run for Congress, Brock began to utilize young people. He grew up in a Democratic stronghold, and he recalled, "no one wanted to listen under fifty."[9] His campaign used the AFL-CIO's Committee on Political Education (COPE), organizing materials to mobilize young volunteers who knocked on thousands of doors. In addition, Brock recruited over three hundred women as Brockettes, who wore white skirts and red scarves while they campaigned for Brock outside supermarkets. Brock claimed that the

Figure 5. Bill Brock with members of his "youth team" after winning his 1962 congressional campaign in Tennessee. This victory made Brock the first Republican to win this district in over forty years. (University of Tennessee, Baker Center)

young supporters also gave his candidacy the allure as the "in thing" and enabled his campaign to persuade independent and even Democratic voters. After becoming the first Republican congressperson in his district in forty-two years at the ripe age of thirty, Brock won the Outstanding Young Republican Award in 1963.[10]

As a congressman, in 1968 Brock recoiled at his fellow colleagues' vituperative reaction to campus demonstrations. Recalling statements on the floor that called for the cancellation of any funding to schools that had experienced violence, Brock called them "probably the most idiotic suggestion I had ever heard." Brock decided to lead a junket of twenty-three youthful Republican representatives who broke up into smaller groups on a national tour of fifty college campuses across the nation in six weeks. As Brock explained: "We would listen. Just sit on the lawn and talk to kids, go have a beer, go into the classes . . . a really serious effort to try to get a sense of what was going on."[11] This tour taught Brock that young Americans could not be simplistically categorized and that most wanted to participate in the system.

Predictably, the Republican junket found antagonism toward

political solutions. The more radical students continually claimed that "violence is justified when proper channels don't work," and a theatrical demonstration on campus displayed a toilet bowl with a sign that read, "Proper channels."[12] Anecdotal accounts from students pointed to one common thread—young people wanted respect. As one Republican congressman reported, nearly all the students fumed at the police's overblown crackdowns on relatively minor student demonstrations. In one incident at Florida State University, cops rushed a protest of thirty or forty students with fastened bayonets. Reacting to this draconian approach, the congressman noted that "the students feel that they're not children . . . and unfortunately from the attitude of some of the faculty and administration, their feeling is that they are children." In addition, students explained their suspicion of the establishment and the political process: "We have a sense of powerlessness because we don't have the vote," one congressman paraphrased, "and elected people are responsive to older people who have a different moral standard than we have." As a result, students argued, "since we can't work within the legal system, for a change, we tend to work in an unlawful way."[13] While the majority of young people rejected the political extremes, convincing them to vote for Republicans seemed a daunting task.

These congressmen found that students on the political extremes— left and right—exaggerated their political significance. When Brock and company visited Florida State University (FSU), the GOP representatives attended a meeting that campus conservatives, the self-proclaimed "98%," organized to counter the widely overblown Students for a Democratic Society (SDS) presence. Rather than embrace the "98%," one congressmen visiting FSU considered them "sanctimonious." Brock agreed and claimed that more students "placed themselves in the middle," rejecting the SDS even as they "isolated themselves also from this so-called silent majority."[14] Thus, a New Republican made progress in mobilizing the moderate majority of students "in the middle."

Brock and his fellow Republican congressmen learned to appreciate the generation gap and recognized youth politics' potential. Brock developed a nuanced approach here, acknowledging that "everyone black or white has a problem with identity. Some find it by adopting this weird garb and beards."[15] Brock recalled that one bearded student explained the political significance of his personal appearance, claiming: "I want individuality. I want to distinguish myself from my elders whom I do not respect." Continuing along this line, the student claimed, "I also want to identify with those concerned about changing things, so it [the beard] becomes a uniform." This grasp for individual identity could be mobilized, Brock claimed, especially after he observed that students at Duke University "have come to a consciousness of their power" and "the students are coming to realize their collective power."[16] Brock's team handed the White House a report that underlined the necessity to alleviate these various frustrations by lowering the voting age and ending the draft.

Rather than condemn beards and student power, Brock developed his political appeal to young voters that could harness this "collective power" for the GOP. After all, while Republicans had gained considerable political traction in the South during the 1960s, the party needed to revitalize its image to wrestle away control of the "Solid South." Running for Senate in 1970, Brock tested his New Republican approach against the longtime Democratic incumbent, Al Gore Sr. Gore's campaign, by contrast, rested its hopes for young voters on his antiwar stance. After the shooting deaths at Kent State, students from more than 450 colleges established local Movement for a New Congress (MNC) chapters to promote peace candidates and animated Gore's confidence in this segment.

Brock's experienced opponent dusted off the tried and trusted criticism of the GOP as the anti–New Deal obstructionists when the incumbent argued, "How did Congressman Brock vote? No, no, no, no, no, no, no, no, 50 times no." Continuing, Gore joked, "His record is so negative that it makes Goldwater look a little socialistic."[17] This contest grabbed the president's attention, as he poured more resources and personnel into the race. Nixon's Southern Strategy for Brock was to think young. Concerning Brock's negative campaign that rejected any and all economic programs that Gore offered, the president warned, "Let him be for something. On the economic issues, he has got to prove he isn't an encrusted old type."[18] As Bill Brock explained, "you can't just run against something and win, you need to offer something positive."[19] Nixon fit this campaign perfectly within his larger agenda to rejuvenate the Republican brand. With its symbolic significance, Nixon also used this campaign to highlight the difference between young people opposed to the president and the sons and daughters of the silent majority.

Swinging through Tennessee on Brock's behalf in October 1970, Nixon consistently met young protesters on the stump. As Nixon answered the "hecklers, taunts and jeers," one journalist noted that the president fashioned "youthful hecklers into part of the political weap-onry." Nixon held up these "shouters" as a symbol of liberalism's failings during the 1960s and told his "silent majority": "they do not speak for youth and they do not speak for America." Connecting the "shouters" in his own audience to the larger youth problem, Nixon warned about those who "try to shout down speakers with obscene words" and pro-claimed, "It is time we draw the line and say we are not going to stand for that." "If the candidate has given encouragement to, has condoned law-lessness and permissiveness," Nixon suggested, "then, you know what to do."[20] For Nixon, the majority of young people knew right from wrong.

Brock could also toss out the red meat on youth issues, as he sounded the alarm over campus turmoil. In one speech, Brock accused liberal politicians of "publicly encouraging 'civil disobedience' and mob pro-test" that resulted in "246 reported cases of arson and at least fourteen known bombings." Claiming, "the minority of trouble-makers among these [students] must be taught that they can't spit in Uncle Sam's face and pick his pocket at the same time," Brock argued, "if we can change the balance of power in the Congress . . . we can put some teeth into the law."[21] Brock mimicked Nixon's tough stance and broke off the rabble-rousing dissenters from the moderates on campus.

Brock's approach reflected the parents' concern that the majority of young people needed protection from the minority. Focusing on parental anxieties, Brock warned: "The onslaught of dope and drugs and pornography . . . is destructive because it's hitting young people before they have a chance to know the difference between right and wrong. . . . Parents feel so frustrated sometimes because we cannot control our children's lives."[22] Rather than high schools and colleges helping their cause, Brock blamed them for influencing this problem negatively: "They are very evil influences in many instances and that is what is so frustrating to us all."[23] Whereas order could revive young people's morals, American institutions had failed.

Speaking to young people allowed New Republicans to sharpen their new appeals for American spirituality and virtues. At Lipscomb University's commencement, Brock found ways that "the trend towards decadence can be reversed." Embracing individualism, Brock argued America could avoid the same symptoms that caused the fall of Rome: "an obsession with sex and a general desire to live off the state." Using their "Judeo-Christian tradition," Brock argued, "if Americans will ac-cept individual responsibility for their individual decisions, then these

Figure 6. A crowd of students at East Tennessee State University gather for Richard Nixon's appearance on behalf of Bill Brock's Senate campaign in 1970. (Archives of Appalachia, University of East Tennessee)

decisions will be geometrically raised on the moral scale."[24] The rise of youth politics handed Brock a new segment to carve out his own constituency on the social issues that threatened the New Deal coalition. One article described the different approaches: "Bill Brock's calculated effort to exploit the attitudes of Tennesseans and Albert Gore's shrewd attempt to play upon their interests."[25] Throughout the campaign, Brock encouraged Tennesseans to vote according to their personal "attitudes" that embraced his square, independent, anti-Washington, and youthful image.

Students on the left feared Nixon and Brock's shared vision of the youth problem, as one campus reporter warned that if Brock won he would end demonstrations at UT and that the board of trustees "set things up" for Brock to go "all the way (to crush dissent)."[26] For Brock's campaign, these critics did not present a significant concern as Brock's aides broadened youth politics to include nonstudents as well. While Nixon limited himself to this more defensive approach that attempted to confront the youth problem as a threat, Brock sought to mobilize the silent majority's youth into a political strength.

Saving room to stigmatize his opponent, Brock also used the youth problem, arguing that Gore did not represent young Tennesseans accurately. "I don't think they are part of the new left, the radical left at all."[27] As Brock's clean-cut young supporters reinforced his moderate image, they also contrasted with Gore's black and antiwar voters. As one car dealer in Tennessee explained: "If you go up to the well-dressed man he'll be for Brock. If you go to a bum or nigger he'll be for Gore."[28] Brock's voters hoped he would clean up Tennessee. Still, Brock's young followers comforted these voters switching over to the GOP; as Rick Perlstein explains, as early as the 1960s, "the RNC launched Operation Dixie, sending fresh-faced young organizers door-to-door to show Southerners Republicans didn't have horns."[29]

Brock cultivated future leaders who shared their generation's concerns but also stood their ground for American virtues. Speaking to the Jaycees, the US Junior Council dedicated to developing future leaders in business and community service, Brock emphasized the need for environmental action and tapping into the reservoir of "unselfish and idealistic vitality of young manhood." While admitting that federal regulation played a role, Brock argued that the private sector and "every citizen in this nation is going to have to reassess his values and be willing to sacrifice to win this battle against the smog, smoke, and filth that is saturating our nation." Far from a liberal cry for government action, Brock continued that personal responsibility extended to confronting other problems such as "crime, drugs and pornography."[30] Offering a solution, Brock proposed to keep the kids down on the farm and away from America's decaying cities. Blaming federal policies that destroyed the family farm, Brock noted that "we've force fed a whole generation of young Americans into the cities." As Kyle Longley explains the role of race in this GOP appeal, this first generation off the farms connected Democrats with civil rights and protecting racial minorities: "They [southern Republicans] understood working and middle-class whites believed the government had become a servant of African Americans." Thus, "any attack on the federal power by Brock implied protection of the 'southern' way of life and its traditions, which included white dominance."[31] Brock argued that if the government could establish rural educational programs, "we can hold our young people in rural areas where they have more opportunity and freedom."[32]

Speaking at a commencement ceremony at another small college in Tennessee, Brock pointed out that this generation could be either the country's worst or greatest. To be the former, Brock warned, all they had to do was "make the tragic mistake of promoting the worth of the individual while supporting a movement toward big government that takes care of all our problems." For the latter, students would have to "build a government that doesn't relieve individuals of their rights in exchange for taking the responsibility for providing their every need." To become "the greatest generation," Brock advised young people to "help create a society that gives everyone the opportunity to grow and prosper in his own way and allows everyone to live their life as an individual."[33] Thus, the GOP used youth's independence to blend its economic and spiritual appeal.

Brock embraced youth issues and charted an appeal directly to young voters. In an interview during his campaign, Brock spoke of the 1968 generation's worthwhile qualities and legitimate concerns. "The great majority of our young people are tremendous," Brock claimed. "They are dedicated, they are concerned, they are idealistic, they really care about this country and about their community and about their families." Brock wanted to bring this generation's sensibility into the system to bring back the nation's "virility," as he glowed, "I think we ought to take the excitement and the sense of challenge that young people bring and channel it into the restructuring of the American Dream."[34]

While Brock offered young Tennesseans an alternative, they made significant contributions to his campaign as well. As Brock recalled, "the energy came from the young, excited that they could change the course of that election." Before Brock's campaign had hit full stride, the College Republicans' Region IV director offered his "prestige and credibility" to organize Brock's youth campaign on each college campus in Tennessee for his January independent study program. Asking for a letter to gain approval for this project, the college senior argued, "I am sure you feel a strong youth organization, both in terms of hardcore workers and public image, is a very vital part of your campaign."[35] This letter predicted correctly, as Young Volunteers for Brock (YVB) energized the campaign.

Considering Brock's positive record with youth, Nixon hoped that the race in Tennessee could offer a new Republican "type" that would help the party redefine itself amid the increasingly youth-centric environment. Brock did just that; as his campaign manager Kenneth Rietz recalled, "not many people thought a three term Congressman from Chattanooga could beat an incumbent Senator." YVB organizations spread across the state; as Rietz stated in retrospect, "Our primary objective in this youth movement was *involvement*." Claiming that the YVB accomplished just that, he bragged that more young people participated in his organization "than any previous youth movement that the state of Tennessee had ever experienced," as "it emphasized Bill Brock's commitment to the youth of Tennessee through Y.V.B. organizations in every county, every city and on every college campus, as well as in most of the state high schools."[36] Rietz explained that Brock offered a "fresh face" that attracted first-time voters on and off campus and that "a lot of people became involved who had never participated in politics before."[37] Even with students, Brock's campaign proved itself as mock elections on campuses, Rietz reported, "won 15, tied 1, lost 1. His [Brock's] campaign was organized, Gore's was not."[38] The rise of youth politics within Brock's organization influenced his image.

Brock's "fresh faced" appeal came through even more forcefully in his extensive television campaign, which made pioneering use of shorter television spots to capture voters looking for an alternative. Planning Brock's advertising, his advisers attempted to "capitalize on all media—but especially television—on Bill Brock's youth, vigor, attractiveness and contemporariness—contrasting these with the older, tired, out-of-date image of the opponent." Another memo pointed out that "especially on television," the campaign should emphasize his "good looks and 'with-it-ness.'"[39] Exaggerating this difference with Al Gore Sr., Brock's campaigners hoped to "bring the Brock image profile in line with the configuration of the 'ideal' Senator."[40] While 30 percent of Tennesseans wanted a "Younger Man," only 15 percent wanted an "Older Man," and less than 20 percent sought a candidate who "Agrees With Me On Most Issues."[41] Merging modern strategies in polling, organization, and image making, Brock's campaign planned to make its candidate likeable through a youth strategy.

Television had elevated the role likeability played in politics, as Brock's advertising coordinators claimed that "this is a far more important factor than most politicians recognize or like to admit. More people vote emotionally than rationally—and that's a fact!"[42] Appearing modern fit this agenda, as Brock's advisers suggested he develop a symbol, or "look," that "should be contemporary and distinctive, but not far-out."[43] As both parties struggled with new expectations in the television era, young voters gave the GOP a way to promote the political attitudes it encouraged. This emotional appeal to attitudes also invited the advent of the negative attack ads. One ad emphasized patriotism and Brock's local loyalty, as a lifelong Democratic farmer explained why he was voting for Brock: "Where was Al Gore when our boys were fighting in Vietnam? . . . He was in New York City at an anti-war moratorium!"[44]

In contrast, Gore banked on issues to motivate his campaign. While he hoped his antiwar stance would attract young voters, he dedicated himself to the more traditional constituencies as the bulk of his campaign in issues and in image returned to the "kitchen table" politics of old. For example, Gore's television ad that longtime Democratic consultant Charles Guggenheim produced aimed at Gore's older voters. Shown playing checkers while discussing Medicare and social security, the commercial focuses on a "wizened, aged" man who approached the incumbent. The man asks Gore, "Didn't I tell you six years ago that I hoped to live to vote for you again? Here I am Albert."[45]

Speaking at one campaign stop, Gore set his terms for reelection on economic concerns of inflation and unemployment: "These are bread and meat questions that come down to the problems that your wife has got to work with paying the bills and keeping the family budget."[46] Gore could match Brock in the traditional crowd gatherings, but when television commercials began bombarding Tennesseans with pro-Brock messages, Gore's traditional speaking campaign could not compete. The quantity of ads helped Brock, as his campaign coffers enjoyed the backing of Tennessee business, Nixon, and the national party. Yet the quality sealed the deal, as the polished and youthful image Treleavan and Rietz developed around Brock's already popular candidacy proved a winner.

Brock admitted: "television was natural for me, I loved it." Brock, recalling the debate, claimed that he knew he had Gore licked even before his debate on *Meet the Press* when old Albert walked in with piles of papers filled with data, facts, and issues. Brock explained, "That's not what television is about."[47] Responding to the advent of the thirty-second ad in 1968, Gore complained, "It's an abomination and I detest it."[48] While Brock spent over $300,000 on television advertisements, Gore spent under $100,000. Brock's campaign mastered this format and captured the emotion of the election that motivated the debate.[49] In the end one journalist commented that this campaign also involved "a race between rival image-makers, media coordinators and advertising agencies . . . in by far the costliest senatorial race in the state's history."[50]

Political observers, expecting the antiwar incumbent Al Gore Sr. to hold a grip on Tennessee's youth, found the exact opposite. Matt Lassiter attributes Brock's victory to Tennessee's more developed two-party state politics, arguing, "Only in Tennessee, one of the most Republican states in the South, did the Nixon administration find small cause for celebration in the 1970 returns."[51] Brock took more credit. As Brock recollected with relish, "Throughout the campaign we had over 8,500 sincere, attractive, articulate young people working day and night for my election." Summarizing the reason his youth campaign succeeded, Brock emphasized, "We gave them a freedom of action sufficient for them to feel a personal sense of responsibility and a measurable sense of accomplishment."[52] Brock's new youth strategy, looking for moderate young people's votes, proved more successful than the Southern Strategy Nixon developed in 1970. As Darren Dochuk argues about that year's midterm election effort, "By shifting to a harder Right, the GOP left the right-of-center open, giving moderate Democrats the opportunity to reclaim lost ground." Within the GOP, Brock gained immediate notoriety for his youth campaign and way to win over the New South.[53]

In his keynote speech at the Southern Regional Republican Conference in 1971, Brock outlined the New Republican approach. Focusing on young people, Brock emphasized their independence, claiming, "Neither party now owns the youth vote. These young people are going to look beyond the labels and surface issues." Urging introspection,

Brock asked the audience to "take a look at ourselves, our system and, in particular, our political party." To avoid apathy or worse, revolution, Brock suggested, "It is time we listen to people, all people—the young, the black and the Wallace voter."[54] After Brock's victory, he submitted a proposal to head Nixon's young voter campaign, the Young Voters for the President (YVP). Summing up his observations, Brock claimed, "this generation is desperate in its search for personal identity and a sense of personal involvement."[55] Nixon's campaign director, Jeb Magruder, quickly suggested that Nixon develop a youth branch of the Committee to Re-elect the President and allow Brock to run it with Kenneth Rietz. While Nixon's attorney general and future campaign manager suggested Nixon downplay this meddling in youth politics, Nixon jumped at the opportunity to get ahead of the youth vote and stop the defensive posture he had assumed thus far. After 1970, Brock's New Republican brand offered the GOP an opportunity to fill the political void.

Political elites set out to connect with youth politics, building an approach that replicated Brock's effort with this increasingly influential and fluid constituency. In May 1971, after becoming Nixon's newly hired point man on the youth vote, Brock argued that the "youth-oriented" campaign Rietz organized proved "this generation is pleading for maximum individual freedom and responsibility." This called for "meaningful involvement," Brock continued, "that means more than stuffing envelopes."[56] Involvement became the central thrust in redirecting young people's notions about politics and the president.

The Youth Offensive

The White House had already struggled with its personnel problem concerning the generation gap. Nixon's domestic affairs chief, John Ehrlichman, wrote a memo before Kent State that decried, "We have loaded aboard a lot of bright, young, able people who can present the President and his program in an excellent light," but "we are epitomized by the Vice President, the Attorney General, and Judge Carswell."[57] Magruder traced this reality directly to the administration's success with appealing to Middle America. Magruder pointed out that there existed a counterpart to the silent majority, "MetroAmericans": college-educated young professionals "who enjoy art, attend the symphony, and read *The New York Times Book Review*." According to Magruder, "MetroAmericans" imagined Nixon's typical voter as a "fat, racist suburbanite sitting at home in front of a television watching a football game and drinking a half-case of beer." Magruder suggested more publicity on the fact "the President has surrounded himself with bright, young, well-educated men who *care*." For example, Magruder argued, "Young Metroamerica won't listen to Mel Laird, but they will to Marty Anderson . . . because he's got more *hair*, a Ph.D., a sexy wife, drives a Thunderbird, and lives in a high-rise apartment."

Haldeman responded favorably, writing "excellent" twice on the memo (which Magruder called "some kind of an all-time high in praise"). *Look Magazine* ran an article on high-level White House aides in their twenties, "Nixon's Youth Corps," claiming that while "most Americans would argue it was John F. Kennedy who brought youth to the White House, Richard Nixon has done more in that regard." Haldeman explained, "It very definitely didn't just happen."[58] Still, this exposure was limited as Nixon felt strongly that "there was only one man in the White House who needed publicity."[59] In March 1971, Nixon's aides worried that "the electorate was not getting a clear image of the President," and Nixon met with four different journalists in one month after he rarely granted interviews in his first two years. Still, despite this effort, the interviews seemed to affirm Nixon's youth problem as he claimed unrest among young Americans resulted from their lack of "old values."[60] Kent State tested this approach, as Magruder's suggestions and many others like his slowly converted the White House to a more youth-friendly public relations campaign that spotlighted the inclusive politics Brock espoused.

The law-and-order emphasis in the 1970 election had not helped. As Colson wrote to Haldeman, "The feeling developed in the campaign that we were 'exploiting' student dissent, using the student issue for political gain and scolding the youth." As a result, "this in Harris' view caused the dramatic shift downward."[61] The White House quickly noticed the need to act on this issue, as Nixon aide Jeb Magruder recommended that the president revisit his 1968 campaign pledge to establish a White House Youth Office.[62]

The debate over a White House Youth Office dated back to the days after Nixon assumed office. In 1969, one White House aide explained the need for a centralized youth effort: "As of late, the pressure to 'do something' has been great. This pressure has taken the form of the Brock report, a report of 22 Congressmen on student disorders."[63]

Then, in 1971, Brock advocated for this change when he sponsored the Youth Council Act that included a Youth Council in the executive office of the president to coordinate all youth programs, advise the president on "policies and programs affecting youth," and strengthen communication between the president and young people. After overseeing campus tours by eight staff members, Magruder concurred, "A youthful member of the White House staff should be designated as the President's liaison with youth."

This fresh-faced representative of the administration would direct a "youth shop" in the White House, something young people from across the spectrum had requested throughout the staffers' research tours. Revealing young people's rising political significance, Magruder wondered if "students can be 'serviced' in the same way Chuck Colson services adult outside groups, Harry Dent the Republican Establishment and Len Garment the minorities."[64] While Nixon had intimated that he would support such an agency, one White House memo revealed, "We plan to propose to the sponsors that the bill be allowed to die."[65]

Nixon's staff agreed to squash it for three central reasons. First, the creation of another bureaucratic institution would only reinforce the press's criticism that Nixon stood distant from young Americans. Bill Gavin, Nixon's assistant secretary of the US Information Agency, instead suggested highly publicized personal interactions with young people that would create "the ring of authenticity" more than some pandering report from "the Third Bureau of the Youth's Under Secretary's Committee for More Equitable Sock It To Em Among Pubescent Males."[66] Second, "Middle America" might see the youth agency as political weakness. Last, the administration feared that it could never find a trustworthy youth spokesman who would "follow our line one hundred percent of the time."[67] Without the right assurances, a Youth Office too close to the president could "create a vehicle for criticism." The results of this inaction, as one aide explained, "has been disastrous for the Administration's image with young people." "American youth are very suspicious of the President," he argued. "The Administration has seemed arrogant yet fearful of young people." Worse, the White House was often "caught off guard" and "constantly reacting" to events in the youth sector, and statements on policy issues "are often insensitive to the prevailing moods of young people."[68] While resisting institutional changes, Nixon's administration found other ways to connect with young Americans.

After the 1970 antiwar march on Washington to condemn Nixon's expansion of the war into Cambodia, the White House began "Operation Dialogue." During a two-day period, the president, White House officials, members of the cabinet, and other high-level officials held meetings with "small groups of young people." In addition, HEW coordinated an effort that received over three thousand calls and set up sixty-one meetings with over one thousand young people followed by eighty-eight meetings during the rest of the month.[69] After stepping down as Nixon's secretary of the interior, Hickel wrote an article in the syndicated *Family Weekly* suggesting that New Politics could be understood on Republican terms. Noting that "both political parties have walked narrow, exclusive paths," Hickel argued, "the young of thought are pulling aside the curtains of phoniness and are demanding the naked truth." Using his department's changes in environmental policy as an example, Hickel claimed that he "left Washington totally convinced that our governmental system is sound." Asking the young not to "try to destroy the system," he admitted that "there is a concern in America, that if 'law and order' stretches too far, it finally becomes hate and order." Sharing the Left's notion of New Politics, Hickel asked government to "welcome the questioning of the young," because "perhaps youth does have part of the solution."[70]

Early in 1971, Nixon committed to a string of public relations moves meant to reverse his image as exclusive and inaccessible. As his administration touted its "open-door" slogan to combat his reputation, Nixon spoke during his return visit to the University of Nebraska about an "alliance of generations." Addressing the reliably welcoming audience at the student-faculty convocation, the president announced a volunteer service corps (Action), a merger between the fledgling VISTA and Peace Corps (the Peace Corps had even begun to recruit older, more technically skilled volunteers). While this move consolidated two large federal programs, Nixon espoused its opportunities for cooperation, claiming, "To those who have thought the system was impenetrable—I say there is no longer a need to penetrate—the door is open."[71] Still, Nixon's move could not avoid cynical interpretations, as this new arrangement placed the leadership with Peace Corps and not VISTA, which conservative politicians labeled "a federally financed hate-Nixon postgraduate school."[72] Clearly, the administration would have to do more.

Recognizing this, Nixon's administration reached out to "young America" through the White House Youth Conference in 1971. Nixon's staff already anticipated a conference on youth and children in 1970, as expected of the White House every ten years. Planning began in 1969, when Nixon unveiled his agenda to form a "youth policy" and named the Urban Affairs Council's (UAC) deputy director, thirty-six-year-old Stephen Hess, as the conference's national chairman. Under Hess, a young aide in the UAC developed two significant reports on the relationship between government and youth in preparation for the decennial event. Modeled on Daniel Patrick Moynihan's writings on national urban policy, Chester E. Finn Jr.'s "The Ecology of Youth" and "Toward a National Youth Policy" explained and proposed solutions to the youth problem. The government, Finn's report asserted, coddled young people and encouraged "dependency" on adult society with college loans and long-term apprenticeships to "prolong their youth." In addition, the system on which young people depended offered little opportunity for them to influence it. Finn suggested the administration consider reforming youth's legal standing, increase government-backed volunteer groups "administered by young people themselves," and make an effort to put young people in "policy making positions."[73] Giving youth responsibilities would both win over young voters and promote the maturity Nixon emphasized in this generation. Considering this added significance, Nixon announced that he would change the conference format to reflect his "open door" by relocating it to a larger venue and expanding the format to include thousands of young people from diverse backgrounds. This conference, unlike its predecessor, would include youth, as Nixon urged Hess to listen "to the voices of young America—in the universities, on the farms, the assembly lines, the street corners."[74] Under Hess's direction, the conference divided the youth issues into three age categories and appointed appropriate adult leadership to each segment's meetings. The eldest group, ranging from fourteen to twenty-one years old, would gather during April 1971 at the YMCA camping grounds in Estes Park, Colorado.

Nixon's administration explained this move as an attempt to isolate the event from the capital's distractions, creating an environment where youth could play a more significant role than in previous White House youth conferences. This decision invited immediate criticism that Nixon meant to remove the conference from the spotlight and relegate it to a remote location where his people could maintain control. "The only authority to protest are the Rockies," quipped one such critic.[75] Outside the limelight, the youth gathering still attracted attention.

The weather initially portended a positive vibe, as young people arrived in Estes Park to sunny conditions. One of the ten task forces, each charged with developing a research study to guide the sessions, prepared a report for the conference titled "Student Participation in Governance." This study underlined the initial optimism about the Youth Conference. "Many of the problems confronting secondary schools in the '70s," warned the paper, "will be those of the colleges of the '60s—student protest and violence and the rapidly increasing drug use." The only solution, for this young attendee, required "student participation." "Many responsible students are ready and willing to solve these problems."[76] Allowing students, and young people, a role in government could head off this expanding youth crisis.

Soon, the snow began, trapping some in their cabins while others shared overcrowded, underheated dorm rooms. A few young people had to be evacuated by helicopter when they fell ill. According to *Rolling Stone* magazine, Nixon's Woodstock "had become another Altamont."[77] The conference carried the same tensions that surrounded the larger youth problem. Over one thousand young people attended, and they brought a wide range of the 1968 generation's political perspectives. Upon entering the conference, a group of students greeted attendees with a flier that read, "The White House Conference on Youth, even before it begins has all the makings of an elaborate fraud."[78] Revealing the problems this generation presented, a group of Puerto Ricans and Chicanos walked out to protest their lack of representation. Young skeptics worried that Hess handpicked the adult delegates, as he held veto power over the selections that attendees nominated beforehand. In addition, many delegates gained access to the event through their governors' nomination, not exactly an open process.[79] However, Hess's choices were somewhat limited, as one White House aide admitted that while a number of invited leaders from the private sector "felt nothing but loyalty and patriotism for the President and their country," they would not attend, as "it was quite another thing to be asked to put their heads in jaws of a tiger."[80]

The young delegates found divisions on cultural issues as well. After a police captain spoke in a session on the marijuana problem, someone stood in protest, saying, "If you are going to lock up everyone for smoking grass, you are going to have to arrest half this conference." After all, a *Rolling Stone* reporter claimed that "the conference pot supply was ample and of good quality."[81] Still, many found the abundance of "squares" conspicuous. One *Time* reporter wrote, "many sported crew cuts" and that they took to the dance floor when a rock band played one night, "dancing in 1950s style, cheek to cheek." James Kunen, veteran of the Columbia University student protests and author of *The Strawberry Statement*, represented the New Left, observing, "I didn't know they could find this many straight kids in America."[82] Claiming that this mixing of American youth produced a curious stew, the *Rolling Stone* reporter continued, "In just four days, Nixon's bureaucrats did a better job of radicalizing middle American youth . . . than a decade of Tom Hayden, Jerry Rubin and Huey P. Newton."[83]

Conservatives also objected to the makeup of the conference's delegation. A twenty-four-year-old Kansas City nurse criticized the conference "because it did not represent either moderate or conservative viewpoints." Bill Brock, the newly elected senator from Tennessee and an adult member of the Values, Ethics, and Culture Task Force, called the group's criticism of America's history of slavery and expansion "masochistic, negative and non-productive."[84] Brock denied young people's radical reputation: "There is a silent majority on every campus," and pointed out that the older generation could not be that bad when they "fought man's grizzliest war . . . fought discrimination . . . built thousands of schools . . . and made a start, although a late one, in healing the scars of the earth and fighting pollution."[85]

Religious youth also vented their frustration, as one member of the United Methodist Church in the United States complained, "I believe our denomination was the only major one to send youth representatives." Conservative students mocked the conference, calling it the "White House Woodstock," and deplored the radical makeup of the young people attending as "unrepresentative" (it even included noncitizens).[86] Referring to the ten task forces of fifteen members that generated reports for the conference, the article continued, "Not one conservative served on the original Task Force in any area issue," while the adult delegates also leaned left when they supported the McGovern-Hatfield proposal to remove all troops more than young people did.[87] Still, as far as one young man was concerned, "This conference was creditable."[88] Although factions contested the conference's representation, moderates were satisfied.

In the end, the delegates voted on a lengthy list of recommendations for the president ranging from abolishing grades in school to ending the war and legalizing marijuana. Putting a good face on it, Hess claimed the event a success, calling it the "fairest conference" ever in the White

House's long-standing youth series and adding that Nixon "has a commitment to take these considerations very seriously indeed."[89] Conservatives recoiled at the final document, as Pat Buchanan recommended, "get the President as far away as possible from this thing." "No serious man can take this silly document seriously," Buchanan jibed; "the children out at Estes Park put this together as a great put-on for Richard Nixon."[90] In fact, Nixon waited a year to respond.

Eventually, Nixon's administration finally released a four-hundred-page "encyclopedia" that answered each of the youth conference's 330 recommendations. Touting his openness, Nixon claimed to accept 60 percent of their ideas "threaded through with basic human values . . . and noble ideals." Furthermore, the president heeded Brock's call to include young people, claiming that he was "soliciting views of young employees when developing policies and procedures of interest to them."[91] Nixon's administration could agree with certain principles concerning civil rights and contraception, but it still opposed the delegates' call for an immediate and complete withdrawal from Vietnam, huge cuts in the defense budget, and the end of nuclear tests that would "emasculate our present defense posture."[92] While the president tentatively bridged the gap and extended an olive branch to America's youth, he made sure to distinguish between the types of young people he would accept and the types who he would not.

Beyond the conference's issues, one young delegate wrote: "this talking together, this trying to understand each other" served a higher purpose—"a spirit of trying a little harder to make America still a better place in which to live."[93] The president wasted little time in using the event for wider political consumption, as he spoke to the rural youth of the 4-H Club months after the event in Estes Park. Speaking of the "most wide open forum 'of, by, and for young Americans' ever held," Nixon claimed that "the time when the young are to be seen and not heard is gone in America—gone for good." The White House report on the conference, bragged Nixon, "will further weaken the myth of an unbridgeable generation gap."[94] Ultimately, his message attracted young people who supported Nixon as he told the attendees, "Your next step should be to focus on a mechanism . . . the American political process."[95] Channeling youth into the system appealed to the moderate young Americans that Nixon targeted.

While these efforts met the growing anxieties over the youth generation, he saw the effort as a sign of weakness. After meeting with one group of student leaders in 1971, Nixon and Haldeman agreed on the "softness of this generation" and that the "quality of student body presidents has changed" for the worse. Voicing his disgust, Nixon complained, "Well it's just crap, we have to sit and talk to these little jackasses," and he told his chief of staff, "scratch all this crap, really, bullshit, all these meetings, this therapy meeting with the little assholes."[96] By 1971, Nixon decided that co-opting his young enemies served little purpose, and that he would have to build his own youth image to counter the visual that linked McGovern with America's future and Nixon with the older set.

The "Open Door" and Policy

The Nixon administration's highest ranks continued their efforts on the youth problem, as they implemented Bill Gavin's repeated advice to hold more media events featuring Nixon and young people. Avoiding the image of "caving in," Nixon made it clear that he wanted to meet with young people "who are on our side, instead of spending so much time trying to pacify those who are against us." The president clarified that he preferred the youth group he met "who support us in Vietnam, rather than the college editors we had in last week, who are opposed to us."[97] In fact, despite the antiwar movement's visibly youthful appearance, polls showed young people "less inclined than their elders to call the war a mistake."[98] Defending Nixon's bombing campaign in Vietnam and neighboring Cambodia, Brock read into the *Congressional Record* letters of support from various young people including the presidents of the Future Business Leaders of America and the Vocational-Industrial Clubs of America, Miss Texas, a twenty-one-year-old state representative, and the Young Republicans' chairman.[99] Encouraged, Nixon's administration sought to fulfill its "open door" slogan and treat young people like adults.

All the White House and domestic staffers under thirty years old signed a "Youth Manifesto," testifying to Nixon's progress in ending the war and the draft and his revenue-sharing plan that would tackle the "leviathan bureaucracy." Sent off to college newspapers, the manifesto refuted the myth that Nixon "did not speak to youth." Claiming, "because we work for the President, because we are young, and because we know the myths are false," this group analyzed Nixon's policies from a "different perspective."[100]

In Nixon's State of the Union speech in 1971, he suggested, "Let us forge an alliance of the generations." In this speech, the president asked Americans to "work together to seek out those ways by which the commitment and compassion of one generation can be linked to the experience of another."[101] Soon after, the Republican Party's newsletter, *First Monday*, included a section entitled "The President and Young Americans," a glossy, colorful collage of headlines, speeches, and images of Nixon meeting with young people. Photographs of Nixon with smiling young boys in the Oval Office announcing the "Newspaper Boy Week Proclamation" or surrounded by leaders of Girls Nation portended a new focus on openness.[102] Seeking to support Nixon's claim to an "Alliance Among Generations," the newsletter packed in headlines such as "Nixon's Draft Plan Vast Improvement" and listed progress in youth issues such as the Vietnam War, the environment, and funding for college.[103] Other changes came through policy as the White House elevated young Americans' position in politics.

Even on international issues that hardly seemed related to youth, Nixon used his achievements to show an openness and leadership that would encourage his own young supporters. These "counterintuitives" complicated the liberal critique that painted Nixon as an "old encrusted type." Nixon's visit to China prompted attention to his prowess and influence on the world stage, but young Americans also found Nixon's détente a compelling case for the president's reelection. As Jeremi Suri argues, youth protest after Kent State forced Nixon to moderate his policy and demanded bold moves such as opening trade with China to counter the problematic Cold War implications of domestic violence on American campuses. As Suri suggests, "At home, the gains in Sino-American rapprochement reduced the influence of inherited ideologies advocated by radical groups—The Red Guard, the New Left and the New Right."[104] Thus, Nixon in China appealed to young moderates.

Looking at how this diplomatic success translated into domestic popularity with young people adds much-needed context to his foreign policy decisions. After all, the opening of trade between China and the United States began with a symbolic ping-pong tournament in Beijing that a nineteen-year-old table tennis player, Glenn Cowan, initiated. As a member of the American Table Tennis Association, Cowan became friendly with the Chinese national champions and gave them red, white, and blue T-shirts with the words "Let it be" across the front. This prompted the Chinese to invite the US team to "Red China." After his return, Cowan appeared before the press in purple corduroy, as "his dark locks hung below a yellow suede pied piper hat." This was the face of ping-pong diplomacy. Describing his stay, Cowan spoke glowingly of China and claimed that after meeting the Chinese premier, "I believe I could mediate between him and Nixon very easily."[105] The Now Generation, increasingly soft on the Cold War, believed in détente.

A campus opinion poll found that only one in twenty students looked at Nixon's trip to China with disfavor.[106] After Nixon returned, ping-pong diplomacy came to American campuses, as the Chinese table tennis team toured America. Inviting the president to attend the match at the University of Maryland, Alan Virta of that school's College Republicans bragged that the club "is proud that the University of Maryland is able to take an active role in the betterment of the relations between our country and the People's Republic of China."[107] Even further, Virta wrote an editorial in the university paper recommending that the new hockey team of Washington, DC, take on the Chinese panda as a mascot.[108]

The White House public relations machine pounced on the popularity Nixon's China plan enjoyed with young voters. Reviewing Nixon's developing Youth Speakers Bureau and Youth Media Services, Nixon's adviser Fred Malek wrote the White House's point man on youth that "we should be pushing the China issue much harder than you seem to be."[109] This advice signified Nixon's turn to build his youth support through actions that appeared presidential and forward looking rather than defensive. Even as Nixon deflected accusations about the Watergate arrests, a poll in September showed that 57 percent of young voters claimed the president was "more sincere" and "believable."[110] Discussing the youth vote with Haldeman, Nixon complained that people expected him to be "colorful" and "exciting" to win young voters, but that he would rather appeal to young people with his accomplishments, as Haldeman agreed, "Who else went to China?"[111]

Nixon's staffers soon organized speaking engagements on campuses to discuss China, and his media campaign distributed TV and radio clips on Nixon's trip to China to 496 television stations and one thousand radio stations.[112] In the summer of 1971, even Nixon's most worldly accomplishments included considerations of the youth problem. Nixon had taken concrete steps to proving he could be a "change" candidate, an image many had thought impossible when looking at the man in 1968. While Nixon's visit to China earned popular praise in America, it also created the impression that young people could influence policy and perhaps elections. As youth politics—conservative or liberal—became a legitimate electoral concern, Democrats' reliance on young voters and New Republicans' effort to revive the GOP pushed Nixon to develop his own youth organization.

5 | "Acid, Amnesty and Abortion"
New Politics and George Mcgovern's Campaign

In 1972, one year after the Twenty-Sixth Amendment lowered the voting age to eighteen, Senator George Mcgovern's presidential nomination offered newly enfranchised young liberals their long-awaited idealist and "sell-out dove on Vietnam." Reinforcing Mcgovern's appeal to youth, the senator himself directed a reform commission after the 1968 election that changed the Democratic Party's rules on delegate selection to include first-time voters. This approach, what the Democrats called New Politics, opened the nomination process through primaries and balanced delegates by race, gender, and age to proportionately represent previously marginalized groups. These two factors drew an unprecedented number of first-time voters to the Democratic National Convention, leading one labor representative to grumble, "There is too much hair and not enough cigars at this convention."[1]

Mcgovern's campaign relied on the senator's strong position against Vietnam "Right from the Start" to recruit young voters. This stance led many traditionally Democratic voters—such as white southerners, Catholics, and labor—to conflate the Democratic nominee's New Politics with 1960s radicalism. Nixon's administration pounced on this opportunity to paint the Democratic Party as "radical-liberal," soft on defense, and socially permissive. As Nixon's chief of staff wrote in his diary, "We need savage attack lines against the Mcgovern positions. Get Mcgovern tied as an extremist." Haldeman pointed out how easily this could be accomplished by "bringing in (*left wing liberal*) Abbie Hoffman, Jerry Rubin, Angela Davis." Exaggerating the differences between the two candidates, the White House aimed to "get the maximum number of pictures of rowdy people around Mcgovern, while we go for the all-out-square America."[2] The youth revolt and student protests during this era wore out many Americans' tolerance for the "hippies" on whom Mcgovern seemed to rely. Democratic political adviser Ben Wattenberg explained

McGovern's problem when he claimed the election "was a referendum on the so-called cultural revolution that has been going on allegedly for four or five years in this country."[3]

Thus, Senator George McGovern's campaign manager, Frank Mankiewicz, faced a political crisis. Mankiewicz desperately tried to moderate McGovern's positions as he infused experienced veterans into McGovern's young leadership, used television to project a more presidential candidate, and appealed to economic "bread and butter issues" such as inflation and unemployment. McGovern's young leaders, however, did not relinquish their control easily, and a widely publicized generational rift developed in the campaign. Despite his attempt to reshape the Democratic coalition to include both young liberals and "party regulars," Mankiewicz could not shake McGovern's reputation as the radical candidate of "Acid, Amnesty and Abortion." McGovern's campaign increased Nixon's motivation to engage in youth politics, and the White House redoubled its campaign for first-time voters. Rather than concede the youth vote as many suggested, Nixon and organizers of the Committee to Re-elect the President (CRP) instead decided to increase its young volunteers' visibility to expose McGovern as the "fraud and super politician that he is."[4] McGovern's original cadre of young liberals made his nomination possible, but this connection to the 1960s youth revolt prevented reconciliation between McGovern and the "old guard" that his New Politics threatened.

Scholarship on youth politics during this era identifies the youth vote's polarizing potential. During the early 1960s, young activists formed New Left groups such as the Students for a Democratic Society and the Student Non-violent Coordinating Committee. These student-led organizations coalesced around the civil rights and antiwar movements to combat their sense of alienation. Consequently, as historian Doug Rossinow has noted, "a fissure opened between older liberals in positions of power and younger activists who fixed their moral gaze on the character and actions of individuals."[5] McGovern's youth-focused campaign continued this fissure, as he built his campaign on the commonly held assumption that youth politics would rejuvenate the Democratic Party with a new liberal constituency. McGovern's campaign, however, overestimated its popularity with the 1968 generation—especially its increasingly independent voters—and overlooked the "sons and daughters of the silent majority."

McGovern's campaign underestimated the organization necessary to run a successful youth campaign. As one young McGovern volunteer at Columbia claimed after McGovern set up headquarters near campus only weeks before the election, "They assumed Columbia and Barnard were for McGovern . . . but they didn't realize the storefront would be a source of volunteering and fundraising." McGovern's media campaign struggled to recruit young supporters as well. Though several Nixon ads featured his Young Voters for the President (YVP) to make his campaign look young, McGovern's television ads—titled, "crime and drugs," "defense spending," and "welfare"—targeted older voters. Not that it would help, as a New York University McGovernite reasoned: "You have to reach them [students] on a more individual basis" because "they also get turned off by TV commercials for candidates."[6] In contrast to the New Republican combination of an organized and media-savvy youth campaign, McGovern's campaign could not secure the anticipated turnout.

McGovern's campaign officials in the spring of 1972 talked about winning 70 percent of the youth vote, however only half of the first-time voters turned out as McGovern won 52 percent of the eighteen-to-twenty-four-year-old vote.[7] The lesson many pundits took from McGovern's loss—beware the Left—essentially accepts the narrative Nixon used to stigmatize Democrats as extremists and attract independent voters. However, the first youth vote carried another lesson for Democrats—young voters required a focused organizational effort. This chapter argues that youth politics elevated the candidates' significance and that McGovern's struggle with young voters influenced his image.[8]

The scholarship on McGovern's campaign remains thin. Two recent efforts to refocus attention on the losing side of this landslide election, Bruce Miroff's *The Liberal's Moment* and the 2005 documentary *One Bright, Shining Moment*, claim that McGovern's may have been the first truly liberal candidacy, but also represented the last.[9] This approach emphasizes that New Politics, and the idealism it carried, could not win at the ballot box. While these limits became clear in 1972, this election opened up politics to American voters, and the campaign cemented a new sensibility in America that saw electoral politics, even in losing, as a process that could be changed from the bottom. Democratic reforms opened up delegate selection with the primary process so young voters, and many other interest groups ranging from women to Latinos, could influence elections and candidates. Similar to a bee sting, the McGovern campaign left its mark before meeting its end. In many ways, then, this was the first "liberal moment"—but not the last.

Youth Politics and McGovern's New Politics

Before Robert Kennedy's assassination, his campaign built a powerful youth constituency that reignited liberals' dreams of another Kennedy who could embody 1960s idealism. Kennedy's national campaign swept across American campuses in the buildup to the California primary, contributing to his surging momentum as he chased Hubert Humphrey for the Democratic nomination. The night Kennedy won the California primary and validated his strategy to use young supporters more prominently, an assassin shot the senator after his acceptance speech. Hours later, Mankiewicz, as the campaign's press secretary, climbed up to a lectern at two in the morning with shoulders slumped and lips quivering to announce Kennedy's death twenty hours after the shooting.[10] After this tragedy, his followers searched desperately for a new candidate that could represent their vision of a youthful, idealistic campaign.

Attempting to continue RFK's campaign, McGovern accepted Kennedy aides' requests and joined the race in August. Heading into the Democratic National Convention, McGovern committed himself to "the goals for which Robert Kennedy gave his life," inheriting about three hundred leaderless delegates and the Kennedy team, including Mankiewicz.[11] While his campaign earned him recognition, McGovern could not offer the same star power that gave Americans confidence in Kennedy's New Politics, as he only won 146 and a half delegates to Humphrey's 1,760 and a quarter delegates. During the 1968 DNC, Chicago's streets erupted in riots, pitting young protestors against Chicago's police force. When Senator Abraham Ribicoff (D-Connecticut) nominated McGovern, he shocked the convention by saying, "With George McGovern as President of the United States we wouldn't have Gestapo tactics in the streets of Chicago." McGovern spoke about this chilling effect when he reflected, "Many of the young people who were beaten in Chicago in the summer of 1968 left with the idea that their cause had been beaten as well." For McGovern, "while their effort fell short, it was, in fact, only the beginning."[12] After the 1968 debacle, McGovern chaired the Commission on Party Structure and Delegate Selection to reform the Democratic Party and include more youth.

The election's consequences frightened the liberal establishment when the Students for a Democratic Society National Council met in Boulder, Colorado, after the convention and adopted a resolution entitled "The Elections Don't Mean Shit—Vote Where the Power Is—Our

Power Is in the Street." To many observers, Humphrey's nomination, the violence outside the Democratic convention, and Nixon's victory ended the young Left's role in the Democratic Party. Yet, the 1968 election had the opposite effect: Nixon's victory sent liberals into a soul-searching reform to convince young Americans that Democrats learned from the loss. One journalist predicted that Mayor Daley and his "city of big night sticks" meant "the last hurrah of the hacks."[13] For this pundit, the problem required that the war and draft end. "That could blunt the radical direction of the New Politics and turn it back to old style liberalism."[14]

While many McCarthy supporters took Humphrey's nomination as a sign that "they should drop out of politics because the system could not be beaten," more felt inspired as another twenty-one-year-old Mc-Carthyite district leader, Simon Barsky, quipped that "they offered too little, too late" in 1968. Barsky explained, "If it ever happened again we would have no one but ourselves to blame," as they sought to re-build the Democratic Party from the ground up.[15] New Politics' prac-titioners demanded open primary elections that decided each state's nominees, and reforms that required delegates to represent each state's population by gender, age, and race. To ensure this change, the DNC chairman, Fred Harris, appointed a twenty-eight-member commission led by Senator George McGovern (D-South Dakota). In one testimonial to the Commission on Party Structure and Delegate Selection, Harris's replacement and political veteran Lawrence O'Brien showed how Dem-ocrats felt the need to adapt. Admitting that the 1968 convention disen-chanted the youth, O'Brien observed: "On this subject, their memories are long, their charity short." Despite the party's culpability, O'Brien promised, "we can pledge that we will do everything *we* can, as a party, to see that it never happens again." As he explained, "that convention in 1968 *did* create the Commission on Party Structure and Delegate Selection. . . . To win, we simply *must change*."[16] The commission heard opinions across the spectrum. One student from Georgia testified that young people did not participate because they distrusted leaders, feared retaliation for voicing controversial views (especially on the war), and felt a lack of knowledge about the process. Recommending new party leadership, this young Georgian stated that his generation demanded "honest politicians" who could counter the fact that "many politicians spend their time trying to be cool and suave."[17] For liberal advocates of New Politics, the emerging emphasis on image stood as an obstacle to their mission. Thus, the Democratic Party's problems with young voters and the need to balance image with authenticity created an opening for Republicans to get the upper hand in the new political styles sparked by television.

Thinking ahead to the 1972 election, Mankiewicz imagined this political potential too, as he wrote in his syndicated article that the "campaign to get out the youth vote may turn out to be as decisive in 1972 as was his [McGovern's] anti-Vietnam campaign in 1968."[18] Mankiewicz, the Latin America Peace Corps director during John F. Kennedy's presidency and an aide for Robert Kennedy's 1968 campaign, had connections to the party's old guard. In addition to his experience, Mankiewicz's faith in youth politics made him the perfect campaign manager to help McGovern's campaign bring together the Democrat's old and new constituencies.

Mankiewicz's version of New Politics, however, rested on his background in Hollywood, which shaped his emphasis on polling and image, or the Kennedy formula. In this approach, young supporters served more as an illustration of a candidate's popularity and energy than a central component of his organization. In fact, journalists widely considered Mankiewicz an honorary Kennedy, and even months after McGovern brought Mankiewicz into his campaign during the spring of 1971, repeated accusations forced him to deny his role as Ted Kennedy's "double agent."[19]

Since McGovern began this second run for president, his campaign had relied heavily on young and untested campaign aides that traveled from state to state to develop his organization. McGovern first hired Gary Hart, a thirty-two-year-old lawyer, to manage his campaign. In turn, Hart brought in twenty-five-year-old Gene Pokorny as the Midwest coordinator, twenty-five-year-old Joe Grandmaison as the New England coordinator, Rick Stearns as the twenty-seven-year-old chief of nonprimary states, and twenty-one-year-old Pat Caddell as the chief pollster and McGovern's director of the "blue collar strategy."[20]

In addition, McGovern depended on the young people's votes more than any other presidential candidate in American history, as he proudly stated, "I stake my hopes in 1972 in large part on the energy, the wisdom and the conscience of young Americans."[21] Party reforms under McGovern had turned the primary elections into the most viable path to the nomination, displacing the old political machines' reliance on the smoke-filled room. In addition, party loyalties weakened among younger voters, and the rise of independents augured a new political approach for increasingly fluid constituencies. In the Midwest, where less than a third of voters over fifty years old declared themselves independent, nearly half of the voters between twenty-one and twenty-four years old claimed no party affiliation.[22] Democratic loyalists watched in horror as many of these independents came at their expense. For McGovern, an outsider, this breakdown provided an opportunity.

Defending the rise of independents, one University of Tennessee student strongly disagreed with critics who claimed "the only way to be *really effective* is to join one of the two major parties." Claiming that "independence is valid," this student saw it as a better way of registering discontent than not voting at all, which confuses the nonvoters concern with apathy.[23] McGovern's campaign research dating back to 1970 indicated that politics became more absorbed with the individual candidate. While McGovern's numbers showed Nixon faring poorly with young voters after the Kent State shootings, one report claimed that moderate, liberal Republicans such as New York City mayor John Lindsay would do much better. "Party allegiance therefore seems to be based on the popularity of individuals," the report argued, "and not any particular preference for a party."[24] As McGovern offered a protest vote, he hoped this sentiment could coalesce into a formidable youth constituency for him.

Before declaring his candidacy for the 1972 election, McGovern gathered six loyal supporters at his farm in Cedar Points, South Dakota, to discuss his own presidential prospects. At this meeting McGovern predicted that the moderates such as Hubert Humphrey, Senator Edmund Muskie, and Senator Henry "Scoop" Jackson would crowd each other out. McGovern touted his unique ability to control the youthful politics that disrupted the 1968 convention by convincing the "party pols and organization Democrats that they're not going to find me leading a Fourth Party or my candidacy producing pickets outside the convention hall."[25] McGovern's initial platform attempted to co-opt groups on the Far Left such as "McCarthyites and the NDC [New Democratic Coalition] people." In addition to his firm antiwar stance, McGovern called for sharp cuts in military spending, support for busing, and a dramatic welfare reform that promised every American $2,000. Thus, McGovern tried to appeal to the young supporters who had clamored for a voice in the 1968 DNC and the New Democratic Coalition's white-collar, eastern liberals to build his campaign's foundation.

At Cedar Points, McGovern also argued that his campaign presented Democrats with the best opportunity to heal the wounds from 1968's confrontational convention. For example, McGovern' prolabor record in the Senate showed his potential to unite the Democratic Party's party regulars and young voters. Joining the campaign after it had begun, Frank Mankiewicz envisioned a wider constituency for McGovern than the idealistic, antiwar youth; as he explained, "I've always thought the blue-collar vote had to be the source of his [McGovern's] strength." Stressing the bread-and-butter issues, McGovern's campaign manager explained, "It always seemed to me that McGovern—not as the antiwar candidate but as the 'change' candidate—would appeal more to Middle America."[26] Healing the party's divisions motivated McGovern's campaign; however, building his youthful and liberal reputation became McGovern's first priority in winning the nomination. Though he was not present at Cedar Points, McGovern's close adviser Frederick Dutton provided the political strategy behind McGovern's attempt to build a new Democratic coalition.

In his book *Changing Sources of Power: American Politics in the 1970s*, Dutton argued that the youth vote deserved attention because a "generation as huge, distinct, and assertive as the coming one still has a life and velocity of its own which must be fed into the calculations of a decade."[27] According to Dutton, the emergence of diverse political groups "indicates a slippage of the older political order and the adjustments it must make sooner or later, however grudgingly."[28] This adjustment required the "older political order" to accept younger people's preoccupation with "culture, morality, communication theory, flux and the interior individual" that shaped youth politics. With these changes came new expectations. Liberal politicians such as McGovern and Dutton expected that young Americans would follow a leader with moral authority.

In a memo to McGovern, Dutton predicted the Democrats could win up to 70 percent of this new voting bloc, or eight million votes, enough to make up the difference between Nixon and Humphrey in 1968.[29] Fueling McGovern's confidence in young voters' liberal leanings, Dutton announced that "Nixon made two fantastic tactical blunders—he approved the 18-year-old vote and the new registration provisions."[30] In many ways, Democrats hoped 1972 could serve as 1968 redux, a "do over." A young Massachusetts Democrat, Barney Frank, mused, "If you reran 1968 with the young people voting, the Democrats would win."[31] The numbers looked good. Among the new voters between eighteen and twenty years old in California, 48 percent identified themselves as liberal, and only 25 percent claimed they were politically conservative.[32] Youth's liberal reputation buttressed McGovern's attempt to outflank the party on the left.

After the Twenty-Sixth Amendment passed, McGovern raised the two remaining questions about young voters, "whether they will participate and how they will participate."[33] Organizations developed to mobilize young voters, indicating that a youth-focused New Politics could be a successful electoral strategy. The Movement for a New Congress (MNC), formed at Princeton University after Kent State, spread to over 450 colleges and claimed seventy-five thousand members who volunteered for congressional campaigns to elect peace candidates. Reflecting on the MNC's work in his 1970 campaign, Representative Parren Mitchell (D-Maryland) claimed, "I don't think we could have won this campaign without the student support."[34] Considering these examples, McGovern believed "they [youth] will work within the system if we open it up to them." Essential to this project, McGovern clarified, "a marriage of truly democratic procedures to humane policies of peace and justice is the essential formula for winning the respect and participation of young people in our political process."[35] This formula and faith motivated McGovern's approach to liberal youth in his campaign.

First, McGovern's campaign immediately flaunted the senator's long-standing antiwar position with the slogan "Right from the Start" to build momentum with student voters. On top of his niche as the antiwar candidate, McGovern rallied to other youth causes such as the environment. Referring to his proposals for citizen review boards to oversee transportation and pollution issues on the local level, McGovern wrote in an editorial for *Parents Magazine* that "many of our young . . . have led the way," following, "I hope that the nation will now move in the direction of greater opportunity for citizen involvement."[36]

Concerning campus politics, McGovern rushed to defend students' concerns about the Nixon administration's law-and-order position toward unrest in American colleges and universities. McGovern conducted polls of student presidents that showed over 90 percent opposition to Attorney General John Mitchell's announcement that FBI agents could investigate people on campus without notifying the institution or local police. In response, the senator fired off a letter to Mitchell, demanding details on the legal authority governing such investigations, and saying that they "should be conditioned on the approval or request of the college president or local police official."[37] To quell the symbolic angst that caused tension between students and cops, McGovern proposed a policemen's GI Bill that would enable men and women in law enforcement to attend college. McGovern argued that policemen would gain "sociological understanding of community problems," but they would also "mingle with students as equals in a way that could bring better communication and mutual respect."[38]

McGovern also addressed marijuana penalties to distance himself from Nixon on social issues. From 1968 to 1970, student support for legalizing marijuana doubled to 38 percent, as McGovern proposed relaxed regulations for smoking pot.[39] In addition, McGovern's daughter had been arrested for marijuana possession and avoided a mandatory five-year sentence only because of a technicality. Speaking at a drug counseling office in Boston, the senator argued that "the grave costs involved in imposing severe sentences and prison terms on usually law-abiding young people and young adults suggests that a more promising route might be to regulate marijuana along the same lines as alcohol."[40] McGovern's tepid defense of marijuana still created a contrast with Nixon.

In the most popular example, a leader in Ann Arbor's antiwar movement received a ten-year sentence in state prison for selling two joints to an undercover agent. This controversy crystallized the youth revolt's transition into politics, as several musicians including Stevie Wonder, Phil Ochs, and John Lennon joined radicals such as Jerry Rubin and Bobby Seale for a "John Sinclair Freedom Rally." As the headliner, Lennon closed the eight-hour program with a song that protested "Law and Order," written especially for the event—"It Ain't Fair, John Sinclair." According to the FBI's confidential dossier on Lennon, he sang, "They gave him 10 for 2, what more can [Judge] Colombo, Nixon, Agnew do?"[41] This protest concert doubled as part political rally and part registration drive to enlist recently enfranchised young voters. After all, many young, first-time voters counted marijuana as one more reason to oppose Nixon.

McGovern's campaign slogan, "I make one pledge above all others . . . to seek and speak the truth," also tapped into the 1960s youth revolt's search for transparency. Pictures of McGovern's rallies relayed the campaign's connection to the counterculture as they quickly conjured images of Woodstock and the Merry Pranksters. Young supporters buttressed this hope, as one of McGovern's eager, young supporters submitted a twenty-page research proposal titled "Thunder in November." Optimistically, this project intended to register 80 percent of young voters, getting them to vote two to one for Democrats, and banked on the "tendency of youths to carry their parents with them."[42] The larger "Thunder in November" proposal included a television commercial that mimicked the quintessential 1960s Coke advertisement—hundreds of young people, clasping hands, swaying to the melody and singing in chorus, "I'd like to teach the world to sing in perfect harmony." Even though the McGovern campaign opted not to employ these particular suggestions, "Thunder in November" captured the hope that this campaign could revive the 1960s sensibility to create a powerful political voting bloc out of America's righteous youth.

McGovern's campaign also carried on the 1960s idealism for more experienced political activists, as one volunteer reminisced in a letter to Mankiewicz, "I think so often of our younger days and all those discussions we used to have and our young idealistic thought." The "first hand report from 'Small Town U.S.A.'" continues, "I believe George McGovern fills a real need for the young of today and their search for ideals."[43] Thus, McGovern's campaign gambled on a strategy that relied on young people to continue the 1960s liberal politics into the 1970s, a strategy that Mankiewicz himself described as "a sort of (hopefully) ever-expanding floating crap game."[44] With young people's involvement, McGovern hoped a grassroots effort could capitalize on the party's new primary system to gain the nomination.

In February 1971, McGovern convened a dozen campus and youth activists to announce the formation of the National Students and Youth for McGovern. While this appeared to copy Eugene McCarthy's strategy to challenge LBJ with a "kiddy corps" in 1968, McGovern targeted young voters as a constituency more than a political adornment.[45] McGovern's youth would also play leadership roles in the organization. By the fall of 1972, McGovern allocated campaign funds to pay thirty student-youth organizers a considerable fifty dollars a week.[46] McGovern's youth campaign framed his attacks on Nixon, as he spoke to students at the University of New Hampshire about the president's failure to "increase the participation of our nation's young people in the decision making processes of our government." Pointing out that Nixon's commissions on campus unrest, marijuana, and education included only one person under thirty ("and Vice President Agnew publicly called for his resignation"), McGovern argued that he had unsuccessfully urged

Nixon "to listen to your generation, to take advantage of your idealism and your intelligence."[47] Explaining that Nixon won New Hampshire in 1968 by only twenty-five thousand votes while there were one hundred thousand potential first-time voters, McGovern stressed that "nothing will happen, nothing will change as you want it to, and as I want it to, unless you register and vote."[48]

The registration process stood as a formidable barrier to McGovern's youth campaign. McGovern had attempted to reform the registration procedure itself to allow as many young people to register as possible, as he sought nothing less than the abolition of the process. His attempt to win young voters motivated McGovern to push for reforming this electoral system as it represented the party machine's ability to control who participated and where. Even before the Twenty-Sixth Amendment's ratification, the McGovern-Fraser Commission issued a report in which the committee advocated a one-time, lifelong registration process. The political system's credibility was at stake; as McGovern argued, "The purpose of registration is to add to the legitimacy of the electoral process." This legislation would provide for enrollment officers to "visit every residence in the land and enroll every qualified person to vote who does not refuse."[49] Most important, this reform would require identification cards that would allow voters to participate politically from anywhere in the country, or abroad for service men and women. The more young voters, these activists thought, the more Democrats. While this effort did not succeed, courts relaxed new registration rules that determined who could register, where, and when.

In October 1971, the senator spoke at a rally in Bend, Oregon, to kick off the McGovern Voter Registration Week. "If potential first time voters are willing to overcome registration obstacles" McGovern cheered, "they have the numbers to determine the outcome of the election."[50] The drives achieved immediate success, as the effort yielded over four million first-time voters registered by McGovern's campaign by September 1972. This effort required money, over one million dollars, and almost a third of the campaign's dwindling budget.[51] To oversee the effort, McGovern handpicked Congressman Frank Thompson, who ran the less robust, but successful registration effort for JFK in 1960. Joining Thompson as the director of voter registration, Anne Wexler easily transferred her experience advocating for youth's political rights for the progressive lobby Common Cause to McGovern's campaign.

One flyer threatened young voters that should they shirk the

responsibility they claimed they deserved, they would invite "the smug-
gest 'I told you so' in history from the cynics and skeptics."[52] Proving
their elder naysayers wrong motivated young Americans to show that
they had a special status in American politics. In a memo to McGovern's
field organizers, Anne Wexler emphasized the tremendous expectations for new voter registration. "By adding blacks, browns and young
people to the registration rolls," Wexler claimed, "we can revitalize the
coalition of working people, city dwellers, intellectuals and small businessmen which has been the backbone of Democratic support since
the Presidency of Franklin Roosevelt."[53] They held the entire New Deal
coalition in their hands. Observers agreed that McGovern would need a
huge youth turnout to compete with Nixon and remake the unraveling
Democratic coalition.

Organizationally, the registration effort drew personnel from young
volunteers or tapped into student government groups such as the Association of Students for Voter Registration. McGovern's campaign
leaders provided these groups with area-by-area registration targets and
radio and television spots, along with literature and manuals to guide
their drives. The registration effort left no stone unturned, as registration officers received orders to set up a centrally located booth on high
school campuses with a list of students eighteen years old or older, and
"those students who were not reached by booth would be contacted in
their homeroom class."[54] One Harris poll predicted a 10 percent advantage for McGovern with youth that could still grow to yield a four-
million-voter surplus, noting that "young people are likely to be voting
differently than their elders."[55] Urging all young voters to register, many
McGovern insiders assumed they would vote for McGovern as his chief
pollster Pat Caddell recommended that they "register all the young people, we shouldn't worry about them."[56]

As liberal youth groups sprouted around the ratification and legisla-
tive process, they soon joined the registration effort. On the face of it,
these groups such as the Youth Citizenship Fund sought to enfranchise
as many Americans as possible to encourage voting after forty-seven
million Americans did not vote in 1968. The YCF directors' political
motivations, however, became clear in their internal communications,
as one report hopefully predicted, "I think youth, if motivated . . . will
vote consistently liberal."[57] For the picture on the YCF poster encouraging young voters to register under the slogan "Register your discontent. Vote," the image shows a voter's bare feet and a guitar under the

curtain of a voting booth. Reaching young people in groups proved the most effective approach and contributed to the herd mentality that campaigns hoped would make voting and the candidates "in." Other efforts attempted to make voting hip, as radicals Abbie Hoffman and Jerry Rubin wrote a book they entitled *Vote* and John Lennon planned a series of concerts leading up to the Democratic National Convention with the sole purpose of registering young people.[58] Relying on college students, who often lived far from their residences, McGovern's campus registration effort still struggled because students had to vote in their parents' home district.

The ensuing registration effort motivated young liberals to bring young minorities in American cities into the political process. Youth Citizenship Fund members lent support to local youth organizations that trained street gangs to use registration as a "tool for extending community control."[59] This optimistic outlook motivated an all-out registration blitz during the summer and fall campaign. A project titled Registration Summer created a collaborative effort between disparate groups including Countdown '72 and Register for a New America. This effort planned eighteen events in swing states as either three-day conferences or rallies that attracted as many as fifteen thousand potential first-time voters.[60]

McGovern utilized his young supporters to exploit the new political procedures and win the nomination. In the primary states, McGovern's youth cadre swarmed contested states with a massive door-to-door campaign. McGovern's twenty-four-year-old point man in New Hampshire, Joseph Grandmaison, organized these young volunteers to build McGovern's impressive following in the country's first and crucial primary. The campaign made use of "beards and 'fuzzies'" that would have been "banished to McCarthy backrooms," and sent them out to knock on doors.[61] Although Muskie was supposed to dominate the Granite State because he came from neighboring Maine, McGovern finished with a respectable 37 percent of the vote and launched his national campaign.

After the New Hampshire primary, under McGovern's twenty-three-year-old national youth director, Ed O'Donnell, Students for McGovern groups popped up in campuses across the nation (although they concentrated on the regions in the East, North, and West that they predicted as McGovern friendly). Students for McGovern included a participatory component, the McGovern Action Corps, led by a twenty-one-year-old Harvard student and son of Kennedy adviser John Galbraith, James K. Galbraith. O'Donnell claimed this wing of each campus group raised

Figure 7. Volunteers await McGovern's arrival at the LA Palladium on
California primary night. As Cathy Bertini explained, McGovernites "were
a little more Woodstock." (Courtesy Stuart Bratesman)

"politics above politics" by engaging activities that included "anti-hunger work, ecology or lobbying," which were not directly connected to the campaign.[62] Thus, the student campaign offered a way to meld the 1960s emphasis on social action with a grassroots presidential campaign.

The key to the campaign, in Hart's words, was "decentralization," with a small national headquarters that empowered youthful local leaders to make decisions.[63] In comparison to the forty people Nixon employed to work on his youth campaign in Washington, DC, alone, the McGovern young voter program counted only four people in Washington and forty out in the field.[64]

One storefront headquarters manager wrote Mankiewicz to describe the grassroots movement's success: "The building was given free, young men painted it at night, after a full day's work, free."[65] In nonprimary states, such as Vermont, McGovern's young supporters manipulated the Democrat's election reforms that "urged" equal representation and gained control of state caucuses to secure delegates. During the caucus in Burlington, Vermont, two Middlebury College sophomores led the McGovern forces to beat Muskie 331 to 138. In contrast, Muskie only managed to drum up support from prominent Democrats. One ward chairman admitted McGovern's success: "I tried, but we turned out zilch for Muskie."[66] O'Donnell developed the youth ranks to include over 150,000 young voters, mostly students, targeting "youth density areas" such as California, New York, and Michigan.[67] Unlike Nixon, McGovern never developed a separate campaign branch or headquarters for young voters, as they became central players in the coordination and planning process.

Many young liberals saw McGovern as a path back into the establishment. In Wisconsin, the president of the Young Democrats endorsed McGovern, claiming he "spoke out against the war long before the other Democratic candidate. He said that he would grant amnesty . . . and he has said that no one should be imprisoned for the use of marijuana." Applauding the senator's "honesty, integrity and concern for all," Young Democrats felt "there *is* a man worth working for and doing so by working 'within the system.'"[68] McGovern attempted to soothe American anxiety about a lost generation while harnessing young people's cynicism. This phase can best be understood through McGovern's mantra, "Identify with young people, but lead them . . . don't capitulate to them as [Gene McCarthy] did."[69]

McGovern's foray into youth politics required tremendous discipline as his rallies could invite a "circus" environment. One rally that "jammed" over two thousand students into an auditorium at the University of Wisconsin, Milwaukee, developed the ambiguous relationship between McGovern's campaign and his young supporters. After a "raucous band" created an air of "electricity and madness," Hart recalled how a "belligerent claque" heckled Warren Beatty when he "tried to direct the crowd's thoughts to politics and to introduce the Senator."[70] McGovern came to Beatty's defense, "challenging the ring leader to come up on the stage or shut up."

To be sure, McGovern had his critics among young voters. Underground newspaper writer Rex Weiner scoffed at McGovern's endorsements from radical leader Abbie Hoffman and the countercultural *Rolling Stone* magazine, as he maintained that they now fell within the establishment.[71] Radicals saw McGovern as just another politician, and their contempt for the system or apathy prevented them from voting at all. Far from united, young voters presented an elusive and fluid constituency.

Richard Scammon, whose book identified the "forty-seven year old housewife" as the target voter for each party, dismissed the 1968 generation's liberal political leaning when he responded, "The idea that the youth group is a solid monolith is sheer nonsense."[72] Even if Scammon was right and young people voted with their parents, hopeful liberals argued, "Democrats have more children."[73] Although McGovern's campaign built its strategy on winning a two-to-one majority of young voters, the Students for McGovern director admitted that "there should be a drastic increase in junior colleges," where "Nixon has a lot of strength," and only briefly suggested that they may want to reach nonstudent youth outside factories and in "entertainment spots."[74] As the campaign entered its final phase in the fall, and hopes dimmed for Democratic monopoly on young voters, the registration process did become more selective, as campaign adviser Anne Wexler pointed out, "We'd be out of our minds doing a blanket canvass in a place like Westport, Conn."[75] Wexler's practical approach also addressed McGovern's financial limitations that hindered his organization and forced a more economical reach for young voters.

Ultimately, this effort to capture the youth vote fell well short of its goal, as students did not register at the rate McGovern's campaigners had anticipated. In New Hampshire, only one-third of the eligible college students registered to vote in the primary, pushing O'Donnell to admit that "the apathy is terrible." As McGovern built his campaign on his antiwar image, his campaign overlooked the organizational opportunities to mobilize young people for the election. For Democrats hoping to capture the youth revolt and convince young liberals that "their generation was on trial," McGovern's camp could not deliver because of young voters' tenuous loyalties to his candidacy.[76] In the end, the campaign registered only half of the intended first-time voters and spent only one-fifth of the intended funds because of budget constraints. While Nixon's war chest increased over the summer, McGovern's campaign had to send out young workers with paper buckets to collect donations at his own rallies.[77] Worse, the registration project drained huge resources from the campaign, as the program's director Frank Thompson resigned when Gary Hart diverted campaign money away from the underfunded registration effort to fund star-studded rallies. Hart, reportedly in tears, begged Thompson to stay on board to no avail. The campaign shrugged off Thompson's departure, but it appeared to crumble from the top as the youth strategy strained its leadership.[78]

Even as Hart attempted to moderate McGovern's image, he continued to channel resources toward these events. Hart's friendship with celebrities such as Warren Beatty proved a valuable resource in organizing youth rallies that attracted young voters to the campaign with musical, star-studded rallies. In one string of "fundraising galas," the candidate sandwiched his political stump speech between live performances by Peter, Paul, and Mary as well as Simon and Garfunkel and Dionne Warwick. For five dollars, McGovern's "children of paradise" got to hand their tickets to celebrity ushers such as Paul Newman, and after some "tried and true 6o's satire, 6o's protest and 6o's idealism," McGovern addressed the young crowd with an anticlimactic, traditional political speech. Defying his reputation, McGovern's "mellow" show created an "image of a McGovern who's not a dangerous radical, a pusher of pot a promoter of abortions or even a fancier of hard rock."[79]

While the advantages to Hart's decentralized approach became clear as McGovern's grassroots campaign succeeded in the early primaries, it also had drawbacks. Rather than shaping his young supporters' image to appeal to a wider Democratic electorate, McGovern's commitment to playing the liberal youth's "pied piper" allowed the youth to shape his own image. In one memo, O'Donnell pointed out that Hart lacked the ground-level control. Complaining about leadership in Delaware, O'Donnell documented problematic personnel, labeling one young female staffer "the most abrasive and immature person in Delaware" and identifying "the other lulu" as "a 19 year old dope freak who has been writing nasty letters to the newspaper . . . and now incredibly is assistant press secretary."[80] Considering these young leaders contributed to, or detracted from, McGovern's image as they spoke for the campaign in Delaware, the decentralized approach amid the increasingly media-focused political environment proved problematic.

In many ways, McGovern's campaign deserved its radical reputation. Hunter S. Thompson, though he exaggerated McGovern's radicalism for his own reasons, painted a picture of pure debauchery on the "zoo plane" devoted to McGovern's press following. In his description, Thompson imagined how the "older and straighter press people must have felt when they saw five or six freaks reeling around the cockpit on takeoff and landing, passing joints around."[81] For McGovern, his reluctance to take a tough line on marijuana considered his liberal constituency, as an anonymous supporter donated one dollar to his campaign, writing, "Dear George, find $1 (one dollar) which would have gone for 2 *joints*. We're going straight for peace. Please stop Nixon now."[82]

His young supporters' language made this radical image believable, as one campus flyer asked "Can we stand FOUR MORE YEARS" that offered "War, Inflation, Repression" not to mention the "murderous racism of Vietnamization."[83] McGovern's strident tone and rhetoric, as he claimed that Nixon's presidency was the "the most corrupt in the history of American politics," along with McGovern's populist focus on economic reform rather than crime control, did little to distance his campaign from its radical image.[84] In combination, the McGovern campaign's rhetoric, permissive campaign culture, and vague stance on abortion, amnesty, and legalization of marijuana invited criticism as he became the frontrunner.

"Middle America" had already lost its patience with the youth revolt, most evident when polls indicated wide support for the National Guard who shot at students, killing four, during Kent State's infamous demonstration. "The Hard Hat Riot" in New York City followed this tragedy, when hundreds of construction workers attacked young protestors, targeting the male demonstrators with the longest hair. Worse, the fact that McGovern depended on youth politics opened his campaign to criticism that it lacked the maturity to soothe the generational tensions in America.

This job—shaping McGovern's image as a moderate "healer"—

appealed more to his other manager, Frank Mankiewicz. As Hunter S. Thompson admitted that even though he wanted to "cut off both of his big toes," he would hire Mankiewicz to handle the press if Thompson ever ran his own presidential campaign.[85] Though McGovern made Mankiewicz his highest-paid adviser, the job appealed more to the forty-seven-year-old journalist as an adventure. As a journalist, Mankiewicz's decision to take a pay cut and join the incipient campaign indicated the opportunities he saw for the Democratic Party to connect the dots between politics and culture. Mankiewicz contended that the Democrats could mine this antiestablishment sentiment for votes with which they could reshape their fractured coalition. Even for Mankiewicz, however, healing the rift between youth and the old guard became increasingly difficult.

Mankiewicz and "Acid, Amnesty and Abortion"

When McGovern gained the nation's attention as a legitimate contender in the winter of 1972, he hired former Kennedy loyalists such as Ted Van Dyke and John Kenneth Galbraith who could help build the national campaign. Throughout the primaries, this change developed an underlying tension between this new leadership and McGovern's young loyalists. This tension became more pronounced as McGovern became the frontrunner and his campaign refocused on healing the party's divisions. McGovern's youth constituency soon became a youth problem, as his campaign could not shed the radical image that its opponents labeled "Acid, Amnesty and Abortion."

McGovern's opponents began the barrage to bolster his radical image in April 1972, as the campaigns focused on the Ohio primary. In a speech in Youngstown, the moderate Democratic candidate, Scoop Jackson, appealed to the blue-collar voters' "Middle America" concerns over drugs, arguing that McGovern's position on marijuana was "virtually to legalize it for the rich." Jackson linked McGovern's permissive approach to marijuana with liberal radicals, claiming that "is a great relief to those who, like the Rubin-Hoffman types, like to mix their politics with pot."[86] The "three A's" smear gained considerable traction, cutting McGovern's lead in half, from a twelve-to-six-point margin in Ohio.[87] Even those in favor of McGovern's antiwar stance feared his radical reputation, as a Chicago lawyer complained that "he [McGovern] had no right to espouse busing, quotas, marijuana."[88] In addition, Senator Hugh Scott, the Republican minority leader, brought the "three A's" attack into the GOP's rhetoric to exaggerate McGovern's permissive politics.

Well before Nixon unleashed his culture war in the 1972 election, the campaign leading up to the California primary revealed McGovern's "three A's" problem. This stretch of the race for the nomination offered Humphrey his last chance to get back into contention. As he battled Scoop Jackson for moderate Democrats' support, Humphrey's campaign trailed McGovern by over two hundred delegates. For Hunter S. Thompson, "Hubert's only hope in California is a savage, all-out attack on McGovern—a desperate smear campaign focused on Grass, Amnesty, Abortion."[89] Though McGovern later claimed to oppose legalization, he had argued that pot should be treated like alcohol as late as February 1972. Desperate for an angle to exaggerate McGovern's radicalism, Humphrey intensified the attack on McGovern as a "Marijuana Sympathizer" that began during the Ohio and Nebraska primaries.[90] McGovern's defensive reaction against these attacks proved their cumulative effect. The night before the California primary, McGovern flew to the National Governor's Conference in Houston to calm Democrats' concerns about his electability. According to journalist David Broder, the governors pledged their support if McGovern could "restrain the 'disruptive tactics' of his youthful supporters."[91]

Though he lost the primary by six percentage points, Humphrey's "three A's" attack cut McGovern's lead in half and cemented popular perceptions of McGovern as "a sell-out dove on Vietnam whose basic constituency is the radical left."[92] Apparently, McGovern's demand for immediate withdrawal linked him too closely to 1960s protest politics. The final vote reflected this trend, as McGovern won 425,000 of an estimated 580,000 youth votes while he lost older voters by twenty percentage points.[93] McGovern's young volunteers also made his victory in California possible, totaling fifty thousand and establishing 180 storefront offices compared to Humphrey's paltry sixty headquarters and fewer than ten thousand volunteers.[94] So, even as McGovern came to appreciate his youth campaign's electoral benefits, he became increasingly sensitive to its stigma. According to Nixon's personal pollster, Robert Teeter, Humphrey's attack on McGovern in California increased Nixon's favorability overnight.

While the generation gap created an image problem for McGovern, youth politics fractured the campaign. Some McGovern campaign aides relished youth's central role. Edward O'Donnell, director of Students for McGovern, emphasized the campaign's reliance on the youth vote when he suggested in a memo that McGovern "say he will defeat Nixon because of it" and that "the reason he is behind in the polls is that students are not polled." Finally, O'Donnell's proposal outlined McGovern's young supporters' symbolic significance, as they would communicate a "message of reconciliation between American young people and others." With his nomination in sight, McGovern moved toward the healing aspect of his Cedar Points plan. This meant that McGovern came to rely more heavily on his campaign's political veteran, Frank Mankiewicz. Mankiewicz always acknowledged the need to reel in McGovern's youthful image, reminding himself on a memo pad to "avoid ideology" and maintain "discipline among troops."[95] Accordingly, Mankiewicz strayed from McGovern's previous strategy and advised a rapprochement with party regulars and mass media appearances to undo the "three A's" image.

The dual leadership structure under McGovern became outmoded as Mankiewicz's strengths seemed better suited to execute the campaign's move for reconciliation with the party regulars. The differences between the senator's campaign managers motivated Van Dyke to repeatedly suggest that McGovern replace Hart with Mankiewicz, claiming, "Gary has been, and will continue to be, destructive and divisive so long as he continues to play any important role in your effort."[96] McGovern even went further as he appointed the former party chairman and archetypal old guard Democrat Lawrence O'Brien as the campaign chairman and the "foremost consultant on . . . overall policy and strategy." This move threatened both Mankiewicz's and Hart's authority, however, it leaned in Mankiewicz's political direction.[97] In the end, McGovern kept both men on his campaign, as Hart "persuaded McGovern that his retention was essential if the nominee was not to lose the backing of the young people who aided his nomination."[98] Even in personnel decisions, McGovern's own youth problem limited his campaign.

McGovern's campaign, largely divided by generation, bifurcated in support of either Hart or Mankiewicz, who personified the cultural divisions that plagued McGovern's campaign. While a witty, jovial personality, Mankiewicz did not drink and often appeared rumpled in traditional attire. In contradiction, Hart embraced a more colorful lifestyle as he ingratiated himself into Hollywood star and McGovern supporter Warren

Beatty's permissive social circles. As for his attire, Hart was described by Theodore White as wearing "gray denim pants, high cowboy boots," and the quintessential "flower-blue open necked shirt."[99]

The fundamental difference between the two became apparent when Mankiewicz shifted the campaign away from the large, young, enthusiastic rallies and toward smaller televised events that could target "issues." Although McGovern's constituency ultimately failed to enlist enough traditional Democratic voters, Mankiewicz's attempt to reach ethnics, Catholics, and labor did not lack in effort. For example, McGovern's more experienced advisers emphasized the rising price of food as they promoted the "bread and butter" concerns, such as inflation and unemployment, which they hoped would resonate with the average American voter, or the forty-seven-year-old housewife in Ohio. Van Dyke even suggested that McGovern tone down his antiwar rhetoric, claiming that the mainstream voter associated McGovern's central issue, Vietnam, with "long haired kids" and "amnesty, which do not attract them."[100] McGovern campaign aide Gordon Weil outlined the basis of this strategy, as campaign strategies increasingly attempted to balance out their candidate's image to ward off stereotypes. Weil asked McGovern to consider the "'consumers' of politicians' public images" in the emerging living room politics and a "public that seems to want its news and opinions spoon fed." Weil pointed out to McGovern that "because of your strong stand on Vietnam and some apparent associations with self-styled radicals, you are classified as a radical. Any stereotype can too easily become a burden and should be counteracted."[101] Young voters exacerbated the problems that image politics created for candidates.

Even younger Democrats understood the need to tone down their rhetoric and broaden their base. In 1971, the Florida Young Democrats received their elders' scorn when their platform urged an end to "restrictive laws" on abortion, divorce, homosexuality, marijuana, and cohabitation. In 1972, they opted for a self-described "all very apple pie and moderate" platform, with the relatively tame calls for the decriminalization of marijuana and a national health insurance plan as its most controversial proposals.[102]

To help rein in the senator's campaign, Mankiewicz pushed McGovern to build a more media-savvy approach rather than continue the large, raucous rallies. This approach stood in direct contrast with Gary Hart's, who placed complete faith in New Politics–style grassroots organization. When Ed O'Donnell reported angrily to Hart that nobody printed the press release announcing five hundred college editors' endorsements, Hart cheered him, claiming "It doesn't matter if they print it or not. What matters is that we've got the people. We're going to win."[103] Annoyed with McGovern's limited exposure early in the campaign, Hart stubbornly confronted members of the press, "To hell with you! If we have to, we'll go to Miami Beach still at 6 percent . . . and we'll win the nomination."[104]As the son of a Hollywood screenwriter, Mankiewicz carried a higher appreciation for the media's role in politics.

At first, McGovern's inexperienced youth cadre played an especially important role in producing his image. Using new techniques to disseminate speeches directly to radio stations, Joe Walker, a recent graduate of Georgetown University, could send out each clip of McGovern's speeches to seven thousand stations a day, dwarfing the one thousand or so who Humphrey and Nixon had reached in 1968. As for television, a Harvard dropout provided the technical support and ensured that McGovern's appearances would be on the news, bragging that there was "not one rally . . . where any television camera failed to get usable footage."[105]

As they moved away from this focus on rallies McGovern's image makers began to belie this youth effort. One day's work showed that Mankiewicz managed the campaign's telegenic effort with more traditional elements of the Democratic coalition when McGovern met a small labor group where he briefly outlined his economic position. He then met 150 Italian American labor and political leaders, followed by radio and television interviews and a 6:30 rally with Ted Kennedy, all in time to get coverage on the eleven o'clock news. While McGovern made an all-media blitz in the final months, his techniques did not adapt to the changing political environment that emphasized image over issues.[106]

McGovern's commercials lacked the condensed political message that Americans could swallow in 1972. Produced as five-minute "man on the street" question-and-answer sessions, Charles Guggenheim's advertisements did not capture the sense of energy, optimism, and stability that the nation desired. These stodgy relics of the 1960s overlooked advertising's central role in the politics of image after 1968. Proving the point, Guggenheim later exaggerated this problem when, partly out of economic necessity, he produced television advertisements that consisted only of text as McGovern spoke the words. Still, a memo to McGovern's press secretary, Kirby Jones, described the press coverage of McGovern's appearance in Portland, Maine, as "not so good," as it "emphasized young crowds, interviewing [a] teenage girl" even though the press officer at the small rally insisted that the "crowd was *not* young."[107] As Mankiewicz attempted to mature McGovern's campaign, its young supporters and popular perceptions of his extremist image undermined this effort.

The Convention and the Aftermath: Failure to Reconcile

The Democratic National Convention in Miami provided the forum in which the Democrats' internal tensions came to a head. Perhaps the party's moderate platform and the relative tranquility that surrounded the convention offered the nation a reassuring picture of McGovern's politics. Even the thousands of antiwar protesters outside the convention were responsible. Only two arrests took place the entire week. One woman demonstrator left her three-year-old daughter at the Miami Headstart Program care center with the words "Please don't feed me—I only eat organic food" in red pen on the child's back.[108] These demonstrators were clearly different from the ones who besieged Chicago's streets in 1968. While technically a success, the convention still exacerbated the "three A's" problem and began McGovern's downward slide in the polls. McGovern's struggles with the liberal and conservative forces in the Democratic Party dramatically colored observers' interpretation of the convention.

Most notably, hundreds of young protestors occupied the Doral Hotel lobby and demanded that McGovern come down from his room and clarify his position on the war after he tempered his antiwar rhetoric.[109] McGovern's advisers debated his alternatives, as they feared both the "undignified" image of McGovern "rapping" with hippies as well as a violent resolution to the protest.[110]

Gordon Weil, McGovern's political adviser, and Eleanor McGovern urged the senator to speak with the protestors and stress his "points of differences with them" to avoid appearing "too much of a radical."[111] First, Mankiewicz met with the crowd and tried to end the confrontation. When the protestors jeered, demanding to speak with McGovern, he eventually came down. Weil saw the protest as an opportunity to show McGovern "handling a group of demonstrators with firmness and coolness." On the contrary, the meeting confirmed Mankiewicz's fears about McGovern's "pied piper" image problem.[112] In reference to the "showdown at the Hotel Doral," a Richmond journalist claimed that McGovern "may be trapped by the fanaticism of his own supporters," describing "McGovern's children's crusade" as an "energetic, over-educated minority."[113] This interpretation melded McGovern's youth image with the lingering bitterness toward privileged campus protesters. The "over-educated" claim also touched on the criticism concerning New Politics' influence on delegates, as 39 percent held postgraduate degrees while only 4 percent of Americans had done graduate work. Aggravating the working-class voters' resentment of New Politics, one reporter quipped, "The old ingredients of money, and education and class still dominate the process."[114]

After this face-off, McGovern returned to his room, and his staff set to finding a vice presidential candidate. That they had not already established a running mate speaks to both the uncertainty surrounding McGovern's nomination and also the lack of traction McGovern gained within the party. The list of possibles, ranging from southerners such as Congressman Wilbur Mills to the northern liberal Ted Kennedy, all brought something different to the ticket. After Kennedy declined the offer, McGovern's people could not decide on a name. After the lobby incident tested McGovern's position on the war and his hold on the youth constituency, McGovern went with Thomas Eagleton, a freshman senator who had campaigned on an antiwar platform in 1968. Eagleton fashioned his own New Politics in Missouri during his 1968 campaign against party favorites, managing to build a constituency of students, labor, rural whites, and urban blacks. While he opposed the war and favored environmental regulation and a lower voting age, Eagleton still chastised "misguided young radicals who measure their political victories in the number of heads split open in violent confrontation with police."[115] Eagleton revealed his social conservatism when journalist Robert Novak quoted his claim, anonymously, that "the people don't know McGovern is for amnesty, abortion and legalization of pot."[116] Eagleton still offered little for southern Democrats and labor to bridge the gap with McGovern. McGovern's aides argued for a "candidate from the camp of party regulars," as one journalist observed that "McGovern was boxed in. He had a scare," after "a noisy demonstration by young anti-war militants at his hotel."[117] McGovern could not fulfill his mantra, "lead them . . . don't capitulate to them" as his attempt to heal the party showed cracks before McGovern even accepted the nomination. Weeks after the convention, Eagleton admitted to suffering from a mental illness that required electric shock therapy. Hesitantly, McGovern dropped Eagleton from the ticket and replaced him with Kennedy's brother-in-law, Sargent Shriver.

While, by convention standards before 1972, the DNC ran according to plan, the vast expansion of media and coverage after the 1968 convention spectacle brought the proceedings under a microscope. The process seemed untidy, as McGovern's campaign leaders intentionally lost a challenge to avoid a parliamentary move that could have awarded hundreds of California delegates to Humphrey. This wrangling pushed the acceptance speech to past midnight, hardly capitalizing on the national exposure. Essentially, New Politics' messy details were laid bare for all to see, and it looked rather old. Shouting matches and arcane backroom strategy dominated, and the outcome lacked the polish one came to expect in the increasingly image-conscious political environment. McGovern finished his speech, quoting the campaign's theme song (lifted from Robert Kennedy's campaign), Woody Guthrie's "This Land Is Your Land." As the nominee recited, "This land was made for you and me," one experienced party leader, Joseph Califano, recalled that Jerry Rubin (who actually won a delegate) and his youthful cohorts, "many in hippie garb," clapped and swayed as they smoked marijuana.[118] Through the wafting smoke that surrounded McGovern on the podium at three in the morning, if Americans saw the senator at all, they found the Democratic nominee hard to recognize. Even though the final platform distanced itself from the controversial planks that supported legalized abortion and legal protections for homosexuals, McGovern's inexperienced delegates, such as a young Alaskan woman who claimed she was elected by "youths and Eskimos," perpetuated his "three A's" reputation.[119]

Thomas and Mary Edsall explain the role racial resentment played in dividing the Democrats, as busing "fell like an axe" through the party and created an alliance of "white, blue collar northerners with southerners against blacks and upper-middle class liberals."[120] In addition, young voters split the New Deal coalition. The convention demonstrated that McGovern's New Politics of inclusion threatened the other end of New Politics that emphasized image. Greeting McGovern in Miami, an ABM ("Anybody but McGovern") campaign briefly emerged around a potential Humphrey/Wallace ticket, setting aside regional politics to consolidate Democratic moderates and conservatives. Southern Democrats led this opposition. "The problem George," George Wallace admitted to

McGovern, "is that our people, even if I was to endorse you, I couldn't get them to support you."[121] Labor also joined the fight. Mankiewicz employed gimmicky tactics such as calling McGovern's campaign "Project GM" when referring to McGovern's campaign with "UAW types"; the reconciliation attempted to downplay McGovern's youthful, radical reputation.[122] McGovern's success, however, motivated AFL-CIO leader George Meany's disdain for the senator. Describing the DNC to a convention of the United Steelworkers, Meany claimed that in Miami "we heard from the people who look like Jacks, acted like Jills, and had the odors of Johns about them."[123] McGovern's labor record scored highly with unions, but his image needed revision.

McGovern's campaign for the young labor vote received outside help as well when a young labor organizer, Kemble Penn, headed the AFL-CIO organization named "Frontlash '72" to recruit the blue-collar youth vote. Hoping to counter "the elitists who come from mostly prestigious universities," Penn claimed that Frontlash '72 worked in fifty communities based on "the New Youth Politics," which he defined as, "not the intellectual gambit of the financially secure . . . but of the insecure." Looking away from campuses, the labor's youth organizers "hit the beaches, the bowling alleys and the lunch wagons where the 'millions of non-elitist working-class-youth' are."[124] While Frontlash also sent off its volunteers to comb bars, unemployment centers, and office parks for the elusive "working youth," its director in San Francisco explained, "Many non-students just feel lost and useless." Fewer noncollege youth registered than students, though this could also be attributed to the difficulty in finding them.[125]

Following Mankiewicz's dictate to refocus on labor, Governor Patrick Lucey from Wisconsin spoke to the Theatrical Stage Employees and Motion Picture Machine Organization on McGovern's behalf (not exactly the AFL-CIO). Lucey took the "three A's" issue head on, arguing that "the Media has emphasized, especially during the recent Democratic Convention in Miami, the visibility of youth and other groups as forces in this revolution." Lucey challenged this popular perception, arguing, "The new politics could not have achieved its success without the full support of the working men and women of America."[126] Still, despite this effort, Meany engineered the AFL-CIO's neutrality vote that denied the Democrats a huge swath of its traditional voting base. Even if McGovern earned Meany's endorsement, blue-collar workers may not have supported him, as only one-third of the representatives at the union's vote wore McGovern pins.[127] While Meany detested McGovern's anti-war stance, McGovern's young supporters clearly alienated the "party bosses" as well as their constituency. New Politics had its limits, as party bosses and organizations still held sway over many voters. In addition, the generation gap became more divisive within McGovern's campaign when Mankiewicz added more seasoned veterans to leadership ranks after McGovern became the Democratic nominee at the convention.

In an internal memo to Galbraith, Humphrey's fifty-seven-year-old former adviser John B. Martin joked, "Single-handed I have raised the average age of the staff to 10 1/2." Martin sarcastically continued, "Most of the betting is being done by 9-year-old experts on National Defense, small barefoot black girls in blue jeans, and boys in long hair and beads."[128] In addition, McGovern's original staffers resented the political veterans and often resisted their directives. This rejection of party leaders also undermined Democrats' hard-earned inroads with urban blacks, as the African American AFL-CIO president in Detroit, Thomas Turner, fumed: "They've got young people running things who don't know up from down. . . . They've got the damnedest attitude, they don't want to be aligned with labor leaders."[129] Mankiewicz learned about this obstacle when he sent party regular Mickey Wapner to help organize the McGovern headquarters in California. Wapner, a Kennedy loyalist and the wife of future celebrity Judge Joe Wapner, immediately reported younger leaders' resistance to her as an "outsider," forcing Mankiewicz to admit that "the complaints we hear constantly about 'exclusivity' and hostility to outsiders are probably all true."[130] This generational rift spread throughout the organization and increased McGovern's struggle to overcome his image as the candidate of "Acid, Amnesty and Abortion."

McGovern's youth-oriented image inspired many Americans to condemn his entire platform as "radical." For example, affluent conservatives feared the senator's plan to increase taxes on the nation's highest incomes, as Eli Sagan wrote to Mankiewicz that wealthy people "are convinced that George McGovern is going to send some blue jeaned, long-haired young men to confiscate that Mercedes-Benz right out of the garage."[131] While the thought of hippie repo men working for the government heightened affluent Americans' anxiety over McGovern's tax proposals, McGovern's connection with liberal students and the counterculture allowed economic conservatives to find radicalism in each of his proposals.

In addition, the steps taken to moderate McGovern's image after the convention alienated his youthful voting base. After Eagleton's revelation, McGovern's campaign conducted an informal poll that showed the senator's office strongly in favor of keeping the Missouri senator on the ticket. In contrast, Mankiewicz's office opposed Eagleton, twenty-seven votes to twelve. This tally correlated more closely to the phone calls that flooded McGovern's headquarters and urged him to "drop Eagleton."[132] Mankiewicz understood the grave reality the Eagleton problem presented to McGovern's campaign, as he wrote in a confidential memo, "many, many people are deeply afraid of craziness."[133] Despite this effort to undo the political catastrophe, the Eagleton affair contributed to McGovern's plummeting reputation and also pushed out many young idealists who believed McGovern had become just another politician. One message from a campaign worker in California bluntly stated, "she has hard evidence that McG has lost youth vote in Cal. over Eagleton affair. They believe that McG has no integrity and they will sit out election."[134]

Landslide

On November 7, 1972, the election results showed George McGovern his campaign's limitations when he managed to win just one state and the District of Columbia. In this landslide defeat, McGovern won 46 percent of the "blue-collar" vote. This statistic's significance becomes more apparent when considering that Democratic candidates garnered at least 56 percent of this constituency (and as much as 73 percent in 1964) since the 1930s. Unfortunately for McGovern, he did not understand the central role that social issues played in this election and the way his young supporters thrust enhanced his radical image.

After the DNC, Nixon's campaign targeted McGovern's with the term "radical elite," which suited Nixon's co-optation of the "three A's" attack perfectly. Pat Buchanan revealed how hard it would be for McGovern to reverse course. While the president's speechwriter acknowledged that McGovern no longer advocated the legalization of marijuana, he stressed that in February 1972, "he favored treating pot like alcohol." Buchanan fumed that "McGovern's catering to young people . . . is the essence of political irresponsibility," warning that his proposal "to remove all criminal penalties amount to a prescription for legalizing marijuana for the rich . . . and giving young Americans easy access into the drug culture."[135] This accusation blamed the elite eastern establishment for spreading the 1960s cultural excesses to young people in the 1970s.[136]

For Catholics, southern whites, and blue-collar defectors to Nixon's "new majority," the young voters catalyzed their motivation to break away from their traditional party loyalties. The late George Meany of the AFL-CIO is reputed to have said of the Democratic Party, "The party of blood, sweat and tears has become the party of dope, sex and queers." Referring to the "'dope, sex and queers' thing," Nixon's major source on McGovern, Ken Khachigian, pointed out to Buchanan that "the time is right . . . to see whether or not we can begin making inroads into these party regulars."[137]

Thus the youth image, and the permissive tag it brought, increased the White House's emphasis on other innovations of the new political environment such as John Connally's Democrats for Nixon. Because of his opposition to McGovern's "dovish" foreign policy, Connally, the former secretary of the treasury under LBJ, broke ranks with his party in 1972 to head the Democrats for Nixon division of CRP. While McGovern's radical image divided his party, Connally attributed his organization's growing ranks to Democrats' repudiation of McGovern's proposed cuts in defense spending. Claiming Democrats "are afraid of George McGovern," Connally insisted that "it is in the best interests of this country that the president be re-elected this year."[138] Even as McGovern built his New Politics on changing the process and building a youth following by going over the heads of the traditional party organization, his image mattered tremendously to young Americans' increasingly independent politics.

This attack outlined two essential components of Nixon's "dirty tricks," proving how Nixon's disregard for authenticity and obsession with image could motivate his notorious predilection for deception.

"Ratfucking" and Going Negative

As youth politics' independent majority demanded a larger role for media in elections, these voters' emphasis on the candidate also pushed campaigns to demean each other. Desperate to tie McGovern to antiwar radicals, Nixon continually pleaded for one hard-hitting advertisement about McGovern's soft stance on draft dodgers that included amnesty.

Although Nixon dismissed the potential damage from a tough approach on amnesty, "you lose the Jewish young, that's about all," his aides and advertising staff urged restraint.[139] Mindful of young independents, one adviser argued with Nixon: "You start into these kids with amnesty, that's when you could lose a portion of your youth vote."[140] Nixon's campaign understood the progress they made with young voters and wanted to play it safe. Nixon could not openly call McGovern's campaign radical. Nixon's aide Charles Colson argued: "Young people tend to identify with individuals much more than with political parties," and that since "all kids tend to identify with each other . . . it is almost impossible to attack one without attacking them all."[141] Thus, Nixon would need to build McGovern's extremist image without contributing to the president's antiyouth reputation that the YVP meant to counter. In Nixon's attack, the YVP gave the CRP a surreptitious political weapon.

Restraint became a challenge after McGovern's liberal and young constituency wandered into Nixon's crosshairs. White House aide Patrick Buchanan took great pleasure in McGovern's primary victories, as he claimed, "Not in our memory has there been such a wealth of material with which to tag a national candidate as an extremist." (Buchanan claimed "'radical' was overused in 1970. The term 'extremist' is a far more difficult one to defend against.")[142] The Democrats' own "three A's" attack on McGovern's campaign during the primaries pleased Nixon's adviser, as he planned to let Humphrey "do the preliminary hatchet work." While Buchanan salivated at the possibility of running against McGovern's youth movement, he sneered, "McGovern's ambitious children seem to be busy 'stealing' [George] Wallace delegates" after a paralyzing gunshot wound forced the former Alabama governor out of the presidential race.[143]

Buchanan appreciated the political punches when the Democratic candidate Scoop Jackson complained that McGovern's passé approach to marijuana "is a great relief to those who, like the Rubin-Hoffman types, like to mix their politics with pot." This critique mirrored the Nixon campaign's "Assault Book," which argued that "Senator McGovern's catering to young people by suggesting we treat marijuana in the same fashion we treat alcohol is the essence of political irresponsibility."[144] Nixon aides begged for McGovern's nomination, arguing "we must do as little as possible, at this time, to impede McGovern's rise." While tempting to attack the senator on "the extremist radical labels;

the pro-amnesty and pro-abortion positions; the radical chic attitude," they thought better, arguing, "Let's not do Hubert's work for him."[145]

Still, Nixon's campaign operatives had set in motion a clandestine effort to attack his enemies that relied on young loyal supporters. Nixon's administration developed its own "dirty tricks," and many of these underhanded strategies filtered down from the White House. This effort did not target McGovern himself until he had secured the nomination in late June. In fact, Nixon's young shock troops' covert political efforts, dubbed "ratfucking," had aimed more at young liberals themselves.

On December 3, 1971, the Association of Student Governments held an Emergency Conference on Youth in Chicago at Loyola University. As one hundred or so student leaders claimed the meeting meant to secure representation at the national conventions in 1972, it soon evolved into a "Dump Nixon" event. Journalists compared this meeting to a similar conference held by Allard Lowenstein in 1968 that set the youth rebellion on a crash course with the Democratic Party and Chicago's finest.[146] While Nixon representatives tentatively scheduled to attend, Rietz called them off as distance became the best strategy. Instead, Rietz had the event "wired" and placed observers, which confirmed his suspicions. The closing statement summed up the one point on which conference attendees agreed; they meant to replace Nixon with "someone who speaks for the young, the poor, and the hopes of America."[147] For most there, that meant George McGovern. Perhaps most telling, pot-toking Mexican comedians "Cheech and Chong" provided Saturday night's entertainment. The liberal Americans for Democratic Action secretly funded the $400,000 meeting, and the event itself ended in "disarray" as blacks and Chicanos demanded a more significant role after a weekend of "fiery anti-Nixon speeches and political workshops." Not even the moderate "fellow from [the] Ripon [Society]," normally known for its Republican leanings, offered a sympathetic voice for the administration.[148]

Contributing to the chaos, Rietz's contact, John Venners, wrote after the fact that "under instructions [from Rietz] to create more turmoil among the already tense and disturbed delegates," he attended workshops to inquire about the event's secretive funding and met with Chicano leaders to discuss the convention's inequality and encourage a walkout with the black caucus.[149] While Rietz's mole claimed that the conference showed radicals' "effectiveness in practical politics will be nil," the conference did plan for a future youth caucus, but Venners claimed the media exaggerated the potential for a threatening organization of young liberals who could form a potent voting bloc.

Capitalizing on the moment, an indignant Republican congressman took up the cause. Speaking on the floor, Representative Louis Frey Jr. of Florida ripped the Emergency Conference as "an assault on the President and the Republican Party." Claiming that the conference denied Nixon supporters' requests to speak, Frey cried foul, as the "non-partisan tax exempt" Association of Student Governments that held the conference "attempted to manipulate the young people for their own political ends."[150] As Nixon's aides attempted to wield the IRS's power, the intimidation did work. As these "non-partisan" registration events revealed themselves as "dump Nixon" rallies, they lost credibility, making it difficult for groups such as the YCF to set up programs. The YCF, an organization formed to register noncollege youth, attracted suspicion that it cared only to recruit Democratic voters and soon became fearful that the IRS would investigate its nonpartisan status. In reaction, YCF organizers replaced the executive director "because he was becoming too political." In addition, a Nixon insider became the organization's director of field operations, allowing the White House to "pretty well decide when YCF should be active."[151] The president's reelection campaign utilized its young supporters as weapons in the clandestine attack politics that made Nixon infamous.[152]

Nixon's men could not resist attaching McGovern's youthful supporters to their differences more obviously. As Buchanan outlined in one memo, "Our great hope in 1972 is to exacerbate the deep Democratic rift between the elite, chic, New Left, intellectual avant garde, isolationist, bell-bottomed environmentalist, new priorities types on the one hand—and the hard hat, Dick Daley, Holy Name Society, ethnic, blue collar, Knights of Columbus, NYPD, Queens Democrats and others. . . . The liberal Democrats should be pinioned to their hippie supporters."[153] But, while calling out McGovern's soft approach on crime maintained Nixon's law-and-order image, Buchanan scoffed that the "three A's" attack was "so 'cute' as to make it appear we are simply political."[154] For Buchanan, "three A's" did not associate McGovern with the extremist label clearly enough. This line of attack would take more work than a simple catch phrase. In addition, CRP's organizers increased its young volunteers' visibility to expose McGovern as the "fraud and super politician that he is" by also offering an alternative to radical youth politics that stigmatized the Left.[155]

Youth speakers soon got hold of the Nixon Assault Book, as the YVP's speakers director asked Buchanan to share "some grape shot for the close range work." The self-described "field artillery," or speakers, focused their speeches based on the audience. For noncollege crowds, or "wage-earners," YVP speakers emphasized McGovern's stance on the issues that fixed him to his radical stigma, "abortion, pot, the war."[156] Nixon's campaign for young voters pulled no punches, and the YVP both encouraged and absorbed that approach.

During October, Nixon's campaign ethics came under further scrutiny when several students contended that a Nixon operative, Donald Segretti, offered cash for clandestine campaign activity. Fresh out of the army, Segretti relished the chance to rehash his college days at USC with Nixon chief of staff H. R. Haldeman. Steeped in the fraternity politics of espionage and subterfuge, where "ratfucking" began, Segretti pulled out his old tricks in the campus campaign and worked through YVP college director George Gorton to locate cooperative young voters who could infiltrate, sabotage, or gather information for Nixon's campaign. The College Republicans' president at George Washington claimed that he received $150 a month from CRP to infiltrate radical groups and report information on individuals that would go to Rietz. While this would not hinder Nixon's juggernaut campaign, it would fall under the larger Watergate umbrella as one of CRP's leaders' many sinister moves that brought down the president. As the Nixon presidency quickly unraveled, a 1973 General Accounting Office audit determined that CRP had maintained a clandestine "Kiddie Corps" that Nixon-busting journalists Bob Woodward and Carl Bernstein claimed to have served as "young spies around the country."[157] In addition to the YVP's reputation as manipulated and contrived, this "tricky" legacy ignores this political moment's larger significance. Nixon's campaign organizers turned McGovern's strength, young voters, into his biggest problem while the YVP turned Nixon's weakness into a political force.

Nixon's campaign managers balanced this attack by building a well-heeled Young Voters for the President organization. Nixon contrasted his version of America's youth with the irreverent, radical liberals that he targeted during his campaign for reelection. The president thanked the YVP at his own convention for "letting us see Young America at its

best at our convention."[158] This showing stirred McGovern's supporters to call into question the YVP members' legitimacy and authenticity,
as Nixon's record did not hold up to the liberal youth's sniff test. Mc-
Govern's youth director, Ed O'Donnell, called Nixon "unworthy of the
youth support he fantasized about" during the RNC.[159] Pointing out his
policy stance, O'Donnell argued that Nixon failed to include young people on commissions investigating important youth issues such as the all-
voluntary army and campus unrest. In September, McGovern claimed
that "any young person or worker who supports President Nixon is too
confused to know which end is up." This approach backfired, as polls
showed this comment hurt McGovern badly, and Buchanan directed the
YVP speakers director to "keep it in the youth public domain . . . and
move it out to campus newspapers."[160] This dismissal of the moderate,
independent young voter who even considered Nixon hit a nerve that
hurt McGovern's image. Nixon's youth cadre followed orders, as one
article written for Calvin College's *Chimes*, titled "Why I'm Voting for
Nixon," displayed the McGovern "which end is up" quotation as the
epigraph.[161]

Mankiewicz tried in vain to balance the New Politics' constituency
with a moderate appeal to the traditional Democratic voting base.
Mankiewicz's papers reveal a wide and varied constituency of interest
groups that included middle-class, liberal reformers of the New Democratic Coalition, migrant workers in Caesar Chavez's Farm Workers
Union, and, of course, students. Nixon's overwhelming victory showed
future Democratic candidates the difficulty of building a new Democratic coalition that embraced diverse ethnic groups, racial and gender
equality, organized labor, and the liberal youth while fending off the
Republican Party's increasingly successful appeal to social conservatives.

Because of young voters' divisive role in this campaign, Mankiewicz
could not convince Americans to overlook McGovern's original proposals for welfare reform, marijuana leniency, huge military budget
reductions, and busing that offered controversial solutions to Americans' problems. After securing the nomination, McGovern's campaign
significantly changed to court the party regulars. By the time the party
gathered in Miami for the Democratic National Convention in July, the
platform differed only slightly from the 1968 convention's. In the end,
however, McGovern's attempt at reconciliation could not overcome his
radical stigma; in addition, his personnel changes to bring back conservative Democrats alienated the original supporters that had aided his

nomination. Consequently, McGovern fared poorly even with his young constituency as only 48 percent of the youth voted, 53 percent of which voted for McGovern.

McGovern's youth did not show up for many reasons. First, the Eagleton episode and other policy shifts to the center led many young voters, such as one Columbia student, to wonder "if someone who acts irrationally and impulsively like McGovern isn't just another politician."[162] One of McGovern's student supporters at Boston University confessed, "McGovern seemed to have an aura of honesty. . . . I just can't get fired up about him now."[163] Reflecting this splintering, weeks before the election, Youth for New Politics formed in October to protest McGovern's "sell-out," objecting to the idea that "you can fool some of the people some of the time, and all of the young people all of the time." Recalling that "we trooped through the snow in New Hampshire" for the "Prairie Populist," these disgruntled young liberals argued that "McGovern had dumped those who helped him get nominated" when he met with the butcher of 1968, Mayor Daley. "Dick Daley!" cried the Youth for New Politics chair, "He's the guy who kicked the anti-war movement in[to] submission. He's the guy whose expulsion from the Democratic Convention was the breath of fresh air we were all looking for."[164] As one journalist observed, McGovern found his image had become "blurred": "He's caught between the old politics he scorned and now reaches for, and the new politics he championed and now leaves."[165]

Second, McGovern's campaign focused only on campuses where politicians and pundits exaggerated both students' liberalism and their political enthusiasm. In fact, the antiwar movement on which McGovern relied took pride in its independence, as one underground newspaper journalist pointed out, "Not every longhaired troublemaker has returned to the system through McGovern."[166] New Democrats such as George McGovern failed to appreciate that young voters had an alternative for the 1972 election. The challenge could not survive, as Nixon's popular position on the environment, the war, and China and his campaign's coordinated effort developed a solid youth constituency that seemed believable to Middle America.

Finally, politics in 1972 involved more than voting. Young liberals could not provide a reliable constituency, as their antiwar and countercultural cohort lacked a clear stake in the election. A political discussion scrawled in a bathroom stall at the University of Tennessee tells the story well. Many of the comments written on the door played out the popular debate over Vietnam and the candidates: One person claimed "McGovern is stupid . . . stupid enough to be honest," while another argued Nixon's Vietnam policy "worked better than Kennedy's or Johnson's." Framing the debate, three comments stand on their own, "Smoke, Dope," "Marijuana Kills," and "Dick is good . . . [signed] Pat Nixon."[167] Alienated students dragged the election into the toilet, as McGovern's divided, decentralized, and inefficient organization could not harness their political culture. This irreverence and profanity marked the counterculture's cynical influence on political dialogue. Fred Faust, the twenty-four-year-old editor of an underground newspaper (the *Outlaw*) in St. Louis, explained that his readers "would rather light up a joint and forget it all."[168] McGovern's antiwar campaign did not offer young voters a forward-thinking campaign.

In the postmortem, McGovern's young voters still split his campaign leaders' interpretation of the election. Frederick Dutton, a key influence on McGovern's youthful approach, pushed Democrats to try harder for the youth vote because "in '76 the younger vote will be four times larger than the likely black vote" and "over twice as large as the so-called 'ethnic vote.'"[169] Less sanguine, Mankiewicz admitted, "If I had to do it all over again, I'd learn when to tell them to go to hell."[170] As the Democrats looked out across the shifting political and cultural terrain, their search for a new coalition in 1972 offered many lessons. The Democratic Party's leaders now faced the daunting task of moderating its image and redoubling its organizational efforts while building a big tent. To this end, McGovern underestimated the damaging role young liberals would play in his defeat. For college students, they punished McGovern for his attempt to shed this youthful image, exposing an "illusion of sincerity, righteousness and honesty."[171]

New Politics in 1972 did have some success. A University of Nebraska student won the seat as the chairman of the state legislature's executive board, a twenty-six-year-old veteran replaced Hawaii's oldest state representative, and an "anti-war farmer" took over as the Athens, Ohio, county commissioner. In addition, congressmen such as the Reverend Andrew Young, the first African American to win that post in Georgia since Reconstruction, claimed that he owed his victory to "the younger, more moderate voters in Atlanta."[172] Young voters' politics could not achieve consensus, but they did enter the system and inspired the ongoing challenge to traditional party politics.

Democratic youth also learned lessons about image and politics from

1972. For young, shrewd, and more optimistic political newcomers such as Bill Clinton and Hillary Rodham, McGovern simply went too far left. In January 1972, Rodham's memo to Bill Clinton painted a rather bleak picture of McGovern's fortunes in Texas. Rodham claimed that the slight increase in voter registration for the Democrats "is black, brown and youth," suggesting that the campaign had become too reliant on minorities and young voters.[173] Clinton witnessed the liberal grasp for youth gone awry and learned to reconcile the Democrat's version of New Politics with the socially conservative direction after the 1960s. While Bill Clinton's presidential campaign used McGovern's youthful strategy to build a grassroots and broad constituency with a celebrity persona, he paid careful attention to the issues that ruled political discourse after the 1960s. As the Republicans dragged him through his antiwar, draft-dodging, pot-smoking days, Clinton's use of MTV to appear youthful, hip, but also authoritative succeeded where McGovern could not. Yet, his image as a product of the 1960s Left, as it did to McGovern, fueled a vehement opposition. The 1972 election and, to some extent, every national election since, has fought over the 1960s legacy and influence on American politics. Looking at 1972 and McGovern's attempt to embrace the previous decade's influence on the Democratic Party through his New Politics, the rise of social and cultural issues in politics instead seared the radical liberal label into Americans' historical memory of the 1960s "youth revolt."

6 | YVP

Reporting on a Washington, DC, demonstration against Richard Nixon's Vietnam policy in the spring of 1972, the president's twenty-three-year-old Young Celebrities Committee director, Robert Podesta, dismissed the idea that this represented "an outraged gathering of the sons and daughters of the middle class to protest the war." Rather, the protest included only "a smattering of fringe type radicals," consisting of "an equal number of McGovern people and communists (they're not the same)." When Podesta asked one high school student at the demonstration about the event after tear gas dispersed the unruly crowd, he replied, "speakers and gas, same old bullshit." Podesta concluded optimistically, "this was *not* the youth of the country."[1]

Scholarship on youth politics during the 1960s and 1970s highlights raucous students and the ones who "dropped out." Nixon's youth campaign organizers thought differently, as they emphasized that 90 percent of the new voters lived with families—61 percent with their parents. In addition, only 26 percent of the new voters attended college.[2] This chapter examines the moderate and conservative youth who came into the political system for Richard Nixon, how political elites reacted to this new bloc, and the new political trends in segmentation that sprang from increasingly independent young Americans' own political organization. Balancing a moderate and "square" political sensibility to develop organizational loyalty, the four hundred thousand Young Voters for the President (YVP) who supported Richard Nixon played an instrumental role in the GOP's ability to win over his "silent majority" in the Sunbelt, the suburbs, and ethnic urban enclaves after the 1960s.

In the early stages of Nixon's reelection campaign, his advisers appreciated that new voters themselves made up 17 percent of the electorate and agreed that the youth generation stood as a "vocal opponent that needed to be neutralized." In March 1972, while 30 percent of Americans declared themselves as Republicans, only 22 percent of young voters between eighteen and twenty-four years old pledged political allegiance to the GOP.[3] Thus, George McGovern's "pied piper" image as the college student candidate challenged Nixon in a vulnerable area. Concerning young voters, Nixon supported the YVP, not because he wanted youth votes, but rather "to avoid the effect on older voters of our conceding the youth vote to McGovern."[4] Nixon's constituency, the silent majority, demanded that he at least appear to be making an effort. Nixon's Committee to Re-elect the President (CRP) treaded lightly here as they feared a visible reach out to young voters, especially students, would invite conservatives' ridicule for pandering to the "shouters." Thus, the YVP leadership made sure they went after the "sons and daughters of the silent majority."

Nixon's in-house public relations team of Madison Avenue's finest admen, the November Group, feared Nixon's problem with the young voters. One Batten, Barton, Durstine and Osborn (BBDO) executive volunteering for the Nixon campaign, Bill Novelli, outlined a youth strategy explicitly suggesting that YVP organizers first "maximize the President's vote among the segment of new voters *who have not attended college and who are employed*," avoiding "general encouragement to vote among 18–24 year olds, especially among college students."[5] This solution to Nixon's youth problem created a new challenge. Reaching the noncollege youth required a targeted and grassroots effort that utilized the most modern elements of Nixon's futuristic campaign. Rietz incorporated CRP's various methods to complement the strategy he employed in Senator Brock's victory, making the YVP a perfect case to study new types of segmentation.[6] Theodore White, author of *The Making of the President* (1972), marveled at the CRP organizers' innovation in polling, communication, advertising, and voting bloc categorization into ethnicity, race, and even occupation when he called Nixon's campaign a "science-fiction preview of future politics."[7]

As YVP director Ken Rietz claimed, "Originally, the folks in the White House felt that they had to do *something*, without confidence that they could do *much*."[8] Nixon's campaign staff cautiously, but with great resources, built the Young Voters for the President. Segmenting young voters while shielding Nixon from any direct campaigning fit perfectly with the CRP leadership's strategy to highlight Nixon's expanding constituency, the "silent majority." Nixon's YVP leaders identified and mobilized different youth to expand his Sunbelt and urban constituency that had traditionally sided with Democrats. This potential source of Nixon supporters included the rising independent segment of young voters.

In fact, Nixon's young voters played a key role in his ability to end the American liberal consensus.

As one University of Virginia student wrote in "Truth: An American Political Anachronism," the "devious" voted for Nixon and the "overbearing" voted for McGovern, "leaving the sensitive and the rational in the undecided, disenchanted category."[9] These voters looked for an alternative to the party politics controlled by Democrats, and New Republicans believed they could provide that choice. Pursuing the independent youth who made up almost half of this voting bloc, YVP leaders pushed the New Republican brand to soothe the transition into a new conservative era. This moderate, square, and youthful movement attracted young voters who opposed one-party rule. As YVP chairman and native of Chattanooga Senator Bill Brock (R-Tennessee) explained, if it were not for the Democratic Party's stranglehold on his home city's politics, young people may not have joined the GOP, claiming: "If my hometown was Republican, it would have been harder."[10] Just as the Democratic Party fractured and lost traditional constituencies in the South and urban ethnic enclaves, the YVP offered independent young Americans an option.

This effort planted seeds in the fresh and fertile soil of youth politics. Examining the YVP forces us to heed Podesta's warning not to pay too much attention to this generation's "speakers and gas." YVP leadership earned the organization's autonomy during the campaign as it became a vehicle for this unheralded youth movement to enter the system and form a network essential to the party's future success. This organization also gave GOP elites confidence that Republicans could forge new party loyalties and thus become the template for both future youth campaigns and segmented appeals to voter groups.

The YVP: Structure and Strategy

After taking his seat in the Senate, Brock went to Nixon to dispute claims that the Democrats could count on the youth vote. Brock recalled: "We had just won, we knew better." Arguing for an autonomous and well-funded effort, Brock claimed, "It is ridiculous to concede the youth vote." He convinced Nixon that most young voters "have a whole different set of values"; as Brock promised, "they are the majority."[11] The president saw merit in the idea, as some polls showed him trailing the youth-friendly Democratic frontrunner, Senator Ed Muskie, by only 8 percent with young voters.[12] Nixon invited Brock and Rietz down to Key Biscayne for a private meeting with Nixon and his "strong man" campaign manager, former attorney general John Mitchell. Brock and Rietz made an offer they could not refuse. If Mitchell could cut them a few million, they promised to deliver the youth vote, emphasizing how the archetypal stereotypes that defined all young people as liberal students thrived only because of the bias of media, Nixon's enemy.

As the chairman of the Young Voters for the President Congressional Advisory Committee, Bill Brock presided over the group's first meeting in June 1971 and opened the proceedings by screening a film on America's youth for the assembled Republican Party representatives. That they would need a primer seems odd, since these were the party's "youth specialists," but Brock emphasized something besides the worn-out "wild in the streets" motif.[13] Conservative journalist James J. Kilpatrick criticized this archetypal image of young people as "long-haired, beaded and bearded, anti-pollution, pro-pot, he despises Nixon and loves McGovern." Popular films and television exaggerated the influence and popularity held by radical youth, Kilpatrick argued, mocking the stereotype that every youth "wants only to get out of college so he can live on food stamps, free love and father's allowance."[14] In contrast, Brock highlighted the majority of young Americans who did not attend American colleges and universities.[15] Brock explained, "The great majority of these young people are not college students but wage earners who care about the economic issues." "Even on campus," Brock suggested, "many of them are scholarship kids."[16] As the YVP set its targets for new voters, this group offered the most likely prospects.

These young people pushed Brock and the advisory board to treat Nixon's young supporters as a voting bloc, more than a symbolic window dressing. To oversee Nixon's youth campaign, the advisory board selected Kenneth Rietz, campaign adviser for Brock's 1970 Senate victory, which included a majority of Tennessee's youth vote. Rietz agreed to leave his position as senior partner in the advertising firm that he ran with Harry Treleavan and assumed control on July 1. Immediately, Rietz set out to create a YVP office in each state, burdened with Brock's prediction that he could recruit five hundred thousand first-time voters to volunteer for the Nixon campaign.

Ken Rietz perfectly fit the role of Nixon's youth vote coordinator. His background in public relations, advertising, and conservative politics propelled him onto the Washington, DC, Republican Party radar. Rietz sought to build a youth campaign through "peer group pressure," which required a robust organization, as he rejected any strategy that simply used "an expenditure of millions of dollars on mass media." Rietz argued: "That would have been a waste."[17] This meant that young people, not superficial image makers, would determine the campaign's effectiveness.

One month after becoming the director of the Youth Division of the CRP, Rietz spurned the November Group's tentative approach. By the fall of 1971, Rietz had wrestled the role of youth guru from the administration's point man, Jamie McLane. After Rietz convened meetings and produced memos over the summer that impressed all, White House aide Gordon Strachan found that McLane's unimpressive monthly report for September largely plagiarized Rietz's recommendations, which "are specific with careful attention given to timing, expenses and keys states."[18] Rietz's approach earned wide praise from the Campaign Strategy Group, eight of Nixon's most trusted advisers who met throughout the fall of 1971 to map out the reelection campaign. While welcoming Rietz's recommendation for "peer group pressure" through "maximum involvement of youth as a means of gaining a fair share of their support," the strategy group warned that the campaign must avoid "the image of making an all-out effort toward youth and meeting failure," clarifying the youth campaign's goals as "high visibility of youth in the campaign organization, but low publicity on our efforts toward their votes."[19] Impressed but fearful the polls would remind people that Nixon had a youth problem, Rietz's superiors still required the cautious approach.

Fundamental to this controlled effort, the YVP structure carefully maintained a hierarchy that assured the CRP's centralized oversight. As for the YVP national headquarters, the original twelve "professional political workers" occupied a quintessentially Nixonian operation run out of a posh office one block from the White House. First, the YVP office's location on the third floor of the city's "lush" First National Bank building was protected by a security man at the elevator and a receptionist who allowed entrance with a buzz lock system.[20] Second, as one reporter described the YVP workers with varying hair length, "nobody needs a bath." Third, it housed the most advanced technology that produced computerized analysis of locations that attracted the elusive noncollege youth.[21] Each state's Young Voters chairman and executive director answered directly to that state's Nixon chairman and met with Fieldmen, a select group of paid Nixon operatives who trained YVP volunteers in Fieldman schools, to maintain a direct connection to the central office in Washington, DC. Informing the YVP director in monthly meetings, a steering committee consisted of preexisting youth organizations such as the College Republicans and Teenage Republicans joined by YVP directors and YVP regional chairmen. Revealing the emphasis on a streamlined, efficient campaign, the plan reminded young voters that "this should be a working committee, not a forum" and that "a big committee gets nothing done."[22] In addition, the state chairman appointed leaders for each of the eight divisions including the Nixonettes, publicity, and registration while the YVP's tripped-out logo, crisscrossing the words "young" and "voters" to overlap on the letter "o," came on all the stationery that the state action plan mandated. Like any successful national franchise, each county or city with a YVP office emulated this same structure with McDonald's-like precision.

The relationship between the local election headquarters, the state youth director, and the national office showed the campaign's organizational strength. Rietz credited this set up, which he called "cooperatively autonomous," for smooth operations with the White House and the November Group.[23] At the top of CRP's organization stood the strong man and Nixon's former attorney general, John Mitchell. Mitchell, however, rarely contributed to the day-to-day operations, and he resigned his post before the convention. This meant that CRP's deputy director, Jeb Magruder, assumed control of Nixon's in-house reelection effort. Reporting to Magruder, Fred Malek headed the campaign's citizens group that oversaw the targeted campaigns to voter groups such as Lithuanians, women, and youth. In addition, the White House maintained its control with its own children as Haldeman, Ehrlichman, and Gerald Ford each had a kid involved in leadership roles within the YVP.

In addition to the familial strings, Nixon's YVP leadership acted in complete loyalty to their cause as the YVP southeast regional director donated his entire month's pay to the YVP, claiming that "all members of a campaign staff should make a sacrifice to their candidate."[24] With this loyalty came a distinct appreciation for discipline. Even when the YVP staffers let their hair down, Big Brother was watching. On one occasion Rietz invited eleven YVP volunteers to join him in the president's reserved box during the YVP-organized "Rock Revival" concert at the Kennedy Center. Apparently, these youngsters pushed the envelope for

CRP's square sensibility. Rietz rejected Magruder's overreaction that they appeared drunk and obnoxious or that they left the box "in an untidy condition." Though they drank champagne, Rietz argued, "we didn't spill it, throw it, or waste it" and "clapped, cheered and danced along with rest of the audience."[25] During the election campaign, CRP organizers did not take any risks, as they brought in each of the YVP state directors to Washington for a "thorough indoctrination into the program."[26] Though the YVP leadership clearly took on a top-down model, it allowed young people new, unprecedented access to the political system. While the Nixon campaign's national office held a tight grip on how they appeared on air, the decision to staff, organize, and fund a separate youth campaign to this extent made the YVP unique.

The CRP director of administration, Robert Odle, warned: "There was a deliberate effort to go after the young voters at the committee [CRP] and more generally in the administration," but it would be wrong to treat YVP as "sui generis," as he clarified, "that effort didn't differ from other groups."[27] While YVP did not achieve favorite status with Nixon or CRP leaders, the relative parity among these various groups shows that the Twenty-Sixth Amendment energized Nixon's campaign for young voters and elevated youth politics from its previously marginal role. Out of over twenty divisions of CRP, the YVP also received far and away more funding from Nixon's coffers and the Republican Party than the other efforts including "Democrats for Nixon" and the various ethnic divisions (Lithuanians for Nixon!).[28] Rietz boasted, "This is no back-of-the-bus thing."[29] Young ambitious Americans followed this opportunity, as the YVP gave them a way into politics. Rietz continued that the YVP should have "separate headquarters where appropriate,"[30] suggesting storefront offices that built Nixon's youthful image by removing his presence from the campaign. Even the name, Young Voters for the President, avoided a direct reference to Nixon and emphasized the organization over the candidate.

In addition, as one YVP director said, "One of our campaign slogans is 'Get Involved!' That's why we have a separate youth headquarters."[31] Creating Youth Headquarters provided young people with the space to play different leadership roles and offered Nixon supporters access to political organization through the "campaign within a campaign."[32] For example, the youth directors also contributed to the overall campaign as they each held a position on the state committee staff. Including the youth directors proved a master stroke. It allowed the campaign to tout

Figure 8. YVP office in Miami that offered young voters the space that Ken Rietz described as "cooperatively autonomous." (Nixon Library)

its "youth atmosphere," provided young supporters with valuable experience, and kept the young directors under CRP's thumb.

Within weeks, Rietz established the model storefront YVP office in DC at Seventeenth and Pennsylvania that quickly employed two young organizers who recruited fifteen willing and able volunteers.[33] These offices felt young, with handmade, colorful, psychedelic posters pasted on the front windows; the slogans "Nixon Now" and "Right On, Mr. President" seemed less Nixon, and more 1970s. YVP offices performed multiple functions in the campaign. First, they helped YVP leaders recruit young people face to face. When the University of Tennessee YVP office first opened in September, national chairman Pamela Powell visited forty volunteers who ran the headquarters and urged them to be "spokesmen" for the president, claiming, "We need a campaign based on personal relationships." Second, the offices offered valuable manpower as the YVP at UT claimed eight hundred members after its first week in operation, pledging to focus on registration and "Bumper Sticker Days."[34]

While Nixon's campaign ensured a well-disciplined crew by dangling jobs as tantalizing carrots, it began to succeed with voters from outside the traditional sources of conservative youth. Recommending a young man to serve as one of Rietz's "shock troops," Jamie McLane vouched that the candidate, "in spite of his work for Humphrey in 1968, is with us."[35] In the ambitious stocking process of the YVP, a former Humphrey man who proved he could help Nixon's youth vote seemed just fine with a campaign that cared less about ideological purity than about dependability.

Youth Politics and the Rise of Independents

While McGovern's campaign developed a stigma that he sucked up to any and all young voters, Nixon's shaky relationship with the Now Generation forced his campaign managers to appeal to only those young voters that supported Nixon for his "new prosperity," his leadership in foreign affairs, or his "square chic" celebrity. To fill the YVP ranks, Nixon's youth campaign searched organizations that fostered sympathy for the president and could offer young supporters to staff YVP offices. While traditional youth organizations such as the 4-H fostered a Nixon-friendly, "silent majority" sensibility, young conservatives and Republicans more focused on politics stood poised to take advantage of new opportunities in 1972.

Young Americans for Freedom (YAF) played a key role in 1964 and 1968, but they became unreliable for Nixon's campaign in 1972. As the YAF's success buoyed its conservative principles, its leaders had not yet become prominent in the White House. Though two former YAF presidents, David Keene and Tom Huston, earned positions as White House aides, Nixon did not actively pursue them to fill his ranks with YAF staffers. While the YAF leadership gained strength and numbers, their libertarian agenda did not lend itself to Nixon's campaign for "Middle America."

Nixon's first term exacerbated the YAF members' suspicions about Nixon's agenda. While Huston spoke on Nixon's behalf during the 1968 campaign, the president's first term fell short of YAF members' expectations in staffing and in policy. YAF members "violently opposed" Nixon's decision to institute wage and price controls, and Nixon's moderation did not resonate with this youth group. Even as Buchanan, a former YAFer himself, wrote Nixon to "suggest strongly that before any youth organization is decided upon, you consult . . . Dave Keene and

Tom Huston," Nixon's youth campaign leadership bypassed the YAF and its ideological purists.[36]

As young liberal voters challenged Nixon, conservative youth also contested the president's reelection as the 1971 YAF Convention title boasted, "*We* Are the New Politics." Speaking to the anti-Nixon tone in Houston, Keene clarified, "The emotionalism of the evening can be explained by the fact that many of the kids participating worked in the '68 campaign and now feel betrayed."[37] Keene reported that the Goldwaterite conservative leader Phyllis Schlafly threatened to conduct a "high level conservative meeting in Houston during the YAF convention to plot an extensive anti-Nixon campaign," as Nixon's advisers decided against sending an administration representative.[38] Nixon divided the New Right, as the White House's resident YAFer explained the larger problem: "they reflect, admittedly in exaggerated form, the feelings of many other conservatives." Keene finished, "There are few identifiable 'movement' conservatives in the administration."[39]

By 1972, internal divisions in the YAF became more visible over Nixon's reelection. His visit to China and Moscow, as well as the Family Assistance Plan that only reformed the welfare system and did not obliterate it as hoped, offended YAF members' principles. As one YAF critic argued, while Nixon could get a pass for China, "it has never made sense to say, 'Only Nixon could have expanded the Great Society.'"[40] One letter to the YAF's *New Guard* newspaper criticized the paper for suggesting that young conservatives should fight only against McGovern, not for Nixon. Complaining about the president's negative image in the September issue, a YAF member counted "a lead article attacking Nixon's SALT agreements . . . three anti-Nixon editorials, three anti-Nixon cartoons and an advertisement for an anti-Nixon bumper sticker" ("Vote Nixon: Republicans for a Socialist US"). This concerned reader feared the YAF would "fall from the ranks of the responsible right into the ridiculous right," arguing, "It is time the YAF stopped waiting for the perfect candidate."[41] And while Reagan urged YAF loyalists to support Nixon, Thorburn observed: "Their resolve to make evident their programmatic disagreements with the Nixon Administration would not go away."[42]

Even though Nixon could not rely on the YAF, another traditional source of young supporters for Republicans, the Young Republicans (YR), seized the opportunity. In addition, the more opportunistic YAFers who supported Nixon moved into the GOP through its youth organization. In 1971, the YR convention saw former YAF members sweep all but one of its eighteen national offices. The New York YR president worried that the national committee "was falling off the right hand side of the world" and that they risked becoming "a party sitting on the razor's edge of ideology." Denying his ultraconservative stigma, the new national chairman, Donald Sundquist, considered himself a "Bill Brock Republican"—moderate and image conscious. By emulating Brock, Sundquist celebrated the senator's free enterprise principles but also embraced his style, as the YR chairman admitted, "We have to do a better job selling young people the idea that we are the party of youth."[43] Thus, YR leadership understood that they needed to package the conservative youth movement to new voters and expand the GOP's appeal.

Several factors, including Nixon's image, motivated young people to vote for Nixon. Nixon's efforts as president, whether ending the draft, passing environmental legislation, or holding youth conferences, also helped his cause. Most important to these young voters, Nixon appeared trustworthy.[44] On the issues, Nixon could claim he stood with young people. And while Nixon's personality earned him only fourth place, behind JFK, RFK, and MLK Jr., in *Newsweek*'s poll of young Americans' most admired men, Nixon's staff found the silver lining as the president remained "the most admired living person."[45] One young Nixon supporter, a twenty-one-year-old YR and advertising salesman in Orange County, pledged, "I trust Nixon as I've never trusted another politician," while another claimed, "With McGovern, I just don't know what to believe and what not to believe."[46] Nixon's successful appeal to young Americans on the trust issue surprised his own people. When one twenty-three-year-old Democrat defected, claiming "McGovern's credibility was one key thing," he laughed that when he walked into the Republican headquarters to switch his allegiance, "You should have seen these little old ladies' mouths open."[47] While Nixon's personal appeal became an asset in channeling "square power" to win over young voters, an economic appeal also worked.

Rietz flaunted Nixon's youthful personnel's national influence on young Americans' emerging roles in the workplace, claiming responsibility for "an atmosphere throughout the country where more industries are hiring more young people for important positions."[48] "There has been a new 'youth atmosphere' created in business," Rietz bragged, "and the administration has played a key role in its development."[49] Taking credit for a younger business climate exaggerated the administration's influence, but Rietz could easily substantiate the claim with his YVP members. This appeal targeted the real "forgotten voter" that one Nixon aide defined as "a 20 year old breadwinner hard at work providing for his young wife and new baby." "His vote will not be determined by party, but by the hope for economic stability, job security and opportunity. . . . His is the voice of common sense."[50]

While one poll showed 64 percent of youth supporting the president's economic plan, a Nixon official claimed, "we found that young people are more interested in the President since his wage-price freeze."[51] Rietz argued that Nixon's young supporters "will vote their pocketbooks instead of the war," claiming blue-collar workers could support Nixon because "they are not as political party oriented as were their parents."[52] As Nixon told Colson, economic concerns separated his youth vote from his opponent's: "The young interested in the economics, that's the young we're getting."[53] The young people who supported Nixon varied, though they all shared the president's faith in the American dream, or Nixon's "New Prosperity."[54]

The 1972 Young Republican convention brought together one thousand members to celebrate Nixon's presidency and America's affluence. Laying out a central theme for the four-day conference, one morning's workshop discussed "the administration's plans for improved prosperity." Lunch offered a suitably prosperous menu: beef shish kebab, filet of sole amandine, prime roast beef, and baked Alaska for dessert. That afternoon, Ken Rietz represented the afternoon panel's "highlight" as he led an open discussion about the YVP. Mixing business with pleasure, the attendees adjourned to the Sheraton-Park Hotel for a "Cold Duck Dance" that featured "all the Cold Duck you can drink." On the last night, YVP celebrities, including football star Bob Griese and actor Clint Eastwood, joined the convention for dinner before the "European style casino and auction with prizes ranging from $100 worth of Coors beer to a special all-expense paid trip to Alaska."[55] Couched in this setting, the YVP promoted Nixon to noncollege youth as an embodiment of political and economic opportunity. As the bland emphasis on prosperity smoothed over potential divisions between conservatives and moderates during the 1972 YR convention, the YVP presence further resolved those tensions as the campaign's opportunities trumped the ideological differences.

Despite the high life the conference promoted, the event performed an important function in bringing local leaders of Young Republican clubs into the national program. As "the dean of the nation's governors and a key figure in the national leadership of the GOP," the convention invited Nelson Rockefeller from New York to deliver the moderate voice of the GOP's eastern establishment. In addition, Nixon's campaign deployed a heavy presence to ensure the YR maintained its distance from conservative ideologues who challenged Nixon's bona fides. For example, John Ashbrook (R-Ohio) offered the YAFers a conservative alternative, sporting the campaign phrase, "No Left Turns" and criticizing Nixon's "liberal" moves. In one memo, Malek suggested that Mitchell attend the YR Conference, claiming that they detected "significant Ashbrook sentiment" in the YR.[56] While the White House passed on the YAF conference, they took control of the YR's annual meeting as the White House could not risk losing this important source of young leaders.

Cultivating this cadre of future GOP organizers, the conference training provided Young Republican leaders with the skills and knowledge to win campaigns. Senator Bob Packwood gave a slide presentation entitled "How to Run a Local Campaign," as other workshops offered strategies tailored to specific challenges ranging from winning urban areas to rural club building. A slew of advertising executives and public relations experts taught new political strategies. Murray Chotiner, a longtime Republican campaign manager whose tactics on Nixon's California gubernatorial race helped to stigmatized him as "tricky Dick," held a "special, off the record session." Next, former YAF member Richard A. Viguerie spoke about new innovations in direct mail fundraising that would eventually earn him the moniker, "the funding father" of modern conservatism.[57] This effort may have been too successful. YR voters soon became the dominant source of YVP volunteers to such an extreme that Rietz wrote to his California YVP director, "We are too heavily YR oriented."[58] While YR support helped, YVP organizers would have to look to independents and students for young voters, intensifying Nixon's campaign for voters outside the party.

The relationship between YVP and other youth organizations had mixed results. In many ways, the reciprocal influence helped both sides as the CR, TAR, and YR ranks swelled while the YVP utilized these organizations to build the campaign. As the Young Republican president, Donald Sundquist recalled a cooperative spirit, arguing: "YVP was a result of College Republicans and Young Republicans." Sundquist recalled one YR training session expecting five hundred in DC actually attracted seventeen hundred members: "We busted the walls down on the

hotel." Thus, YVP helped YR groups as well. "I think that was a byprod-
uct of YVP," Sundquist claimed, "I think it was a great team effort and
everybody believed in Brock and in Nixon." In 1970, however, College
Republicans split with the Young Republicans, and in 1972 the RNC
added the College Republicans, not the Young Republican National
Federation (YRNF), as only its third official wing that held a seat at the
party's executive committee.

However, this relationship with the College Republicans was more
serendipitous than intentional as the YVP continually stressed that their
job was to reelect the president. As Thomas Bell explained, these conflicting goals could strain the YVP's affiliations: "This [YVP] was not
about the party, we didn't even get along that well with the Young Republicans. They were all about the platform and we were all about the
candidate."[59] Nixon's YVP leaders emphasized the pragmatic political
effort while other young activists on the right sought less compromising positions, especially on international affairs. Compared to the more
ideologically driven conservative groups such as the YAF, Davis made
clear: "YVP was not a hard right group, not YAF, Nixon was hardly a right
winger." Gary Burhop stated it more bluntly: "I thought they were nuts."
Explaining the "barbell theory," Bell believed that the fringe on each
side enjoyed too much attention and that the YVP proved the majority
was in the middle.

While many factors divided this generation, young Americans during this era overwhelmingly rejected the two major parties and identified as independents. For example, one stewardess declared her party
affiliation as "Gemini," claiming that "an independent is more willing
to say what he feels, than what the party thinks is right."[60] One student
called party-line voters "indifferent," suggesting that it "deemphasizes
the value of the person running for a public office and places him in a
mediocre pile labeled 'Republican' or 'Democrat.'"[61]

These independent youth made up an unwieldy segment that one
journalist described as the "invisible youth . . . battered by the forces of
tradition and change, more pragmatic than ideological, cynical about
politicians, and not very confident in their ability to influence them."
By 1972, polls showed that 49 percent of the 1968 generation described
their politics as "middle of the road."[62] Young people had increasingly
identified themselves as politically independent since 1949, but the process accelerated after 1964. Though Republicans' claim to 23 percent
of the youth vote remained constant, Democrats among voters in their

twenties dropped from 51 percent in 1949 to 39 percent in 1970. Independents over this same time increased from 26 percent of young voters to 40 percent of young voters.[63] Thus, the process of declaring themselves as independents allowed young people the transition from traditionally Democratic areas into Republican hands. After registration closed in Jacksonville, Florida, 86 percent of the electorate there signed up as Democrats while only 53 percent of young voters did so. Thirty percent of these young voters declared themselves as independents, well above 3 percent of Jacksonville's total voters who did not commit to a political party.[64] As one journalist warned, "The stakes in this contest are high. If distrust of both parties continues to grow, the entire fabric of US political life eventually will be threatened."[65] Instead, YVP leaders saw this distrust as a clear opportunity in the South and in urban ethnic enclaves. Brock's politics welcomed people outside the student milieu: "We were open, honest, welcoming, nobody ever said 'he doesn't belong to us.'"[66]

Brock's original YVP strategy proposal stated bluntly, "Party labels have become increasingly meaningless" as a means of classifying young voters.[67] Charles Colson issued a report to Haldeman on the causes, claiming that although the conventional wisdom that tied young people to their parents' politics held true to a degree, this was "much less so than ever before." "There is increasing independence and in many instances defiance and rebellion against parental behavior patterns."[68] YVP leaders struggled to develop young voters' party loyalty. The eighteen-year-old director for Nixon's youth campaign in Cincinnati complained about independents' increasing role, reminding young people that "a vital force of our democracy is the two party system."[69] As the YVP campaign reached outside the party, the pursuit of young independents magnified Nixon's young supporters' effort to present the GOP as a political alternative.

Thus, Bill Brock, known as a "pragmatic Republican," welcomed young voters' desire for "some measure of independence."[70] Nixon's young supporters followed this welcoming approach. A twenty-three-year-old director of the RNC's youth activities, Nancy Payne, proposed a "New Alignment of Youth" organization to tout Nixon's policies on important youth issues such as Vietnam, the draft, volunteerism, the environment, and concerns about the federal government's growth to capture increasingly independent young voters. Considering independents in the short and long term, Payne argued, "The non-affiliated young person is vital to the Republican party for the election and the future growth of the GOP."[71] While GOP partisans among young voters including Young Republicans, College Republicans, and Teenage Republicans played traditional "political roles" such as "office workers and warm bodies at rallies," independents required a new thrust in Nixon's campaign, "education." Teaching young people that Nixon "is listening, is responding, and is doing a good job" could be enough to win over this segment.[72]

After all, political ignorance prevented many noncollege young people from deciding; as one youth organizer observed, "Many do not even know the names of the political parties, and feel powerless to influence public events. . . . Many nonstudents just feel lost and useless."[73] This sense of powerlessness inspired Brock's politics, as he explained his appeal to youth: "They were fed up with the system . . . thought nobody was listening. . . . My message was that if you don't like what is going on, it's your fault, if we don't like what they look like then we should look in the mirror."[74] This stress on new voters forced Republicans to reach out to working, "nonstudent" young people they could persuade.

To win over these young voters, Rietz suggested that the national convention for the largest vocational groups in the country provided the perfect forum. The Distributive Education Club of America (DECA) gathering would include seven thousand of the most organized, "as well as patriotic," vocational education students "and should provide the most outstanding reception."[75] With its working-class appeal and affinity for tradition, one vocational student group promised Nixon an especially receptive audience, as the invitation for the president to speak promised "you will not need to be concerned with egg throwing or rude behavior."[76] Nixon's White House point man on youth, Jamie McLane, agreed. "This group is important," explained McLane, "because these young people are the real working youth—mechanics, bricklayers, metal workers, etc."[77]

In June 1972, Nixon met in the Oval Office with presidents of six major vocational education organizations to celebrate the one-year anniversary of the Twenty-Sixth Amendment and reaffirming the president's call for "career education." Among the groups represented at this meeting, leaders of Future Homemakers of America, Future Business Leaders of America, Future Farmers of America, and Future Industrial Clubs of America joined Nixon for a fifteen-minute talk and photo op.[78] These efforts paid off. Representing over 1.5 million members, an unprecedented nine vocational organization presidents endorsed Nixon. Rietz credited the success to "high Nixon visibility in this group," a validation of his emphasis on "peer group pressure."[79]

Speaking to members of his Young Labor for Nixon at the White House, the president thanked them for understanding his policy in Vietnam "more clearly than some people in the media, some people in the universities."[80] As Nixon celebrated the war's end slightly prematurely, the audience clearly appreciated his announcement that, for the first time since 1965, no Americans had died in Vietnam the previous week. Still, Nixon laid down the patriotism especially thick here, suggesting that this group should instead be called "Young Labor for America." Campaigning against McGovern, without mentioning his opponent, Nixon explained that his young voters "know that strength in the hand of America is not bad thing. It is a good thing. It is a necessary thing."[81] Nixon's campaign managers deemed the exercise worthy, as 21 percent of young people not attending school claimed to be conservative, only 6 percent higher than students did, and working youth claimed to be of radical or liberal sentiment half as often as those attending college. Using this appeal to patriotism played an especially significant role in winning over working youth who overwhelmingly preferred to identify as "middle of the road."[82]

The harsh reality of economic responsibilities, said many onlookers, would even turn college graduates into potential Nixon supporters. While SDS philosopher Herbert Marcuse anointed students as the carriers of revolution because they existed "outside society," one journalist observed that a student "two to three years out of college is no longer 'outside society.'" Instead, "he is on his way to becoming a 'square,' just like President Richard Nixon."[83] Young families provided a logical target for Nixon's reach to working youth. As Nixon's campaign manager in Hamilton County, Ohio, the young advertising man Peter Glaubitz claimed that youth who "have had to provide for young families tend to be for Mr. Nixon. They seem to be better able to deal with realities."[84] As nine out of ten young people below thirty lived with their families, many young voters also lived with—and influenced—older voters.[85]

Nixon's campaign organizers could not agree on whether young voters would follow or challenge their parents' political loyalties.[86] Young liberals clung to the idea that they would vote differently from their parents and convince their folks to give McGovern a shot. Meanwhile, Operation Kinfolk, a YVP program, provided Nixon's young voters with

Figure 9. Young Labor for Nixon visits the White House: Spiro Agnew meets young "noncollege" voters who Nixon's campaign coveted. (Nixon Library)

postcards that requested a statement of support for the president. After the program's youth volunteers gave postcards to relatives, they collected them once completed and sent them to CRP for future contact by election workers. As one report suggested, "This will negate any conclusions that all youth are against Republicans, or against this administration." In addition, the report observed, "mothers and fathers can be influenced by what is happening among their offspring, as we all well know."[87] Although many pundits and political scientists consider kids' politics dependent on their parents' beliefs, Operation Kinfolk's organizers considered another possibility—parents could follow their kids too. Young voters also gave the GOP a beachhead into Democratic families.

In fact, many young Nixon supporters in the South and in urban white enclaves ran to the right of their parents and the GOP. Almost 20 percent of eighteen-to-twenty-year-old voters supported the socially conservative firebrand George Wallace. While Wallace predictably won over youth on southern campuses, he also polled around 50 percent with young voters in white working-class neighborhoods in the North. Kevin Phillips attributed this Wallace youth support to a young "counter 'counter-culture,'" defining this young blue-collar voter as "the 20 year-old garage attendants who hate the college kids with their new convertibles, pliant girlfriends, peace and freedom bumper stickers, and big allowance checks from home."[88] Young policemen, truck drivers, and steelworkers, Phillips argued, dismissed their parents' "depression based concern with economic liberalism and Democratic fidelity" and instead "lean towards a kind of hippie stomping, anti-intellectual, social 'conservatism' in the George Wallace vein."[89]

YVP represented the various groups Nixon courted. Most came from suburban communities and either attended college in Washington, DC, or pursued political careers on their own campuses. One described himself as a "political animal," and the term could be applied to almost all of them. Many started their work in politics even before they could vote, volunteering for Nixon's 1968 campaign. In both the North and the South, these YVP leaders usually followed their parents' politics. For the most part, YVP's young leaders came from Republican families. While Hank Haldeman, Jack Ford, and Nixon's own children formed a reliably GOP stock, other young Nixon supporters were often inspired by their parents' and grandparents' political activism at the local level for the Republican Party. Still, many shocked their parents; as David Chew recalled, "I sort of ran ahead of them, they were surprised."[90]

But in many cases their support for Nixon indicated this generation's move to the GOP and away from their families' political loyalties. YVP played an important role in expanding the party's reach. Tim Carey grew up in a New York, blue-collar, "very conservative Democratic family," as his mother was a maid and his father was a butcher. Carey's grandmother was a leader in local party politics as part of a "long line of Democrats." Underlining the generational break from party loyalty, when Carey became an elected official as a Republican after Nixon's re-election, his grandmother refused to attend the swearing in ceremony. This move to the GOP could be just as rebellious for young people in the South. When Jerry Gilbreath ran for state representative as a Republican and won at twenty-four, his folks did not approve. As he exclaimed: "I had to talk them into voting for me!"[91]

While some claimed nonideological motives, all YVP professed their faith in the "free market" and "individual responsibility." Moderates like Haldeman saw a limited role for government in the economy, stating: "I believed then and continue to believe in properly regulated free market economy" and "fiscal responsibility."[92] Others saw the economic principles as a way of life; as Perry Bacon explained his political identity, "I didn't drink, I wasn't guilty about anything, I believed in the free enterprise system."[93] This faith in capitalism also separated Nixon's young voters from McGovern's "prairie populism," as Bell argued: "populists really don't understand market economics."[94]

In the South, they even used their faith in competition to explain why a conservative Republican Party was important to give people a choice and end one-party rule. As Asbell claimed: "I grew up in Alabama, and forever and ever Alabama was Democrat, reasonably corrupt. . . . If there was some competition that maybe it would help, 'free market economy' for giving people a choice, one party rule had not been great for Alabama." To these young, ambitious political newcomers, the GOP barely existed except for the patronage jobs such as postmasters, creating a small Republican leadership cadre given the pejorative title "Post office Republicans." Donald Sundquist explained how his effort to break the one-party rule in the South replaced the elitist county chairmen he called "knife and fork Republicans," as they only showed up for major events. Following the organizational emphasis espoused by Congressman Walter Judd (R-Minnesota), "the Rush Limbaugh of the day," Sundquist formed twenty-five different Republican Clubs and increased participation. Sundquist remembered: "I wanted to change things," and he did, as he converted his district to the Republican Party.[95]

In Mississippi, Jerry Gilbreath agreed: "In the South, we did not have Republicans. . . . That was the main reason I became involved, because it was a one party system." Gilbreath, elected as one of only three Republican state representatives in Mississippi at twenty-four, joked: "We were called the leader, the whip and the whippee, I was the whippee." Under Clark Reid, the state's Republican chairman, who Gilbreath admired "like god," Gilbreath bragged that he and his peers were "the nucleus of the beginning of the GOP [in the South]." Converting southern Democrats took effort but did not require an ideological shift. In fact, many young GOP leaders saw the older generation of conservative, southern Democratic leaders as mentors. Recalling his campaign approach to lure voters away from the Democratic Party, Gilbreath remembered telling old men at the gas station: "First thing, I know you are all southern Democrats, I want to talk you into being a conservative Republican, I am as conservative as Senator Eastman [D-Mississippi] and all those people.

I went back to that store two or three times and convinced them, and I won."[96] Young southerners provided the political organization that had been sorely missing from the GOP in states like Mississippi.

In each region, YVPers embraced their counterintuitive, almost antiestablishment affect. The YVP's political activism channeled a direct challenge to liberal Democrats as Bacon recalled: "We were told by the media that young people would not support Nixon, we had a chip on our shoulder to prove the establishment wrong." Rejecting what YVP organizer Tom Davis called the "self-righteous group speak" on New England's prestigious campuses, Bacon realized, "when I went to Amherst [Massachusetts], I just wasn't a part of it."[97]

YVP members were also overwhelmingly white. This issue elicited varied explanations from YVPers, as Bell felt: "We went where the young people were, campuses, sporting events. I would say that our representation of minorities was reflection of that . . . plus that is where the party was."[98] After all, Nixon won less than 20 percent of African American votes. Still, many southern YVP leaders pointed out the schools they attended in the 1960s were barely integrated, if at all, and many college campuses where YVP recruited had not been thoroughly desegregated. Speaking about his time at Ole Miss, Mississippi's state YVP chairman Jerry Gilbreath recalled race as a major issue that motivated young conservatives' politics. Only a decade removed from the ugly and tense controversy surrounding James Meredith's admission as the university's first black student, Gilbreath observed that students he recruited were "all not in favor of integration." "We began losing with Supreme Court, it was a major issue" Gilbreath recalled, "but for YVP, I didn't see it."[99] However, while Ottosen described the YVP politics as moderate and pragmatic, he admitted: "It was Schizophrenic. We had very conservative leaders on the local level." According to Tom Davis, "busing worked for him [Nixon] in the South," though his opposition to Great Society programs such as affirmative action played an important role in Nixon's reach for white ethnic voters in the North too.[100]

Samuel Freedman explains YVP leader Tim Carey's transition to a Republican coming from a New York, working-class, Democratic family, claiming: "Most important for the conservative he would become, he [Carey] saw white liberals indulging the impulse of black nationalists toward a kind of *re*segregation, rewarding the rioters with programs and dollars earmarked for 'equal opportunity.'"[101] According to Thomas Sugrue and John Skrentny, Nixon's appeal to white ethnics "appeased white working class discontent by embracing law and order rhetoric, rolling back many Great Society programs, and nationalizing the southern strategy."[102] Still, Bell asserted that young voters appreciated the president's comparatively moderate position, "he was not a Southern Democrat . . . not Goldwater."[103]

Both sides did poorly with young African American voters. While half of the youth vote turned out in 1972, only 37 percent of young blacks cast their ballots. As another YVP member explained, race was not an explicit category used to target voters. YVP members argued that conservatives' emphasis on individuality explained why the reach out to young blacks did not get more attention. According to Carey: "Democrats deal with groups and Republicans deal with individuals," offering instead the YVP's color-blind categories that identified voting groups by occupation such as the blue-collar Young Labor for Nixon and young airline stewardesses known as Nixonaires. These vocational groupings indirectly reaffirmed racial categories that marked YVP's lack of diversity. As Dean Kotlowski explains Nixon's effort to recruit black Republicans with "Black Capitalism": "The president and his aides sought to replace the melting pot concept, where distinct ethnic and racial cultures disappear, with one blending economic opportunity and separatism."[104] This emphasis on prosperity did not win over young black voters.

Not that they did not want to have blacks involved. When one young African American, Don Johnson, earned a spot as a YVP "Fieldman," his superb resume, which included high positions in the Office of Economic Opportunity and the Urban League, earned unanimous approval. Observing Johnson's positive attributes, Magruder first listed, "Black."[105] Thus, because the president, and the GOP, struggled to find a reliable constituency with African Americans, Nixon's campaign for black votes lacked support within the administration.

Even when CRP's leadership did consider a plan to recruit twenty thousand black youth volunteers called Young Black Friends for the Re-election of the President, the program sought Nixon sympathizers only on college campuses. Rietz thought ambitiously, "we have had good luck this far with young blacks . . . and I feel this is worth the additional $20,000." Malek scoffed, claiming, "I doubt the President has any substantial support among blacks on college campuses."[106] Both sides agreed that noncollege black youth, such as the urban blacks who rejected McGovern's appeal to American cities, were outside the realm. Despite this reluctance, Nixon campaigned for black voters in 1972

through an expensive and effective targeting of young black professionals through *Jet* magazine. As Leah Wright Riguer explains, one Nixon
aide defined the campaign's emphasis on the black middle class as an
attempt to "neutralize a portion of black voters which cannot be won
over."[107] This reach for young blacks added to Nixon's increasing ability
to marginalize his most vocal young detractors. In fact, one of Nixon's
highest-ranking African American officials, assistant secretary of HUD
Samuel Jackson, hinted that Nixon could break generational loyalties to
the Democratic Party by blacks, claiming: "Most of the older blacks will
go to their graves voting Democratic but young people are more interested in issues."[108] This counterintuitive approach pushed Nixon's youth
campaign to also challenge McGovern's claims to American campuses.

The YVP turned to student politics for several reasons. First, Democrats claimed that they owned the student vote. After one *Newsweek* poll
in 1971 named the Democratic frontrunner, Senator Ed Muskie (D-
Maine), as the most popular candidate among students, one Nixon aide
needled Rietz, "we haven't forgotten you and your promises of youth."[109]
Second, campuses provided a rich resource of personnel. Voices in the
administration suggested that any youth would do. As secretary of health,
education and welfare and Nixon's initial point man on the youth issue,
Robert Finch, reported: "In a controlled situation, long haired, mod-
dressed youth in one precinct v. neatly-dressed youth in a like precinct,
the candidate's vote increased in both cases."[110] Nixon's campaign organizers understood the need to match the Democrats ground game and
that the YVP leadership would have to start with student politics.

New Hampshire and Student Politics

By December 1971, Rietz had staked out new territory for Nixon's youth
campaign; Brigham Young University, free of radicals, offered Nixon a
visit and a "most positive reception on a campus held in great respect by
those in the Southwest (and much of Middle America)." While Rietz acknowledged that liberal college students would criticize Nixon for playing it safe, Rietz easily dismissed them: "Their views should not dictate
our appealing to our kind of people." Besides, Rietz argued, "we will not
get the others' vote anyway."[111]

Nixon's effort for student voters underlined the symbolic role his youth campaign played in building his constituency. Nixon conceded his weakness with young voters, and Rietz even admitted that he did not anticipate how successful they would become while he planned and executed the YVP campaign.[112] Still, Nixon's youth campaign stood for the "counterintuitive" and undermined the stodgy, ideological, and cold portrayal of Nixon that his critics projected. As one Nixon aide admitted, "Nixon isn't going to carry the college vote," though "the margin by which he loses it is important."[113] If Nixon could show he had student supporters, that the bomb throwers on campuses represented the fringe, he could more easily speak about holding demonstrators accountable without alienating moderate and conservative youth or their parents. Stressing the need to start organizing a year in advance, Rietz hired an up-and-coming campus vote organizer, George Gorton, in January 1971.

Gorton, in his early twenties himself, had earned his reputation as a youth guru in 1968 after he ran James Buckley's unsuccessful campaign to unseat the liberal Republican incumbent, Senator Jacob Javits (R-New York). Though the papers misspelled Gorton's name, he got the credit for Buckley's strong showing among disaffected conservatives, and Peter Wilson quickly hired him to run his campaign for mayor of San Diego.[114] After Wilson won in 1970, Magruder visited Gorton and offered him the job. Setting his sights on the New Hampshire primary, Gorton quickly showed why he deserved the position.

As Nixon prepared for the New Politics that Democrats developed after 1968, he used mock elections against liberal Republicans to practice campus politics. Nixon's primary opposition came from Congressman Pete McCloskey (R-California). McCloskey wanted to replace Nixon's "war, pollution and deceit" with "peace, conservation and honesty." His candidacy showed the potential problem Vietnam presented to Nixon's reelection campaign, as one flyer hearkened back to 1968, claiming that "if thousands of young people register to vote for McCloskey, the same kind of pressure the McCarthy campaign applied to Johnson can be applied to President Nixon."[115] Most troubling, a January poll at Iowa State University showed 53 percent of the students opposed Nixon's election. Reporting on the "the need for increased efforts in the youth area," one aide explained, "This is a school in which we should do much better," claiming that these students "feel he is too 'political' and they don't trust him" as "they feel he isn't getting US out of Vietnam fast enough."[116] To counter this impression, the campaign needed a visible YVP presence to support the president's claim to a silent majority on campuses. As the YVP scrambled for young people, Gorton organized students for an immediate injection of young volunteers.

The New Hampshire primary tested the YVP's ability to generate a youth-oriented appearance for Nixon's campaign. In one of his first campus visits, Gorton walked into a room of students at the University of New Hampshire and announced his role. As Gorton recalled, "I asked, 'who here supports the President,' and a guy hit me in the face."[117] Thus, the campus political culture made it difficult for those who supported the president to admit it. Gorton believed this could be reversed, as he and other YVP leaders showed Nixon supporters they were not alone and that they too belonged in the "silent majority." This required the YVP to make Nixon's campaign "cool," which Gorton characterized as "standing up with other people—coming out with the crowd."[118]

Hoping to build "peer group pressure" for Nixon supporters who had hesitated to actively participate in the campaign, Gorton focused on the student mock elections. Mock elections had been a college tradition, and Nixon's campaign organization utilized this long-standing political exercise to show Nixon had young supporters in the most unlikely places. YVP members on campuses across the nation manipulated mock elections to exaggerate Nixon's popularity with students. As Rietz put it, this strategy would build momentum, "to make it look like everyone is supporting the candidate."[119] Thus, while the young campaign targeted young Americans' attitude, it also looked to change it.

The YVP state action plan on mock elections encouraged local organizers to first develop a positive attitude: "Your campus contact will probably tell you that the President can't win on his campus." The key to success in mock elections, wrote Rietz, "is to be better organized. So much better organized that we can identify and deliver to the polls a high percentage of our supporters while the opposition is relatively inactive."[120] First, a local organizer contacted a "supporter" in student government to approach the school's student body president, as a "non-partisan," to sponsor an election. Ensuring YVP control, the "non-partisan" Nixon supporter would then "offer to do the work and set it up."[121] This control allowed YVP campus leaders to designate times and places for mock elections that lowered turnout.

YVP members quickly canvassed door to door in dorms and fraternities and positioned a YVP table to ensure that "every Nixon voter passing the poll will vote." As Gorton explained, after the YVP convinced student leaders to hold mock elections, they sent "a good looking girl and guy" to hand out Nixon literature and make sure all the pro-Nixon kids voted.[122] YVP directors suggested that polls should be easy to locate but emphasized that the election "must not be connected to regular student elections, the selling of football tickets, or anything else that will cause an unusually large voter turnout."[123] Nixon's top emphasis on selectivity guided the YVP's grassroots effort as well. After Nixon's antiwar Republican challenger, Congressman Pete McCloskey, ate in the Dartmouth student cafeteria three times leading up to the New Hampshire primary, CRP's organizers feared that the "general student apathy that usually allows us to control a mock election does not now exist" and cancelled it.[124] For this reason, high schools offered a special challenge, as Rietz reported: "There is, however, some difficulty in controlling these elections since voting is mandatory and we need exactly the right situation."[125] In fact, Gorton admitted, "there was no way we could have won if voting was mandatory" on campuses. Because the "silent majority" on campus made up a minority, Gorton gave credit to the organization: "We canvassed everyone . . . we got a large percentage of Nixon supporters on any given campus to do something."[126] This ability fed into the "silent majority" mythos that has shaped modern politics since 1972.

In addition, Rietz claimed, "the general psychological effect of winning straw polls, especially on college campuses which are supposed to be the stronghold of our opposition, is beneficial to the entire campaign."[127] This plan came to fruition, as Nixon's campus victories piled up from smaller, controllable, and reliable campuses such as Florida's St. John's River Junior College, where Nixon even managed to win that campus's Democratic primary through write-in votes.[128] Combined with this success in campus mock elections, the YVP needed to make Nixon's young supporters more visible and active before the first primary in early March 1972.

Gorton looked to his old haunts, the New York conservative youth crowd, to bring in more YVPers. Before Cathy Bertini took over as the YVP state director in New York, Gorton asked her to help him prepare for the primary in New Hampshire to counter McCloskey's claim to the youth vote. When Gorton called Bertini, he offered to pay for "any vehicle, planes or trains, that you can fill with organized kids," as Bertini sent 250 young people to work in New Hampshire for Nixon.[129] In addition, the young campaign workers cost very little. As YVP members in New Hampshire rang over ten thousand doorbells one day, costing Nixon's campaign "two kegs of beer and some Coke."[130] YVP members' performance in the primary gained attention from within and outside the campaign.

In one rally that attracted over four hundred Nixon supporters, Rietz's college director reported that "the crowd looked good." While the media coordination did not come through as Rietz had hoped, the press learned about the rally only one day in advance, and the YVP's sudden and impressive arrival evoked criticisms of a contrived and cosmetic effort.[131] Magruder listed off YVP's successes, arguing that the event created "great public relations with locals" while it "demoralized McCloskey headquarters," "developed credibility for the idea that youth support the president," and "increased morale among local troops."[132] In addition, CRP unveiled its new system for distributing sound clips to radio stations, as thirty-three stations in New Hampshire and all the Boston stations played recordings from the rally.[133] Promising to "rebuild the responsive, progressive element of the Republican Party," McCloskey fared poorly in the primary, carrying only 20 percent of the vote to Nixon's 68.[134] This election, and the YVP contribution, effectively closed any opening for a youth-oriented challenger in the GOP.

Mitchell rewarded Gorton's ability to win campus mock elections, and the emphasis on students suddenly became central as the CRP supplied the college director with an "unlimited budget" and thirty-eight paid field people. After New Hampshire, the CRP leadership reversed its strategy to avoid student voters as Gorton expanded the Nixon campaign on American campuses and fueled a more ambitious youth effort. As Gorton recalled, "We had speakers, money and possible future jobs."[135] These opportunities at once eliminated the turf wars that plagued Nixon's youth campaign in 1968 and also attracted the career-minded young voters across the silent majority.

Gorton next focused on Florida, where Nixon needed to shore up the large youth vote, and utilize the YVP volunteers to develop the campaign in this crucial state that held the earliest primary in the South.[136] Campus organizers in the South found a more receptive audience. Agreeing that winning mock elections on "border" state campuses was easier than campaigning in the North, Bell claimed, "I don't think there is any question about it," pointing out that of the thirty-two student elections he organized, "we only lost UVA because it was a more national university . . . we got crushed." As Nixon's popularity gained ground in the suburban Sunbelt as southern conservatives considered themselves part of the "silent majority," the independent-minded youth bloc allowed the administration to expand its national approach to include the South. Across the South, as a Louisiana State University poll showed, though many students could not yet join the Republican Party, 66 percent preferred Nixon over any Democratic candidate. Even better for the president, though only 29 percent in the poll preferred the Republican Party, 43 percent of the registered students favored the GOP.[137] With its structure and momentum, the 150 paid YVP organizers began to capitalize on their work and recruited volunteers on campuses. In one week, twenty thousand students joined the YVP ranks, fifteen hundred in one day volunteered at the University of South Carolina.[138] Any states below the Mason-Dixon line would provide an enormous cushion to Nixon's claim to a national mandate.

College Republicans played a central role in reinvigorating the GOP with future leaders. Young leaders, such as the Republican National Committee's twenty-three-year-old domestic affairs writer, Brian Smith, argued that the youth support for Nixon should assume a more central role in Nixon's reelection campaign. Denying that students could not be won and thus lacked significance to the YVP, Smith claimed, "They're going to be the leaders of tomorrow, and if the Republican Party is going to be a viable party . . . we've got to attract the leaders." Smith's twenty-three-year-old peer agreed on the youth campaign's larger significance, bristling at Nixon's previous efforts that included "pompom girls and the cheerleaders and the nostalgia," warning that "if that's all we have to offer then this party is in trouble."[139] Though many CR members studied business as a major, an overwhelming majority majored in political science, and their participation in the campaign served as a career opportunity.[140]

Cathy Bertini, the YVP state director in New York, stated, "Not a soul was just there to get Nixon elected." In New York, the YVP included mostly college students and tapped into the influential youth network that Rockefeller had formed as that state's governor. Calling it "a movement," Bertini recollected "a huge hope that the administration would be full of young people, and the government would be more inclusive to young people."[141] George Gorton, the YVP college director, pointed out the advantage this gave the YVP, as they faced very little opposition from College Republicans when they set up shop. While Nixon's youth campaign set off local turf wars in 1968, no such tension existed in 1972; as

174 | CHAPTER 6

Gorton explained, "we just blew them [CR] away. . . . We had speakers, money and possible future jobs."[142] If naked opportunism played a role here, so did genuine curiosity in the Republican Party.

Nixon's YVP depended on willing and able student leaders who understood the youth vote's larger implications for the GOP. College Republican National Committee chairman Joe Abate's letter welcoming activists back to campus in the fall argued that the 1972 election offered a unique chance to realign American politics for the future and encouraged members to "bring collegians into the Republican fold." Claiming that "the 18 year old vote, the President's initiatives and the reaction to the New Left have all moved most students into a more moderate, independent mold," Abate called for a "well-informed, well-organized effort" to "bring strength and vitality for our Party for years to come."[143] The title for the Maryland College Republicans Convention, "Youth! Tomorrow's Responsible Republicans," spoke to their moderate and mature appeal.[144] In contrast to the radical student image that the media popularized, Bertini claimed, "We were almost a counter-culture on campus."[145] This period saw impressive CR gains, as the University of Maryland's CR club's membership jumped from two hundred to eight hundred.[146] As College Republican chapters grew, they maintained an important emphasis on professionalism and developed a more significant role in Republican politics.

Their primary contribution, Fieldman schools, organized workshops to train young people in modern politics. The CR began the National Leadership Training School in 1968 to recruit members and create future Republican organizers, or Fieldmen. Pointing out the success of the National Leadership Training School in Washington, DC, for seven hundred students, CR president Jack McDonald called for similar schools overseen by the CR Leadership Development Team in each of the nation's eleven regions and eventually within each state.[147] Starting in 1971, CR leaders initiated thousands of Fieldman schools that offered training for "future 'Youth for . . . ' Chairmen and full time salaried youth campaign fieldmen."[148] The schools averaged 23 attendees per seminar and offered "an exhaustive curriculum. . . . Voter registration, campus organization, press, literature, communication, the campus canvass"—all the techniques needed for a well-run, successful collegiate election. During the weekend-long program, participants received a two-hundred-page "massive notebook of 'how-to' materials" and "the sacred texts of the CR organizers, such as Saul Alinsky's *Rules for Radicals,* David Ogilvy's *Confessions of an Advertising Man,* and Sun Tzu's *The Art of War.*"

As the twenty-two-year-old CR executive director, Karl Rove oversaw the expansion of the controversial schools after 1971. Rove devised and taught workshops to teach young people the ins and outs of campaigning. As a college student, Rove proved his persuasive personality when he won the American Legion's national oratorical competition and the title of Utah's 1969 State Champion Orator.[149] As a college student, Rove joined the YR and quickly climbed within the ranks. After Rove convinced his peers and party elites he could lead the CR, he strengthened the organizational ability to recruit voters.

In July, the Maryland Federation of College Republicans conducted a workshop for "regional people for Youth for Nixon" at Towson State College. Hoping to attract College Republicans, a memo claimed that "well-meaning amateurs can help a campaign, but trained leaders are the ones that really get things done."[150] And while the Maryland State Central Committee chairman and vice chairman hardly added star power, the memo concluded, "Carl [*sic*] Rove will travel down from the National Fieldman School in Pennsylvania to speak to us and give us an idea of some of the interesting activities going on there."[151] Another flyer promoting the Towson State event mentioned that "CR leaders will be trained by professionals, (one of them is the infamous Karl Rove)."[152] The speakers at these events revealed their multifaceted purpose, and influence. A Georgetown University campaign workshop brought in young Republicans to hear the voices that shaped the New Majority: the YAF's *New Guard* editor, a public relations expert, a former CR executive director, and Jeb Magruder from the CRP.[153]

While Rove and his fellow CR members saw the Fieldman schools as organizational necessities, opponents saw him as a teacher of "dirty tricks." In a leaked tape of a Rove-led workshop, he can be heard describing how he sabotaged a Democratic rally by handing out fake invitations. Distributed to "vagrants, homeless and drifters," the "faux invitation" read, "Free Beer, Free Food, Girls and A Good Time for Nothing." Rove claimed this tape did not include the instructional context; this was not a "how-to" but a parable warning the audience "not to duplicate the stupid thing I did." Still, it seemed to substantiate Rove's nefarious reputation. After the tape surfaced and RNC chairman George Bush called him in for a few congenial questions, Rove was the subject of a *Washington Post* article titled "GOP Probes Official as Teacher of 'Tricks.'"[154] This cynical label missed the point that these schools operated outside of the YVP. Connecting Rove's underhanded tactics to Nixon's, many in the incredulous press explained incorrectly that these future Republicans took their marching orders from the White House.

These schools served as a gateway into the YVP, as the College Republican National Committee chairman, Joe Abate, wrote to perspective Fieldman school attendees, "If you want to play a meaningful role in the 1972 campaign . . . then the Student Fieldmen School is for you."[155] Building a sense of national unity, College Republicans developed a coherent vision of responsible Republicans in 1972 as way to legitimize their role in the 1968 generation. The Now Generation's sense of alienation that motivated young liberals to get involved also pushed conservative and moderate youth to demand a more significant part in the process.

The University of Maryland's CR president Alan Virta bragged: "We no longer serve solely as auxiliaries to be used by the regular party and campaign organizations in the outside areas. We now *are* the regular party and campaign organization."[156] One College Republican paper editorialized, "the Nixon organization is concerned about getting the youth vote and has money and talent to back up these concerns," continuing that if students could increase their influence and usefulness, College Republicans could "move away from the kiddie politics that College Republicans often engage in."[157] In a letter to the county's Republican Central Committee chairman, one CR president requested "the full responsibility of running an entire precinct." The CR leader made it clear that "we are not afraid of hard work," as he stressed that his club's volunteers "would look forward to more person to person contact with voters and candidates . . . more than simply distributing literature."[158]

One CR club advertised these unique opportunities to recruit more members, underlining that they do much more than grunt work. Along with the weekend-long political training sessions and "great parties" they held with CR clubs from Kentucky, Virginia, West Virginia, and other schools in Maryland, the University of Maryland College Republicans' members met with Senators Beall, Mathias (R-Maryland), Goldwater (R-Arizona), Javits (R-New York), Percy (R-Illinois), Brooke (R-Massachusetts), and Thurmond (R-South Carolina).[159] This effort reached a wider audience, beyond the College Republicans, to enlist the independent majority on campus. As the campaign shifted to registering first-time voters, CR members also understood the average student's priorities. One College Republican registration drive at the University of Tennessee offered the fraternity and sorority that registered the most voters a keg of beer, prompting one student to write, "if you can't interest them in politics, woo 'em with music and booze."[160]

While the CR clubs offered personnel to the YVP, the CR's Fieldman schools also influenced the Nixon campaign's youth strategy. In late June, YVP organizers held a three-day National YVP Conference in rural Tennessee. This event duplicated the Fieldman School formula, offering seminars on the YVP program for sixty representatives, or Fieldmen, from each state's YVP office.[161] Fieldmen extended the Republican Party's laser-like focus on campaign discipline throughout the nation. If Nixon's campaign offices in Washington, DC, functioned as CRP's brain, the YVP Fieldmen who trained aspiring Republicans served as the brawn.[162] Nixon's staffers still orchestrated the personnel and leadership training for YVP volunteers, but this approach encouraged local youth efforts that duplicated this approach. This growth benefited Nixon, as he could boast by September that polls showed he had tied McGovern for student votes at 48 percent.[163]

Despite these successes with GOP youth auxiliaries, Nixon's campaign advisers wanted workers committed to the president, not the party. The YVP "Organization Manual" instructs students, "Avoid relying solely on Young Republicans as they already have obligations to the party, and state and local office seekers that will prevent them from putting their maximum effort into the Nixon campaign."[164] While Rietz felt "YR's are OK for a start," he stressed that "a real effort has to be made to involve other young people as we build."[165] The YVP search for young voters looked beyond party loyalists as Nixon's central command maintained its agenda to expand its youth constituency and reach independent voters. As the campaign turned into the summer of 1972, YVP volunteers targeted young independents through this organization to register first-time voters.

Speakers and the Issues

Nixon ended the draft, wound down the war, passed environmental protection, lowered the voting age and age of majority, went to China, and more. Several of Nixon's policies motivated young moderates to support him. Most important to these young voters, Nixon appeared trustworthy.[166] Speaking with YVP leaders in the White House, Nixon urged their speakers to hit two points, "the draft has ended" and "Vietnam has virtually ended." "When we came in we had a war. . . . We are ending that in a way that does not destroy the respect Americans need among its allies."[167] Perhaps the most popular move with moderate young voters, going to China, enhanced Nixon's presidential image after the summer when his poll numbers showed his growing success. Certainly, youth were more pro-China than their "silent majority" parents. A campus opinion poll found that only one in twenty students looked at Nixon's trip to China with disfavor.[168] Nixon's moderate appeal to independent-minded young voters also extended to his foreign policy. As Davis recalled: "Nixon understood that Soviet block was not a monolith. . . . Nixon was a pragmatist."[169] Hank Haldeman, when considering Nixon's visit to China in comparison to domestic issues, added: "much more important was the larger international affairs successes." Thus, the YVP mirrored Nixon's moderate image in comparison to other young conservative groups.[170]

Even as Nixon deflected accusations about the Watergate arrests, a poll in September showed that 57 percent of young voters claimed the president was "more sincere" and "believable."[171] In a meeting with YVP leaders, Nixon emphasized this issue for the youth campaign: "The world will never be the same . . . and who can you best trust to deal with the Russians and make the world safer? . . . Why do you put in an experienced quarterback?"[172]

As party loyalty waned disproportionately with young voters, political observers hoped they would become more knowledgeable about policy positions to make more individualistic choices at the voting booth.[173] Nixon's campaign managers combined these "issues" to provide a message to youth about Nixon's presidency that built on political realities to enhance his presidential reputation. So if it came down to image, Nixon's surrogates made sure young people got the right impression. Colson explained, "Credibility is an even more critical issue with the youth than with the public at large. . . . The answer here relies more on what we say and how we say it rather than what we do."[174] The messenger mattered as much as the substance. Thus, Nixon's speakers offered young voters the perspective they found most trustworthy, sporting the moniker, "the youth truth team."[175] These carefully tailored messages and messengers provide an insightful lens into the different groups

Figure 10. YVP leaders meet the president. *Left to right*: Tricia Nixon Cox, Tom Davis, Ken Smith, Angela Harris, Ken Rietz, Richard Nixon, Lea Jablonsky, George Gorton, Angela Miller, Edward Cox. (Nixon Library)

Nixon's youth campaigners targeted. Many local youth volunteers participated in the speakers program, as YVP classes held sessions for up to fifty people to train them on "the best approach during a speech to a youth audience."[176] One session trained 125 young people who "covered" forty-nine high schools in only fourteen days.

As for issues, opinions of the Vietnam War became a test of patriotism that divided young voters. Many YVP men proudly served in the military, and Nixon's promise of "peace with honor" mattered to these voters. "The war was major, our pitch was Nixon would get us out correctly, not capitulate."[177] The war and the draft were unpopular with most YVPers, but the rhetoric and sentiment of American pride distinguished their position on the war from McGovernites'. This emphasis had a targeted appeal. As Tom Bell clarified, "The South is much more patriotic." In the North, patriotic and military families also found a new home in the GOP, as Carey explained: "My older brother was buried in Arlington. My father was very patriotic. . . . I think the GOP was more willing to show their patriotism."[178]

Haldeman agreed, stating that one difference between young voters for McGovern and those for Nixon was youth's "attitude towards the war and perception of patriotism." Still, there was room to criticize the war in the YVP ranks, as Haldeman himself remembered that as a ponytailed student in the spring of 1972, "I was marching on the UCLA campus . . . two weeks later I was working on the campaign and honestly feeling there was not a conflict there."[179] Rather than a matter of whether or not to support the war, these YVP differed from Democrats on the degree to which they opposed it. Bacon summed up this distinction, claiming he was "opposed to the war but not enough to vote for McGovern. . . . I was more middle of the road."[180]

YVPers also believed class was a distinction between McGovern and Nixon youth. Haldeman characterized this widely shared opinion: "YVP was less well off than McGovern activists. . . . We tended to have kids that were independent and self-sufficient and grew up in different environments . . . perception was that the bulk of McGovern youth came from campuses and were dependent on parents." This perception proved true, though clearly Nixon fared much better with college voters than many had predicted. Dietrich explained that the YVP was "huge with kids not in school" as the YVP's cultural appeal cut across class lines: "You can have square blue collar or square executive."[181]

As the speakers program became more popular, Nixon could contrast his supporters with McGovern's. In the South, a young Baptist journalist and White House aide, Wallace Henley, spoke to the Mississippi State Youth Congress on Nixon's behalf. Speaking to this conservative audience, Henley joked that real change could not come "by one glorious week's rampage through the streets." Ridiculing campus culture, Henley followed Nixon's focus on noncollege working young people, mocking students, "you come out of the ivory tower of drugs and protest and into the very real world."[182] Citing a recent Gallup poll that found 30 percent of young Americans did not care "if America was the best," Henley claimed that the youth feared real work and could not "perceive greatness." While "the screaming generation wanted the luxury of dropping out, of evading reality by means of drugs," religion offered an alternative, more participatory path as the young Baptist, and future minister quoted the Bible, "where there is no vision, the people perish."[183] The audience received Henley well. When these students divided themselves into a mock legislature, they labeled themselves Republican by a 2–1 ratio.[184]

Melding religion, economics, and patriotism, Henley hit just the right tone for this crowd that sought an authentic renewal of the American spirit after the 1960s turmoil. One notable name absent from Nixon's speaker list, Billy Graham, revealed the awkward relationship between Nixon and the religious conservatives he courted. Even though the celebrity evangelist ranked as young Americans' most highly regarded person, garnering 44 percent of young people's admiration in a Gallup poll, Graham did not stump for Nixon.[185] While Nixon moved to create a moral presidency, he could not yet merge his campaign with the religious celebrity. Still, Graham put the campaign in touch with fifty major Christian youth groups and their vast mailing lists.[186] In addition, Graham coordinated a partnership between Nixon's campaign and evangelical Oral Roberts University's successful basketball team that Nixon's aide Harry Dent described as "clean-cut youth."[187] When asked how religion played a role in their politics, Tom Davis claimed: "YVP never catered to that [evangelicals]," adding, "we did have a cultural appeal though." Avoiding direct pleas for evangelical votes, its YVP leaders' emphasis on free enterprise and "square" values came close enough. Evangelical leaders could easily connect their politics with Nixon's. As Darren Dochuk shows, Californian migrants from the Bible belt transformed the Sunbelt politics by fusing free market ideals with evangelical theology to develop modern grassroots conservatism. For example, Bill Bright's Campus Crusade for Christ formed in the 1950s and 1960s across California and the South to counter permissive campus culture. One of Bright's youth leaders, Lipscomb University graduate William Banowsky, explained the Nixonian appeal to these "square chic" youth: "I have seen joy come to the lives of young men and women who have found something more significant to do than take pot or go to bed."[188]

In 1972, Campus Crusade for Christ held its largest meeting since the organization formed. Held in Dallas, Explo '72 convened almost one hundred thousand evangelical youth from across the nation for this milestone event. While Nixon wanted to appear, Bright decided against the obvious political affiliation. However, the attendees obviously supported the president, as a poll showed they chose Nixon over McGovern five to one, denounced student protest, claimed American attitudes toward sex were too permissive, and favored stronger penalties for marijuana possession. Nixon's recorded speech thanked this crowd for its "deep and abiding commitment to spiritual values." As John Turner argues about these young evangelicals' politics, "Explo '72 provides evidence of conservative evangelical activism typically over-looked in historical accounts of the 1960s and 1970s."[189] At Graham's urging, Bright met Nixon's campaign organizers about the youth effort over several dinners and served as a liaison between evangelical campus groups and the party leaders.[190]

As the YVP stepped up its efforts on campuses, Rietz utilized youth-friendly cabinet members such as the first EPA director William Ruck-elshaus, HEW secretary Elliot Richardson, or the YVP chairman, Pamela Powell. While one could predict visits at the University of San Fernando's College of Law Enforcement, community colleges, and religious campuses, surrogates also went to larger northern universities such as Princeton and the University of Michigan to offer students a version of Nixon they would find more appealing than the man himself.[191] Though Nixon's campaign carefully structured the YVP to ensure direction but preserve autonomy during the campaign's early stages, CRP's leader-ship would take a more hands-on approach to ensure a return on its youth effort during the campaign's final months.

Registration

After the Twenty-Sixth Amendment's ratification, the need to register young voters concerned the Nixon administration. When YVP Fieldman Tom Bell attended one of many voter registration workshops that in-cluded mostly left-leaning groups such as the National Student Associa-tion, Young Socialists, and the NAACP, he advised that YVP leadership should utilize "their supposedly non-partisan registration efforts for our own partisan ideals." Acknowledging that registration of "blacks, poor whites and 18–20 year-olds is going to be very harmful to us," Bell noted that "it will be necessary to exert as much control as possible on their activities."[192] This thinking inspired the White House to pursue its own registration effort to counter the optics of McGovern and new voters. After all, registration played a central role in youth politics as first-time voters totaled over twenty million in 1972.

Throughout June and July 1972, Haldeman peppered different cabi-net members, asking Secretary Finch, "what are our plans, specifically in regard to youth?" and criticizing Magruder that "no effort is cur-rently being conducted to register people in the 18 to 21 year old age bracket."[193] In response, CRP leadership increased its control over its youth branch as the registration effort took shape. The daunting task of locating Nixon's young voters sharpened CRP's advanced capabilities to segment voters. Many aspects of youth demographics distinguished between the generations, as 36 percent changed addresses in one year. Still, only 7 percent moved out of state, and 63 percent of male voters had joined the labor force while 47 percent of women between eighteen and twenty-four years old had jobs.[194] Hardly the college provocateurs or the commune-dwelling dropouts seen on American film and television.

Under these circumstances, selectivity became the guiding principle behind this effort; the project's name, Target '72, revealed the focus on registering Nixon voters. Malek urged precision and reminded Rietz that any attempt to register young people "would have to be done on quite a selective basis."[195] Rather than rely on students, Nixon's campaign carefully sought out the less concentrated majority of young people who did not attend college. Earliest estimates acknowledged Nixon's national approval ratings among students dipped to 29 percent, while it remained at fifty percent for "18–20 year old non-students."[196] The YVP registration guide reminded its members that the "average income of an 18–24 year is $8,000 per year, so don't go into high cost housing areas." Nixon even saw this as a way to bolster his conservative populism, as he suggested his staff spin the YVP's selective focus on noncollege young voters to emphasize that "McGovern people are limiting themselves to the elite youth."[197]

The YVP registration guide followed this logic and suggested that door-to-door canvassing proved the most effective strategy, and concentrations of young people could be found in metropolitan centers with new housing construction. In addition, field workers looking for young Nixon voters compiled lists of new parents, newlyweds, and new home owners to get to noncollege voters. For example, his researchers discovered that almost all of California's 2.5 million youth lived in ten of that state's fifty-eight counties, concentrated in the rapidly expanding residential areas of the Southland.[198] Nixon's home state, flush with young voters, looked endangered. He had barely won California in 1968, and Rietz admitted that in that state "we are in very bad shape with 18–24 year olds." With millions of potential first-time voters in California, his campaign knew exactly where to go.[199] Even though McGovern's campaign could brag about a 57 to 41 percent edge over Nixon among registered voters that August, the growing YVP organization aimed to catch up. Confident in their ability to shrink the difference, YVP leaders pointed to the polls that showed 46 percent of those who had not yet registered supported Nixon while only 43 percent supported McGovern.[200] Fifty-nine percent of young people between eighteen and twenty-four who did not attend college had not registered as late as August.[201] Clearly, Nixon's approach required more work than McGovern's campus-focused youth campaign. Eventually, over four hundred thousand young voters joined the YVP and supplied over half of the entire campaign work.[202] Nixon's incipient youth following may have flown below the radar, but it stood ready and able to help his reelection.[203]

Conclusion

Richard Nixon's youth campaign, despite popular predictions, had become a powerful weapon in his campaign for reelection in 1972. As Nixon's campaign peeled young, noncollege voters away from the Democratic Party, party loyalty appeared to weaken. However, YVP members injected a new independent sensibility that the GOP channeled. The 1968 generation infused the 1972 election with a new appreciation for a targeted campaign that this shifting electorate required. In addition, young voters provided the ground troops and the wedge to loosen traditional regional political loyalties and build new ones among urban ethnics and in the Sunbelt.

Nixon and his young supporters both deserve credit for this unexpected result. As locating and mobilizing young Nixon supporters posed a logistical problem, the YVP leaders required discipline, and the administration assured that it controlled the organization's structure and hierarchy. Combining its vast resources and groundbreaking campaign tactics in polling, registration, and organization, the YVP sharpened Nixon's "science-fiction preview of future politics."[204] The YVP story shows that this "campaign within a campaign" set a model organization for future youth efforts.

In doing so, the YVP opened the political process to a segment of this generation that considered itself a movement. These young activists utilized the YVP as a vehicle to announce their presence and rejuvenated the GOP with a leadership cadre that would exert lasting influence. As YVP leaders agreed Nixon had little to do with the energy behind the YVP members' enthusiastic effort, his presidency still became a signature moment in the mobilization of the conservative movement. As Hunter S. Thompson bemoaned the fact that his hopes for youth politics failed in 1972, scholarship on the history of youth politics has continued the argument that McGovern's effort fell short. Remembered as a lost opportunity, or moment, McGovern's candidacy is still alluded to as the first and last youth campaign. However, Nixon's young voters proved more influential.

Nixon's loyal young voters here helped the transition of Democrats to Republicans. Even though many voters making this transition registered as independent during this election, young people saw it as the right political position. This cannot be defined as a pure realignment as the party politics did not drive the political environment. Cathy Bertini claimed, "Young voters didn't want to be the party, and CR didn't want to be consumed by the campaign."[205] Still, this Nixon-friendly version of independents varied greatly from the liberal-leaning, antiparty independent youth who McGovern courted (and encouraged). While independent voters assumed a fluid reputation, their political direction charted a larger shift in party politics to the politics of image. As the next chapter shows, young independents required an image-conscious campaign that Nixon could not provide up to this point. Now that he could claim a portion of the Now Generation, Nixon's advisers found a way he could transition from the law-and-order image that defined his original relationship with young Americans. Nixon had finally gotten past the youth problem.

7 | "Right On, Mr. President"

Young Voters and the Politics of Image

The night before Richard Nixon accepted his renomination at the 1972 Republican National Convention in the Miami Convention Center, his clean-cut, well-mannered, but exuberant Young Voters for the President (YVP) volunteers attended a concert in nearby Marine Stadium. In the audience, over six thousand young people combined to celebrate the president and their own emergence on the political scene. Only one year earlier, the Twenty-Sixth Amendment had lowered the voting age to eighteen, enabling over twenty-seven million young Americans to join the electorate as first-time voters.

Sammy Davis Jr. kept the crowd going until the chairwoman of the YVP, Pam Powell, led Nixon to the center of the floating stage, where he addressed the crowd that one journalist described as the "not-so silent young majority."[1] In his memoirs, Nixon recalled the event's electric environment, as he wrote, "Hands above their heads, four fingers outstretched, the thousands of young people took up a chant that I was hearing for the first time: 'Four more years! Four more years!' It was deafening." Observing the moment's significance, Nixon glowed, "It was music. This was a new kind of Republican youth: they weren't square, but they weren't ashamed of being positive and proud."[2] The event marked the culmination of Nixon's four-year struggle to disprove the popular perception that young people disliked him.

Speaking to the audience, Nixon emphasized his young supporters' independence, telling them, "nobody has the youth vote in their pocket." Then, after Nixon praised Sammy Davis Jr., the rat packer snuck up behind the leader of the free world and squeezed him with both arms. As one journalist explained Nixon's awkward reaction, the president's "entire body curled in on itself with an instinctive tremor the way a man's body will when it senses the end is near." While "the hug" lasted only seconds, it brought the crowd to a frenzy and created a

Figure 11. Sammy Davis Jr.'s famous hug during the RNC youth concert surprised Nixon, the six thousand YVP in attendance, and the media. (Nixon Library)

sensation in the popular press; *Time*, for example, dedicated a two-page spread to a photograph of the brief embrace in Miami.[3]

To Nixon's detractors, this moment with Sammy Davis Jr. exposed the president's inability to be hip.[4] One self-proclaimed "young liberal Democrat" and fan of Davis fumed in a letter to *Life Magazine*, "I am disgusted with all the publicity given to his recent sellout to the President."[5] This appeal to young voters elicited a wider criticism of the image-focused political style. "Nowadays we press youth out of the young as quickly as possible," complained journalist Russell Baker. "With the national genius for packaging, [we] merchandise youth to the aging as something that can be put on like a plastic wrapper."[6]

To Nixon's advisers, the event hit just the right note, as they agreed that young Americans "just wanted to be taken seriously and heard."[7] Furthermore, simply appearing with young supporters showed voters, young and old, that Richard Nixon could be "in." As Bill Brock recalled the hug, he explained: "Man, that is powerful television, to have that going on in the middle of four thousand young people hootin' and hollerin'."[8] Nixon's success in youth politics involved a fundamental change in American politics—a vehicle for young voters to revive and reframe the Republican Party. Although Nixon initially hesitated to support a youth campaign for his reelection, he appreciated the young voters' significance after the Miami rally. His young voters sure appreciated it, as Laura Jordan recalled her impression of the hug: "Whoa! Who knew?—Sammy Davis, here's this boring old guy, and then you get Sammy who is so cool." Thus, while the YVP event proved Nixon's control of youth politics, it also revealed his domination of image politics. Kathryn Cramer Brownell explains that Nixon's polished 1972 election "served as a triumph of Nixon's ability to project an effective and powerful media message through a full-scale studio production that showcased him as the premier star of American politics."[9]

Youth politics in 1972 owed much of its popularity to the intermingling of politics and public relations; as Haldeman told Nixon, "The young voting bloc, that's another media created thing."[10] While dismissive of the youth vote's origins, Nixon's campaign utilized its impressive YVP organization to challenge popular perceptions that Nixon widened the generation gap. With the YVP, Nixon's administration contradicted McGovern's widely accepted image as the young voters' candidate—their only choice. Thus, Rietz emphasized the youth vote's symbolic significance, boasting: "We will beat them in the area that McGovern has made a key element of his campaign."[11] Rietz had predicted this necessity and built the youth campaign, from its beginnings, around a strong YVP presence at the RNC. On this stage, the plan suggested, "We can show him [Nixon] constantly surrounded by young people—our kind of young people; young people who will not turn off the electorate viewing the convention."[12] Though critics such as Hunter S. Thompson dismissed the YVP as "waterheads," and one prominent anchor compared them to "sewer workers," this robust cadre of loyal supporters substantiated Nixon's image as the president for all Americans. As David Greenberg explains, "Public opinion, Nixon understood, could not only be ascertained but crafted."[13]

Nixon's staff identified the special significance the youth vote carried, pointing out that visible and potent youth support for a candidate would "allay fears that the young people, and indeed many adults, would not accept him."[14] Without a compliant press, CRP leaders combined their own resources to make Nixon's campaign image; the YVP and the high-powered executives who volunteered for Nixon's personal ad agency, the November Group, worked together to counter the conventional narrative that depicted young Americans as hostile to the president. Nixon's youth politics would have to compensate for his reputation.

As the social issues connected to the politics of youth emphasized how voters felt more than any political loyalty, emotional and image-conscious appeals became more effective than the "bread and butter" issues.[15] When asked to characterize the YVP's reputation, New York's YVP state director Cathy Bertini recalled, "We were a little bit more establishment and they [McGovern's young supporters] were more Woodstock." After YVP leaders visited the president at the White House, he described them as "tough, strong, bright, good looking," and "damned impressive."[16] Thus, young voters gave Nixon a chance to perfect his own version of "square chic." As YVP's college director George Gorton explained, YVP's members played a crucial role in the CRP's ability to make voting for Nixon "cool" for all voters, young and old.[17] While continuing the attempt to marginalize the rebellious youth that dominated the 1968 campaign, the reelection effort offered a more convincing alternative.

YVP: An Image Strategy and Independents

Nixon's effort to reach independent young voters further motivated a carefully constructed media effort to display the YVP. In pursuit of this welcoming image, Nixon's reelection campaign focused disproportionate attention to building a visible youth presence. Nixon's campaign used young voters to highlight the president's credibility as they often carried signs reading, "Nixon's the One," and produced songs with the chorus, "more than ever, we need Nixon now." Predictably, opponents challenged the YVP's legitimacy, as one student quipped that while McGovern's "long hair" youth aimed to "end lies and deceit," the YVP's well-manicured members "traded their David Cassidy buttons for Nixon banners."[18] Thus, while Nixon's campaign avoided cheerleaders and nostalgia, it projected a "square" image to continue a segmented appeal.

Universally, when YVPers defined their image and politics they did so in contrast to McGovern's. YVPers described McGovern as "out there" and "off the charts." As for his young voters, they also seemed "out there" to YVP leaders. "I think the Democrats took the college students for granted with 'sex and drugs and rock'n roll.'" These differences mattered in practice, especially during recruitment: "When you are recruiting on a college campus, and some student is wearing a long dress, tie dye shirt or not wearing a bra, that's not somebody you are going to recruit. We were more button down. . . . I was not into the hippie lifestyle."[19] As a recent graduate of American University and YVP organizer in key swing districts such as Michigan's coveted Macomb County, Gary Burhop explained, "The perception was that McGovern had the dirty smelly college kids and the non-college kids were trying to find a career." Burhop relayed what he thought about the counterculture: "I'm trying to work my ass off, you are over entitled."[20] This argument resonated with noncollege youth, but also appealed to resentful college students.

In addition, YVPers inspiration combined the young Left's protest politics and culture, as they recalled, "it was a time when there was still a smell of the riots in the air." This sentiment had a political memory and went beyond McGovern's image, as Dietrich recalled: "I'm from Chicago, and we really didn't like the Democratic Party after 1968. . . . We had such a distasteful view of riots. We didn't like it, I think the majority were going about their lives."[21] As another YVP leader summarized: "If you're working, maybe in night school, [you] don't have time to scream and protest, and you don't have time to smoke pot."[22] Recalling the RNC in 1972, one YVP leader remembered protests, or "hate demonstrations" that included imitation blood, as a catalyst, claiming: "When we went to [the] convention, we had men surround the women, the first time we had ever seen that and it solidified young people for Nixon."[23] As protesters fulfilled the wild-in-the-streets motif, Nixon countered with "square" youth who believed in the president.

Reflecting on the 1968 Youth for Nixon campaign, Nixon's adviser Mort Allin pointed out the potential for this effort to provoke more creative spectacle through different media forms in 1972. "Youth, with its flair for the unique and far out," prodded Allin, "can be the division that flies in the face of traditionalism."[24] While Allin focused on posters, this creative space in Nixon's otherwise stodgy campaign allowed for Nixon's YVP to spice things up. It would be this area where the "creative revolution," a new advertising era that sold with youth but also sold to youth, would exercise its fullest potential in merging Madison Avenue with the White House. Nixon's youth campaign in 1972 owed much of its attention to the rising role of image politics. "The new era," Theodore White explained, "is one where emotions and ideas are manipulated by the mass media." As a result, "television commentators will be more influential . . . than Mayor Daley."[25] Tom Wicker of the *New York Times* agreed, as he pointed out that television "allows candidates to go over the heads of organizations and delegates" and "focuses on personality rather than record of party service."[26]

During the 1960s, media became the central tool for candidates to reach voters. Federal Communications Commission figures showed that political spending for television and radio quadrupled between 1956 and 1968, far beyond the increased prices and inflation during this period.[27] As Nixon admitted in his memoirs, "since the advent of television as our primary means of communication modern presidents must have specialized talents at once more superficial and more complicated than those of their predecessors."[28] Nixon campaigned from the White House, even refusing to debate his challenger.[29] This "non-campaign" strategy entrusted Nixon's campaign managers with freedom to create the president's image. As YVP's college director George Gorton pointed out, "In addition to Ken [Rietz] getting them [youth], it was a matter of showcasing them."[30] In the summer of 1972, CRP leader Fred Malek expressed concern about "how little we have done in a broad PR sense." When one YVP organizer contacted Malek about obtaining a *New York Times* film clip on the new voting rights to be shown in high school classrooms, Malek responded, "Quit worrying about this peripheral shit and let's get going on a media plan."[31] This new impetus came as the campaign shifted its sights toward the convention and looked to expand its reach beyond the GOP base. Nixon's advisers anxiously pushed the YVP leaders to utilize their symbolic value and improve the president's standing in image politics.

Rietz carefully targeted the youth vote, underlining the president's ability to segment particular voter groups (Polish for Nixon!). While Jeb Magruder set up plans to attack enemies with a rifle, rather than shotgun technique, he issued a lesser known "rifle memo" to his boss, John Mitchell. "There has been evidence that certain techniques of direct, targeted, 'rifle-shot' communications to voters can substantially augment a candidate's mass media image," argued Magruder. "These techniques use past voting data, socia-economic data and public opinion."[32]

Nixon saw this shift to a youth and image focus as problematic. After all, his efforts to counteract a generally hostile media environment with Madison Avenue–style campaigning in 1968 evoked even more criticism. Joe McGinnis's *The Selling of the Presidency: The Classical Account of the Packaging of a Candidate* ridiculed the growing role of public relations experts in shaping Nixon's contrived image. Thus, Nixon's CRP leaders decided to in-source the public relations campaign to limit expenses, control outside access to the operation, and assure its advertising team's loyalty to the president, as Jeb Magruder admitted: "So many of the creative people in advertising are liberal Democrats." Creating Nixon's own agency, the CRP leaders controlled "hiring, salaries and loyalties."[33] Looking to utilize Nixon's internal resources, the high-powered advertising executives who volunteered for Nixon's in-house PR team, the November Group, featured the YVP.[34] Joining the November Group, advertising executives that included Peter Dailey, Bill Novelli, William Taylor, and Phil Juneau set out to change popular perceptions of the president. Melding of this new advertising style and politics emphasized the ways in which American politics had moved into the living room, and away from the bread-and-butter issues that dominated the kitchen table.

For Nixon, the YVP allowed his administration to make full use of the modern image politics that he had found so problematic as a candidate and as president. Since McGinnis's biting criticism of Nixon's 1968 packaged candidacy, scholars have followed the notion that the New Nixon in 1968 marked the beginning of the "image-is-everything president."[35] Judging by the youth vote, Nixon's image politics in 1972 provides a more complete picture of a modern campaign. In his campaign for reelection, Nixon's image relied on a more segmented, focused organizational approach that reached new voters for the GOP.

Many observers continued to criticize the new superficial, image-based political style, as one study came to the conclusion that "*1972 could scarcely be labeled an issue election.*"[36] Another political insider quipped, with television, "you could run a candidate who is maybe in a mental hospital" as "the techniques of political image makers often work in the service of distortion . . . life-and-death issues disposed of in ten seconds."[37] Popularized in 1968, this cynical interpretation pushed political observers to overlook important ways political segmentation could engage a constituency. Rather than separate issues from image, the November Group's advertising gurus built on their relationship and created a youthful campaign by collaging Nixon's record on the Vietnam War, the draft, the environment, and the voting age. This powerful connection between the YVP and his personal media wing showed that the image-making process in politics developed as a telling window into the period's larger and structural concerns. In this case, Nixon's politics of image shows that young voters reinvigorated Republicans to aggressively pursue new constituencies. In addition, the new segmentation efforts that targeted specific voter attitudes changed the way candidates fashioned their image.

In planning the organizational outline in September 1971, Rietz asserted that young people would not simply change tune and buy Nixon.[38] Still, Rietz's background as a public relations expert colored his view of the youth's significance, as he revealed the project's ultimate goal to get youth actively involved "so the overall campaign takes on a young flavor."[39] While the College Republicans increasingly felt they had become part of the campaign, not just window dressing, they also understood their symbolic role. In one CR newsletter, Karl Rove asked if some volunteers could come to the headquarters early for a photo shoot of "young people stuffing envelopes alongside little old ladies."[40]

On August 12, over twenty thousand YVP volunteers in twenty-three different states led a registration drive that targeted hundreds of thousands of young voters. While Rietz admitted that the number of new voters registered fell short of expectations, "primary emphasis was placed on media attention, not registration." Rietz's report on the coverage claimed that over forty newspaper articles and television or radio programs featured the YVP volunteers' canvassing. Nixon's daughter and her husband, Tricia and Ed Cox, received special attention as they reached out to new voters in suburbia's center of leisure, the shopping mall. Thus, Rietz argued, "the registration drive can be considered successful in terms of publicity," and Malek agreed "the media attention was well worth the effort."[41] Rietz saw the organization's visibility as a way to both soften Nixon's image for voters of all ages and make supporting Nixon the "in" thing.

In many ways, Nixon flaunted his youth campaign to older voters first. As Finch clarified in a memo to the president, "Parents expect public officials to work with youth. Adults want their youth to participate legitimately, even though unproductively, within the system." Finch argued that "if youth turns off a candidate it can mean adult rejections."[42] Thus, the November Group's ads harkened back to the 1960s youth Nixon would rather remember.[43] One J. C. Penney executive claimed: "The appeal to the young is heard by many who are in their 30s and 40s." A BBDO study went even further, arguing that "since the need of a 'younger' image appears quite suddenly (at about 25), it should probably be kept in mind that in selling to people under 25, the 'youthful' appeal may not be effective."[44] While YVP organizers felt older voters would appreciate the YVP's image, the youth campaign focused on winning over young voters.

Young Republican leaders learned the centrality of image in campaigning, and though pictures with "little old ladies" did not exactly make Nixon hip, Rove tried to help make the president "in." Selling buttons that read "I Give a Damn," Rove wrote, "This is just the thing for the socially-concerned, right on Republican."[45] Referring to another, "VotePower" button, a CR official wrote Rove, "The button really did wonders for me, it boosted my ego."[46] With this growth in morale, the president's young supporters could stand up and be counted.

November Group observers found Rietz's focus groups with young people surprisingly successful.[47] For example, after a room full of young people almost unanimously opposed the president, these same first-time voters proved much more "sympathetic" to Nixon's presidency when YVP leaders separated them into smaller groups and discussed his policies on major youth issues.[48] When young people felt involved, many of the subjects dropped their concern to be hip in their peers' eyes and admitted they supported the president. Thus, as the YVP image helped Nixon contrast his "square" campaign with McGovern's "extremists," it also gave Nixon's campaign the motivation to hone its argument to a particular voting bloc.

Young voters, more than any other segment, looked at the candidate and not the party. As Robert Finch wrote to the president, "Since youth are not locked into party they will join with and adhere to individual candidates."[49] While Mort Allin admitted, "The hippies, yippies and malcontents will never be ours," he held faith that there existed "a majority of latent moderate student supporters who will work for a man whom they respect and who shows an interest in their support."[50]

This emerging political emphasis on independents and image relied heavily on targeted research, data, and polling to reach a particular, desired youth segment. In the campaign's earliest days during the summer of 1971, Rietz obtained the services of the Playboy Enterprises subsidiary College Marketing Corporation, "a successful firm having a revenue of $1,300,000 in the 14 months they have been in business." With its experience in surveying students for corporations concerning "brand preference studies, brand name testing and brand package testing," Rietz quickly found this developing field in marketing especially useful in "finding out what the youth vote is thinking about." This research also gathered information on campus leaders, publications, and radio or TV stations with influence. The firm's director and New York Stock Exchange member W. Peter Hass pledged the support free of charge, as Rietz reported that "they are all Republicans."[51] While Nixon protested the liberal media establishment, his allies on Madison Avenue brought him a strong advantage. The youth campaign offered an important vehicle to combine political appeals for votes with businesses' appeals for customers. With the giant resources this alliance provided to Nixon's campaign, the November Group worked closely with YVP research to both find common ground among this emerging youth constituency and isolate the differences they could exploit.

Young Americans' first concerns, the environment and the Vietnam War, stood out as priorities in the early polling data of eighteen-to-twenty-four-year-old new voters.[52] The CRP even had nonvalid postage stamps made that read Generation of Peace (GOP) with Nixon's picture. However, this hardly mapped out a clear route for the youth campaign. CRP Citizens Division director Fred Malek pointed out this changing dynamic in March 1972: "I do not think we can lock in our posture regarding Vietnam for several months."[53] Nixon as the peace candidate could not yet work, but Bill Novelli's research showed the November Group could start with the candidate's reputation. The president ranked poorly in the categories of "relaxed," "warm," "extroverted," "sense-of-humor," and "up-to-date." One November Group executive, Bill Novelli, pointed out the line Nixon had to straddle, warning in a March 1972 memo: "To present the president as a mod candidate of youthful orientation would perhaps: invite disbelief, invite ridicule, damage the Nixon image held by the 35+ voter."[54] While Nixon's campaign to recruit young voters rested on his accomplishments and hoped to soften his image, his campaign aimed to be "believable" by emphasizing Nixon's strengths as he received high rankings in categories such as "experienced," "trained," and "informed."[55]

Last, presenting Nixon as a beloved leader could quell his aloof public persona. Bill Gavin, assistant director of the US Information Agency, claimed that the "Nixon machine was animated by an unspoken but fierce love on the part of all of us for the Boss. That same love can be communicated by the President to all young Americans (and of course to the media)."[56] Undeniably, a mod Nixon in an unusual double-breasted jacket, loud patterns, long hair, a wide belt, and tight low-rise pants would have been hilarious. Thus, Nixon in control, but not out of step, became the desired balance. Nixon opted for a paternalistic relationship with youth, as Rietz explained: "Most young voters do not want a president who is one of them . . . just as the majority of young people do not want a father who is a pal."[57] This meant the YVP needed more attention, but also that it had to develop an appropriate image for the GOP brand.

One poster depicted the president from behind his hunched shoulders, as he stood hands in pockets, leaning against a wall in the oval office and peering out his window. The slogan claimed that America needed "coolness," "intelligence," and "a sense of history" more than it needed "clarion calls," "charisma," and "histrionics."[58] Nixon's advisers disagreed over this image's effectiveness, as it turned Nixon's back to the viewer and could reinforce his distant reputation. After extensive polling, young voters rated this highest among Nixon's posters, receiving a more favorable response than both the "Peace in Vietnam" and "Environment" posters. This picture made Nixon presidential and thoughtful, something the children of the silent majority welcomed amid this period's vitriol and exhaustion with the 1960s turbulent legacy. The November Group attempted to soften Nixon's image, as another poster of the president walking with his wife especially resonated with Nixon's young voters. One of his twenty-three-year-old campaign workers approved: "You know that one picture of him walking along the beach in sports clothes? I think that's the most effective shot we have of him."[59] Contradicting his square reputation, the YVP posters presented a slightly more casual Nixon. Beyond the traditional youth appeal, this image targeted young voters more likely to support Nixon.

Under this assumption, CRP dissected and courted the youth segment more than any other. Behind this ambitious plan, Rietz laid out the strength of "peer group pressure," which he defined as maximum involvement and exposure of youth as a means of convincing more youth to join in Nixon's reelection effort. While Rietz focused on building the YVP membership, Nixon's young supporters also developed the symbolic significance CRP leaders needed to improve Nixon's image for all voters.

Rietz acted cautiously concerning public relations as he emphasized that organization made the media and not vice versa, and he made sure to separate the two. For example, when the YVP chairman consulted a state Young Voters Committee, consisting of young celebrities and athletes who actively supported the president, Rietz urged that "the Young Voters Committee have as much of a separate identification as possible."[60] While Rietz valued the role these big names played, to confuse them with the organization would risk stigmatizing the YVP as commercial.

Despite Rietz's hesitance, young celebrities played an important role in publicizing Nixon's youth campaign and attracting new voters. Nixon developed a wide and varied group of television stars, athletes, and entertainers to counter critics who handed the youth vote to the "in" candidate, McGovern. After *Newsweek* published one article that predicted Nixon would suffer with the youth vote, the Celebrities for the President's director, Raymond Caldiero, fired off a letter to challenge the premise. The article seemed especially dangerous as it ignored Nixon's celebrities and rallies and questioned his star power with young voters. Caldiero listed the new members of the "Performers for the President," including the Carpenters and Allen Osmond among others, who would provide "entertainment suitable for rallies for young people." Caldiero fumed that *Newsweek* instead ignored this effort, and focused on "a so-called division . . . a division in which the young always support Senator McGovern."[61]

Although Rietz downplayed the YVP's image politics, his higher-ups emphasized it. In May 1972, the YVP's Celebrity Division proved effective in defending Nixon as "in," and Magruder suggested to Rietz that "it would be useful for us to have many more young celebrities who are appealing to young people."[62] Young Voters for Nixon also became useful in drawing celebrities to speak on the president's behalf. Buchanan wrote Magruder about one such celebrity, Elvis Presley, who promised to "pop for some loot" if granted a position on "some antidrug commission." Buchanan added, Presley would contribute only if approached "by the right young guy" as he was "turned off by older folks."[63] Of course, the King never joined the Nixon campaign, but the story proves that youth became an indispensable resource in negotiating "showbiz politics."[64]

While John Lennon staged concerts to register young McGovern supporters that doubled as protests against Nixon's War on Drugs, Nixon used celebrities to communicate his antidrug message to young people. As one memo advised, "drugs seem to be the best issues to involve celebrities with the President. Witness the success with Sammy Davis Jr."[65] Nixon's campaign managers used surrogates to counter McGovern's Woodstock image, meaning they could not resist athletes' growing celebrity. Besides, O. J. Simpson projected a more wholesome personality than the "limousine liberals" from Hollywood. When Shirley McClain and Warren Beatty rounded off McGovern's so-called "sparklies," Nixon sent Miami Dolphins linebacker Nick Buonicotti or Miss USA, Debbie Shelton. In addition to the celebrities, Nixon's rally organizers displayed young women in matching outfits, the Nixonettes, to differentiate his young supporters from hippies.

In fact, CRP developed two campaign divisions under the YVP for young women: the Nixonettes, young women in matching Nixon campaign regalia, and the Nixonaires, airplane stewardesses who attended rallies in their flight uniforms. Most visible, the Nixonettes added vitality to Nixon's appearances, as they always popped up adorned in their red wrap-around skirt with blue borders, cotton flop hat in white or blue, a silk YVP scarf, and a button that read, "Get to Know a Nixonette."[66] The manual for "rally men" instructed them to recruit "good-looking college girls. . . . Get as many as possible . . . hundreds, thousands." Their presence played a central role in Nixon's image, as the manual suggested, "Always attempt to have these girls at the front of the crowd so they will be picked up by the TV and wire photos cameras."[67] Led by Angela Miller and Pam Powell from the YVP national office, this effort crystallized New Republicans' effort to soften the GOP's image while reaffirming gender lines in the early 1970s.

Laura Jordan Dietrich, a twenty-year-old student from Chicago, headed Illinois's impressive Nixonettes branch of the YVP as she explained: "We had a Nixonette chair in every county in Illinois, that campaign was extremely organized with structure." This explained the YVP's larger success, Dietrich laughed: "Nixonettes became the youth campaign, where there are girls there are guys." Dietrich described their ebullient effect as "perverse" in contrast to what she called the "demeaning peer pressure of feminism." "I don't want to say we were cheerleaders," Dietrich admitted, "but you've got cute girls in cute little uniforms." Still, Dietrich remembered, "we had a lot of pride": "You're cute you're fun, nobody's making you do this."[68] Representing the YVP's virtuous and charismatic appeal, young women also found the YVP as an opportunity to get involved. In fact Phyllis Schlafly became the role model for many of these conservative young women who found space to play important roles as foot soldiers and recruiters or as top-level organizers.

Powell, the twenty-four-year-old daughter of actors June Allyson and Dick Powell, became the national chairwoman of the YVP. While her first memory of a campaign was handing out bumper stickers for Nixon in 1960, she admitted her father was one of Nixon's debate advisers often blamed for his disastrous first performance against John Kennedy. After she had been a Nixonette in 1968, Powell emerged as the prominent leader in Nixon's youth effort. As one journalist put it, the "fresh faced, petite blond" became the "youth symbol of the Nixon campaign."[69] Speaking on the president's behalf, Powell praised his efforts to hire more women, claiming, "I've never had a problem being a woman. It has, in many cases, helped me."[70] The press certainly took note of young women such as Powell, as one headline under a photo of her pinning a Nixon-Agnew button on the Pennsylvania lieutenant governor read: "A pretty girl makes politics more palatable."[71] Personally, Nixon's view of his young women volunteers betrayed this outdated perspective, as he thanked a group of campaign staffers, "I know what you men do . . . I know it's difficult for your wife to think about you out there with all those cute little 'Nixonaires' and 'Nixonettes' and everything."[72] Still, even as Nixon's campaign used young women to spice things up, it also targeted the forty-seven-year-old woman in Ohio who Scammon and Wattenberg defined as the average American voter.[73]

Figure 12. YVPers in a Nixon car, making Nixon "with it." (Nixon Library)

As Madison Avenue's segmented public relations techniques moved into modern politics, campaigning with younger women became even more important. As for the women at home, the campaign's "Program for Women" stressed the "sensitivity to the new self-awareness of women," pointing out that "women watch twice as many television hours as men, and hear three times as many radio hours." In addition, the research showed that with the advent of the birth control pill, more women worked and had more money and influence over family expenditures. As a result, media-savvy women often "know far more than her husband about public events."[74] Nixon's clean version of America's youth offered an appealing vision to American women with children, as a Harris poll in 1970 showed the "difficulty to raise children, drugs, generation gap" as the greatest problems in being a woman.[75]

Researchers in Nixon's Women Voters for the President relied on polls that Virginia Slims conducted in preparation for an ad campaign launching a new cigarette "geared essentially to the 'liberated' woman." For younger women, "not enough jobs, equal opportunity, salaries" topped the issues that revealed resentment about their role in society. The Nixonaires accomplished a slightly different image, as their

Figure 13. YVP chairwoman Pamela Powell bangs the gavel to commence the 1972 Republican National Convention. (Nixon Library)

occupation had become synonymous with the new, exciting opportunities for young women in the 1960s. A group of Pan-Am stewardesses up front greeting Nixon at the airport produced exactly the desired effect to communicate Nixon's support for what Virginia Slims called "the liberated woman." To reach this constituency, Nixon's campaign decided to integrate women throughout the campaign. Under this plan, "women will be seen everywhere and on all levels of the Nixon 1972 campaign."[76] Women did hold important positions in the YVP, as Bertini, Miller, and Powell showed. The YVP campaign appealed to both younger women and their mothers.

In Nixon's campaign, the participatory politics mattered, but making it look good became the focus. Still, Nixon's campaign combined issues, organization, and image to create a single objective—counter peer group pressure that worked against the president. One way to do this, mass media, gave the YVP direct access to young voters and the opportunity to take Rietz's work with small groups and test it on a larger scale. If YVP leaders could persuade young people to support Nixon in a small room, a similar argument on the issues through posters, television, and radio could do the same.

Youth and Media

Making Nixon's campaign image more hip and believable required a media effort to highlight the president's young supporters. Entrusted with this mission, Nixon's campaign managers brought together the best and the brightest of American advertising. Many of Nixon's CRP directors shared a background in public relations and advertising. The November Group, made up entirely of advertising executives, followed this pattern. A publication on the election published in 1973, *Financing the 1972 Elections*, described the November Group as CRP's "advertising arm," which produced television programs, documentaries, and specialized campaign materials such as posters and campaign brochures targeted toward specific voting groups.[77] Peter Dailey, the in-house PR firm's director, exemplified the high-caliber pedigree they all shared. While Dailey ran his own high-priced LA firm, other members such as Phil Joanou came from the prestigious Doyle, Dane, and Bernbach. Dailey's first priority was to build Nixon's campaign on a "peace generation." According to Dailey, the campaign set out to build on the incumbency and highlight Nixon's accomplishments to emphasize Nixon's presidential noncampaign. "There was only one candidate," explained Dailey, "and then there was the President."[78] This strategy showed a substantive openness to youth politics concerning the war but also maintained his leadership position above the fray. Although Nixon stayed off the campaign trail, he could not avoid the living-room politics waged through television.

As Aniko Bodroghkozy asserted in *Groove Tube: Sixties Television and Youth Rebellion*, "Baby Boomers would not only have their huge numbers in common; they would also have their shared rearing with the television set to knit them together." In addition, baby boom historian Landon Jones argued that this was the first generation to receive such intense marketing attention: "From cradle, the baby boomers had been surrounded by products created especially for them, from Silly Putty to Slinkys to skateboards."[79] During the 1960s, on Madison Avenue, selling *with* youth became a necessary way to sell *to* youth. Older American consumers also saw youth as a stand-in for hip, new, and nonconformist.[80] As media and marketing efforts defined the way young and old viewed

Americans between eighteen and thirty, the youth generation also carried this emphasis on image into the political system.[81]

After Nixon's first term, Magruder pointed out that people had already developed a static idea of Nixon's television image.[82] Supporting this mission, the November Group hit the airwaves to publicize Nixon's interactions with young people. Thus, Nixon's campaign managers recorded songs, sung by YVP, for distribution to YVP supporters, along with other folksy tunes that always incorporated the lyrics "Nixon Now." This combination balanced the slogan's urgent call for a strong, disciplined leader with the soft harmonies of 1970s pop music. Nixon's image makers saw the YVP as a way to dull Nixon's stigma and the public's sharpest criticism that he lacked a human side and charisma. For example, the November Group's George Karalekas complained to radio and television station managers that he would "rather be up against a nice Coke, or Pepsi, or Canada Dry than a banging Excedrin spot." The soft drink branding set the tone they desired, as Karalekas made clear: "We'd prefer non-abrasive commercials around us."[83]

Soft drink advertisements offered a model style for the November Group. As an early proponent of "lifestyle marketing," Pepsi targeted consumers with a "young view of things," the Pepsi Generation. Pepsi's youth-centered television commercials began with an ominous beginning: a car driven down a hill toward a lake, young people whizzing around on strange contraptions, or a camera zooming closer and closer into a road on a hillside. In each case, the dangerous image and music become lighthearted as the commercials show thrill-seeking young people before the soothing Pepsi jingle calms viewers and urges them to "Come Alive!!!" All in thirty seconds, the ads project the frenetic energy of a generation and a comforting resolution. Pepsi-Cola president Roger Enrico summed up the youth's appeal to consumers, explaining, "We can appeal to the broader audience through the eyes of youth." Youth culture had achieved new significance in America, as Pepsi exhibited the blueprint for putting "a youthful mindset on the product emphasizing vitality, excitement, being on the cutting edge."[84] Nixon's in-house advertising team included BBDO's high-powered executives from the Pepsi Generation who developed and duplicated this effort to sell the president.

When Nixon did use television, the YVP played an important role in undermining his "static," "abrasive" image. One commercial, titled "Youth," speaks directly to the November Group's efforts to build his youth image on his record and the Pepsi formula for selling with youth. Beginning with a menacing, dark, dangerous, and fast-paced riff, a deep voice in an accusatory tone lists the youth's demands over images of young people protesting, "You ask for an end to the war, you wanted peace, you said the draft was unfair, you asked for a say in our government, you wanted a voice in your future, you said why isn't something being done to save our environment." The music and announcer rise to a crescendo, "you spoke out for change, you asked for reform, you wanted a better America," when they both cut out giving way to Nixon's inauguration speech as he calmly suggests, "we cannot learn from one another, until we stop shouting at one another." The ad then lists Nixon's achievements in winding down the war, ending the draft, supporting the Twenty-Sixth Amendment to lower the voting age, and reforming environmental policy. As a candidate of change, this approach to young voters communicated that the job remained unfinished, and that "we need President Nixon, now more than ever."[85]

One similar Nixon ad begins with an upbeat tune as Young Voters for the President members sing in chorus, "making dreams reality, more than ever Nixon Now for you and me." The montage of still shots shifts from a butterfly on a flower to other pastoral landscapes and then begins to show young people filled with extreme joy as couples embrace in a sun-splashed open field or frolic in the ocean. Thirty seconds into the two-minute commercial, Nixon can finally be found wading into crowds of jubilant young supporters when the image shifts to a YVP office and its window adorned with signs reading, "We Luv the Pres" and "Happiness is Nixon." As the song continues, "reaching out across the sea, making friends where, foes used to be," the montage continues with close-ups of Nixon's notable visits to China and the Soviet Union. Cognizant of his silent majority, the ad continues with footage of Nixon's visit to a construction site teaming with loyal young hardhats. Then, the commercial flashes a still shot of a young smiling couple, holding hands as they run barefoot through puddles. As one critique observed about these ads, "They are various and inclusive. They appear, in catchy tunes and in specific directed issues, to reach out to all Americans, not simply the 'average' ones in the factory."[86] Ironically, with its targeted and focused youth effort, Nixon's campaign deflected his youth syndrome and tried making Nixon likeable to everyone. While this reach to "all Americans" reinforced Nixon's claim to a "silent majority," his strategists understood that Nixon's constituency had to be segmented.

Rather than being nostalgic and old-fashioned, Nixon's YVP showed that the GOP offered an alternative youth image. This Pepsi-like version of youth culture that dominated ads of the early and mid-1960s focused on the squares within this segment. As one Pepsi executive admitted in 1969, "overnight, those tanned, frolicsome happy go-lucky people began to become advertising anachronisms." Now, Pepsi's youthful fantasy "became square to the very people we were aiming at."[87] While soft drinks hoped to stay in fashion, fearing "square" status, Nixon could afford to choose the 1968 generation's attributes that his voters would appreciate most. Despite this conservative approach, this outreach to young people had limits as one ad quickly yielded a conservative critique that Nixon had "aligned with the hippie vote."[88] Congressman Ben Blackburn from Georgia, annoyed after watching the ad that showed "the President has done many of the things the kooks wanted," called Nixon's campaign aides to complain that "straight citizens resent catering to that element."[89] In turn, CRP leaders pulled the ad, while Magruder explained that television commercials were not as effective in reaching young people as "activities on college campuses and elsewhere."[90] Magruder's decision showed that the silent majority's persistent anxieties about adolescents and law-and-order politics pushed Nixon's campaign to tread carefully with the youth image. While television and media played an important role in Nixon's effort to highlight his YVP, the campaign had to show that it included young voters as well. Specifically, the YVP convention plan aimed to "take advantage of the coverage of the national news media to identify the President with young people."[91]

"Right On, Mr. President": The Republican National Convention

In the months leading up to the RNC, Nixon made it clear that more had to be made of the YVP's members on the PR front. After all, CRP leaders designed an "Open Door" theme for the convention to counter McGovern's quota system.[92] After years of planning made the YVP successful, the Republican National Convention thrust Nixon's cadre of young supporters into the limelight. In an article on the convention, *Variety* magazine described it as "the biggest commercial freebee since television began," and the administration would not miss this opportunity to showcase the YVP in action.[93] When they arrived, "the boys beardless, the girls firmly bra-ed," over three thousand members broke up into three sections.[94] Leadership for the sections came from the national youth campaign headquarters' salaried staff, while each section then divided into ten one-hundred-person "units," consisting of ten "teams" of ten young people.[95] The order exhibited here served the perfect contrast with young people who either supported McGovern or opposed the president.

Once congregated in a nearby school that one cynic dubbed "the pen," the YVP's steering committee assigned each group to a job, ranging from transportation to sign painting. Maintaining the priority on discipline, they all stood on call for rallies, unplanned events, and presidential appearances.[96] As the YVP staff director explained, "If the President calls and says, 'I need 500 kids at a press conference,' we can get them there in 20 minutes."[97] YVP members who studied journalism interviewed their colleagues and sent tapes or stories back to their hometown newspapers. The College Republicans executive director, Karl Rove, directed the youth desk, operated out of a room at the Fontaine-bleau, that informed reporters about youth activities while he recruited potential CR club organizers. The CRP leaders still took precautions as the YVP made Nixon's advisers nervous about controlling the square Nixon brand. While the YVP volunteers selected to attend the convention represented the cream of the crop, Nixon's campaign managers saw controlling thousands of young people as a potential problem.[98] YVP's leadership developed a legal assistance program with forty volunteer attorneys to make sure young volunteers did not get arrested, and if they did, to get them out of jail as quickly as possible.[99]

In contrast, representing Nixon's enemies, a "carnival of protesters" built a tent city in nearby Flamingo Park. Here, Yippies, Zippies, Vietnam Veterans against the War (VVAW), Jesus Freaks, and others welcomed visitors to the "people's liberated zone of revolutionary living, organizing and non-violent direct action."[100] These groups varied in concerns, as the Yippies' leader Abbie Hoffman attempted to organize young working-class Americans around a class-based critique of America while the Jesus Freaks urged their drug-consuming counterparts to find an authentic life through religion. This park symbolized the fractured state of the New Left's factions, and their differences caused constant chaos and confrontation between them. Furthermore, some groups that focused on more political issues, such as the VVAW, moved to another part of the park to avoid the counterculture's stigma. Nixon's staff had discussed several plans to head off any disruptions including pushing local universities to hold finals for summer classes during the convention, shutting down the schools altogether, or holding an alternative conference for young people that would "draw the crowd from the inevitable march on the convention center."[101]

Still, the networks mostly ignored the presence of the protestors and the tumultuous activity outside the convention that resulted in small-scale rioting and thousands of arrests. Abbie Hoffman complained, "We got a fucking elephant dragging a fucking coffin down the street and we can't even get on the 11 o'clock news."[102] The network's reporters had reason to comply owing to the Nixon administration's barrage of attacks unleashed against network executives, reporters, journalists, and newspaper editors for their perceived liberal bias. The Republican Party's poster boy, California governor Ronald Reagan, claimed that broadcasters "pander to the drug culture, allow obscenity on the air, and turn over their facilities to those who shout revolution."[103] More concretely, Nixon pushed Federal Communication Commission officials to demand information on documentaries such as CBS's *The Selling of the Pentagon* owing to accusations of "news staging." Morley Safer, the cohost of the documentary-based program *60 Minutes*, confirmed the defensive posture networks consequently assumed, accusing Nixon's administration of carefully planting "doubt in this country about what we print or show or say." Continuing his criticism of this "planned program of misinformation" and its chilling effect on the press, Safer complained that Nixon's administration had "done for the truth what the Boston Strangler has done for the door-to-door salesman."[104]

While the network's reporters ignored Flamingo Park, some print journalists acknowledged the protestors. These articles usually enhanced the protestors' disorganized image in contrast to Nixon's orderly convention. For example, David Lamb, a *Los Angeles Times* reporter, interviewed a VVAW protestor, a twenty-five-year-old Miami policeman, and an eighteen-year-old YVPer for an article titled, "3 Young Men in Same City Different Orbit." After quoting the VVAW protestor, Rusty Bronaugh, who claimed "The war in Vietnam is just one of the issues," Lamb immediately pointed out that Bronaugh first smoked marijuana at age eleven.[105] Meanwhile, a Harvard student wrote, "By comparison, the YVPs were mindless hordes."[106] Thus, youth politics at the RNC hardened the perceived differences between the candidates.

Hoping to get a more authentic perspective, a group of self-described "video freaks" formed a production crew, Top Value Television (TVTV), armed with portable Sony porta-pak cameras, and filmed a documentary on the RNC, *Four More Years*. In making *Four More Years*, TVTV's members used cinema verité and distorted fishbowl lenses to stage their own version of the convention. *Four More Years* introduces the Nixon Youth in a compromising situation. In the first scene, a young man, floppy topped with side burns, and a young woman with long straight hair rehearse in a studio for a convention appearance as they repeat the chorus, "Nixon now, all we need is Nixon now," and a softer verse, "Reaching out to make dreams reality." The footage then shifts to shots of YVPers shouting and clapping, "Hey hey, what do you say, Nixon-Agnew all the way," while lined up to greet the president at the Doral Hotel. TVTV's editors interspersed this image with their own chant, "Hey-hey, ho-ho, Tricky Dick has got to go!"[107] Thus, TVTV's editors immediately framed the contest over America's youth that appeared throughout the documentary.

After this opening, a segment labeled "Right On, Mr. President" begins with a tight shot showing a young man on the convention floor screeching, "Yee haw, Right On!" Continuing with its focus on the YVPers, TVTV's crew filmed a formal gathering that Nixon's daughters, Trish and Julie, hosted with the Nixonettes. Before the party that included dignitaries such as Secretary of State Henry Kissinger, one Nixonette organizer commends the YVPers working the room, "just the decorations alone will give us the fun we need." Despite this obvious critique of Nixon's attempt to appear hip, TVTV's reporters offered the YVPers an opportunity to refute allegations that they only served as a "propaganda mill." In this candid moment, five YVPers excitedly emphasized their voluntary commitment and autonomy to chant whatever they wanted; however, they admitted to a rather strict transportation and work schedule. Contradicting their defense, the YVPers answered in unison with a perfectly synchronized "NO!" when TVTV's reporter asked whether the Republican Party forced them to work.

Hunter S. Thompson joined TVTV reporters in ridiculing the Nixon Youth. In his book, *Fear and Loathing: On the Campaign Trail, '72*, Thompson recalls with glee the shocked reactions of a young Nixon supporter ("a poor, ignorant young waterhead") after he told her NBC anchor John Chancellor dropped LSD in his drink.[108] Firing back, one YVP volunteer who attended the convention argued, "We were there because we love and respect Mr. Nixon, and our demonstrations were spontaneous and sincere."[109] Not all YVPers agreed, as one of Nixon's young supporters acknowledged the YVP volunteers at the convention mattered more for image, complaining that "nothing has anything to do with politics. It's all cheerleading." Another protested, "I just got fed up with it. I just couldn't stand every five minutes and cheer, cheer, cheer."[110]

Thus, the YVP members' authenticity became contested territory for Democrats and Republicans. Democrats claimed the GOP paid YVPers to come and that they did not represent American youth politics. In fact, this select group of YVP's "hardest workers" who made the six-day trip received a special rate for transportation and a room, paying half the cost had they attended on their own.[111] Though congressmen usually contacted them directly with an invitation to attend the convention, they came of their own will, paid their own way, and made their own political commitment. Their work was rewarded; the YVP organizers provided the volunteers with "a swimming pool, tennis court, rock bands and games."[112] The GOP also offered youth events in venues throughout Miami such as a youth speakers program and a Youth Appreciation Luau that would bolster the YVP volunteers' morale as well as create photo opportunities. Still, YVP members who attended the convention received nothing in return. This explains the YVP volunteers' thin skin when NBC News anchorman John Chancellor compared them with Mayor Daley's controlled and paid "sewer workers" from the 1968 DNC. After over five hundred complaints from Republicans, Chancellor apologized—to the sewer workers.[113] Reacting with "Sewer Workers for Nixon" signs, the YVP got the last laugh. In many ways, this response reflected the YVP humorous group persona.

Even career-minded YVP leaders such as Tim Carey admitted, "we all wanted to have fun," as YVPers often echoed this sentiment. Describing his trip from Mississippi to Miami, including a stop at Disney, Jerry Gilbreath recalled with nostalgia: "I drove down to Miami with 5 other wild young Republicans in an old station wagon with 'Republican Convention or bust' on the back singing the Beach Boys on a 8 track."[114] These warm memories fostered lasting friendships that created a strong personal and professional network. But they also provided a glimpse into the new enthusiasm young voters brought into campaigning at the height of youth politics' popularity.

During the RNC, Nixon finally perfected the "square chic" version of celebrity. Describing Nixon's "well-mannered" YVP members at the RNC who stood in a holding area dubbed "the pen," one reporter explained: "there is no aroma of marijuana wafting through the air."[115] Outside the convention, predictably, other reporters found that amid the protestors who congregated at nearby Flamingo Park, "marijuana is widespread."[116] Nixon's image makers used youth to enhance the distinctions between his campaign's "square chic" and McGovern's radicalism. The convention served as center stage for Nixon's performance in 1972. From the three enormous screens behind the podium, a collage of Nixon's achievements splashed across the convention, and consequently across the nation; whether shown sipping champagne with Brezhnev or sauntering down the Great Wall of China, Nixon appeared presidential.[117] Although YVPers represented only 3 percent of the delegation, the convention featured them prominently. Projected on the convention's screens, hundreds of YVPers welcomed the Nixon family upon their arrival at the Hotel Fontainebleau, chanting thunderously, "Four More Years!"[118] Furthermore, compensating for the low percentage of delegates under thirty, the seating arrangements for the convention assigned YVPers to the perimeter of the floor to shape a youthful appearance that the *New York Times* described as "efficiency in Bermuda shorts."[119]

CRP organizers developed a schedule laced with young speakers but also included the fifteen hundred YVP volunteers inside the convention as "props." For example, on the night of Nixon's nomination, the press center erroneously received the Republican Party's choreographed itinerary for the evening's events. Though the proceedings did not match up exactly with this script, the Nixon Youth's "spontaneous" cheer, "Nixon Now!"—slated to last from 10:33 to 10:45—only missed by a half hour.[120] They waved signs that helped bridge generations, such as one that read "Ron Baby, We Love You," which they waved enthusiastically for the sixty-one-year-old Ronald Reagan's speech. The convention's proceedings included Nixon's young supporters and displayed the emerging role youth played in politics that year.

Donald Sundquist, president of the Young Republicans, addressed the convention's opening session, arguing: "Never sell our young Americans short." Rather than some monolithic liberal bloc, Sundquist pushed for the more independent-minded generation: "We are not going to be taken for granted. We speak for ourselves."[121] Through young voters, Nixon also appealed to the precious blue-collar vote he planned to peel away from the Democrats. Utilizing the intense media coverage, Nixon's campaign managers carefully selected delegates to target the working-class independents who became more common with the youth vote. The final session of the convention began with a "salute to working youth." In addition, the White House invited a twenty-year-old boilermaker from Pittsburgh, Ross Scumaci, to second the president's nomination. Scumaci fit the bill perfectly after the Democrats' rules excluded him from the delegation and pushed him to support Nixon. In addition, one aide drooled, "He is husky, and wears a moustache . . . [and] will be heading up Working Youth for Nixon in the fall." While Scumaci's seconding speech criticized McGovern's quotas that blocked his own role in the Democratic Party, he celebrated Nixon as a friend of the working man and, in the eyes of one union leader, "galvanized ethnic and labor Democrats around RN."[122] Three "working youth" also offered floor resolutions on the RNC's first night.

Still, the nomination rally the night before the president's official coronation as the Republican presidential candidate stood out as the convention's highlight. While the rally in Marine Stadium did not begin until 8:30, YVPers arrived two hours early for a rally "warm-up" to hear speeches and organize for the ensuing concert.[123] Denying the damning criticism of the YVP as square, tightly choreographed cheerleaders—fighting words for the 1968 generation—one YVP volunteer bragged, "It's not true what they say about us!" "We drink, smoke and cuss all the time . . . we have great parties and some of us even smoke the other stuff."[124] This cultural contradiction had regional origins as well, as *Rolling Stone* took great pleasure in reporting that "all three plane loads of the California YVPs arrived stoned."[125] While Nixon's youth dabbled with their own counterculture, the YVP during the convention emphasized "square chic."

To enhance his image as "hip," the president applauded the Nixon Youth during his speech at the Marina Bay concert, starring Sammy Davis Jr., only one hour after his official nomination. The president argued against the premise that the youth vote "is in anybody's pocket." After his speech, and an awkward hug from Davis, Nixon's youth followed the president to the airport, where they were granted special access to his farewell. Here, Nixon proclaimed, "Those who have predicted that the other side is going to win the young voters are simply wrong."[126] Highlighting the YVPers, Nixon's campaign communicated to voters that his youth was the majority. This political moment signifies two essential points about the YVP. First, Nixon showed how much he had learned about youth politics and image since his narrow victory in 1968. Not only did Nixon perform enthusiastically, but his campaign managers skillfully surrounded the president with cheering young faces while he embraced the role of showman-in-chief. Second, his youthful audience forces historians to confront the strange reality that young people liked Nixon.

After the convention, the polls showed Nixon's lead as high as twelve points among voters between eighteen and thirty years old. By September 28, however, a Harris poll showed the lead down to two. The differences could have been technical, and the students' return to campuses accounted for the surge in McGovern supporters. Still, as one memo made clear, the change was significant.[127]

Following the successful Marina Bay rally, Rietz also planned a series of eight similar events. Finding students came easy, but the concerts helped bring together the working youth. As Brock explained, the concerts "let us connect with them where they were." These shows presented a different picture of Republicans and Nixon, as they "put up some pretty people who could play a pretty good sound" and "make it fun."[128] Special youth events scheduled in cities across the nation included a "traveling rock and roll revival show—one of the most popular forms of entertainment with young people," modeled after the Marine Stadium event.[129] These events targeted suburban communities that fit the YVP organizers' demographics, as the "Legend of Rock 'n' Roll" tour traveled to eight locations in the campaign's last month. The tour's finale at Fairfax High School outside of Washington, DC, performed under a large Young Voters for the President banner and was flanked by large cutout silhouettes of Nixon, featured late 1950s and early 1960s performers such as the Coasters, the Five Satins, and Gary U.S. Bonds. Even Nixon's music targeted a particular youth segment.[130]

After the convention, YVPers then shifted gears and focused on local efforts. Headquarter YVPers were "scattered hither and yon" to establish phone bank operations in areas where the GOP wanted to make inroads, as Gary Burhop set up in Michigan's crucial Macomb County to court its traditionally Democratic voters for Nixon. The YVP rallies, however, grabbed the media's attention. A traveling rally that mimicked the Marina Bay concert preoccupied many YVPers' time and effort. As Fred Asbell explained, "The premise of YVP from the get go was that there was a tendency of the press to define everyone under thirty as against Nixon, our efforts were to put together events that allowed people who were supportive of Nixon to realize that they weren't the only folks that felt the way." YVP leaders hoped that getting rid of Nixon's stigma would allow youth to recognize other like-minded voters. As Asbell recounted:

Figure 14. The Nixonettes' appeal to traditional campaign gender roles, despite the powerful role women played in the YVP organization, helped delineate Nixon's young supporters from the young McGovernites. (Nixon Library)

"We would advertise, and roommates would show up not realizing the other one was coming, students were not open about it." Organizing these rallies fell on YVP leaders, requiring them to assume roles in transportation and media. As the music groups traveled by caravan, YVPers did advanced talk shows, and developed "tremendous publicity" to make newscasts, and when buses came in to towns, they made sure YVP volunteers were there cheering them.[131]

As the master of ceremony for the rallies, Tom Campbell suggested the rally format through concerts to reach working and high school youth. While oldies wouldn't alienate older demographics, avoiding the "kidlash" aimed at rebellious and permissive youth, Bobby Lewis, Gary U.S. Bonds, and Danny and the Juniors could still attract young people. The entertainment value helped build the enthusiasm for the finale when the young crowd ranging from sixteen to early twenties stood in the aisles as the band played "Nixon Now." The oldies worked for Nixon's young crowd; this also separated Nixon's youth from McGovern's. Comparing the sedate, sitting audiences at McGovern's student rallies with his concerts, Campbell bragged: "The YVP looked more energized." YVP leaders were well aware of their significance in Nixon's campaign, claiming: "I think it was as much image as getting out the youth vote. When Trish [Tricia Nixon] came to rallies . . . our goal was to get out young people for her, we were always getting them out front."[132] Thus, YVP crowds also added to the Nixon campaign's command of the new political emphasis on the candidate as a father.

As a speaker, Nixon's daughter Tricia, clad in a "short white knit dress and white vinyl boots," stirred up crowds that numbered more than one thousand Nixon supporters. Keeping it clean, Tricia modeled square power. Taken aback by the audience's wild cheering, Tricia joked, "Your E.Q.—enthusiasm quotient—must be at least in the genius category." These rallies earned Nixon's youngest praise as "really great," "dynamite," "lovely," and "delightful."[133] Aimed at maximum press coverage, the publicity created "peer group pressure" to support Nixon.

Theses rallies revealed the calculated and savvy political planning that went into Nixon's campaign image. For example Nixon's youth rallies also reflected the YVP organizers' limited but nuanced outreach to young black voters. As Tom Davis explained, the use of supportive celebrity black groups, including Sammy Davis and the Five Satins, represented a strategy to exhibit the president's moderation. In addition, including celebrity black groups opened the party to other young blacks: "that's why we brought them there," he added; "brings in the whites too." "We want to be inclusive and send the message: 'We're not the polarizing ones.'"[134] Alienating Nixon's critics, this plan utilized YVP rallies to extract as much political capital as possible from this counterintuitive strategy.

Lessons Learned: Youth and Image

In the end, Nixon's youth campaign succeeded. On voting day, only eleven million of the twenty-five million voters under twenty-five showed up at the polls. While McGovern won this segment by a 52 to 46 percent margin, Nixon fared better when including all the voters under thirty, who Nixon's youth campaign managers targeted.[135] Over 28 percent under thirty registered as independent, and Nixon won an overwhelming majority of this segment as only 26 percent identified themselves as Republicans.[136] It did not win the majority, but it played an important role in Nixon's landslide victory by a sixty-one-to-thirty-eight-point difference. Nixon's YVP also helped draw a clear distinction between his campaign and his opponents, a necessity in the candidate-focused environment that these increasingly independent youth fostered. As pundits remarked that this election marked "the year the independent voter 'arrived,'" they predicted its influence on the political system—personality and media savvy would overcome competence.[137] Nixon's square affect countered this concern, when one youth spokesman readily admitted, "there is no question the President is not the most charismatic character out there."[138] Still, Nixon's young voters offered this necessary political ingredient. Youth politics opened up this election to new and creative strategies that changed campaigns in modern American politics. Consequently, YVP's members attracted attention as a model of distortion in America's image-based politics by his opponents, but a model of authenticity to his silent majority.

Convinced that the mass media worked against Nixon, especially on the youth problem, Nixon turned to his own resources in the November Group and the YVP to win the image war. Furthermore, as youth politics emerged in 1972, young Americans brought their image-conscious outlook into both campaigns' strategies. While one leadership group in the YVP focused on public relations and rallies, the larger leadership cohort focused on registration and "the get-out-the-vote program."[139] These two thrusts encapsulate the competing visions of young people's role in politics after 1972—youth as symbol versus youth as voter. In Nixon's campaign, youth politics merged the participatory politics and a PR effort. This new political approach may have offended traditionalists and idealists, but it also opened up politics to new groups and required tremendous organizational discipline. Thus, the politics of image changed the American political system but did not replace it. As youth's influence on image shows, this process involves more than changing optics. Instead, this book reveals that the policies and political organization that meant to both placate and harness young voters began a new, youth-focused era in modern American politics for both parties.

Some in Nixon's administration believed Rietz belonged on a short list to become the RNC chairman. After young Nixon supporters achieved "movement" status in 1972, YVP leaders such as Rietz and Gorton would have to participate in congressional hearings on Watergate—damaging their career trajectories. This project looks beyond Nixon's "dirty tricks" and focuses on his presidency's larger, structural significance in modern politics. Still, Watergate does explain the YVP's limits. Even YVP leadership on the ground level felt Watergate's stigma. As Cathy Bertini recalled, "everyone lost everything," when she described watching Nixon's resignation speech while sitting in a room of crying coworkers.[140]

Rebuilding the GOP, however, required young leaders to continue the Republican Party's search for a new majority. Pam Powell, the YVP's chairperson, served as the first White House Youth Affairs Office director, revealing two important ways that Nixon's youth campaign influenced the Republican Party. First, leadership and training personnel who helped build the YVP became important leaders in Nixon's second-term administration and beyond. Cathy Bertini became the White House's second Youth Affairs director in 1975 during Gerald Ford's presidency. In addition, the need to establish a White House Youth Affairs Office shows that youth politics became entrenched in politics generally. Nixon's campaign charted a new approach to youth issues and young people's attitudes as the YVP mobilized young voters and included young people in the process as the White House built young Americans' trust in the president through policies.

YVP leaders' campaign for young voters marked the New Republican reach to expand the GOP's constituency. Reflecting on the role of image, even Bill Brock came to join the concerned chorus protesting its negative influence on democracy. Speaking years later, Brock testified that thirty-second ads had "tended to create the impression that solutions are simple" and that "it also leads to polarization in politics."[141] This targeted and divisive messaging challenged the forward thinking approach Brock encouraged. Bill Brock, considering the YVP legacy, remembered that the organization relied on "a belief that we need to get more people involved and believing that they can make a difference." "We would never have considered ourselves the kind of right we see today," Brock argued. "We were open, honest, welcoming."[142] As he understood, unraveling the GOP constituency that built its majority would undermine the Republican Party's effort to unite a lasting coalition for conservative principles.

While the youth craze ran its course after 1972, the struggle to define this generation's politics had just begun. Even in recent politics, both conservative and liberal politicians, pundits, and activists hold up this era's protest politics or memories of radicals to rekindle our hopes or fears that we trace to the sixties experience. Understanding the political environment they entered, and changed, this story shows that baby boomers brought politics into a new era that placed culture above bread-and-butter issues, elevated image above party loyalty, and merged grassroots politics with modern communication methods. And while youth politics shaped Nixon's "silent majority," young voters also learned from Nixon.

After Richard Nixon resigned, many young Americans found it quite believable that Tricky Dick had broken the law. But for many of the young voters in America who cast their ballot for the president, their image of Richard Nixon from the 1972 election could not be reconciled with the long list of dirty tricks connected to the White House. He ran as the statesman, the trustworthy and steadfast leader, and the moral voice to calm the decade of permissiveness and protest. To those who chose the moral Nixon, they were let down. To other, more libertarian-minded conservatives among the youth, Nixon did not represent the solution, but a vehicle with which conservative youth could gain entry into powerful and influential positions. Nixon's policies fell short for many young ideologues on the right, but his tactics and methods (both overt and covert) could not be beaten. While Watergate dragged down the CRP's reputation, the YVP story shows that this "campaign within a campaign" introduced modern politics to a political generation and vice versa.

8 | From Watergate to Reagan

After Watergate, youth politics' glow tarnished rapidly. As politicians and pollsters surveyed the damage in 1974, attention quickly turned to the concerning rise of apathy and cynicism among the nation's young citizens. After all, more than six out of ten young adults believed that society was "democratic in name only."[1] This trend continued as Gerald Ford assumed the presidency when 70 percent of young people believed "corruption and dishonesty are widespread at the highest levels of government." As for their future, only 3 percent expected to be active in politics later in life.[2] On campus, one undergrad stoked Americans' worst fears about the youth vote's future, admitting: "Most students aren't interested in politics. They're interested in sports and beer."[3] Even in campus elections the system struggled to attract voters as one embarrassed class president-elect refused the job because "not enough students turned out for the election."[4]

Still, owing to its sheer size, the under-thirty segment after 1972 continued to supply voters, campaign workers, and future leaders in both parties. In 1960, there were sixteen million eighteen-to-twenty-four-year-old Americans. In 1978, that number had increased to twenty-nine million.[5] Even though the percentage of young people who actually voted decreased over the seventies from the 50 percent level it reached in 1972 to 43 percent in 1980, voters under thirty still made up over 20 percent of the total electorate.[6] The youth vote had become deceptively significant and a required piece to any successful campaign.

In addition, young voters and their widely reported demise added new significance in 1976 as a symbol of Watergate's civic fallout. In keeping with Ford's pledge to "the maintenance of a climate of trust and confidence in our nation and its leadership," he appointed former chairwoman of the Young Voters for the President (YVP) Pamela Powell to direct the first Office of Public Youth Liaison (OPL), with the goal of "improving communication between our national and local leadership."[7] In this capacity, labeled "Ford's Girl Next Door," Powell conducted weekly Tuesday meetings between government representatives and young leaders, organized field conferences across the nation, and maintained frequent contact with more than 250 national youth organizations. Still, while Powell's position indicated a new openness to youth politics, Ford struggled to win the popularity Nixon achieved with this segment in 1972. The post-Watergate stigma, the economy, and Ford's own mixed record on youth issues such as college loans and marijuana made the president's reach to young voters difficult, as he lost to his Democratic opponent, Jimmy Carter, 54–46 percent with the under-thirty vote.

This chapter first explains youth politics' changing terrain during Ford's presidency. In addition to Watergate's negative influence on the GOP brand, polls found that young Americans in the 1970s produced a more fluid range of opinions on social issues that had worked for Nixon. For example, while noncollege youth had served as the GOP's most reliable base of young voters, their concerns about campus unrest and drugs became less significant. One study comparing youth issues in the late 1960s to the early 1970s isolated the most noteworthy development: "non-college youth have virtually caught up with college students in adopting the new social and moral norms." In the 1960s, the "new code of sexual morality, centering on casual premarital sex, abortions, homosexuality and extramarital relations" remained "confined to a minority of college students," however, fears grew that this "new morality" had recently spread to both mainstream college youth and mainstream working-class youth.[8] In addition, marijuana use continued to rise, even becoming more commonplace with the same blue-collar youth Nixon relied on to support his attack on drugs.[9] Thus, Ford could not wield Nixon's culture war on permissiveness that had helped separate his young voters from McGovern's.

Also, Watergate emboldened increasingly conservative youth leaders who took control of the Young Republicans that had previously aided Nixon's campaign. These leaders represented the emerging New Right in the GOP, who had gained power amid the party's post-Watergate decline. As Donald Critchlow explains, "Because members of the New Right were a minority within a minority party, they were able to press with impunity an agenda that interjected new issues and policies into the political arena."[10] This political landscape introduced a new irony; while young voters could moderate the GOP image and broaden its message, Republican youth politics moved to the right and required a conservative leader to unite its ranks. And though the GOP's youth politics as measured by voters registered and votes cast struggled to regain the prominence it achieved only four years earlier, YVP strategy played a central role in rebuilding the GOP youth effort. Young voters' political apathy benefited the Republican Party in this case, as the organizational approach to student and young voters it had developed in 1972 equipped GOP youth campaigns with the strategy, party network, and funds to overcome these obstacles better than their Democratic opponents.

Even though youth politics changed drastically in 1976, this effort continued the YVP's targeted effort to pry independent, moderate young voters from traditionally Democratic voter segments in the South and in white, ethnic, urban enclaves. In this project, the YVP's strategic uses of youth politics in 1972 inspired institutions within the White House and GOP campaigns to professionalize the outreach to this vital segment. In addition to Pam Powell's role in the Ford administration, Bill Brock became the RNC chairman, and several YVP personnel joined both Reagan's campaign and his administration.

This chapter also explains that Ronald Reagan's youth effort challenged Ford in 1976 by rallying the New Right and then built a winning campaign in 1980. Under Morton Blackwell's supervision, Youth for Reagan also balanced the Young Americans for Freedom (YAF) heavy youth effort with young voters from the South, white ethnic enclaves, and students. Although the results at the polls showed the Democrats' slight hold on the youth vote, the election marked the resurgence of young voters identifying as Republicans. During the late 1970s, the College Republicans counted only 250 viable CR clubs. After Reagan's election, College Republicans peaked at eleven hundred clubs and approximately 110,000 members.[11] In 1980, only 20 percent of the young voters identified themselves as Republicans and 42 percent as Democrats; the rest registered as independent. By 1988, while the Democrats maintained a slight edge in party affiliation, more voters under thirty registered as Republicans than did so as Democrats.[12]

This new prominence continued young voters' influence on the Republican Party's shift away from the YAF's grassroots, ideologically focused cadre to candidate- and party-based youth organizations. This approach to expand the party and win over new voters for the GOP made an especially careful effort to win the young, blue-collar voters Ford and Nixon had courted as ethnic youth. It also pushed the youth politics to the right. Wayne Thorburn explains this change for the YAF, arguing: "It was harder to be a right-wing radical defending what now appeared to many to be the establishment."[13] Youth on the right no longer appeared extreme and pushed their way into the system as campaign operatives, political leaders, and policy makers.

At first glance, Reagan's personal popularity created a significant difference between his youth campaign and Nixon's effort. Even the title of Nixon's youth organization, Young Voters for the President, avoided direct mention of the candidate's name; Reagan's reach for young voters, Youth for Reagan, made the connection more obvious. Outsiders attributed Reagan's youth following to the "favorite grandfather factor."[14] Reagan's image also attracted the large independent segment of young voters with his claim to patriotism, leadership, and trust.[15] Yet, even in image politics, the "square chic" culture that Reagan's "nicely dressed and spotless" young supporters brought to his campaign borrowed directly from the political culture that Nixon inspired.[16] Despite Blackwell's claim to originality in 1980, Youth for Reagan's square style, semi-autonomous organization, and targeted strategy to win over independents built on the YVP model.

These factors continued and strengthened Nixon's successes with young ethnics and established fertile ground for future GOP candidates on campuses, in the South, and in northern, industrial states. Young voters' party loyalties were weakest in these regions. While scholars and pundits credit Reagan for winning over the voters in the South and in Macomb County, those inroads resulted from a long-term courtship that emphasized its youth effort.[17]

Youth Politics after Watergate

After Nixon's victory, the White House staff continued its youth effort into the president's second term. Nixon himself set the agenda, as he ordered his staff to develop a strong youth presence and entrusted Anne Armstrong with his youth outreach. Armstrong, the former RNC chair and newly appointed White House aide, required each department to submit one youth representative. In many ways, the young YVP leadership assumed they would soon enjoy the career benefits they deserved after earning national credit for their surprising youth campaign for Nixon in 1972. Ken Rietz emerged as a frontrunner to replace Bob Dole as the RNC chairman, as Haldeman told Rietz: "To move us forward, we think we need a youthful look to the RNC."[18] In addition, Pamela Powell became the first White House director for youth activities. As the chairman of Nixon's YVP and then serving the same role for the Nixon inaugural concerts, Powell's hard work, charisma, and loyalty made her an obvious fit for this unprecedented position that organized several facets of public relations and youth outreach as well as the Bicentennial operation. Other programs included a work-study program for college seniors and graduate students of international relations, and another initiative brought in over two hundred "young professors" to participate in briefings and speaking engagements on campuses.[19]

Watergate quickly put Powell's loyalty to the test, as she maintained the president's innocence throughout the crisis and Nixon's fall. Always the optimist, Powell doubted Watergate would dampen the progress the GOP had made with young people, claiming in 1973, "they haven't dropped out."[20] Imagining a future Republican administration as she assumed her role in 1973, Powell recommended an intense increase in young appointees to advisory councils to ensure lengthy terms "so that we would have a continuing influence within the next administration."[21] Powell even suggested a group called the Future of the Republican System (FORS) to utilize the YVP approach and sustain the youth effort. Powell underestimated the immediate political losses the GOP would suffer in 1974 as the Democrats gained forty-nine seats in Congress and three Senate seats to make it a sixty-to-thirty-eight majority over the Republicans. But also, her suggestions to increase youth outreach overlooked the long-term challenges that Watergate posed to the RNC's young voter recruitment.

However, as Watergate unfolded, this faith quickly shattered. The Republican Party faced an uncertain future after Nixon resigned. Even worse for YVP leadership's rising young stars, the promising paths to political success that the 1972 campaign opened abruptly closed, while Watergate also challenged Nixon's youth on a personal level.[22] YVPer Donald Sundquist remembered his emotional response to Watergate's deep significance as "one of the tragedies of my political career"[23]; another called it "soul searching."[24] George Gorton never faced a fine or charge for his activities on the Nixon campaign, but his professional and social worlds both came crashing down as he lost his job, his girlfriend, and his friends. Owing to this alienation, Gorton recalled, "I thought of myself as a shady character." "It was a very dark period of my life."[25] Considering the organizational impact, Tom Bell thought about the "what ifs" surrounding Watergate and explained his own disappointment: "That's why Nixon's resignation was so damaging because they were betrayed. . . . we made a difference. We had all sorts of plans for ways to keep people involved."[26]

After Nixon resigned, White House aides hoped this youth outreach would continue. In fact, many Ford aides argued that Watergate highlighted the need to develop an "open door" that welcomed transparency and dialogue with various youth groups. Ford began his presidency by following Powell's emphasis on young Americans, as he met national officers from twenty-two major national student organizations in his first month in office to "solicit their ideas and suggestions with regard to the fundamental issues confronting youth today: drugs, unemployment, education, juvenile delinquency." This reach out to youth promoted collaboration with social institutions he called the "fifth branch," which included family, religious bodies, fraternal and civic societies, unions, interest groups, and various voluntary organizations.[27]

As one student wrote for a "Bicentennial Minute" radio announcement, "We have lost our flare, our energy, our amusing audacity, and our novelty."[28] Polling of young people in 1973 supported these concerns. In 1969, 44 percent of noncollege young adults felt the government needed "fundamental change." After 1973, that number had jumped to 64 percent. For black youth, the problem was even worse. Among minority youth, 55 percent called American society "sick"—76 percent said it was "non-democratic."[29] As one student explained why she planned not to vote, she argued about the candidates: "I think they're screwed . . . it's impossible to tell what they're really like. Look what Nixon did."[30] While the solutions in the 1960s and early 1970s focused on channeling youth's stunning campus protests and the politics of the street into the system, politicians after Watergate attempted to rescue the youth vote from apathy.

The Ford White House courted young people to work in important and previously unattainable positions. Ironically, the post-Watergate rehabilitation effort appropriated Nixon's youth strategy. Promising "honest, fresh, bright" government, Powell described her three-year plan to organize Ford's youth outreach.[31] Powell dusted off a plan from the early days of Nixon's presidency to create a focused Youth Office in the White House. Despite Powell's pressure to develop a targeted approach, the White House created the "Citizen Participation" division that included women, youth, and ethnics; as Powell admitted, "This means that there will be no separate areas for any of these special interest groups nor will there be staff provided who will work solely on individual areas."[32] Powell quickly learned that the youth effort would face several obstacles as moderate voices of youth engagement had lost their momentum in Ford's administration.

Young Ford supporters understood their party role in the post-Watergate context; as one member in Nebraska wrote in the Teen Age Republicans' (TAR) monthly newsletter, *Target*: "We must show that Watergate was not planned or executed by any person involved in the party and that we aren't selling out because of public misconception." In fact, this young TAR member argued that conservativism offered "one sure way to prevent future Watergates. . . . Only through the Republican philosophy of limited government and government close to the people can government stay honest." Another New York TAR leader called his members to action: "Let us act *now* to forge a new faith in our American system and to involve more young people in our Republican Party." Or else, this teenager warned: "Our system will suffer an even harder blow as our classmates become of voting age still believing that all government and politics are corrupt."[33]

Scholarship on this era focuses on the "malaise" that defined the period after Vietnam and Watergate. These interpretations debate the state of modern conservatism after the Nixon presidency.[34] While some historians argue this period stunted the American shift to the right, others contend this actually contributed to conservatives' influence in the Republican Party. Concerning youth politics in the GOP, the membership in the Republican Party's auxiliaries such as the College Republicans dropped, creating an opening and opportunity for the New Right movement conservatives to take leadership positions and develop a wider influence.

In many ways, Watergate actually created new opportunities for young people, as one twenty-year-old county chairman, the youngest in the country, explained: "Older Party members had a tight hold on leadership . . . but now the structure has opened up and more young people are on their way up in the Republican Party."[35] This opening created room for new leaders who would challenge the party's direction and promote the New Right's vision for a conservative party. In addition, as Bruce Schulman argues, "The scandal reinforced a generalized antigovernment passion whose main effect worked against Democrats and liberals and for Republicans and conservatives."[36]

Reflecting the ideological split between moderate Ford supporters and conservative Reaganites, Young Republicans' move to the right that year provoked an internal struggle for the party's future. While some of this was the usual turf war infighting, the policy ideas espoused by the New Right directly challenged the party platform as they advocated for nuclear superiority, Cuban liberation, and full recognition of anticommunist Rhodesia and attacked UNICEF funding of Vietnam to challenge the party's pragmatic détente. Domestically, the Young Republicans adopted a platform "unalterably opposed" to busing, gun control, postcard voter registration, the ERA, and "environmental hysteria." In addition, they wanted a constitutional amendment mandating a balanced budget and repayment of the national debt.[37]

Elected chairman of the YRNF in early 1975, Jack Mueller represented the most conservative elements of the leadership that supported Governor Ronald Reagan over the incumbent. While claiming his victory assured "harmony," YR leader Paul Manafort admitted Mueller appealed to an exclusively conservative element who trusted only "Republicans of our philosophy."[38] As Richard Viguerie's *Right Report* newsletter crowed, conservatives made up over 60 percent of the GOP delegates, early New Hampshire polling showed 25 percent of young voters favored Reagan over the 6 percent supporting Ford, and the Gallup polls showed that almost 25 percent would support a conservative third-party ticket.[39]

In fact, well before the 1976 campaign, as Ford assumed the presidency and selected his vice president, YR supported Barry Goldwater as the vice president in 1974. Claiming Nixon's reelection as one of ideology, the YR argued, "Senator Goldwater's political and moral leadership are highly respected by a nation longing for the implementation of the principles it mandated in 1972."[40] Many on the right attributed Nixon's victory to conservatism, not the candidate. Instead, to the ire of these movement conservatives, Ford selected a representation of the East Coast party establishment, New York's former governor Nelson Rockefeller. Further division revealed Ford's difficult challenge to rally the Republican auxiliaries to his cause for reelection.

While Ford still extended his hand to Young Republicans in 1975 by speaking at the White House with a select group of leaders from the

Young Republican Leadership Conference (YRLC), they proved problematic. Powell described the event as marred by a "few minor problems" due to poor "receptivity by national officers." That day, the YR presented a resolution at the YRLC that denounced Ford's policies on the deficit and criticized his choice of vice president as liberal, blaming the president for "the possibility of a conservative third party." Forming a Committee for Conservative Alternatives, this resolution urged the Ford administration to "readopt the conservative principles that brought about the massive Republican mandate in 1972."[41] An informal tally showed only seven YR state organizations could be considered "solid Ford" while eight were "totally against" and the rest split.[42] Despite YR executive director Peter MacPherson's success in stopping anti-Ford elements from endorsing Reagan, one report summed up the rift, "with friends like MacPherson, these moderates feel, Ford doesn't need enemies."[43] As moderate YR leaders such as Paul Manafort and MacPherson found jobs in the White House, the remaining YR leadership was divided along allegiances to Ford. For middle-of-the-road Young Republicans, things got worse. Almost one year after receiving Ford's congratulations by phone for winning the election as the YR chairman, Mueller endorsed Reagan. Rather than heal youth's post-Watergate apathy, the campaign would expose the political schism in the GOP that created new problems for organizing young voters.

Campaign 1976

The Ford reelection campaign developed its own youth program in January 1976, tapping Carolyn Booth to direct Youth for Ford. In forming this organization, Ford aides looked back to Nixon's YVP for direction. Repeating YVP director Ken Rietz's catch phrases, the Youth for Ford proposal claimed: "Young people are more susceptible to 'peer group pressure'" and can be convinced that "it is the 'in thing to do' to work for the President."[44] Powell agreed, as she suggested: "a specific youth program based on peer group pressure (e.g., the 1972 Young Voters campaign) has proven more and more successful and has been politically sound."[45] Thus, citing model youth campaigns such as Bill Brock's, Nixon's Young Voters for the President, and the College Republicans for Buckley in New York, the Young Voters for Ford plan opted to develop a "mini-organization under the Ford umbrella." Compared to the preceding efforts it emulated, however, Youth for Ford's leaders found more obstacles to developing a potent young voter organization. While Republican auxiliaries gladly assumed a deferential role in the Nixon effort, the 1976 youth campaign struggled to find the relative unity of 1972.

This youth focus forced the GOP's debate over how to expand the party, as the RNC gathered in 1975 to consider "positive action" programs that included "participation by women, young people, minority and heritage groups and senior citizens in the delegate selection process." This program stemmed from "open door" changes to Rule 32 that the 1972 RNC revised, mandating the GOP to take "positive action to achieve the broadest possible participation by everyone in party affairs." Targeting youth troubled some GOP leaders, as Mississippi RNC chairman Clark Reed recalled: "This emulates the very thing that took the Democrats down to defeat in 1972."[46] Thus, RNC leaders feared that by allowing a vote on Rule 32 to wait until the 1976 convention, this "extremely divisive issue . . . will exacerbate the conservative-moderate split which has already appeared."[47] While Reed and other conservatives held concerns about groups sabotaging the GOP principles, he exaggerated their moderate influence in the post-Watergate era.

The YR continued its steady drift right in confidence that they could move the whole party, as one YR conference delegate in 1976 bragged after hearing the moderate Republican commerce secretary "thunder" against wasteful spending: "Why, it's even getting so that some liberal Republicans are sounding like Republicans." Richard Viguerie stridently claimed, "the Ford youth vote folded at the conference" and boasted that Roger Stone had built Reagan Youth "into the most effective youth campaign ever run for a GOP presidential candidate."[48] While White House aide Skip Watts represented Ford in the conference's Presidential Forum, Ronald Reagan was the banquet speaker.[49] Reagan's popularity and Ford's tensions with increasingly conservative youth groups slowed the incumbent's traditional ability to utilize these groups for his election effort.

As for the college voter program, this effort also exposed Ford's limited popularity with moderate youth. Ford had taken a conservative position on student loans and earned one Michigan student's title, "enemy of education," based on his track record in Congress. This student editor mocked Ford's presidential campaign announcement at his alma mater in Ann Arbor, joking it was "akin to Hitler making the first donation to the United Jewish Appeal."[50] Despite the moderate reputation Ford earned with the New Right, the alienated students on the left found the White House's youth outreach just as selective as the preceding administration's. The National Student Association (NSA) executive director, Drew Olim, complained about the selective approach Ford took to youth groups. After several unreturned requests to meet at the White House, Olim griped to Powell: "It was typical for USNSA to be snubbed during the Nixon days and we were proud of our appearance on the 'Enemies List.' But I had thought things had changed since then. Apparently not." While he claimed NSA would prefer to work "with the Ford administration rather than outside it completely," he admitted that "it is beginning to appear that we have no alternative."[51]

Despite his moderate, open-door approach, young Americans saw Ford as a continuation of the preceding White House's approach to student politics. The campaign for students became more urgent as polls showed Ford's problem with young voters. In March, before Carter emerged in the Democratic primary, polls showed that Ford led the youth vote in the anticipated matchup with the predicted party leader, Hubert Humphrey, 50 to 46 percent.[52] By May, after Carter emerged as the potential nominee, he led Ford by a three-to-two margin with young voters.[53] As one student explained early in the primaries, "Jimmy Carter's getting the youth vote. . . . The Allman Brothers gave a concert for him and a lot of young celebrities have supported him."[54] Still, there was room on campuses for a solid pro-Ford block, as the CR conference in 1976 passed its first resolution to endorse Ford. Ford enjoyed a 59 percent approval from students, while 77 percent approved of him as a father and man. As one student said, "I was really impressed by how open Mr. Ford was about his feelings, about his kids smoking marijuana. . . . The Fords didn't cover it up."[55] In fact, using Jack Ford, the president's popular though controversial son, became a focus for the effort on campuses. The moderate congressman Stewart McKinney (R-Connecticut) "strongly recommended that the presidents use his son Jack heavily on college campuses," as he told Ford that he would not get elected without the support of college students, complaining: "My God, first McGovern and now Carter!"[56]

When Jack met eight hundred students at Bowling Green, however, the message challenged the messenger. Aside from defending his father's attempt to challenge Supreme Court mandates for busing to integrate schools, Ford also had to spin the president's law-and-order position on marijuana. While socially conservative, square young voters supported Ford's antimarijuana position against decriminalization, monthly marijuana use among high school seniors had risen from less than 10 percent in 1968 to over 35 percent in 1976, and over 40 percent of baby boomers supported legalization.[57] Admitting his own opposition to harsh marijuana penalties, Jack pointed out that he and his father disagreed, "but I'm glad he and I can discuss it like rational human beings."[58] If this meant to make Ford more hip, it paled in contrast to Carter's full-throated call for cannabis decriminalization during a student rally in March.

Amid this shifting cultural sensibility, Ford struggled to connect with young voters. Speaking to Young Republicans, Ford joked that in a popular play, *Picnic*, one actor tells Paul Newman's character to "loosen up and get sexy," and Newman answered: "I can't do that. I'm from Ohio and I'm a Republican!" Thus, Ford told this group, "Young Republicans, more than ever before, will be a key element in bringing a new and more vital image to our party."[59] Still, even the public relations efforts backfired. After receiving answers to five questions for each candidate, *Scholastic* magazine's editor blasted the president's answers as "stuffy, makes the President appear pompous and is a put down to kids." As a result, the note warned: "Congratulations. The Republicans—through the PFC (President Ford Committee)—have just written off the youth of America and undoubtedly countless votes."[60] Internal notions of youth also lagged, as Karl Rove reviewed the youth fact book, complaining: "The picture it gives of young people is a VD-infected ROTC grad interested only in the draft."[61]

As Carter built his popularity with students, Ford's campaign struggled on campuses, especially since College Republican clubs had declined. While 43 percent of the higher education institutions reported a College Republican group in 1970, only 28 percent had CR clubs in 1977, as they fell from over five hundred nationally to just over two hundred in 1976.[62] Many college students, especially the upperclassmen most familiar with Watergate, associated the GOP with corruption. In addition, Ford's opposition to expanded college loan funding, his pardon of Richard Nixon, and his conservative position on social issues failed to engender the type of support on campuses that usually followed Republican presidents.

Aside from utilizing Jack Ford, the organizational approach on campuses also had mixed success. Ford's campaign looked back to the New

Republicans in Tennessee such as Lamar Alexander for a program that concentrated its efforts on registration drives on campuses. In his losing bid for governor in 1974, Alexander registered sixteen hundred students at UT in one day and won 62 percent of the student vote. Utilizing a shared "hustle" script, this approach encouraged aggressive but targeted work through tables, dorm activity, and phone banking to get volunteers involved even before registration.

Still, Youth for Ford leaders advised young people to organize these drives through the general campaign, and "*always* be very nice when dealing with them" since "the local office is usually nervous about students voting as a block."[63] Perhaps they had reason for concern, as Alexander's fish-in-a-barrel approach to locating potential student volunteers and voters in Tennessee turned up less sympathetic students in the North, as one Ivy League poll showed Ford trailing Carter 45 to 55 percent.[64] The College Republicans' presence on campus, while loyal to Ford, lacked the organization and numbers to challenge Carter nationally for the student vote.

Making matters worse, Youth for Reagan chapters enlisted movement conservatives who consistently banked their hopes on his candidacy. Before the battle with Ford for the Republican nomination at the Republican National Convention in Kansas City, Reagan met with Youth for Reagan members for breakfast in California, sending off four busloads of young supporters that left on a sixteen-hundred-mile trip to rendezvous with the former governor.[65]

The Republican National Convention presented the first real test for the Ford youth effort. As Ford shifted his focus from healing Watergate's effect in American politics and rejuvenating confidence in the democratic system to mending intraparty divisions, he hoped the convention could develop the GOP unity necessary to win the election. Speaking to TAR leaders in the White House one month before the nomination, Ford explained: "it makes no sense for us to scramble down to the wire for the nomination and then have our party fall apart the next day." Rather, the president suggested, "we must strive to prevent it from becoming a grudge battle." "Following Kansas City [RNC]," Ford said, "I want a united, I want an enthusiastic Republican Party."[66] This spirit of unity extended beyond party politics, as Ford observed: "In the past ten years we have heard a great deal about generation gaps and communication gaps." Ford claimed his goal was to "break down some of the barriers that divided this country during the sixties and early seventies."[67] With his strategy to unite the country, the Ford convention plan required visible young supporters.

While Nixon could afford a national youth campaign in each state, and designated over fifty YVP staff to focus solely on the convention, the planners of "the Presidentials" admitted, "this plan is modest" and that "the purpose of this youth convention plan is different from the '72 effort." Rather than focusing on media exposure, this approach prioritized training a "nucleus of youth volunteers in each state for the general election effort."[68] This youth campaign made clear that young voters would now be seen as part of the larger campaign and on the same level, as its organizers warned not to include "demeaning groups" such as the Nixonettes in 1972. "Therefore," the proposal concluded, "it is recommended that there be no 'Fordettes' or any other type of organized cheerleading squad for women or men."[69] The intended message here framed the youth vote's more institutionalized position in the senior campaign, though it also came from necessity as the campaign needed these volunteers.

The Ford campaign's low expectations for a strong youth showing at the 1976 RNC in Kansas City created a realistic goal, as the President Ford Committee (PFC) leaders planned for only 850–1,200 young people to participate in its convention youth organization, named "the Presidentials." Still, almost two thousand young volunteers paid $130 to join the Presidentials program,[70] gathering to offer manpower, visibility, and training programs with fellow young Ford supporters.[71] Desperate to build Ford's charisma, the campaign organizers also hoped that youth could add "color" to the usually mundane convention procedures. The Presidentials program emphasized that rallies and demonstrations created "welcome breaks from the routine convention business for the millions of TV viewers," explaining, "no single group of the population is better suited to provide enthusiasm and spontaneous support than young people."[72] And while it lacked the electric moment when Sammy Davis Jr. hugged Nixon during his convention rally of over four thousand YVPers, Betty Ford performing "the bump" on stage with Tony Orlando in front of thousands of Presidentials energized the party image. After Watergate, young Republicans at the 1976 RNC, including stewardesses, wore "Republicans are people too" pins that betrayed their rehabilitative purpose.[73]

Many volunteers for Ford spoke highly of their experience at the convention, as one Ford supporter asked: "Where else are you going to

Figure 15. Jack Ford and Tony Orlando add star power to a Presidentials' rally. (Ford Library)

get all of these experiences and meet all these VIPs in one opportunity?" Still, the housing crunch scattered the Presidentials as far as fifty miles from the convention, and many of the volunteers complained about the food.[74] More significantly, one twenty-three-year-old woman and longtime Ford admirer voiced her disappointment in the Presidentials program's structure and organization, stating, "I expected more to do than be a part time 'cheer leader,'" though she still intended to support Ford.[75] Other negative feedback indicated that the youth effort at the convention did more harm than good, as this post-Watergate sentiment engendered an emphasis on authenticity that had been previously reserved for those on the left.[76] As one young man complained after the convention, he was "shipped around from one TV stage to another deceiving both the TV public and more importantly the delegates." Claiming he was "disgusted," this young voter concluded: "If this is how you plan to run our government through deception and deceit—Carter's my man."[77] Though Powell was thrilled that the Presidentials attracted a slightly larger group than anticipated, this turnout strained the program, exposing its lack of resources. Despite the best efforts by Carolyn

Booth and former YVPer David Chew to execute the Presidentials plan, Reagan won considerable platform victories against abortion and détente. In addition, his Youth for Reagan leaders in the convention led an hour-long demonstration that pushed Ford's acceptance speech back to midnight.[78] Reagan's failed campaign to win the nomination at the 1976 RNC scored pyrrhic victories; Laura Kalman argues that "Reagan won in losing."[79]

After the convention, Ford's campaign made progress in uniting Republican youth as the YR chairman Jack Mueller shifted his support from Reagan to Ford in exchange for a full-time paid position on the campaign for its last two months. This addition provided some optimism, as Ford's youth campaign director, Carolyn Booth, commented: "Mueller has been very successful in turning Reaganites around—especially the youth."[80] There were successes; the campaign gained steam in October. A weekly report to the state chairman began, "Wow! Have you had a week . . . the entire National Youth Office is buzzing with excitement about *your* accomplishments."[81] As one manager bragged: "Unlike previous campaigns, volunteers are not limited to licking stamp[s] and stuffing envelopes." Rather, she explained, Youth for Ford organizers "put the young people up front with the party leaders and the candidates themselves."[82]

Although these public exchanges spoke enthusiastically, Ford's campaign assumed less sanguine perspectives on the youth effort's shortcomings behind the scenes. First, PFC fell well short of its goals for colleges to establish campaign organizers. In Florida, where the campaign intended to build its reach to at least seventeen colleges, it managed to include only seven campuses under its umbrella. When the Florida youth director reported some progress in its lackluster campaign for Ford, morale still faltered as "his suicidal depression has become cautious optimism."[83]

Ford tapped into patriotic, free-market principles, emphasizing that Carter threatened these ideals. As one nineteen-year-old Ford supporter from Oklahoma wrote the president: "You have done a lot to bring respectability and integrity back to the Republican Party. . . . What this country does *not* need is some klodhopping [*sic*] dingbat socialist like Jimmy Carter."[84] In addition, the GOP reach for young voters reflected a break from the one party system they inherited, as one twenty-four-year-old from Tennessee wrote: "The youth of the South aren't as 'die hards' as their parents and grandparents."[85] Still, Ford's youth campaign set its sights low in this region as it targeted only one college in Mississippi, the same as its goal for Massachusetts, but well below the forty-one campuses it worked on in Michigan. In fact, one of Ford's Michigan field workers reported, "The President's strongest area in the state is the 18–24 year old range and he's uncommonly weak with people 45–60 years old."[86] This youth effort, robust in some places, evidenced a limited geographic focus.

While one report praised the youth effort in Illinois, claiming its "high visibility campaign" surprised PFC leaders, reports from Florida explained: "We have no surrogate program for campuses, we have no rallies, we have no parties—there is no opportunity for young people to get together and plan activities."[87] These weaknesses in the South and on campuses pushed Ford's youth campaign to expand its constituency of young voters. Pleas for more help in southern states found little support, as one young Ford supporter wrote Booth asking for supplies, "Notwithstanding the rumors that we hear that the PFC is writing off the South, we are striving towards victory here."[88] Despite bringing on Nixon's Southern Strategy specialists Bo Callaway and Harry Dent to build on the 1972 success below the Mason-Dixon line, Carter and the GOP's divisions stemmed this shift as many young Republican operatives in the South rejected Ford's invitations to help his campaign.

This meant courting a more diverse group of the youth segment, as a conference Powell organized for Young Republicans held a seminar on "how to entice black voters away from the Democrats." Here, too, the strategy looked to bypass traditional party politics and leadership groups, as the Reverend Kim Davis, a local black minister, suggested these Young Republicans "sit down and do some honest rapping" with potential young black voters. Telling the YR members to avoid the communities' "super-niggers," Davis suggested that they instead "develop some new leadership . . . spread it around."[89] Most problematic for this effort, the GOP lacked black leadership at the local level, as Jesse Jackson explained: "An all-white Republican national, state and local leadership apparatus designing a strategy to win black voters will not work!"[90] As one student, Nancy Jackson, wondered about Powell: "She was a Nixon supporter, she was successful and had glamorous parents, I'm not sure what she could say to youth in blighted areas and to minorities." Furthermore, she argued, "she was more a public relations person than anything else."[91]

However, one local black businessman in Michigan took up the challenge and decorated several vans for Ford and drove "groups of mini-skirted Black girls and music into Black neighborhoods" with campaign flyers for the president. Still, this outreach fell short as it lacked money and resources. As Leah Wright Riguer diagnoses the cause for Ford's lackluster campaign that earned only 8 percent of the black vote, "Republicans sought African American voters, but they wanted to secure this without exerting meaningful effort."[92] While this campaign to win young black voters failed to win, Ford continued the GOP's outreach to white nonstudent young voters.

Predicting the campaign's geographic and demographic realities, the GOP Ethnic Group Program explained: "Due to Carter's advantage in the South . . . a Republican victory strategy must add to the normally Republican Mountain and Plain states [and] most of the big electoral vote states in the Northeast and Industrial Midwest." In Rustbelt states, Ford's advisers worried about Carter's "Southern down-home appeal" in Southern Ohio and with large Appalachian white populations in Cincinnati.[93] In addition, Carter's popularity with evangelical and traditionally Republican rural voters caused concern.

Fortunately for Ford, many young rural voters still identified with YVP's square chic. When it came to law and order, non–college students supported life sentences for drug dealers more than their campus cohort, 45 percent to 30 percent, and opposed legalizing marijuana, 53 percent to 40 percent.[94] Supporting this trend, rural youth responded well when one hundred members of Future Farmers of America (FFA) visited Ford in the Rose Garden; the FFA president Alpha Trivette welcomed the president as an official member of their five-hundred-thousand-person organization that Trivette called "probably the largest group of squares in all the world."[95] Attracting these voters required a focus on the cultural conservatism and suspicion of government that could also win over independent youth. The noncollege youth quickly emerged as a necessity for Ford' electoral hopes.

Meeting with the US Youth Council, Powell spoke to hundreds of young leaders at the conference titled "Youth and Politics after Watergate," where she explained ways to reach "non-student youth."[96] Less than a third of the eighteen-to-twenty-year-old segment attended college as the rest filled almost 15 percent of the nation's employment needs. While 37 percent of working youth claimed white-collar jobs, blue-collar workers made up 36 percent of the employed youth, 21 percent worked in the service industry, and 5 percent included farm workers.[97] Ford's campaign faced even more pressure to win over urban ethnic voters, mostly second-generation Italians and Polish, as one memo stated: "If Ford or Reagan is to carry Ohio against Carter they must cut into the normally heavy Democratic margins in ethnic neighborhoods in Cleveland and other North Ohio industrial centers."[98] This intensified the appeal to young, independent-minded, ethnic working voters in cities: "Youth voters have [been] shown to be the most responsive to campaign issues rather than party lines."[99] Ford hoped that several issues such as abortion and resentment over liberal Great Society programs would move these young voters away from the Democratic Party.

These blue-collar voters also embraced conservatives' rejection of pluralism and underlined ethnic nationalities to challenge the melting-pot theory of diversity. As the columnist Ellen Goodman defined "ethnicity" in the 1970s political terms, "they don't mean African or Mexican ethnics, better known as 'minorities.' They mean White non-WASPs . . . white working class."[100] In his 1972 book *The Rise of the Unmeltable Ethnics,* Michael Novak envisioned a conservative future for Eastern European and Catholic blue-collar voters. Amid the context of the busing crises such as Boston's that sparked violent outbreaks between working-class blacks and whites, this effort increasingly targeted younger members of this population who identified as independents and distanced themselves from what one young carpenter in Boston called the "Gold Coast liberals" who pushed for integration in working-class communities but not in their own.[101] The plan to recruit ethnic voters for Ford in 1976 pointed to the Democrats post-1968 strategy as alienating to these voters, pointing out that they "no longer consider themselves to be solid supporters of the 'New Politics of the Democratic Party.'"[102]

As Robert Moss explains, Novak's "New Ethnicity" resonated especially well with young, third- and fourth-generation, blue-collar voters who challenged their parents' assimilation; as one claimed, "we cannot be like our fathers, we cannot live like our mothers."[103] Goodman described young Americans role in what she called "ethnic chic," joking: "The ethnic celebrations at which candidates are watched to see if they can digest kielbasa seem to me to be typical third generation America."[104] Thus, when the National Republican Heritage Group (NRHG) formed in 1971 to expand the GOP reach out to ethnic voters, it quickly identified young voters as a vital component to its strategy. This organization soon became an umbrella organization to offer resources to over

Figure 16. Young Polish for Ford marching with "Fordski" banner. Young voters helped court ethnic voters for the GOP. (Ford Library)

four hundred Republican nationalities groups such as the Republican State Heritage Groups Council, the National Republican Nationalities Federation, and the Republican State Central Committee.[105] As Ford assumed the presidency, the NRHG sharpened its focus on youth outreach by organizing a conference for NRHG Young Leaders in Washington, DC, and sponsoring its young leaders' visit to the White House and meeting with Powell. Speaking with this group about their electoral role in 1976, Powell emphasized "the crucial importance of nationality and heritage in politicizing the two-thirds majority of American youth that does not attend college."[106]

Powell remembered this segment's significance during the 1972 YVP campaign and pushed to follow that electoral success when she came into the White House as the youth liaison. RNC chair George Bush agreed with Powell that despite her "great contact" with noncollege youth groups, "she points out quite correctly that there does not appear to be room in the official party structure for these people."[107] NRHG offered one potential place where this could be accomplished. NRHG leaders quickly organized its youth leadership cohort into a formalized youth program.

Targeting white ethnics, the National Republican Heritage Group Council's Youth Committee, established in 1976, provided young people, "who by preference identify with their nationality," an opportunity in Republican Party politics.[108] In their local areas, these young leaders wrote articles for local foreign-language newspapers, appeared on ethnic radio shows, and arranged cultural events that doubled as rallies. As its stated mission, one Ford aide explained: "The Ethnic Youth Committee is desperately trying to combat the overwhelming influence of the Democratic Party in the ethnic community."[109] This continued institutionalization of young voter projects indicated the youth vote's new significance in American politics. One year later, this group returned to the White House for its second annual conference as a permanent standing committee with a full vote on the NRHG executive board. In addition, this visit included speeches from Powell and the other prominent Republican figures such as assistant to the president William Baroody Jr., NRHG's cochair Mrs. Anna Chenault, and the College Republican leader and former Nixon campaigner Karl Rove.

In many ways, Nixon's young campaigners in 1972 fueled this organization. While the Nixonette leader Angela Miller became the NRHG cochair of the Activities Planning Committee, New York's YVP state chair Cathy Bertini served as the first director for the organization's newly formed Youth Division. For holdovers from the Nixon campaign such as the NRHG Youth Council's chairman Manuel Iglesias, "much of the 1972 Nixon margin over McGovern reflected a large swing of ethnic voters, particularly young workers, to the Republican presidential ticket." Reflecting on Nixon's success with this segment in 1972, the youth program attributed young voters' swing to three factors. First, PFC leaders credited "an adverse reaction to the strong counterculture aspect of the McGovern campaign." Second, antigovernment suspicion also sharpened these voters' concern with corruption and party politics. In Chicago, for example, the strategy argued, "the Republican campaign can capitalize on this same anti-machine sentiment, particularly strong among younger ethnics."[110]

Last, with the breakdown of the Democratic coalition, Republicans contributed to this shift with "careful targeting of various ethnic voters."[111] Watergate intensified young voters' rejection of party politics, as even one Young Democrats' leader in New Jersey, Salvador Desantis Jr., wrote Ford, "Apathy has reached a frightening peak and must be reversed," arguing that even his cohort could support Ford if he would just offer an honest outreach that included a meeting at the White House with a representative for an "exchange of viewpoints." Concluding with an enticing possibility, Desantis made clear, "Mr. President, today's youth respect men not party."[112]

Winning over these young voters would build on Nixon's successful rebranding of the GOP as the home for the "silent majority." Adding to Ford's motivation to court these voters heading into the general election, his outreach to white ethnic voters had already delivered in important states. One month before the convention, the New York Republican State Committee's Heritage Group's Council, representing thirty-two organizations that included nineteen nationality groups, endorsed Ford over Reagan twenty-six to one.[113]

However, here too the conditions in 1976 undermined Ford's youth effort. While Watergate "reinforced anti-Republican feelings" among ethnic voters who supported Nixon, the "Ethnic Youth Plan" also acknowledged: "The economic recession of 1974–75 had a particularly adverse impact among younger blue collar ethnic voters."[114] Of course, Ford's infamous statement during his debate with Carter that "there is no Soviet domination of Eastern Europe" did require considerable damage control. Additionally, as Powell observed in comparison, "the Republican Party is not particularly enthusiastic in its efforts to recruit young people compared to the '72 campaign which involved Young Voters for the President."[115] Still, the party's project of attracting young, Catholic, ethnic voters continued to mine Novak's New Ethnicity for Republican voters.

The Ford campaign, however, cautiously limited young voters' focus to reaching older voters—avoiding the events and concerts that marked Nixon's appeal to young voters. In contrast, Carter's campaign attempted to use his young supporters to attract a wider youth segment: as one manager bragged, "These kids are going out of their way to get involved," praising the "new awareness" that struck the young voters in 1976. The primary approach for the campaign as it headed into the final months of the campaign—car caravans of Youth for Ford volunteers—organized young supporters to guzzle across their home states in groups of ten to thirty automobiles and meet at a central location where they would attend rallies, distribute bumper stickers, set up lawn signs, and answer questions at tables in targeted locations. This approach allowed Ford's young supporters to reach people in small towns and rural America and created "personal contact with citizens who are not always in the spotlight." For example, calling their program "take Ford to the people," one caravan of over ten cars and fifty Ford youth volunteers from Florida State University left the steps of the state capitol to stop in counties west of Tallahassee and of course, finished in Panama City.[116] Still, a September Harris poll showed youth leaning heavily, fifty-eight to thirty-seven, for Carter.[117] Ford represented a connection to Richard Nixon for young voters who participated in 1972, and Carter offered these resentful youth an alternative described as "folksy," "down to earth," and "non-political."[118] The year 1976 failed to live up to the buzz around registration, attending rallies, and voting that young Americans embraced during the first youth vote in 1972. But a new youth politics was emerging, as activism became professionalized. As one student said, "There's some political organization, but it's not like four years ago." But while the large-scale activism had waned, something else had taken its place, as a student paper explained: "Campus activism hasn't exactly flourished in 1976. Most of the politicking has been left to student hacks, the future ward leaders and state senators."[119]

1976 and Vote Splitters

In the end, while Carter won as predicted, Ford closed the gap in the final months and lost by 2 percent of the popular vote. Crucial to this victory, Carter won over 54 percent of the under-thirty vote.[120] Still, the election results revealed the post-Watergate realities for these young voters. The total youth vote exceeded expectations, barely, as 45 percent of the under-twenty-nine segment turned out at the polls. Although well over 60 percent of the college students cast a ballot, the noncollege youth vote fell to less than 40 percent.[121]

Dividing the youth vote by age, over half the twenty-one-to-twenty-nine-year-olds voted, choosing the Democrat 56 to 44 percent. The eighteen-to-twenty-four-year-old voter turnout fell considerably from over 55 percent to 48 percent.[122] Among black voters under twenty-four, only 26 percent voted.[123] Surprisingly, Ford fared better than Carter with eighteen-to-twenty-one-year-olds, who supported the president 51 to 49 percent.[124] Even college polls showed mostly eighteen-year-old freshmen considerably more supportive of Ford than upperclassmen, who sided with Carter.[125] Meanwhile, Carter won 52 percent of the student vote, splitting the working youth of college age.[126] Still, this youngest segment of the youth vote revealed the steepest drop off, decreasing from 48 percent in 1972 to 38 percent.[127] While the novelty of first-time voting for this age group clearly wore off five years after the voting age was dropped to eighteen, the post-Watergate apathy also undermined these voters' enthusiasm. As one nonregistered eighteen-year-old complained: "How is my vote going to affect the outcome of that foul bureaucratic machine called the election?"[128] Times had changed dramatically from the optimism that surrounded the previous presidential election's youth politics.

One youth politics trend continued from 1972—as Democrats outnumbered Republicans, 37 percent to 22 percent, 41 percent of young voters claimed no party affiliation—as Ford continued some of Nixon's success and won the majority of independents. Carter regained the Democratic Party's victory with labor, winning 62 percent of union household votes,[129] but this group's shift to the Democratic Party showed its weakness as Ford continued the GOP's inroads with traditionally Democratic white ethnic voters. Most significantly, young blue-collar voters showed the decline of party loyalty. In blue-collar industrial regions such as Mon Valley, Pennsylvania, where Nixon won in twenty-seven steel towns, Ford won only five "bedroom communities" in the bellwether region. While Carter won the majority of young voters in this region, these same voters also supported the moderate Republican H. John Heinz III for Senate, proving to one observer: "If it was young voters who put Carter in the Mon Valley, [then] they apparently have learned early to split-vote."[130] In addition, Ford matched Carter with noncollege youth, especially with blue-collar Catholics who had consistently given the Democratic Party over 60 percent of its votes before 1972. As one journalist observed, "Catholics were the soft-underbelly of the Carter-Mondale strategy for reconstructing the Roosevelt coalition."[131] Rather than a sudden, issue-based shift to the Republican Party on abortion, the youth effort shows the GOP's growth was gradual and contingent on a wider party effort to undermine Democratic loyalties.

Reflecting on the loss, one journalist explained that "conservatism began to be confused with racism by minority and young voters," and that "too much of Republican campaign appeals were directed at middle aged, white and reasonably affluent Americans."[132] While critics claimed Ford's camp had lost its moderate touch, those on the right saw differently. As Donald Critchlow argues, "If Ford had done more to placate the Right . . . he might have unified the party going into the

1976 presidential election, and a united Republican party probably would have defeated Jimmy Carter."[133] Thus, if the Republican Party could channel this blue-collar frustration with government and win over independents while offering a candidate capable of courting the New Right, a new majority could be rekindled.

1980 and Reagan's Youth Vote

During Governor Ronald Reagan's campaign for the Republican Party's presidential nomination in 1980, he overwhelmed his competition in the GOP's primaries. Reagan won the New Hampshire primary in a landslide, however, he only split the youth vote with his closest competitor, George H. W. Bush.[134] Even worse, Bush won 59 percent of the voters under thirty when he beat Reagan during the Pennsylvania primary.[135]

Concerns about Reagan's youth effort pushed his campaign manager, Bill Casey, to recruit a former College Republican leader and youth expert, Morton Blackwell, to head the Youth for Reagan campaign. Dubbed "the eyes and ears of the New Right," Blackwell quickly diagnosed the campaign's problems: "no student voter registration," "no program to train pro-Reagan student activists," and "no budget to accomplish anything significant." Still, Blackwell held out hope: "If implemented, the program of mass based youth political organization will have a very major impact on the general election."[136] In two ways, Blackwell delivered.

First, Reagan's youth campaign turned out volunteers and votes. Youth for Reagan included two hundred thousand volunteers and twenty-six paid coordinators, as Reagan won 44 percent of the under-thirty segment. Because the former moderate Republican and independent candidate John Anderson won 11 percent, this was enough to split the youth vote with President Jimmy Carter.[137] While this result fell short of Nixon's youth effort that won close to 50 percent of young voters in 1972, Youth for Reagan rebuilt the organization YVP had developed and ensured Reagan's eventual success with an overwhelming majority of young voters in 1984. In addition, Youth for Reagan contributed to the candidate's image. Blackwell predicted a robust youth campaign would "defuse the residual 'age issue'" as Reagan vied to be the oldest sitting president in American history.[138]

Second, College Republicans attributed their success to the party leaders who funded the project. Predictably, Bill Brock gained acclaim as one editorial from the *College Republican* labeled him the "Architect of the Republican Victory, 1980" and claimed: "His commitment to the youth of our party has been without parallel." Praising the RNC chairman's generous budgeting for youth programs, the article explains that the approach Brock formulated in the early 1970s, as Nixon's youth director, "realized that a majority party is not only built on tactics of get out the vote and candidate appeal, but strategies based on growth . . . training future leaders and involving thousands of college men and women for the first time in politics."[139]As Craig Shirley claims, Brock "would become one the most effective chairmen of the GOP's history, credited with bringing it into the modern political world." Coming into this position in 1977, Brock focused on rebuilding from the youth level, as only 11 percent of young voters belonged to the Republican Party.[140]

Despite Brock's generosity, the funding differences between Youth for Reagan and the YVP stand out. Under the constraints of new campaign finance laws after Watergate, budgeting emerged as the first consideration for any program. As Ford experienced, federal election laws held Reagan's campaign to $30 million, one fourth of Nixon's budget. While Nixon's demise stigmatized the Republican brand and stunted the GOP's growing efforts with young voters, its effects on campaign reform also hampered Youth for Reagan's resources. In addition, the Reagan-Bush Committee's chief house counsel, Loren Smith, found the YAF "linkage" to Robert Heckman's Fund for a Conservative Majority "is sufficiently close as to raise possible legal questions." Smith decided Youth for Reagan and YAF should not share "any organizational ties" beyond personnel "not connected with an independent expenditure organization."[141]

In addition, Reagan's campaign managers looked to moderate youth on campuses and in the GOP's expanding southern and urban white ethnic constituencies, as one aide warned, "The campus YAF image is right-wing extremist."[142] While Nixon and Ford failed to win over the YAF, Reagan pushed the conservative youth organization away. Thus, to limit costs, avoid scrutiny under the new campaign laws, and expand the GOP's reach on campuses, Blackwell focused on the College Republicans' role and the campaign's influence on party building. Still Blackwell remained confident, bragging, "The leaders of the Carter and Anderson youth efforts may have more funds than are proposed in this national Youth for Reagan effort, but we will clobber them."[143] Dismissing Nixon's 1972 campaign accurately as "expensive" and inaccurately as "useless," Blackwell claimed that Young Voters for the President consisted mostly of "chartered buses, hired halls for youth rallies, hired bands to entertain the bussed in students, and very little in the way of work done."[144]

Aside from these differences, both Nixon's YVP and Youth for Reagan courted a wide range of youth beyond the campuses, as Reagan continued this appeal to these traditionally Democratic young voter groups. The Republican Party's youth effort continued its regional focus and success in Sunbelt states that reflected the GOP's opportunity to expand into a majority party. Although many of these leaders came from traditional sources—TAR, YR, CR, and YAF—Youth for Reagan also sought young activists from organizations such as National Republican Heritage Youth Group Council, Student Right-to-Life groups, libertarian student groups, the InterCollegiate Studies, and Hillel Foundation. As Blackwell wrote to youth organization leaders, "There can be no policy of 'Republicans only' or 'long-time Reagan supporters only.' We are recruiting young people who want to help us elect Ronald Reagan President of the United States. Period."[145] Specifically, the new Republican auxiliary, the Heritage Youth Committee, gained favored status, as the campaign literature stated: "Every effort should be made to place each and every Heritage Youth volunteer into a meaningful Republican Party Organization and/or campaign as soon as possible."[146] While Reagan could rely on southern youth, he also returned the urban white ethnic voters to the Republicans.

Last, both YVP director Ken Rietz's plan for "peer group pressure" and Blackwell's Youth for Reagan "mass-based" organization relied on a separate, "semi-autonomous" youth campaign that targeted recruitment, well-trained leadership, and a mass media effort to attract moderate young voters beyond the original, conservative youth organizations that previously staffed the GOP campaigns. While Blackwell dismissed Nixon's youth campaign, the structural focus on creating a separate youth leadership stands out as an obvious influence. Blackwell's coined phrase, "Give 'em a title and get 'em involved," described the same inclusive sentiment that Rietz's campus activists in the YVP carried into the 1972 election. Following Nixon's lead, the GOP offered young Americans leadership opportunities, patriotism, and prosperity.

The Takeover: Blackwell and the YAF

Morton Blackwell quickly emerged as the most qualified, loyal, and willing person to organize Reagan's youth effort in 1980. Blackwell's career began in 1960 when he led Students for Nixon and Lodge at Louisiana State University. In 1964, as one of the eleven original members of the National Youth for Goldwater steering committee, Blackwell served as the youngest delegate to the national convention. Though he supported Reagan's failed bid for the GOP nomination in 1968, Blackwell eventually worked closely with Nixon's campaign as the executive director of the College Republican National Committee and then consulted with Nixon's youth effort in 1972.[147] The need for young leaders to organize Blackwell's "mass-based" youth campaign made him an even more attractive candidate for the job, as he founded a PAC in 1972, Committee for Responsible Youth Politics (CRYP), which "trained, placed and often funded the youth coordinators for conservative candidates."[148] While the Youth for Ford and GOP campaign for young voters struggled to organize its resources after Watergate, youth politics matured and turned right through institutions such as the newsletter *Right Report* published by Blackwell and fellow young conservatives such as Richard Viguerie.

Blackwell worked for Reagan's 1976 presidential campaign as the floor leader during the state convention in Virginia, and at the Missouri convention he devised the winning strategy that resulted in Reagan's upset sweep there. At the request of Reagan's campaign aide John Sears, Blackwell suggested a plan for the Reagan youth effort in 1975, though, as Blackwell claimed, "a critical element of publicity for Reagan student support was vetoed by campaign so that 1976 youth effort never could snowball on campus."[149] While Blackwell argued that the Youth for Reagan effort in 1976 failed because of internal campaign decisions, competing with Ford and Jimmy Carter on campuses and the larger backlash to Watergate also made student voters elusive for the GOP.[150]

In 1980, when Reagan became the clear frontrunner during the initial primaries, Reagan's campaign managers again turned to Blackwell to revive youth politics in the GOP. Explaining how "mass-based youth politics" worked, Blackwell bragged about his system's ambitious goal to "organize on behalf of a candidate a significant percentage of virtually every local student body, both college and high school." The plan ambitiously promised to yield considerable results: to place recruitment tables at 2,750 of 3,300 colleges, to canvass two million of the five million students in America, to identify and register six hundred thousand students who supported Reagan, to recruit roughly 375,000 student volunteers for Reagan, to process two hundred thousand absentee ballots for Reagan, to establish Youth for Reagan organizations in "virtually all congressional districts," and to enlist twenty-five thousand nonstudent activists (over four hundred thousand members combined).[151] The campaign's managers quickly approved his plan in mid-April, and Blackwell assumed control of the operation immediately.

Staffing leadership positions became the first priority in filling out the complex structure necessary to execute Blackwell's system. In Blackwell's first move as Reagan's newly hired youth adviser, he hired Steve Antosh as the Youth for Reagan national coordinator. As the twenty-four-year-old chairman of Blackwell's CRYP, Antosh had risen through the political ranks as a prominent College Republican at Oklahoma State University. Most important, as CRYP focused on organizing youth politics and supplying conservatives with well-trained and determined young organizers, Antosh shared Blackwell's emphasis on leadership schools.

The program Antosh inherited had many problems, as Blackwell summarized: "Thus far, the 1980 Reagan campaign has had a useless youth effort."[152] Blackwell carefully devised a structure that harnessed the various organizations and broadened Reagan's appeal through cooperation. At the top of the pyramid in the "single campus canvass structure," the Reagan campus coordinator shared control of political activities with the CR chairman, the local Republican House and Republican Senate candidates' youth campaign organizers. This system created clear lines of communication from Antosh through the four national regional coordinators to the fourteen paid field staff they oversaw. Thus, with little expense, directions from the most elite organizational levels could reach the rank-and-file volunteers about short-notice projects such as crowd swelling, media activities, literature drops, and poster making. Beyond its significance in Youth for Reagan, leaders intended this system to "create a strong campus organization for all cooperating GOP candidates," "increase existing club [CR] membership" and begin an "organized means of rapid, personal contact after the elections between CRs and all students."[153]

Reagan had already developed his powerful influence on College Republicans' leadership. In 1977, Roger Stone became the CR president and assured the organizations' loyalty to the governor. As a former young CRP operative in 1972, Stone had begun his career ominously when he was cited by the Senate Watergate Committee for sabotage and espionage. In 1976, however, Stone headed Reagan's youth campaign and then served as the National Conservative Political Action Committee (NCPAC) treasurer. Observing Stone's rise to power, columnist Robert Novak claimed, "the Reagan inner circle" had engineered a takeover of the CR that built "a party within a party."[154] Thus, even in the early stages of the CR revival, Reagan's campaign further institutionalized and professionalized conservative youth politics in the GOP.

Beyond the CR apparatus, Reagan's campaign meant to build the party's future managers. "Not only is it a source for workers," the Youth for Reagan Canvass Manual claimed, but the Organization Committee concept also "has uncovered a crop of new leaders each place it has been tried."[155] In addition, Antosh and Blackwell intended to tap non-student youth groups such as the Future Farmers of America and 4-H for positions in the senior campaign such as "precinct captain, telephone boiler room director, and projects chairmen."[156] As Blackwell aimed to replace the Youth for Reagan leadership and structure, he moved Reagan's youth campaign away from the YAF.

Dating back to the beginning of his political career, Ronald Reagan's popularity with young conservatives had few rivals. During his 1966 campaign for governor in California, young conservatives such as Young Americans for Freedom rallied to his cause, as that election inspired the first incarnation of Youth for Reagan. Reagan's victory stirred this youth cadre across the nation to recruit the governor for a presidential run, as they established Youth for Reagan offices in several states.[157] In protest against President Richard Nixon's plans to visit China before his reelection in 1972, YAF leaders formed Youth for Reagan chapters in thirty-seven states even as the governor declared allegiance to the president and asked them to stop campaigning on his behalf.[158]

During the YAF's 1979 mock nominating convention, Reagan won 78 percent of the delegates.[159] Ironically, just as their chosen leader finally became the frontrunner for the GOP primary, the YAF lost its role in Reagan's youth politics. Reagan's initial appeal for a national youth vote suffered as his youth campaign, Youth for Reagan, relied on the conservative youth organization YAF. YAF members gave Reagan the moniker "Republican Messiah" and saw the governor's candidacy as their opportunity to finally put one of their own in the Oval Office.[160]

However, political, economic, and organizational factors shut the YAF out of the Reagan campaign.

Blackwell complained that Youth for Reagan's campaign became too reliant on this cadre. Reagan himself had contributed to the YAF leaderships' significant role in the campaign after the New Hampshire primary, when he called the organization's national chairman, James Lacy, to "express his appreciation for YAF's efforts there and in the other early primary states." However, Lacy complained, once Blackwell arrived the Reagan campaign stopped returning his calls.[161] While reliable, Reagan's campaign eyed a national campaign that would extend its reach to other, less ideologically driven voters. This effort became even more significant as Reagan's critics questioned whether he would control the party's "right-wing" or become "the prisoner of a determined minority."[162]

Reagan's advisers looked to youth politics to defuse the "Reagan-as-bad-guy" myth. Reagan himself made this line of attack challenging, as one columnist admitted, "by himself, Reagan makes a pretty poor excuse for a menace," and Congressman Mickey Edwards (R-Oklahoma), director of the policy task force for Ronald Reagan's 1980 presidential campaign, agreed that Democrats could not paint Reagan as another Goldwater extremist: "His style and personality just make it impossible to sell him as an ogre." Instead, Reagan's opponents emphasized his vulnerability to his conservative supporters and advisers.[163] To ensure that "the less ideological elements of the effort be given maximum exposure and the more conservative elements less," Edwards called for more visibility to Reagan's work with youth-friendly "'acceptable' Republicans" such as Bill Brock and George Bush.[164] As Antosh recalled after the election, older voters found it "very hard to believe the barrage of mudslinging about Reagan being a right wing crazy when young people so consistently expressed a preference for Reagan."[165] The emphasis on the Youth for Reagan's image benefits helped court the campaign's targeted constituency in the middle.

While Craig Shirley explains that Blackwell's appointment caused a "hue and cry from Washington's establishment Republicans,"[166] this plan also angered YAF leaders as the organization's chairman complained to Reagan's national campaign director, William Casey: "I must admit my disappointment at not having been consulted, and my surprise at the establishment of any youth operation that does not take advantage of the organizational structure of the YAF."[167] YAF leaders quickly submitted their alternative youth plan to Casey, hoping they could build themselves more clearly into the Youth for Reagan structure with a carefully detailed approach that outlined activities, budgeting, and resources necessary to execute a successful youth campaign. Claiming, "We are thus in somewhat of a quandary as to the current status of the Reagan youth effort," YAF leaders reminded Blackwell, "The cadre is in place, ready to move."[168]

Youth for Reagan leaders never granted the "green light" that YAF organizers desired. While the YAF plan called for a "cadre-based effort," Blackwell dismissed this approach. A "youth cadre campaign," argued Blackwell, "is possible where the candidate has a strong identification with either the liberal or conservative viewpoint. In such cases, it is possible to attract numbers of students who are committed to the candidate's philosophy." As the GOP learned in 1964, however, this required a level of exclusivity that limited the program's size and impact. "It is too big a country, and the aggregate resources employed are too massive for a few hundred willing hands to affect the outcome one way or the other."[169]

Even as Reagan furthered their cause, Blackwell reported to Reagan adviser Max Hugel: "I have spent much of the last week holding hands with outraged conservatives." Young critics from the right complained, "There is no place in this campaign now for movement conservatives," and they warned Blackwell, "They have been using you to keep us in line through the convention. Watch. They will drop you now."[170] This concern proved wrong, or misplaced. Perhaps, for YAF leaders, they were learning the ironic reality that the increased roles New Right conservatives played in Reagan's campaign moved the party closer to YAF's philosophy as their organization became less necessary. As Wayne Thorburn explains its fractured state in the early 1980s, "part of YAF's difficulties arose from its own success."[171]

As YAF leaders bemoaned Youth for Reagan's plan, CR leaders understood that Blackwell's campus-based approach would benefit their organization the most. Separating themselves from YAF's cantankerous leaders, CR chairman Stephen Gibble wrote Casey: "To alleviate any possible ambiguity, the College Republican National Committee *supports* the Reagan Youth Plan developed by Morton Blackwell," while complimenting Blackwell's experience and understanding as "unparalleled" and the plan as "ambitious, realistic and cost effective."[172] While Barry Goldwater relied on YAF's organization to build his youth campaign in 1964, Reagan's campaign managers in 1980 had to keep their distance.

As a former YAF leader, Antosh reluctantly broke the news, claiming, "this decision is not at my request or to my liking."[173] Unfortunately for YAF, Youth for Reagan leadership's close relationship with the RNC fit neatly into Blackwell's larger emphasis on institutionalizing youth politics behind the party and its candidates.

Recruitment and Training: "A Broad Base"

During the summer in 1980, the Youth for Reagan training schools began to recruit and initiate young people into the campaign. First, these schools served as tryouts for sixty full-time coordinators that Blackwell's plan required.[174] In addition, Reagan's campaign developed its own youth organization and leadership because these auxiliary groups' membership had steadily declined over the decade. In 1979, of the over three thousand four-year colleges, only 670 could claim a College Republican club.[175] Putting the leadership schools directly under Reagan for President control opened up the training program and positions to young people outside the traditional organizations that fed the party such as the YR, CR, and YAF.

The schools had two main goals. First, they trained young activists in campaign tactics and organization. The seminars were not "rah-rah sessions at all," said Antosh; "we teach seminars on how to find volunteers, how to plug them into the regular projects of the campaign, and how to do special projects with students."[176] Over two days, the Youth Staff Training Schools covered every aspect of the mass-based campaign: the structure to set up Youth for Reagan headquarters, ways to coordinate the campaign with other Republican candidates' youth programs, and how to involve nonstudents. The schools focused primarily on the canvassing process, requiring first that campus organizers gather volunteers who supported either Republicans, Reagan, or both. While this approach opened the campaign up to young independents who supported Reagan for reasons beyond his ideology—personality, trust, and leadership—it did not try to convert voters, as the plan flatly states its limits: "Do not argue or engage in long conversations with one individual." "It is not worth the time and energy to argue with opposition supporters. Forget them!"[177]

The schools also enabled Youth for Reagan to select the full-time coordinators, as Antosh claimed: "Based on the exercises and tests covering the material presented at the school, decisions can be made on filling the sixty youth slots on the youth field staff team." The schools proved to be a success on all fronts, as the students' evaluation forms showed the overwhelming majority found the training "outstandingly useful" and the sourcebook "excellent." In addition, Antosh claimed that the first school held before the convention at George Washington University included "at least twenty top-notch students whom we would feel very confident in placing in Reagan youth field staff positions."[178] The training proposal intimated the GOP's newfound confidence in a youth majority. "Leadership participation must not be limited only to those with a history of activism in GOP youth groups or conservative organizations," the report argued. "Youth for Reagan must have as broad a base as possible."[179] Ever since Nixon's landslide in 1972, the GOP maintained its hopes for a coalition that included young working-class voters.

Scholarship on ethnic voters in the 1970s has shown how the realities of America's faltering economy and the socially conservative appeal of the GOP fractured the New Deal coalition.[180] Examining the GOP's reach to white, ethnic working-class voters explains the mechanics of this transition. Influential Republican pollster Bob Teeter criticized politicians' shared stereotype of the blue-collar voter as balding, fifty-five years old, and a World War II veteran, claiming: "They are more likely to be twenty-four years old, wear a rag around their head and drive a van to work."[181] Reaching out to these young voters followed the opportunities Nixon and Ford cultivated with their own youth efforts.

The GOP appeal for America's twenty million ethnic voters looked to young people to break party loyalties that had handed Democratic candidates success with this segment. Attempting to rebuild the party in the Watergate aftermath, Bill Brock's strategy as the chairman of the RNC borrowed from the YVP playbook. In meetings that the RNC named Concord Conferences, teams of RNC staffers recruited "young people who look like the people from their community." After all, Brock explained, "Polish people need Polish leaders." These conferences trained young people on activism and recruited them into local offices. As a result, Brock claimed, voters would think, "hey, Republicans look like us." "That was where I think it [YVP] made lasting differences. Give that community a voice."[182]

After working on the YVP campaign, Fred Asbell continued working with Brock as the RNC chair and testified to the Concord Conferences' success: "I cannot begin to tell you how many places we had gone, all manner of folks, who say, 'I got involved in politics through a Concord Conference, and today I am a member of congress.'" Asbell noted that Concord Conferences did much the same thing as the YVP, focusing instead on "local elections," allowing the national party to recruit and train people for school boards elections and elect state legislators to "build a farm team." Similarly, the Heritage youth plan utilized recognizable young Republicans from each nationality group, "whose name ought to be familiar in local heritage circles."[183] This effort capitalized on what the Heritage Council called a "tremendous reawakening of ethnic spirit" with a "special emphasis on their cultural uniqueness."[184] Republicans hoped to use this "uniqueness" to peel away these traditionally Democratic voters.

This effort aided the main strategy to win traditionally Democratic voters in industrial regions, or the Rustbelt, as Casey explained young ethnics helped make Reagan's campaign "positive," claiming: "We need to change this public perception of Reagan as conservative. He is pragmatic."[185] The Heritage Youth Committee's literature claimed, "We are the future and we must be involved in all aspects of the Party," quoting the prominent conservative Catholic leader Michael Novak's prediction, "The young are more ripe for the new ethnicity than the old. . . . The new ethnicity is oriented toward the future, not the past."[186]

Republican leaders saw the Heritage Youth as an opportunity to continue growing the Republican Party through young voters. As one recruitment letter stressed, "The Party acknowledges the potential of the Youth groups who possess an immeasurable amount of energy and talent . . . to accomplish pertinent changes within the Party. The Heritage Youth Committee wants to make those changes at the 'grassroots' level." Growing the party's constituency through young voters, Heritage's youth effort claimed that it "opens a door of the party that best relates to young people who 'recognize their roots.'"[187] As for the YVP's inroads into traditional Democratic territory, those voters already discovered the GOP as an alternative. Tim Carey, a former YVP leader, worked in the 1980 campaign for both Reagan and Senator Al D'Amato (R-New York) on Staten Island, where Reagan split its white working-class voters in New York City. Carey appreciated this relationship. "I don't have any data to support that position," Carey admitted, "but my mother-in-law research; in bars, veteran halls, with blue collar workers etc., leads me to believe that the YVP's, in some ways led to the 1980 Reagan Democrats phenomenon."

The Republican appeal to these ethnic young voters in 1980 rested on three central themes. First, the Heritage Youth Committee tapped into urban white ethnics' resentment over issues such as busing and taxes. One Heritage flyer celebrated the unmeltable ethnics and smaller government by stressing, "The Republican Party is the party of the individual, we want to keep you unique. Free. Independent. Without unnecessary government restraints." Second, the Heritage appeal offered job opportunities in registration efforts, canvassing, working in headquarters and research, as the flyer continued, "There's a whole open road of opportunity—just waiting to be conquered." Last, the outreach included a cultural appeal. "But it's not all politics," Heritage Republican Youth advertised, as the campaign included community action projects, heritage festivals, and folk dances.[188] While scholars argue that working-class voters cared mostly about racial resentment or jobs, Republicans also offered young ethnics carefully targeted appeals to nationality and culture.

The party cherished these volunteers, as the program's instructions about using them indicated young ethnic campaign workers had earned a favored status. In a letter to prospective Heritage Youth volunteers, the campaign announced: "We feel that it is necessary to open the door for young Heritage people to get involved in the Party's activities."[189] Once they signed up to join the cause, the Heritage Youth Committee Volunteer Recruitment and Organization Program explained, these volunteers held special value and deserved extra attention, suggesting: "Campaign assignments that would include the Heritage Youth Committee volunteers should be stressed so that a recruited volunteer does not feel neglected or ignored." Indeed, former Heritage Youth leader Toula Drakatos catapulted into one of five highly desired and paid positions in the CR's Victory Force '80 program.

To support this effort, Heritage Youth Committee leaders recruited volunteers and established training schools to teach young Heritage members how to campaign in ethnic communities using "native tongues . . . usage of ethnic fraternal organizations, festivals and churches."[190] Thus, young voters continued to play a crucial role in rebuilding the GOP after Watergate and pushed the party to redouble its efforts for traditionally Democratic voters. Beyond the Heritage groups, Youth for Reagan leaders also recruited groups such as the Future Farmers and students from vocational schools who overwhelmingly supported the governor's probusiness and antigovernment stance.

As Blackwell explained, "one of the significant benefits of a youth campaign is its ability to garner a considerable amount of media attention which would otherwise have been lost to the campaign." All youth training schools included instruction in the "art of writing news releases" to increase news coverage of Reagan's campaign and "reinforce the Governor's image as a youth-supported candidate."[191] This plan relied on traditional grassroots organization tactics; it also met new expectations for image politics in 1980.

Convention and Youth Activity

The youth vote held a different significance for each candidate in this election. As Blackwell explained, while President Carter tried to revive his "status as the college cult candidate" that provided early momentum in 1976, independent candidate John Anderson "counts on continued campus support to provide credibility to his campaign." For Reagan, "While his opponents are likely to maintain that Reagan's conservative ideology is antiquated," Blackwell suggested, "Reagan's mass-based youth support will lend an air of freshness to his public image."[192] The RNC in Detroit proved the perfect stage to enter into the mass media phase of Youth for Reagan. Preparing for this schedule, Reagan's national chairman of Youth for Reagan delegation, Donna Tuttle, had two weeks' notice on the list of the over fifteen hundred young people attending the convention. The young voters' carefully planned presence in the convention lessened the stigma that all GOP leaders sought to shake. One columnist called Youth for Reagan "the vanishing cream on the face of a middle-aged convention" and observed that "the world saw a jiggling, squealing mass of Reaganite enthusiasm."[193]

The Republican National Committee program director, former YVP director Ken Rietz, admitted: "The whole idea is to make the event into a TV production instead of a convention."[194] This approach reversed the 1976 strategy that Blackwell claimed "had a virtual prohibition against any publicity, on or off campus, regarding the student support of Ronald Reagan." Blackwell emphasized that "kids are photogenic and exciting. . . . Even the Geritol ads featured young looking-old people." In addition, "Evidence of student support, if fed back to the campus has a snow ball effect" that makes the campaign "the thing to do."[195] While young voters meant to moderate Reagan's image, the seventy-year-old's "age problem" made young voters especially important as well. As Laura Kalman writes, "Both Republican elites and reporters seemed doubtful that America would choose someone so many viewed as an elderly, out of it right winger."[196]

This high publicity strategy elevated Youth for Reagan members' role during the convention. Starting the celebration before the nomination, Reagan for President convention planners arranged a youth rally with Donnie and Marie Osmond performing for thousands of young voters at the Ford Auditorium the night before the nomination. Before the rally, as Youth for Reagan delegates filled in the audience, the rally coordinator exhorted, "We're going to raise some pandemonium for Governor Reagan. . . . We're going to have all kinds of hell-raising." One observer claimed, "The energy they throw off could microwave the Republican elephant." The Osmonds then joined the rally and explained why the nation needed Reagan to win. Telling the crowd, "We have just returned from an extensive world tour," Donny recalled "the decline of the United States' prestige and respect throughout the world." The Osmonds encouraged this youth to vote for a change, claiming: "I think we can safely say that all of us want to make America great again."[197]

While not everyone could be an Osmond, Reagan's campaign suggested the Osmonds' comments should emphasize that they "are a part of the kids all over the country . . . doing the same thing the kids in the audience were doing."[198] Connecting celebrities' lives with young Americans' economic concerns, Donny slammed Carter for the rising inflation, unemployment, trade imbalance, high interest rates, and deficit spending. As the twenty-three-year-old star pointed out, "I am buying a home just like everyone else and I am paying the same high interest rates."[199] This image-focused appeal emphasized the Republican Party's effort to become the more trustworthy steward of the economy and the proper inheritor of the incipient Yuppie voter segment.

Despite their shiny image, Youth for Reagan did not always live up to their reputation. For entertainment, Youth for Reagan planned wholesome activities such as a Detroit River cruise, tours of the Ford and General Motors plants, shows, and dances. But, even though Blackwell's convention plan emphasized "sufficient supervision that youth supporters will be kept constructively busy and out of trouble," several Youth for Reagan members vandalized their Eastern Michigan University room, destroying over thirty pillows to use the stuffing as decorative sand during a "simulated beach party."[200] Youth for Reagan leaders in another dorm had to institute a curfew to curtail "wee-hours rowdyism." According to Youth for Reagan delegates, adults feared any discipline for these "excesses" would alienate young supporters who contributed the precious commodity—enthusiasm. Reagan for President leaders hoped the more prominent image of the Osmonds and "clean-cut," "nicely dressed and spotless" young Americans made the most noticeable impression on convention watchers.[201]

While these young conservatives found plenty to celebrate at this convention, they also had work to do. The youth delegation formed convention demonstrations, headed a Youth for Reagan news bureau and newspaper, and distributed literature for the senior campaign.[202] In their spare time, the youth delegation members attended "addresses by top political mangers and candidates" and campaign management programs.[203] During the convention, the Young Republican chairman announced "Operation Persuasion" to register nonvoters and enlist independents or Democrats to vote for Reagan—a costly project that relied on a "massive media blitz to convince young Americans that the GOP wanted them."[204] Though Representative Jim Leach (R-Iowa) admitted in 1980, "The Republican label is not an advantage on campus," he noted, "but it's no longer a millstone."[205] "Six years ago, youth were the greatest reservoir of Democratic votes," Leach continued optimistically. "Now they are the greatest reservoir of independent voters."[206] After Ronald Reagan's campaign, those young independents completed their transition. The candidate-focused effort to expand Reagan's constituency beyond Republicans became clear during one workshop for students in the youth delegation. Advising Youth for Reagan volunteers on campus recruitment, one CR leader suggested, "Don't admit you are a Republican unless pressed."[207]

Inside the convention, Youth for Reagan's more visible effort also aided their candidate's image, as the plan reminded them to "generate enthusiasm," and "provide photogenic proof of Reagan support."[208] The party emphasized young people during the proceedings, as three youth leaders spoke during prime convention time. The desired crowd effect, spontaneity, required a balance of organization. As Blackwell explained that while "hand-printed signs would look more spontaneous . . . young supporters need some directions on where to assemble and what slogans to chant to be most effective."[209] One columnist described Youth for

Reagan as "legions of freshly scrubbed young faces, all carefully coached and choreographed . . . to stream through the entrances and onto the convention floor at just the right moment," explaining, "their job was to appear on television as often as possible to convince any young TV viewer that youth is behind 69 year-old Ronald Reagan."[210] In addition, the GOP emphasized youth's diversity, when former Texas governor and Democrat John Connally spoke to a Youth for Reagan gathering: "The delegates here represent the broadest base of working class people of any Republican Convention."[211] Still, Reagan's campaign managers came to a crossroads with the youth effort after the convention, as the budget decisions they made on Blackwell's plan dictated the youth campaign's size and approach.

After Reagan's campaign spent the bulk of its allowed expenditures in the early primary process, the original proposal for a $300,000 program—1 percent of Reagan's available coffers—became unrealistic. After Hugel told Blackwell that the Youth for Reagan budget was on the chopping block in late July, Blackwell protested, "I confess to being profoundly disturbed by our conversation today." "If the program falls through it will be a tragedy for our campaign and for the Republican Party."[212] Blackwell produced a scaled-back proposal that could function with a $150,000 budget.

Fortunately for Youth for Reagan, a GOP youth vote pioneer held the purse strings for the party. Reagan's campaign managers easily convinced the Republican National Committee chairman, Bill Brock, to house and compensate Youth for Reagan coordinators as they claimed the funding could be considered "non-allocable" because of the party-building aspect of this effort. This enhanced the growing connection and institutional role the CR played in the GOP, as it had split off from the Young Republicans only in 1970 and shortly became the third official auxiliary for the Republican Party in 1972. After Hugel's make-or-break meeting with Brock, the longtime youth expert predictably pledged to help Youth for Reagan. Attesting to the youth program's cooperation with the larger party efforts, the RNC matched Reagan's campaign funds and dedicated $75,000 to Youth for Reagan to be spent on salaries.

Finally, in mid-August, Youth for Reagan began to place over sixty coordinators in locations determined by careful polling. With this crisis averted, a reenergized Antosh promised Hugel: "Max, it has been a long, hard struggle. . . . We will put together a youth effort that you will be immensely proud of."[213] Youth for Reagan, scaling back its original plans for a national campaign, focused its resources on a more limited group of swing states: Texas, Florida, Louisiana, Mississippi, Pennsylvania, Ohio, Illinois, New Jersey, and Washington. In these states alone, Youth for Reagan recruited twelve thousand "hard core volunteers, each of whom volunteered on an average of 20 hours per week" and identified one hundred thousand "strong supporters" to participate in special events and mock elections.[214]

Immediately after Youth for Reagan avoided a budget crisis and began its campaign program, the results proved the mass-based plan's merit. With its newly hired staff that included twenty-six coordinators, regional coordinators, two secretaries, a youth events scheduler, and a youth media director, Youth for Reagan campaigners started to implement the latter stages of Blackwell's mass-based strategy. The first step here, according to Blackwell's cautious and targeted approach, required a Nixonian polling system to identify the issues and groups for Youth for Reagan. Foreign affairs, unemployment, and inflation quickly surfaced as the issues that motivated young voters. On the positive side, young people perceived Reagan's strengths as a leadership image and an ability to improve the economy. For negatives, however, the polls showed young people held a "stereotyped perception of Reagan as right-wing conservative."[215] Student positions on social issues especially concerned Reagan's campaign managers. While the national support for the ERA reached 55 percent, 65 percent of young voters wanted the amendment. Concerning abortion, though the issue divided the nation, 60 percent of youth favored it. As a solution, the student campaign took every effort "to portray the candidate as a compassionate man concerned with people and their problems."[216]

Reagan also shared the Nixon youth campaign's emphasis on polling and public relations strategies as Richard Nixon's former media and advertising expert from 1972, Richard Dailey, headed Reagan's version of the November Group, "Campaign '80." To court first-time, noncollege voters, Reagan's campaign invested heavily in television advertisements. Teeter predicted that many alienated young Americans who did not vote in 1976 because of Watergate and Vietnam would cast their first votes in 1980, claiming those with less than a college education "are not going to go through their entire lives not participating in the process."[217] The Republicans launched an unprecedented $8.5 million television campaign that targeted young high-school-educated voters. Here, the campaign's emphasis on voters' attitudes also directed their commercials' messages. Whether these ads showed Reagan speaking about peace during the convention or about America's openness to immigrants on Liberty Island, the advertisements emphasized his audience's youth. In addition, the focus on young voters' attitudes dictated when to show the commercials based on the target audience. Referred to as "adjacencies," ads during nighttime television programs offered the most exposure to young voters. Still, while Democratic candidates such as Ted Kennedy placed his campaign commercials on *Saturday Night Live*, Reagan's team opted for Friday night's nostalgic and family-friendly program *The Waltons*.[218]

Youth for Reagan activities in public relations revealed youth politics' influence on all voters. During "Operation Kinfolk," for example, Youth for Reagan distributed postcards on campus with a picture of the governor and young supporters through the canvass organization. Young voters who supported Reagan then mailed the cards to older friends and relatives to endorse his candidacy and request their vote. As the plan outlined Operation Kinfolk's purpose, it claimed, "This project is well suited for creating a youth image for Gov. Reagan and will give many undecided voters a good reason to decide to vote for Reagan for President."[219] Another project "designed to increase Gov. Reagan's youth identification" included Operation Windshield Wash, which instructed Youth for Reagan members to hit parking lots with Windex, paper towels, and flyers that read: "Now that you can see clearly, we hope that you will vote for Gov. Reagan for President on Nov. 4."[220] This organization was recruited as an important voting segment but served as a walking, talking political advertisement. Operation Burma-Shave borrowed directly from the iconic ad campaign that placed consecutive road signs for motorists to develop a sequenced, gimmicky message. While Burma-Shave brand shaving cream ads read on separate boards, "No matter / How you slice it / It's still your face / Be humane / Use / Burma-Shave," Youth for Reagan signs claimed: "You want to fight / That big tax bite / So listen to our news / If Reagan wins / Tax cuts begin / If Carter wins, you lose / Youth for Reagan." As Burma-Shave road signs had been most popular during the 1930s, this simple and nostalgic approach spoke to Youth for Reagan's style. Youth for Reagan tried several other projects that gained free publicity such as carefully coached letters to the editor of school newspapers and "Bumper Brandings" that placed Youth for Reagan stickers on cars at Republican rallies, sporting events, and shopping centers (with permission).[221]

In the closing weeks of the campaign, as Carter's popularity on campus slipped considerably, Youth for Reagan targeted the president and went on the offensive. "Operation Rain on Carter's Parade" organized a "rapid deployment force" to appear at any Carter surrogate speech with signs that read "We Support the Guv" and "High Inflation, High Taxes, No Jobs, Inflation + Unemployment = Carter." While the program intended to embarrass Carter, "and what could be a better place than a Carter or Mondale appearance where there is always plenty of national press anxiously looking for controversy," Youth for Reagan leaders made sure "there should be no booing or heckling."[222] When Carter officials attacked Reagan in a speech, Youth for Reagan members held up "Stop Your Gutter Politics" signs. Even as Reagan falsely connected Carter's campaign to the Ku Klux Klan and Reagan's campaign ran attack ads on television blasting Carter's handling of the Iran hostage crisis as "weak and indecisive,"[223] Youth for Reagan directives promoted their morally upstanding, conscientious, and respectful effect, reminding its members, "You must be careful to not get too vicious in your attacks, or people may react negatively."[224] This type of discipline demonstrated Reagan's plan to channel this young supporters' activism and still target moderate voters.

Youth for Reagan's success in campus mock elections helped Reagan's public relations as well but also provided a morale boost that made a "terrific impact on the entire campaign." Blackwell argued, "a series of wins across the country can create a 'win psychology.'" Thus, mock elections focused campus leaders on organization and discipline; as the Youth for Reagan plan admitted, "the voting must be optional. . . . Otherwise 'election' becomes a survey of student opinion and our organizational strength is diluted." Despite this emphasis on selectivity, Blackwell stressed that the mock elections still needed legitimacy: "the object is to structure mock elections so they are unquestionably honest. . . . With representatives of all candidates present," as the Youth for Reagan's superior GOTV organization would succeed without the deception and Nixon's youth program relied on in campus elections. Blackwell's plan gained its confidence from the campaign organization, not a solid majority, as it explained to Youth for Reagan campus leaders, "Without a canvas (it is rare for the opposition to conduct one) it will be very difficult for Reagan's opponents to win."[225] The plan paid off, as Reagan won all but three out of more than eighty mock elections held in late

October. Two of those losses came to the independent candidate, John Anderson, indicating the weakness in Carter's student organization.

Youth for Reagan's success on campus also contributed to the GOP's confident reach to the Sunbelt. Antosh bragged about his youth organization, daring the "doubting readers" who polled Ivy League schools: "ask the opinions of the following people from the South, Midwest and West."[226] One Youth for Reagan news release boasted, "Reagan's strength in this area provides a glimpse of things on the horizon."[227] Reagan's 59 percent support in the mock election at the University of Georgia, Carter's home state, provided the "man bites dog news" that Antosh claimed Youth for Reagan would deliver.[228] As one student claimed after a Reagan victory in Baltimore's Mt. Saint Mary's College's mock election, "If Ronald Reagan can win on a college campus, then he can win anywhere."[229] While the organizational efforts boosted Reagan's chances with young voters, their contributions to Reagan's image also became more influential in the campaign.

One young leader complained that the press initially ignored Youth for Reagan, explaining that if a reporter attended one of their events: "They would have seen true typical examples of American youth and what motivates them." This meant that "there were no drunken yahoos. There was instead a real . . . patriotic sing a long." Still, the "Youth Staff" claimed success, explaining Youth for Reagan with the "popcorn theory"—"at first it warms up, then a few kernels pop, then it really gets going, pop, pop, pop."[230] Youth for Reagan also energized the campaign, as a final review explained: "On the whole, these young people have worked extremely hard—and all hours–day and day out." Not only did Youth for Reagan provide important foot soldiers, "their enthusiasm and follow through has been infectious!"[231] Reagan's success with young voters inspired all Republicans. Even in Massachusetts, that state's national committeeman bragged, "It wasn't just the manpower but the esprit of the young people." "When some of the older people saw them out there working, it gave them a sense of hope."[232]

If young voters inspired Reagan's older supporters, the election results must have elated them. Despite a close race during the campaign, Reagan won 51 percent of the total electorate, defeating Carter, who could muster only 41 percent. Voters in the eighteen-to-twenty-year-old bracket sided with Reagan by 6 percent, 44 percent to 38 percent.[233] However, while Reagan claimed a decisive victory, he split the under-thirty youth vote with the incumbent. If the Republicans wanted a mandate for the future, they would have to build on the Youth for Reagan effort in 1980.

Thus, Reagan's inaugural "extravaganza" made sure to include his young supporters. First, the official planners scheduled a Beach Boys concert for thirty-five hundred Youth for Reagan that had the crowd "dancing and surfing in the aisles the night before the inauguration." After Reagan's inaugural speech, based on the theme "America: A New Beginning," his young supporters attended the "Youth Gala" to hear the Pointer Sisters and then the Washington Jazz Battalion, which the CR's executive secretary, Sandra Webb, appreciated as "a wonderful alternative to Rock and Disco." The president and First Lady made the "Youth disco" their second of ten visits that evening after attending the veterans ball to announce Iran had freed its American hostages.[234] Vice President Bush and his wife, Barbara, also stopped by the Youth Gala unannounced as the crowd "went wild." Nobody at the party slept that night; as Webb exclaimed, "Everyone was too excited about the new beginning for America."[235] And while Nixon first held an inaugural celebration for young supporters in 1972, the Reaganesque version realized the GOP's rise to the majority party that YVP leaders envisioned. This promising beginning opened the door for a new constituency of conservative and moderate youth that could ensure Republicans' prominence in American elections.

Epilogue

Only fifteen years before his 1980 campaign, Reagan blasted students on California's campuses as "malcontents, beatniks, and filthy speech advocates."[1] In contrast, the quintessential 1980s American family sitcom *Family Ties* proved the clearest indication of youth's conservatism as Michael J. Fox played the seventeen-year-old "Reagan-worshipping" son of aging hippies during that decade. One article described Fox's character, Alex P. Keaton, as a "conservative, supply-side besotted teen" with "greed that flowed like sap." His lefty father wondered out loud: "Do you think he was switched at birth and the Rockefellers have our kid?"[2] Still, while Alex loved Reagan, Nixon loomed larger as the cultural godfather of the 1980s conservative turn for youth. Alex kept Tricky Dick's framed photo next to his bed, even consulting him in times of need. Popular opinion supported the show's depiction of a realignment in youth's political culture, as one journalist observed, "The students of the '60s, those ragged, raging rebels who burned the flag . . . have given way to a generation of conformists in neat polo shirts."[3] Other champions of the bygone youth rebellion reinforced youth politics' new image as square. The forty-year-old former radical Yippie leader Jerry Rubin, who warned young people in the 1960s "never trust anyone over thirty," changed his slogan in 1980 to "Never trust anyone under 30—they're too conservative."[4]

Youth politics had shifted to an outlook more sympathetic to the Republican Party. From 1970 to 1978, the number of first-year college students calling themselves "far left or liberal" fell eleven percentage points. Liberals could barely stomach it. One *New York Times* article, "The 80's Generation: The Lost Ideals of Youth," explained this change as a "harsh, dry, materialistic wind sweeping away the political passion and the heedless idealism of 60's and 70's." A Princeton student told the author, "People here are interested in jobs and sex, in that order. It's no longer a crime to want to be a millionaire."[5]

Contrasting the 1980s youth culture with the 1960s and 1970s image of young people, one journalist explained, "The Vietnam War is lost and forgotten. They want big jobs, small mortgages and careers."[6] This shift in the 1980s, attributed to Reagan's presidency, actually indicated that Richard Nixon's emphasis on the economy and attack on the 1960s political and cultural liberalism in youth politics had succeeded. In 1984, leaders at Washington and Lee University asked the faculty to require that undergraduates wear neckties to classes, prompting conservative columnist George Will to gloat, "America is back and standing tall, and it has a nice sharp crease in its trousers."[7] The enduring hippie myth still inspired these young voters, as even one Youth for Reagan coordinator recalled: "I remember when I was five or six years old and I saw hippies on the street, I was turned off."[8] Thus, this presidency also vindicated Nixon's "square chic" culture to challenge the 1960s permissiveness. Speaking to young people during his reelection campaign, Reagan glowed, "Your generation really sparkles. . . . I've seen enthusiasm and patriotism in your eyes that convince me that you get high on America."[9] This new confidence mythologized straight youth to exaggerate the shifts in young people's cultural attitudes. Still, one researcher admitted Reagan's image reached young voters but maintained that this did not reflect a conservative turn on all of the issues: "their social values are as liberal as their counterparts in the 1960s."[10] Thus, while Reagan could win over younger independents, youth's shift to the Right had limits.[11]

Despite these accounts that highlighted young Americans' new conservative sensibility during the 1980s, the careful organization and planning in GOP youth politics that Richard Nixon's presidency had begun over a decade before shaped Reagan's youth vote plan. Blackwell argued that developing future leaders became a key to building the Reagan majority and leaving a long-term mark for conservative politics: "In the long run," Blackwell predicted, "the most important impact the Regan administration will have is to have 'credentialed' a whole generation of conservatives in Washington and in government." As one article explained the Reagan administration's opportunity to reverse the Democrats' enduring hold on entry-level positions, "Now, with the ascendency of the Reagan administration, conservatives are taking steps to construct such a farm system, identifying bright young people." "Planting them in the government," Republican leaders hoped, would provide a harvest later on: "what sprouts is a perennial presence here."[12] Young men and women who took titles such as "executive assistant, personal assistant, special assistant" now came from an entirely different source, as the conservative study group the Heritage Foundation maintained a computerized bank of young conservatives with the proper credentials requested by the administration.[13]

Organizations such as the YAF that stood as counterrevolutionary, conservative forces on campuses were replaced by more savvy campaign institutions that targeted and mobilized young voters.[14] In addition, this group became a victim of its own success. As one former YAFer complained: "YAF seems increasingly interested in high-publicity projects that advance the careers of its aging Yuppie inner circle but have only a tangential connection to the lofty sentiments on which the organization was founded."[15] The YAF, like their generational cohorts on the left, had sold out.

While Reagan's presidency coincided with, and perhaps caused, the YAF's demise, the College Republicans enjoyed unprecedented gains. The leadership for this new wave came from an unlikely place, Massachusetts, indicating Reagan's popularity and the GOP's rise to majority status. Taking over the reins in 1981, a twenty-one-year-old Brandeis University student, Jack Abramoff, won the election for CR chairman after directing the surprisingly successful Massachusetts youth campaign in 1980 that placed over five thousand volunteers, produced over sixteen thousand votes on Massachusetts campuses, and made an "impact with regard to visibility" that helped Reagan become the first Republican to win the state in twenty-five years.[16]

The 1984 election, of course, indicates the culmination of the GOP's youth politics. The results from this election gave conservatives great reason for hope. Reagan did best in the South, winning 68 percent of the under-twenty-five segment. Even in the Northeast, 57 percent of the voters under twenty-five chose Reagan.[17] As former YAFer William Rusher explained the changing demographics in the nation, as Americans poured into the Sunbelt, he predicted an enduring Republican majority. The narrative that Nixon had espoused gained from this apparent victory. As Rusher channeled the 1972 campaign message, he explained the effects of this structural shift in American politics: "The response of the left . . . was to try to poison the whole Vietnam generation, and especially its college element, against American society in general." While this made a "political shambles out of the early 1970s," Rusher took solace in that it "only delayed the general rightward trend."[18] In 1987, speaking to the College Republicans about their Democratic counterpart, Ronald Reagan jabbed, "They don't realize that it's cool to be conservative."[19]

Figure 17. "Rebuilding a country that once was": Reagan at a rally at Bowling Green State University in 1984. (Reagan Library)

This transition serves as a reminder that the GOP's rise to the majority party came from an extensive youth organization that both aided and benefited from Reagan's image. Republicans' effort to lure young independent voters away from the Democratic Party shows that first-time voters from the baby boomer generation shifted the electorate but also sparked the modern political campaign. Ronald Reagan's campaign mastered the segmented marketing approach that Nixon also borrowed from Madison Avenue. As executive director of Youth for Reagan in 1984, Liz Pickens explained Reagan's appeal to young voters: "President Reagan is kind of an Indiana Jones in their eyes."[20] While the Republican Party's rise to a majority rallied a fragile youth coalition of independents and conservatives, YVPers, Youth for Ford, and Reagan's young supporters played a vital role in both the rise of image politics and the shift in party politics after 1968. In addition to the YVP and subsequent youth efforts that made possible the Republican majority, these young political professionals easily transitioned into successful careers.

Their experience in youth politics created a launching pad for key operatives and several candidates in the following decades, and created a lasting "strong fraternal bond." Reviewing the YVPers who attended the organization's reunion in 2012, the list reads like a who's who in the Republican Party. As one former YVP leader recollected the reunion meeting forty years after Nixon's reelection: "I was dumbstruck about how consequential we were."[21] While rank-and-file YVPers went on to become loyal party members and also major political figures, the YVP leadership produced future state representatives, US congressmen, and one two-term governor of Tennessee, Donald Sundquist. Many became political consultants, heading campaigns for notable candidates such as Arnold Schwarzenegger, Boris Yeltsin, Haley Barbour, Dan Quayle, and Jack Kemp. Still others held remarkable political positions that included highly influential lobbyists, chiefs of staff for major state and national politicians, an executive director for the UN World Food program, and a chairman for the US Chamber of Commerce. Reagan included several of these YVP leaders in his own administration, as Nixonette leader Laura Jordan Dietrich rose to become the highest-ranking woman in the US State Department during the Reagan administration when he appointed her as his deputy assistant secretary of state for human rights. One of the YVP's RNC organizers, David Chew, even served as staff secretary and deputy assistant to the president after 1983.[22] In addition, other young leaders who worked with YVP on behalf of the College Republicans and the RNC, such as Karl Rove, also developed important leadership experience with young voters in 1972 that would propel their influential careers.

In hindsight, YVPers often attribute their subsequent career successes to what Sundquist called, "one of those magical times." During this election, young political operatives in Nixon's campaign gained incredible hands-on experience. As Hank Haldeman explained, it was the first youth campaign "run by young voters separately, a complete campaign structure with all the counterparts of a senior campaign," adding: "that structure is unique and created an opportunity for leadership for people under thirty or even twenty."[23]

The professional opportunities appealed to the less idealistic and more career-driven young activists, as Bacon admitted: "personally, politics intrigued me as a career, it was not about the issues. . . . A lot of us were that way."[24] Thus, YVP's leadership structure professionalized youth politics in ways that resonated with ambitious young moderates. Gary Burhop credited YVP's director: "Rietz empowered us to do the best job we could," as he chuckled: "there was not a whole lot of oversight." Burhop bragged: "I chartered 30 737's, I was 22."[25]

In 1985, as the chairman of the Committee for Responsible Youth Politics (CRYP), Blackwell opened his organization's roast of Jesse Helms and announced the name change of his conservative group to Conservative Leadership PAC (CLPAC), pointing out that CRYP, established in 1972, had begun before the Heritage Foundation, the House Republican Study Committee, and the conservative caucus; Blackwell joked that "all of those organizations and many others have suggested that we stop calling ourselves a youth group since we're so old."[26] While the PAC's emphasis remained on supplying conservatives with well-trained and determined young organizers, the CLPAC leaders' decision to change its name revealed how much youth politics had matured in the GOP since 1968.

Notes

Introduction

1. Nick Thimmesch, "Hold Back the Pigeons!," *Telegraph-Herald* (Dubuque, IA), January 17, 1973, 6.

2. Marjorie Hunter, "Second Nixon Inauguration Will Put Accent on Youth," *Index Journal*, January 4, 1973, 8.

3. James Brown committed but then declined the invitation after his recent album was boycotted in response for endorsement of Nixon in 1972.

4. Mary Hilt, "Averill Park Girl Thrilled by Inaugural Dance with President," *Times Record*, January 24, 1973, 3.

5. AP, "A Night of Dancing for Exuberant Nixon," *Des Moines Register*, January 21, 1973, 4.

6. Dale Wittner, "Young Voters Surge to Enroll in the System," *Life Magazine*, October 15, 1971, 28.

7. Wittner, 28.

8. R. W. Apple Jr., "Youth Vote Likely to Aid Democrats," *New York Times Magazine*, May 10, 1971, 18.

9. William F. Buckley Jr., "A Way Out on Voting Age Pledge," *Washington Star*, February 17, 1970, 17. Jeb Magruder claims Teeter recommended the CRP leaders "halt all activity among young people" after his first wave of polls in 1970. Jeb Magruder, *An American Life* (New York: Atheneum, 1974), 171.

10. Richard Nixon, "Remarks to a Student-Faculty Convocation at the University of Nebraska," John T. Woolley and Gerhard Peters, *The American Presidency Project* (online). Santa Barbara: University of California (hosted), Gerhard Peters (database): http://www.presidency.ucsb.edu/ws/?pid=2955 (accessed October 12, 2012).

11. Rick Perlstein, *Nixonland: The Rise of a President and the Fracturing of America* (New York: Scribner, 2008), 565.

12. Richard Ivan Jobs, "Youth Movements: Travel, Protest and Europe in 1968," *American Historical Review* 114, no. 2 (2009): 376–404. Jobs compiled a useful bibliography on this topic that has emphasized the transnational and global nature of 1968: Ronald Fraser et al., *1968: A Student Generation in Revolt* (New York: Pantheon, 1988); George Katsiaficas, *The Imagination of the New Left: A Global Analysis of 1968* (Boston: South End, 1987); Carole Fink, Philipp Gasser, and Detlef Junker, eds., *1968: The World Transformed* (Cambridge: Cambridge University, 1998); Arthur Marwick, *The Sixties: Cultural Revolution in Britain, France, Italy, and the United States, c. 1958–c. 1974* (New York: Bloomsbury Reader, 1998); Jeremi Suri, *Power and Protest: Global Revolution and the Power of Détente* (Cambridge, MA: Harvard University Press, 2002); Andreas W. Daum,

Lloyd C. Gardner, and Wilfried Mausbach, eds., *America, the Vietnam War, and the World: Comparative and International Perspectives* (New York: Cambridge University Press, 2003); Gerd-Rainer Horn, *The Spirit of '68: Rebellion in Western Europe and North America, 1956–1976* (Oxford: Oxford University Press, 2007); Martin Klimke and Joachim Scharloth, *1968 in Europe: A History of Protest and Activism, 1956–1977* (New York: Palgrave Macmillan, 2008); Belinda Davis et al., eds., *Changing the World, Changing Oneself: Political Protest and Collective Identities in 1960s/70s West Germany and the U.S.* (New York: Berghahn Books, 2009); Martin Klimke, *The "Other" Alliance: Global Protest and Student Unrest in West Germany and the U.S., 1962–1972* (Princeton, NJ: Princeton University Press, 2009).

13. On history of youth politics during this era, see John Morton Blum, *Years of Discord: American Politics and Society, 1961–1974* (New York: W. W. Norton, 1991); David Frum, *How We Got Here: The 70's, the Decade That Brought You Modern Life (for Better or Worse)* (New York: Basic Books, 2000); David Greenberg, *Nixon's Shadow: The History of an Image* (New York: W. W. Norton, 2003); Walter L. Hixson, *The Vietnam Antiwar Movement* (New York: Garland, 2000); Mark Hamilton Lytle, *America's Uncivil Wars: The Sixties Era from Elvis to the Fall of Richard Nixon* (Oxford: Oxford University Press, 2006); Bruce Miroff, *The Liberal's Moment: The McGovern Insurgency and the Identity Crisis of the Democratic Party* (Lawrence: University Press of Kansas, 2007); Perlstein, *Nixonland*; Doug Rossinow, *The Politics of Authenticity: Liberalism, Christianity and the New Left in America* (New York: Columbia University Press, 1998); Alan Sica and Stephen Turner, eds., *The Disobedient Generation: Social Theorists in the Sixties* (Chicago: University of Chicago Press, 2005); Melvin Small, *Covering Dissent: The Media and the Anti–Vietnam War Movement* (New Brunswick, NJ: Rutgers University Press, 1994); Theodore Windt, *Presidents and Protesters: Political Rhetoric in the 1960s* (Tuscaloosa, AL: University of Alabama Press, 1990); Jules Witcover, *Very Strange Bed Fellows: The Short and Unhappy Marriage of Richard Nixon and Spiro Agnew* (New York: Public Affairs, 2007).

14. Perlstein, *Nixonland*, 497.

15. Robert E. Weems and Lewis A. Randolph, "The Ideological Origins of Nixon's 'Black Capitalism' Initiative," *Review of Black Political Economy*, Summer 2001, 58.

16. Suri, *Power and Protest*, 5.

17. Ronald Reagan Speech at CPAC, February 6, 1977, http://reagan2020.us/speeches/The_New_Republican_Party.asp (accessed May 24, 2018).

18. John Andrew, *The Other Side of the Sixties* (Piscataway, NJ: Rutgers University Press, 1997), 1; Wayne Thorburn, *A Generation Awakes: Young Americans for Freedom and the Creation of the Conservative Movement* (Ottawa, IL: Jameson Books, 2010).

19. Colson to Haldeman, Folder: Youth Optional Proposals [2 of 2] [CFOA 336], Box 43, PRF.

20. Arthur H. Miller and Warren E. Miller, "Issues, Candidates and Partisan Divisions in the 1972 American Presidential Election," *British Journal of Political Science* 5, no. 4 (October 1975), 393–434, http://www.jstor.org/stable/193436.

21. Louis M. Seagull, "The Youth Vote and Change in American Politics," *Annals of the American Academy of Political and Social Science* 397 ("Seven Polarizing Issues in America Today," September 1971): 91.

22. Rowland Evans and Robert Novak, "Young Republicans to Elect Trickster," *Eugene Register Guard* (April 27, 1977), A15.

23. For the fall of the New Deal order, see Jefferson Cowie, *Stayin' Alive: The 1970s and the Last Days of the Working Class* (New York: New Press, 2010); William Crotty, *Decision for the Democrats* (Baltimore: Johns Hopkins University Press, 1978); Miroff, *Liberal's Moment*; Rossinow, *Politics of Authenticity*; Allen Matusow, *Unraveling of America: A History of Liberalism in the 1960s* (Athens: University of Georgia Press, 2009); Gary Gerstle and Steve Fraser, *The Rise and Fall of the New Deal Order, 1930–1980* (Princeton, NJ: Princeton University Press, 1990).

24. For the rise of conservatism, see Lisa McGirr, *Suburban Warriors: The Origins of the New American Right* (Princeton, NJ: Princeton University Press, 2002); Matthew Lassiter, *The Silent Majority: Suburban Politics in the Sunbelt South* (Princeton, NJ: Princeton University Press, 2007); Bruce Schulman and Julian Zelizer, *Rightward Bound: Making America Conservative in the 1970s* (Cambridge, MA: Harvard University Press, 2008); Rick Perlstein, *Before the Storm: Barry Goldwater and the Unmaking of the American Consensus* (New York: Hill & Wang, 2001).

25. For the rise of image in politics, see Richard W. Waterman, Robert Wright, and Gilbert St. Clair, eds., *The Image-Is-Everything Presidency: Dilemmas in American Leadership* (Boulder, CO: Westview, 1999); Markus Prior, "The Incumbent in the Living Room: The Rise of Television and the Incumbency Advantage in U.S. House Elections," *Journal of Politics* 68, no. 3 (2006): 657–673; Edwin Diamond and Stephen Bates, *The Spot: The Rise of Political Advertising on Television* (Cambridge, MA: MIT Press, 1992); David Mark, *Going Dirty: The Art of Negative Campaigning* (New York: Rowman & Littlefield, 2006); Kathleen Hall Jamieson, *Packaging the Presidency: A History and Criticism of Presidential Campaign Advertising* (Oxford: Oxford University Press, 1996).

26. See David Greenberg, *Nixon's Shadow*; Daniel Frick, *Reinventing Richard Nixon: A Cultural History of an American Obsession* (Lawrence: University Press of Kansas, 2008); Mark Feeney, *Nixon at the Movies: A Book about Belief* (Chicago: University of Chicago Press, 2004); Gill Troy, *Morning in America: How Ronald Reagan Invented the 1980's* (Princeton, NJ: Princeton University Press, 2005).

27. Greenberg, xxxii.

28. For more on young conservatives, see Perlstein, *Before the Storm*; John Andrew, *Other Side of the Sixties*; Alan Crawford, *Thunder on the Right: The "New Right" and the Politics of Resentment* (New York: Pantheon Books, 1980); Rebecca E. Klatch, *A Generation Divided* (Berkeley: University of California Press, 1999); George H. Nash, *The Conservative Intellectual Movement in America since 1945* (Wilmington, DE: Intercollegiate Studies Institute, 1996); William A. Rusher, *The Rise of the Right* (New York: National Review Books, 1993); Gregory L. Schneider, *Cadres for Conservatism: Young Americans for Freedom and the Rise of the Contemporary Right* (New York: New York University Press, 1999); Thorburn,

Generation Awakes; Craig Shirley, *Reagan's Revolution: The Untold Story of the Campaign That Started It All* (Nashville, TN: Thomas Nelson, 2005).

29. Samuel Freedman, *The Inheritance: How Three Families and America Moved from Roosevelt to Reagan and Beyond* (New York: Simon & Schuster, 1996), 22.

30. Mark Bauerlein, *The Dumbest Generation: How the Digital Age Stupefies Young Americans and Jeopardizes Our Future (or, Don't Trust Anybody under Thirty)* (New York: Tarcher, 2009); Henry Giroux, *Youth in Revolt: Reclaiming a Democratic Future (Critical Interventions: Politics, Culture, and the Promise of Democracy)* (New York: Paradigm, 2013); Henry Giroux, *Politics after Hope: Obama and the Crisis of Youth, Race and Democracy (The Radical Imagination)* (New York: Paradigm, 2010); Dan Cassino, *Consuming Politics: Jon Stewart, Branding, and the Youth Vote in America* (Hackensack, NJ: Fairleigh Dickinson University Press, 2009); Michael Connery, *Youth to Power: How Today's Young Voters Are Building Tomorrow's Progressive Majority* (New York: Ig, 2008).

31. Robert Mason, *Richard Nixon and the Quest for a New Majority* (Chapel Hill: University of North Carolina Press, 2004), 26.

32. Colson to Haldeman, "18 Year Old Vote in 1972," December 9, 1970, Folder: Youth Optional Proposals [2 of 2] [CFOA 336], Box 43, WHSOF PRF, NARA II.

33. Michael Flamm, *Law and Order Street Crime, Civil Unrest and the Crisis of Liberalism in the 1960s* (New York: Columbia University Press, 2005), 181.

34. Cathy Bertini interview, July 18, 2012.

35. Ralph De Toeledano, "Poll Confirms Public Support for Nixon," *Reading Eagle*, December 23, 1969, 8.

36. Recent scholarship on Nixon's "silent majority" has emphasized Nixon's role in realignment as liberalism unraveled politically. Lassiter, *Silent Majority*; Bruce Schulman, *The Seventies: The Great Shift in American Culture, Society, and Politics* (Cambridge, MA: Da Capo, 2002); Robert Mason, *Richard Nixon and the Quest for a New Majority* (Chapel Hill: University of North Carolina Press, 2004).

37. Tom Wicker, "In the Nation: The New Politics," *New York Times*, March 21, 1968, 46.

38. Jack Anderson, "The Washington Merry-Go-Round: Former Nixon Spy Now with Reagan," *Wilmington Morning Star*, December 19, 1975, 2.

39. Perlstein, *Nixonland*, 629.

40. Mason, *Richard Nixon and the Quest for a New Majority*, 131.

Chapter 1. New Nixon and the Youth Problem, 1968

1. Richard Nixon, "Today's Youth: The Great Generation," NBC Radio (October 16, 1968).

2. "People Want Safety on the Streets: Nixon Says Law and Order Concerns Americans Most," *Reading Eagle* (Reading, PA), October 27, 1968, 21.

3. Flamm, *Law and Order*, 164.

4. Michael A. Cohen, *American Maelstrom: The 1968 Election and the Politics*

of Division (New York: Oxford University Press, 2016); see also Lassiter, *Silent Majority*, 234, "The law-and-order platform at the center of Nixon's suburban strategy tapped into Middle American resentment toward antiwar demonstrators and black militants but consciously employed a color-blind discourse that deflected these charges of racial demagoguery and insulated the Republicans from direct comparisons to Wallace."

5. Paul Hoffman, "Coalition to Seek Candidate for '68," *New York Times*, June 13, 1966, 19.

6. Russell Baker, "The Observer: The Pied Piper of Minnesota," *New York Times*, March 21, 1968, 46.

7. Jeff Cox, "A Kind of Magic: Even Young Moderate Conservatives Seem to Flock to Eugene McCarthy," *Victoria Advocate*, April 30, 1968, 4.

8. Edith Evans Asbury, "More Youths Join McCarthy Forces: Pour into New Hampshire for the Final Push," *New York Times*, March 10, 1968, 48.

9. Sam Brown interview with Elizabeth Deane, WGBH, August 11, 1982.

10. Robert F. Kennedy, *To Seek a Newer World* (New York: Doubleday, 1975).

11. Cowie, *Stayin' Alive*.

12. DeMar Touscher, "Student Polls Come On Strong for Bobby," *Deseret News*, May 16, 1968, A11.

13. "Kennedy Girls," Anne Berkovits for Carol Breshears, Folder: Research Division, Youth, Box 69, Papers of Robert Kennedy, JFK Library, Boston, MA.

14. "SRO for RFK," Folder: Research Division, Youth, Box 69, Papers of Robert Kennedy, JFK Library.

15. Russell Baker, "Observer: The Newest Wrinkle in the Youth Game," *New York Times*, May 21, 1964, 34.

16. Baker, 34.

17. "Youth Says Kennedy 'Archaic,'" *Syracuse Herald*, July 22, 1967 Folder: Research Division: Youth File, Box 69, Papers of Robert Kennedy, JFK Library.

18. Ruth Montgomery, "Bobby's Charm Fades," *Mid Cities News*, July 23, 1967, 4.

19. "Youth Says Kennedy 'Archaic.'"

20. Volunteer Office to Campaign Staff, File: Correspondence File, Research Division, Box 46, Papers of Robert Kennedy, JFK Library.

21. Anthony Ripley, "National Students Parley Finds Unity Only in Dissatisfaction," *New York Times*, August 20, 1968, 23.

22. AP Report, File: Wire Service Clips, Press Division, Box 22, Papers of Robert Kennedy, JFK Library.

23. Walter Sheridan, recorded interview by Roberta Greene, August 5, 1969, 18–21, John F. Kennedy Library Oral History Program.

24. Sheridan, recorded interview by Roberta Greene, August 5, 1969, 18–21.

25. "Students for Kennedy," Folder: Research Division, Youth, Box 69, Papers of Robert Kennedy, JFK Library.

26. Martin Waldron, "Chicago Police, 'Best in World,' Reject Criticism," *New York Times*, August 30, 1968, 15.

27. Paul Bullock, "Rabbits and Radicals: Richard Nixon's 1946 Campaign

against Jerry Voorhis," *Southern California Quarterly* 55, no. 3 (1973): 319–359, 324.

28. Vote by Groups, 1952–1956, http://www.gallup.com/poll/9451/election-polls-vote-groups-19521956.aspx (accessed July 1, 2014).

29. Dwight D. Eisenhower, Republican National Convention, August 23, 1956, http://millercenter.org/president/speeches/detail/3359 (accessed July 1, 2014).

30. Ronald Docksai, "Welcome to the Remnant," *New Guard*, Young Americans for Freedom, 1965–1972. 1961—Sterling, VA, Serial Publication, Boston Public Library, Boston, MA, October 1971, 4.

31. Docksai, 4.

32. Schneider, *Cadres for Conservatism*, 79.

33. Mort Allin, "Youth for Nixon Final Report," 14, Folder: Subject Files, Alphabetical (JSM) Youth [2 of 3], Box 27, Papers of JSM, Nixon Library, Yorba Linda, CA.

34. "Nixon Plans New Image in Campaign," *Spokesman Review*, May 31, 1968, 14.

35. Flamm, *Law and Order*, 177.

36. Greil Marcus, "Books," *Rolling Stone*, December 7, 1968, 24.

37. De Toeledano, "Poll Confirms Public Support for Nixon," 23.

38. Marcus, "Books," 24.

39. Loudon Wainwright, "One More Try for the Heights," *Life Magazine*, March 1, 1968, 60–68, 61.

40. Wainwright, 61.

41. Schneider, *Cadres for Conservatism*, 46.

42. Richard Smith, *On His Own Terms: A Life of Nelson Rockefeller* (New York: Random House, 2014), 412.

43. Gore Vidal, "The Best Man, 1968," *Esquire*, March 1963, 59.

44. Rowland Evans and Robert Novak, "Inside Report: Nixon's Youth Movement," *Victoria Advocate*, September 8, 1966, A4.

45. Evans and Novak, A4.

46. David Keene, "The Conservative Case for Richard Nixon," *New Guard*, Summer 1969, 11.

47. Boisfeuillet Jones, "The Young Republican Plight," *Harvard Crimson*, July 7, 1967, https://www.thecrimson.com/article/1967/7/11/the-young-republican-plight-pthe-overwhelming/ (accessed November 12, 2013).

48. Jones.

49. Jones.

50. McDonald's Action Plan, Folder 52, Box 15, William Emerson Brock III Papers, MPA.0106. University of Tennessee Libraries, Knoxville, Special Collections.

51. McDonald's Action Plan, Box 15, Folder 52, PWEB.

52. McDonald's Action Plan.

53. McDonald's Action Plan.

54. Memo, February 1968, Folder 10, Box 1, Papers of University of Maryland College Republicans (UMDCR), Presidential papers, Karel Petraitis, 1967–1969, Hornbake Library, University of Maryland, College Park, MD.

55. McDonald's Action Plan.

56. Allin, "Final Report," 10.

57. "Bliss Announces Youth Conference This Fall," *Maryland Republican Banner*, October 1968, Folder 10, Box 1, Papers of UMDCR, Presidential papers, Karel Petraitis, 1967–1969. UMD, College Park, MD.

58. Allin, "Final Report," 14.

59. Gavin to Garment, Folder: Gavin [1 of 3], Box 69 WHCNF, SMOF Papers of Len Garment, 1968 Campaign File, Nixon Library.

60. "Young Adults for Richard Nixon," Folder: 1968 Political Campaign File, Young Adults for Nixon, Box 82, SMOF Papers of Leonard Garment, Nixon Library.

61. William Dowd to Garment, "Campaign Film for TV Spot Use: Using Law Students." June 7, 1968 Political Campaign File, Young Adults for Nixon, Box 82, 1968, SMOF Papers of Leonard Garment, Nixon Library.

62. Allin, "Final Report," 19.

63. Allin, "Final Report," 19.

64. Lamar Alexander to Leonard Garment, "Youth and Television," September 4, 1968, Folder: 1968 Political Campaign File, Youth for Nixon, Box 82, Papers of Len Garment, Nixon Library.

65. REH to RMN, March 29, 1968, Folder: 1968 Political Campaign File, Youth for Nixon, Box 82, Papers of Len Garment, Nixon Library.

66. Charles McWhorter to Len Garment, August 23, 1968, Folder: 1968 Political Campaign, Students for Nixon, Box 82, Papers of Len Garment, Nixon Library.

67. Joe McGinnis, *The Selling of the Presidency: The Classical Account of the Packaging of a Candidate* (New York: Simon & Schuster, 1969), 138.

68. Allin, "Final Report," 19.

69. Illinois Citizens for Nixon, September 28, 1968, 1968 Political Campaign Topical File, Students for Nixon, Box 82, SMOF, Papers of Len Garment, Nixon Library.

70. Allin, "Final Report," 5.

71. Gavin to Garment, February 2, 1968, Folder: Gavin [1 of 3], Box 69, 1968 Campaign File, WHCNF, SMOF Papers of Len Garment, Nixon Library.

72. Richard Nixon at Syracuse University, October 29, 1968, Folder: 1968 Political Campaign—Topic Files, Syracuse, October 29, Box 8, Papers of Len Garment, Nixon Library.

73. James M. Naughton, "Nelson (Zap) Rockefeller and Richard (Cool) Nixon," *New York Times*, July 28, 1968, 176.

74. See James Gilbert's *A Cycle of Outrage: America's Reaction to the Juvenile Delinquent in the 1950s* (New York: Oxford University Press, 1988).

75. NBC Radio, August 10, 1968.

76. David Murray, "Payoff for Loyalty: Watch Lindsay in 1972," *Youngstown Vindicator*, August 12, 1968, 11.

77. "Textual Highlights of Republican Platform," *Gettysburg Times*, August 5, 1968, 3.

78. Harvey Stone, "The G.O.P. Follies," *Rag* 2, no. 36 (August 15, 1968): 1.

79. James K. Batten, "Politics 1968: Obeisance at the Altar of Youth," *St. Petersburg Times*, July 18, 1968, 1.

80. "Youths Say G.O.P. Convention Was Irrelevant to Their World," *New York Times*, August 19, 1968, 30.

81. John Herbers, "Conservatives Laud Choice; Moderates Dismayed," *New York Times*, August 9, 1968, 19.

82. "People Want Safety on the Streets," 21.

83. John W. Finney, "Humphrey Visits Discotheque and an Auto Plant," *New York Times*, October 18, 1968, 34.

84. Douglas E. Kneelands, "Politics Hollow for Missouri Students," *New York Times*, October 14, 1968, 40.

85. Sylvan Fox, "Scores of Youth Seized in Anti-election Protest across the Nation," *New York Times*, November 6, 1968, 3.

86. Carl Rowan, "Nixon's Coronation Need Not Be Boring," *Eugene Register Guard*, August 21, 1972, 12A.

87. Allin, "Final Report," 14.

88. Allin, 14.

89. Allin, 9.

90. Seagull, "Youth Vote and Change in American Politics," 95. James Lamare, "Inter-or-Intragenerational Cleavage? The Political Orientations of American Youth in 1968," *American Journal of Political Science* 19, no. 1 (February 1975): 81. While Wallace won only 14 percent of the voters over thirty, 24 percent of non-high-school graduates under thirty supported his candidacy in 1968.

91. Gallup Election Polls by Groups, 1968–1972, http://www.gallup.com/poll/9457/election-polls-vote-groups-19681972.aspx (accessed October 13, 2011).

Chapter 2. Law and Order

1. Gavin to Keogh, February 7, 1969, Folder: Attitude Study [CFOA 336], Box 43, PRF, NARA II.

2. "Student NEA Beefs Up Political Image," guest column, National Education Association, *Florence Times Daily*, August 29, 1970, 4.

3. Richard M. Scammon and Ben J. Wattenberg, *The Real Majority: An Extraordinary Examination of the American Electorate* (New York: Coward-McCann, 1970).

4. Bernard Shaw, "20th Century Brings Changes to the American Voter," December 28, 1999, http://archives.cnn.com/1999/ALLPOLITICS/stories/12/28/millenium.voter/index.html (accessed October 20, 2012).

5. Mason, *Richard Nixon and the Quest for a New Majority*, 17.

6. Perlstein, *Nixonland*, 737.

7. Joshua F. J. Inwood, "Neoliberal Racism: The 'Southern Strategy' and the Expanding Geographies of White Supremacy," *Social and Cultural Geography* 16, no. 4 (2015): 407–423.

8. Geoffrey Kabaservice, *Rule and Ruin: The Downfall of Moderation and the Destruction of the Republican Party* (New York: Oxford University Press, 2012), 273.

9. Tom Davis to Haldeman, July 2, 1970, File: Youth Programs [1 of 2], Box 158, SMOF H. R. Haldeman, Papers of Richard Nixon, NARA II.

10. Mason, *Richard Nixon and the Quest for a New Majority*, 99.

11. Lassiter, *Silent Majority*; Schulman, *Seventies*, 38.

12. "Nixon Popularity Is Found High, Especially among Young Voters," *New York Times*, June 5, 1969, 24.

13. Colson to Kehrli, Folder: Youth-General, Box 56, Papers of James McLane, Nixon Library.

14. Oval 690-11, March 21, 1972, White House Tapes, Richard Nixon Presidential Library. 1:00 p.m.–2:15 p.m.

15. Matthew D. Lassiter, "Impossible Criminals: The Suburban Imperatives of America's War on Drugs," *Journal of American History* 102, no. 1 (2015): 127.

16. Khalil Gilbran Muhammad, *The Condemnation of Blackness: Race, Crime and the Urbanization of America* (Cambridge, MA: Harvard University Press, 2011); Lassiter, "Impossible Criminals," 128.

17. John Chamberlain, "Nixon Courting 'Square Power,'" *St. Joseph Gazette* (Missouri), May 12, 1969, A4.

18. Schulman, *Seventies*; the quote is from George Packer, "The Decade Nobody Knows," *New York Times*, June 10, 2001, http://www.nytimes.com/books/01/06/10/reviews/010610.10packert.html.

19. Richard Nixon, "Remark to Members of the Association of Student Governments," Public Papers of the President. September 20, 1969, http://proxychi.baremetal.com/csdp.org/research/shafernixon.pdf.

20. Harold Buckner to President, December 28, 1970, Folder: Presidents Commission on Campus Unrest 1/1 January 1, 1971 to March 27, 1971, Box: FG 288, Papers of Richard Nixon, NARA II.

21. Kenneth Keniston and Michael Lerner. "Campus Characteristics and Campus Unrest," *Annals of the American Academy of Political and Social Science* 395 (1971): 39–53, 44.

22. Richard Nixon, "Statement on Campus Disorders," Public Papers of President, March 3, 1969.

23. Arnold Stenberg, "The Creative Society: Where the Action Is," *New Guard*, Campus Issue, March 1967, 12.

24. Joseph Kraft, "Foes of War Can Help to Rally Voters," *Youngstown Vindicator*, May 11, 1970, B2.

25. Michael Rossman, "The Sound of Marching, Charging Feet," *Rolling Stone* 30 (April 5, 1969): 6.

26. "Rules a Result of Immaturity," *Lipscomb Babbler*, December 5, 1969, 2.

27. "Hustler's Editorial 'All Wet': Fails to Show 'Provincialism,'" *Lipscomb Babbler*, June 1968, 2. In fact, Vanderbilt's campus was calm because its president, Alexander Heard, became concerned and established an open speakers series

that included MLK Jr. and Stokely Carmichael. For more on Heard, see http://www.insidevandy.com/drupal/node/10277.

28. "Student Leaders Becoming Stereotyped; Moderation Often Fails to Be Considered," *Lipscomb Babbler*, November 1, 1968, 2.

29. Karilyn Barker, "How Will Nixon React? Asks Interested Youth," *Palm Beach Daily News*, April 21, 1969, 1.

30. "Student Violence—a Means to What End?," *Lipscomb Babbler*, May 22, 1970, 2.

31. "Much Ado about Nothing," *Lipscomb Babbler*, October 3, 1969, 2.

32. Flyer, University of Tennessee Special Collections, Folder: Student Unrest 1970s, June 1970.

33. David Lawrence, "Campus Unrest Linked to Drugs," *Palm Beach Post*, May 28, 1970, A14.

34. McGovern Press Release, November 9, 1970, Folder: Youth 1970, Box 921, PGM, Mudd Library, Princeton University.

35. Dr. Lev E. Dobriansky to the President, "The Crucial Ethnic Vote in the '72 Campaign," Folder: Re-election Committee [Folder 2 of 3], Box 9, PPB, NARA II.

36. Duncan Spencer, "The New Voters: Factory Workers Turning Nixon," *Evening Star*, Folder: McGovern [3 of 6], Box 8, PPB, NARA II.

37. Isserman papers, *Record Courier*, May 8, 1970.

38. Isserman papers.

39. University of Tennessee Yearbook, 1969–1970, 102.

40. *Daily Beacon*, June 1970, University of Tennessee Special Collections, Folder: Student Unrest—1970s.

41. Robert S. Diam, "Q & A: The Fortune 500–Yankelovitch Survey: Shaken Faith in Nixon," *Fortune*, June 1970, 60.

42. Letter from the People. "Must Learn Cause," *Modesto Bee*, July 29, 1970, 49.

43. "1970: A Time of In-Betweenity." *Christian Century*, December 30, 1970, editorial page.

44. "Hickel Tells Nixon: Heed Youth Cries," *Modesto Bee*, July 7, 1970, 17.

45. Nixon, "Remark to Members of the Association of Student Governments."

46. Tom Davis to Haldeman, July 2, 1970, Folder: Youth Programs [1 of 2], Box 158, SMOF H. R. Haldeman, NARA II.

47. Research to Mitchell, "Dividing the Democrats," October 5, 1971, Folder: Alphabetical, B, Box 15, PJM.

48. "Hickel Tells Nixon: Heed Youth Cries," 17. "President's Youth Advisor Is Quitting, Nixon 'Image' with Young Dissenters Said Bad," *Florence Times-Daily*, May 5, 1970, 15.

49. Haldeman to Tom Davis, July 2, 1970, File: Youth Programs [1 of 2], Box 158, H. R. Haldeman Papers, NARA II.

50. Magruder to Haldeman, October 20, 1970, File: Youth Programs [1 of 2], Box 158, PHRH, NARA II.

51. Magruder to Haldeman, October 20, 1970, File: Youth Programs [1 of 2], Box 158, PHRH, NARA II.

52. Magruder to Haldeman, July 24, 1970, Folder: Attitude Study [CFOA 336], Box 43, PRF, NARA II.

53. Magruder to Haldeman, July 24, 1970.

54. "Redundant Commission" (editorial), *New York Times*, June 16, 1970, 46.

55. Donald A. Clelland, Thomas C. Hood, C. M. Lipsey, Ronald Wimberley, "In the Company of the Converted: Characteristics of a Billy Graham Crusade Audience," *Sociological Analysis* 35, no. 1 (1974): 45–56. See also Garry Wills, "How Nixon Used the Media, Billy Graham and the Good Lord to Rap with Students at Tennessee U," *Esquire*, September 1970, 119–122, 179–180.

56. Richard Rosser, "Graham: Curiosity Leads to Christ," May 26, 1970, University of Tennessee Special Collections, Folder: Nixon-Graham Crusade, 1970.

57. Susannah Taipale, *Thou Shalt Not Kill*, Appendix, Nixon speech at University of Tennessee, May 30, 1970, University of Tennessee, Special Collections, Nixon-Graham Crusade.

58. Taipale, *Thou Shalt Not Kill*, "Nixon's Remarks at Dr. Billy Graham's East Tennessee Crusade, May 28, 1970," Appendix 2, University of Tennessee Special Collections.

59. Flyer, University of Tennessee Special Collections, Folder: Student Unrest 1970s, June 1970.

60. Albert Minor, "Billy Graham the Impregnable," University of Tennessee Special Collections, Folder: Nixon-Graham Crusade, 1970.

61. Sanford Jay Rosen, "The Greening of the Scranton Commission," *AAUP Bulletin* 57, no. 4 (December 1971), 506–510, 509–510.

62. Scranton Commission, https://files.eric.ed.gov/fulltext/ED083899.pdf.

63. Scranton Commission. The first was the October 15 Moratorium against the Vietnam War.

64. Scranton Commission.

65. John Zoller, "On Student Unrest," *Triton Times* (UCSD) 11, no. 8 (October 23, 1970): 1.

66. Richard Delgado, *Critical Race Theory: The Cutting Edge* (Philadelphia: Temple University Press, 2013), 2.

67. Scranton Commission.

68. "Campus Unrest Panelist Says 'Real' Issues Are Being Ignored," *New York Times* (1923–Current file), November 2, 1970, 38.

69. "Talk of the Nation: Kent State Shooting Divided Campus and Country," National Public Radio, May 3, 2010, https://www.npr.org/templates/story/story.php?storyId=126480349 (accessed May 5, 2010).

70. Isserman papers.

71. Analysis by Robert C. Byrd, October 16, 1970, Folder: President's Commission on Campus Violence [May–October 1970], EX FG 288, NARA II.

72. Analysis by Robert C. Byrd.

73. Analysis by Robert C. Byrd.

74. Isserman papers.

75. Flyer, University of Tennessee Special Collections, Folder: Student Unrest 1970s.

76. Nixon to Scranton, December 10, 1970, Folder: President's Commission on Campus Unrest [May–December 1970], FG 288, NARA II.

77. Mort Allin to George Grassmuck, "Thoughts on the Lincoln Speech," Folder: Eighteen Year Old Vote [1 of 2], Box 43, PRF, NARA II.

78. Mort Allin to George Grassmuck.

79. James Naughton, "Nixon Is Seeking to Limit His Role as Conciliator," *New York Times*, January 19, 1971, 31.

80. Arthur Levine and Keith R. Wilson, "Student Activism in the 1970s: Transformation Not Decline," *Higher Education* 8, no. 6 ("Student Activism," November 1979): 627–640.

81. David Broder, *The Party Is Over: The Failure of Politics in America* (New York: Harper & Row, 1972), 120.

82. As reported by *New Guard*, Summer 1967, NG2.

83. Lawrence, "Campus Unrest Linked to Drugs," A14.

84. Oval 690, March 21, 1972, White House Tapes.

85. Oval 690, March 21, 1972, White House Tapes.

86. Krogh interview, PBS, 2000, http://www.pbs.org/wgbh/pages/frontline/shows/drugs/interviews/krogh.html.

87. Lassiter, "Impossible Criminals."

88. William F. Buckley, "End the Pot Penalties," *Washington Star News*, November 10, 1974, C4.

89. David T. Courtwright, "The Controlled Substances Act: How a 'Big Tent' Reform Became a Punitive Drug Law," *Drug and Alcohol Dependence* 76 (2004): 9–15; David F. Musto and Pamela Korsemeyer, *The Quest for Drug Control* (New Haven, CT: Yale University Press, 2002); Radley Balko, *Rise of the Warrior Cop: The Militarization of America's Police Forces* (New York: Public Affairs, 2013); Dan Baum, *Smoke and Mirrors: The War on Drugs and the Politics of Failure* (New York: Little Brown, 1996).

90. Kathleen Frydl, *The Drug Wars in America, 1940–1973* (Cambridge: Cambridge University Press, 2013).

91. US Congress, Committee on the Judiciary, House US Congressional Hearings to Provide for the Establishment of a Commission on Marihuana, HRG-1969-HJH-0003, October 15 and 16, 1969. 13.

92. Dana Adams Schmidt, "President Orders Wider Drug Fight; Asks $155-Million," *New York Times*, June 18, 1971, 1.

93. McGirr, *Suburban Warriors*, 204.

94. William J. Robbins, "Congress Gets Nixon's Bill to Curb Drug Abuses," *New York Times*, July 16, 1969, 51.

95. "Letters from Readers," *Spokane Daily Chronicle*, November 22, 1971, 4.

96. Del Rosa Federated Junior Women's Club in San Bernardino to Nixon, March 2, 1972, Folder: Commission on Marihuana and Drug Abuse, Box 1, FG 308, Nixon Presidential Materials, NARA II.

97. "Vote at 18 and Reforms in Draft Backed by Violence Commission," *New York Times*, November 26, 1969, 29.

98. Jeremy Kuzmarov, *The Myth of the Addicted Army: Vietnam and the Modern War on Drugs* (Amherst: University of Massachusetts Press, 2009), 106.

99. Dan Baum, "Legalize It All: How to Win the War on Drugs," *Harper's Magazine*, April 2016, https://harpers.org/archive/2016/04/legalize-it-all/ (accessed August 10, 2017.

100. Theodore Roszak, *The Making of a Counter Culture: Reflections on the Technocratic Society and Its Youthful Opposition* (Berkeley: University of California Press, 1995), 169.

101. Jerome L. Himmelstein, *The Strange Career of Marijuana* (Santa Barbara, CA: Greenwood, 1983), 132; Jeffrey Hart, "Marijuana and the Counterculture," *National Review*, December 8, 1972, 1348.

102. John Herbers, "Thousands in the Capital Express Faith in America," *New York Times*, July 5, 1970, 32.

103. Edward Fiske, "The Closest Thing to a White House Chaplain: Billy Graham," *New York Times*, June 8, 1969, SM27.

104. Larry Eskridge, "'One Way': Billy Graham, the Jesus Generation, and the Idea of an Evangelical Youth Culture," *American Society of Church History* 67, no. 1 (March 1998): 84.

105. Eskridge, 84.

106. Will Herberg, "Conservatives and the Jesus Freaks," *New Guard*, November 11, 1971, 15.

107. "State Attorney Says War on Drugs Succeeding," *Sarasota Herald-Tribune*, October 7, 1968, 2.

108. Don Oakley, "New Appraisals of Marihuana: Harsh 'Pot' Laws under Fire," *Prescott Evening Courier*, November 3, 1969, 6.

109. Antoni Gollan, "The Great Marijuana Problem," *National Review*, January 30, 1968, 74–80.

110. *The Elephant's Memory* 1, no. 1 (Spring 1972), Folder 13, Box 1, NFCR Presidential Papers, Alan Virta 1971–1972. University of Maryland, College Park, MD.

111. Lassiter, "Impossible Criminals."

112. US Congress, US Congressional Hearings to Provide for the Establishment of a Commission on Marihuana, 21.

113. US Congress, 21.

114. US Senate Hearings before the Subcommittee to Investigate Juvenile Delinquency, HRG-1969-SJS-0027, Committee on the Judiciary. Senate, September 15, 1969.

115. US Senate Hearings before the Subcommittee to Investigate Juvenile Delinquency.

116. US Senate Hearings before the Subcommittee to Investigate Juvenile Delinquency.

117. US Senate Hearings before the Subcommittee to Investigate Juvenile Delinquency.

118. Oval 690-11, March 21, 1972, White House Tapes.

119. "Senate Debates Laws on Marijuana Use," *Day* (New London, CT), January 28, 1970, 11.

120. Bill Kling, "Senate OK's Nixon's Drug Control," *Chicago Tribune*, January 29, 1970, C56.

121. Kuzmarov, *Myth of the Addicted Army*, 57.

122. "Nixon Calls for a War on Drugs," *Palm Beach Post*, March 21, 1972, A4.

123. Mark Shiel, "Banal and Magnificent Space in *Electra Glide Blue* (1973): An Allegory of the Nixon Era," *Cinema Journal* 46, no. 2 (2007): 91–116, 103.

124. FBI, Uniform Crime Reports, 1972–2000, http://www.csdp.org/research /shafernixon.pdf.

125. Baum, "Legalize It All."

126. *Volunteer*, UT Yearbook, 1971–1972, 102. University of Tennessee Special Collections.

127. Robert Finch to Jon Huntsman, Folder: Youth—Optional Proposals, 2 of 2 [CFOA 336], Box 43, PRF, NARA II.

128. Oval 473-5, March 25, 1971, White House Tapes.

129. US Congress, US Congressional Hearings to Provide for the Establishment of a Commission on Marihuana, 123.

130. Lassiter, "Impossible Criminals," 128.

131. Michelle Alexander, *The New Jim Crow: Mass Incarceration in the Age of Colorblindness* (New York: New Press, 2010).

132. Alexander, Oval 690-11, March 21, 1972, White House Tapes.

133. Ian Brailsford, "'Madison Avenue Takes On the Teenage Hop Heads,'" *Australasian Journal of American Studies* 18, no. 2 (December 1999): 45.

134. Interim Report of the National Commission on Marijuana and Drug Abuse, December 14, 1972, 2, Folder: Commission on Marijuana and Drug Abuse, 1971–1972, Box 1, FG 308, NARA II.

135. US Congress, Hearings, Drug Abuse Education Act of 1970, HRG-1972-EDL-0039, July 20, 1972.

136. "Pot Penalty Recommendations Called 'Sane,' 'Frightening,'" *Sarasota Journal*, March 22, 1972, B9.

137. Geoff Shepard to Ken Khachagian, Alphabetical File, Box 1, FG 308, NARA, II, College Park, MD.

138. James Walsh to Nixon, March 28, 1972, Folder: Commission on Marihuana and Drug Abuse [1971–1972], Box 1, FG 308. NARA II.

139. Novelli to Dailey, "Women Voters," April 27, 1972, Folder: Subject Files Alphabetical (JSM) Women, Box 27, PJM, Nixon Library.

140. Del Rosa Federated Junior Women's Club in San Bernardino to Nixon, March 2, 1972.

141. Oval 690-11, March 21, 1972, White House Tapes.

142. Robert Finch to Jon Huntsman, Folder: Youth—Optional Proposals [2 of 2] [CFOA 336], Box 43, PRF.

143. Oval 504-2, May 27, 1971, Conversation, White House Tapes.

144. Schmidt, "President Orders Wider Drug Fight," 1.

145. "Excerpts from President's Message on Drug Abuse Control," *New York Times*, June 18, 1971, 22.

146. James Kilpatrick, "Conservative View: The Matter of Marijuana," *Tuscaloosa News*, September 27, 1972, 3.

147. Kilpatrick, 3.
148. Oval 504-2, May 27, 1971, White House Tapes.
149. "Students of America!," *Esquire Magazine* 78, no. 3 (September 1972): 75.
150. Flamm, *Law and Order Street Crime*, 181.

Chapter 3. "The Orderly Process of Change": Nixon and Youth Issues

1. Richard Reeves, *President Nixon: Alone in the White House* (New York: Simon & Schuster, 2001), 225. Despite Nixon's efforts to stir up opposition, this was the most quickly ratified amendment in American history.
2. Allin to Grassmuck, "Thoughts on the Lincoln Speech," January 15, 1971, Folder: 18 Year Old Vote, 1972 [1 of 2], Box 43, PRF, Nixon Library.
3. Robert Finch to President, "Youth," April 8, 1971, Folder: Youth Progress Report and Paper, Box 45, PRF, NARA II.
4. "Student Radicalism Changes Faces," *Lipscomb Babbler,* January 14, 1972, 2.
5. Odle to Magruder, "Brock Strategy Proposal," Folder: Subject Files, Alphabetical (JSM) Youth No. 1 [1 of 3], Box 27, PJSM, Nixon Library.
6. "Vote at 18 Described as Danger to Nixon," *Milwaukee Journal,* June 29, 1971, 8.
7. Kabaservice, *Rule and Ruin,* 286.
8. For the environment, see Brooks Flippen, *Nixon and the Environment* (Albuquerque: New Mexico University Press, 2012); John C Whitaker, *Striking a Balance: Environment and Natural Resources Policy in the Nixon-Ford Years* (Washington, DC: American Enterprise Institute Press, 1987). For economy, see Allen Matusow, *Nixon's Economy: Booms, Bust, Dollars and Votes* (Lawrence: University Press of Kansas, 1998). For draft, see Julian Zelizer, *Arsenal of Democracy: The Politics of National Security—from World War II to the War on Terrorism* (New York: Basic Books, 2010). See also, Schulman, *Seventies,* for an overview of the administration's liberal tactics for conservative goals.
9. Karilyn Barker, "How Will Nixon React?," 1.
10. Colson to Haldeman, "18 Year Old Vote in 1972," December 9, 1970, Folder: Youth Optional Proposals [2 of 2] [CFOA 336], Box 43, WHSOF, PRF, NARA II.
11. "Young People and Their Political Power: A Special Report on the 18 Year Old and the Vote," Folder: Youth Vote, 1972, Box 107, PGM, Mudd Library, Princeton University.
12. Rebecca de Schweinitz, "The Proper Age for Suffrage": Vote 18 and the Politics of Age from World War II to the Age of Aquarius," in *Age in America: The Colonial Era to the Present,* ed. Corinne T. Field and Nicholas L. Syrett (New York: New York University Press, 2015), 209–236.
13. US Senate, *On Lowering the Voting Age,* Hearings before the Subcommittee on Constitutional Amendments, US Senate Committee on the Judiciary, 91st Congress, February 16, 1970, HRG-1970-SJS-0040, 284.
14. Milton Kaufman to the President, February 21, 1969, Folder: Lowering

Voting Age, Correspondence, 1969, Box 494, PGM, Mudd Library, Princeton University.

15. US Congress, *Extending Voting Rights Act of 1965*, 91st Cong., 2nd sess., *Congressional Record* 116 (June 17, 1970): 20190.

16. *Extending Voting Rights Act of 1965*, 20190–20191.

17. US Senate, *On Lowering the Voting Age*, 56.

18. US Senate, *On Lowering the Voting Age*, 35.

19. US Congress, *L.B.J.: A President Who Understands Young People*, 90th Cong., 2nd sess., *Congressional Record* 114 (June 27, 1968): 19079.

20. US Senate, *On Lowering the Voting Age*, 11931.

21. US Congress, *On Lowering the Voting Age*, Amendments to Senate Joint Resolution 7, 92nd Cong., Judiciary Committee Report, February 17, 1971, 6.

22. US Congress, 6.

23. Jeb Magruder, *An American Life* (New York: Atheneum, 1974), 172.

24. Perlstein, *Nixonland*, 509.

25. Rebecca Logan, "Project 18," http://hin.nea.org/home/48614.htm (accessed October 29, 2011).

26. Rietz to Magruder, "26th Amendment to the Constitution," Folder: Alphabetical Files (JSM) Youth [4 of 4], Box 29, PJM, Nixon Library.

27. Ron Walker to Dwight Chapin, "Young Americans in Concert at Carnegie Hall," July 2, 1971, Folder: Declaration of Independence, Bill of Rights, Constitution [January 1, 1971–December 31, 1972], EX FE 4, Papers of Richard Nixon, NARA II.

28. Ron Walker to Dwight Chapin.

29. "Ceremony Marking the Certification of the 26th Amendment," July 5, 1971, Folder: Declaration of Independence, Bill of Rights, Constitution [January 1, 1971–December 31, 1972], EX FE 4, Papers of Richard Nixon, NARA II.

30. "Ceremony Marking the Certification of the 26th Amendment."

31. Steven V. Roberts, "Youths Meet on 1972 Drive, and Politicians Pay Heed," *New York Times*, December 5, 1971, 65.

32. John Elrod to Marquis Childs, "Comments on Russo Letter to Washington Post," Folder: Student Vote, Box 219, PCC, Mudd Library, Princeton University.

33. Michael McDonald and Samuel L. Popkin. "The Myth of the Vanishing Voter," *American Political Science Review* 95, no. 4 (2001): 963–974, 970.

34. Kenneth Guido Testimony to Subcommittee on Census and Statistics, US House of Representatives. June 27, 1972, Folder: Voting Rights Project, Box 220, Common Cause Papers, Mudd Library, Princeton University.

35. "National Student Lobby Alerts Students to Issues," *Daily Titan* (University of California–Fullerton), October 25, 1972, 5.

36. "Denying the Youth Vote," *New York Times*, June 8, 1972, Folder: Youth, 1972, Box 107, PGM, Mudd Library, Princeton University.

37. Adam Rome, "'Give Earth a Chance': The Environmental Movement in the Sixties," *Journal of American History*, September 2003, 525.

38. "Speech from California's Survival Fair," *Rag* 4, no. 21 (April 13, 1970): 13.

39. Whitaker, *Striking a Balance*, 4.

40. James Bowman and Kathryn Hanaford, "Mass Media and the Environment since Earth Day," *Journalism Quarterly*, Spring 1976, 164.

41. Mels Stephens to Charles Colson, "'Youth' Strategy," July 28, 1971, Folder: Youth Programs [1 of 2], Box 158, PHRH.

42. CIS 70, Environmental Protection Act Hearings, S-3575, May 12, 1970, 13.

43. Congressional Hearings on Environmental Education Act. HR-14753, March 24, 1970, 32.

44. Whitaker, *Striking a Balance*, 5.

45. Flippen, *Nixon and the Environment*, 12

46. Flippen, 15.

47. Randal Cornell Teague, "Environmental Pollution and YAF," *New Guard*, April 1970, 10.

48. Editors, *Fortune Magazine*, eds. *The Environment: A National Mission for the Seventies* (New York: Perennial Library, 1970), 168–169.

49. CIS 1972, S-261-59, 131.

50. "BBDO-LA Raps with Students about Business," Folder, Alphabetical (JSM) Youth [1 of 4], Box 29, PJM, Nixon Library.

51. See also J. Louis S. Warren, ed., *American Environmental History* (Carlton, Australia: Blackwell, 2003), 271–288.

52. Nixon, "Remarks to a Student-Faculty Convocation at the University of Nebraska."

53. YVP Brochure, Folder 4, Box 2, Papers of UMDCR.

54. Diana Ralph to the President, June 7, 1969, Folder: Youth Advisory Committees, Begin—December 31, 1970, FG 216-3, Papers of Richard Nixon, NARA II.

55. "People Should be Individuals," editorial page, *UT Beacon*, October 26, 1972. University of Tennessee, Special Collections.

56. Gerald Jerkins, "Draft Deferments Hard for Graduates, Undergrads," *Babbler*, February 21, 1969, 2.

57. "Vote at 18 and Draft Reforms Backed by Violence Commission," *New York Times*, November 26, 1969, 29.

58. Richard Nixon, "Nixon's Special Message to Congress." Public Papers of the President, May 13, 1969.

59. Zelizer, *Arsenal of Democracy*, 203–236.

60. *House Review of the Administration and Operation of the Draft Law*, US Congress, Special Subcom on Draft, Committee on Armed Services CIS 91-2 70, July 23, 1970, Committee on Armed Services Serial No. 91-80, Selective Service, H.R. 18025; 91 H.R. 18578, 12562.

61. *House Review of the Administration and Operation of the Draft Law*, 12562.

62. *House Review of the Administration and Operation of the Draft Law*, 12562.

63. March 3, 1970. Papers of Richard Nixon, Folder: February 6, 1970–March 22, 1970, FG 216, NARA II.

64. Ken Cole to Flanigan, October 13, 1969, Folder: October 1, 1969–December 31, 1969, EX FG 216, Papers of Richard Nixon, NARA II.

65. "Meeting with Curtis W. Tarr, March 4, 1970, Folder: February 16, 1970–March 22, 1970, EX FG 216, Papers of Richard Nixon, NARA II.

66. Letter to Tarr, Folder: February 16, 1970–March 22, 1970, EX FG 216, Papers of Richard Nixon, NARA II.

67. Richard Nixon, "Statement on Establishing Nationwide Youth Advisory Committee to the Selective Service System," June 6, 1969. Public Papers of the President.

68. Robert B. Semple Jr., "Nixon to Form Youth Panels in All 50 States to Advise on Draft," New York Times, June 7, 1969, 2.

69. Letter to Richard Nixon, June 7, 1969, Folder: Youth Advisory Committees, Begin—December 31, 1970, FG 216-3, Papers of Richard Nixon, NARA II.

70. Flanigan to Hunt, June 13, 1969, Folder: Youth Advisory Committees, Begin—December 31, 1970, GEN FG 216-3, Papers of Richard Nixon, NARA II.

71. Tarr to Honorable William Steiger, March 9, 1970, Folder: February 16, 1970–March 22, 1970, EX FG 216, Papers of Richard Nixon, NARA II.

72. Tarr to Rose, July 21, 1970, Folder: July 1, 1970–August 31, 1970, EX FG 216, Papers of Richard Nixon, NARA II.

73. House Review of the Administration and Operation of the Draft Law, US Congress, Special Subcom on Draft, Committee on Armed Services, July 23, 1970, 12562.

74. News Release, Selective Service System National Headquarters, "1969–1970: Time of Change in Selective Service," Selective Service System [January 1, 1971–December 31, 1972]. [3 of 3], EX FG 216, Papers of Richard Nixon, NARA II.

75. Tarr to Rose, July 21, 1970, Folder: July 1, 1970–August 31, 1970, EX FG 216, Papers of Richard Nixon, NARA II.

76. Rose to Tarr, July 8, 1970, July 1, 1970–August 31, 1970, EX FG 216, Papers of Richard Nixon, NARA II.

77. Rose to Rabb, June 12, 1970, April 1, 1970–June 30, 1970, EX FG 216, Papers of Richard Nixon, NARA II.

78. Ken Rietz interview, June 6, 2012.

79. Richard Nixon, RN: The Memoirs of Richard Nixon (New York: Simon & Schuster, 1990), 673.

80. H. R. Haldeman, Haldeman Diaries: Inside the Nixon White House (New York: G. P. Putnam's Sons, 1994), 359.

Chapter 4. Nixon and New Republicans

1. T. Harding Jones to Finch, Folder: Youth Programs [1 of 2], Box 158, PHRH, WHSF: SMOF, NARA II.

2. Finch to President, Folder: Youth Optional Proposal [2 of 2], Box 43, PRF, NARA II.

3. Steven P. Miller, *Billy Graham and the Rise of the Republican South* (Philadelphia: University of Pennsylvania Press, 2009), 142–143.

4. Rietz interview.

5. Oval 385-14, December 2, 1972, White House Tapes.

6. Feeney, *Nixon at the Movies*, 225.

7. Oval 795-1, October 10, 1972, White House Tapes.

8. Hope, "Nations Youth Being Courted for Votes," 22.

9. Bill Brock interview, December 12, 2012.

10. Allen Jones to Brock. Georgia Federation of Young Republican Clubs, June 14, 1963, Folder 53, Box 15, PWEB.

11. Brock interview.

12. Tape 2, 4, Folder 2, Box 31, PWEB.

13. Tape 2, Disc 8, Folder 2, 4, Box 31, PWEB.

14. Tape 2, Disc 7, Folder 2, 4, Box 3, PWEB.

15. Tape 6, Folder 6, 13, Box 31, PWEB.

16. Tape 6, Folder 6, 24, Box 31, PWEB.

17. "Tennessee's Senator Gore Faces Toughest Race of Political Life," *Sarasota Journal*, October 6, 1970, A8.

18. Mark, *Going Dirty*, 81.

19. Brock interview.

20. Walter R. Mears, "President on the Stump: Hecklers' Taunts, Jeers Give Weapons to Nixon," *Freelance Star*, October 20, 1970, 1.

21. Press Release, October 6, 1970, Folder 18, Box 17, PWEB.

22. Press Release, October 6, 1970.

23. Brock interview, Folder 17, Box 17, PWEB.

24. Brock Commencement Speech at Union College, Jackson, TN, Folder 94, Box 14, PWEB.

25. Tom Wicker, "The Bitter Senate Struggle in Tennessee," *St. Petersburg Times*, October 21, 1970, A14.

26. Log Cabin no. 7, Student Unrest Flyer, Folder: Student Unrest, 1970s, University of Tennessee Special Collections.

27. Log Cabin no. 7.

28. Kyle Longley, *Senator Albert Gore, Sr.: Tennessee Maverick* (Baton Rouge: Louisiana State University Press, 2004), 233.

29. Perlstein, *Nixonland*, 464.

30. Brock to Jaycees, January 8, 1971, Folder 85, Box 15, PWEB.

31. Longley, *Senator Albert Gore, Sr.*, 234.

32. Brock interview, Folder 17, Box 17, PWEB.

33. Brock at Union College. May 30, 1969. PWEB, Box 15.

34. Brock interview, Folder 17, Box 17, PWEB.

35. Eddie E. Williams III to Brock, October 29, 1969, Folder 16, Box 31, PWEB.

36. "Critique of Young Volunteers for Brock Tennessee Senatorial Campaign 1970," Folder 20, Box 31, PWEB.

37. Rietz interview.

38. Rietz to Magruder, "Mock Election," Folder: Alphabetical (JSM) Mock Elections, Box 22, PJM, Nixon Library.

39. Brock Campaign Objectives, Folder 17, Box 17, PWEB.

40. Brock Senate Campaign Meeting, October 12, 1969, Folder 19, Box 31, PWEB.

41. Brock Senate Campaign Meeting, October 12, 1969.

42. Advertising Objectives, Folder 19, Box 19, PWEB.

43. Advertising Objectives, Folder 17, Box 17, PWEB.

44. David Helvarg, *The War against the Greens: The "Wise-Use" Movement, the New Right, and the Browning of America* (New York: Johnson Books, 2004), 89.

45. "Tennessee's Senator Gore Faces Toughest Race of Political Life," A8.

46. "Tennessee's Senator Gore Faces Toughest Race of Political Life," A8.

47. Brock interview, December 12, 2012.

48. Letters, *Time*, September 21, 1970.

49. "Tennessee's Senator Gore Faces Toughest Race of Political Life," A8.

50. Mark, *Going Dirty*, 83.

51. Lassiter, *Silent Majority*, 272.

52. "Young Voters for Nixon Proposal," Folder 20, 5, Box 31, PWEB.

53. Darren Dochuk, *From Bible Belt to Sunbelt* (New York: W. W. Norton, 2011), 331; Lassiter, *Silent Majority*, 271.

54. Brock at GOP Southern Regional Conference, Folder 103, Box 15, PWEB.

55. Brock, YVN Proposal, Folder 20, Box 31, PWEB.

56. "Senator Brock Concerned with Youth Vote," *Times-News* (Henderson, NC), May 3, 1971, 9.

57. Magruder, *American Life*, 105.

58. "Nixon's Youth Corps," *Look Magazine*, February 10, 1970, 48.

59. Magruder, *American Life*, 105.

60. James M. Naughton, "Nixon, on TV, Attributes Youth Unrest to Loss of 'Old' Values," *New York Times*, March 16, 1971, 20.

61. Colson to Haldeman, "18 Year Old Vote in 1972," December 9, 1970, Folder: Youth Optional Proposals [2 of 2] [CFOA 336], Box 43, WHSOF PRF, NARA II.

62. Magruder, *American Life*, 113.

63. Jamie Bennett to Bud Wilkinson, September 1969, Youth Status, Box 16, PPF, Ford Library, Ann Arbor, MI.

64. Magruder to Haldeman, July 24, 1970, Folder: Attitude Study [CFOA 336], Box 43, PRF, NARA II.

65. McLane to President, November 1971, Folder: Youth Programs [1 of 2], Box 158, PHRH, WHSOF, Nixon Library.

66. Gavin to Haldeman, January 12, 1971, Folder: Attitude Study CFOA 336, Box 43, PRF, Nixon Library, NARA II.

67. Magruder, *American Life*, 125.

68. Engman to Cohen, Proposal, March 24, 1972, Folder: Youth Status, Box 16, PPF, Ford Library.

69. Rockefeller Youth Task Force Summary, January 12, 1971, Folder: Attitude Study [CFOA 336], Box 43, PRF SMOF, NARA II.

70. Walter Hickel, "America Is Tired of Hate: Walter Hickel on New Politics," *Sarasota Herald-Tribune*, December 12, 1971, 6.

71. Gary Wills, "The Forgotten Promises to Youth," *St. Petersburg Times*, January 25, 1971, 14A.

72. "The Administration: Getting It All Together in the Name of Action," *Time*, June 7, 1971. In fact, Dr. David Gottlieb of Pennsylvania State University, who conducted the study, decided that most volunteers in VISTA found it an opportunity to work for change "within the system."

73. Robert B. Semple Jr., "Nixon Aides Plan Policy for Youth," *New York Times*, December 8, 1969, 54.

74. "Report from White House Youth Conference," *Rolling Stone*, May 27, 1971, 25.

75. "Report from White House Youth Conference," 25.

76. Harold Hodkinson, *Student Participation in Governance*, Education Task Force Paper, Center for Research and Development in Higher Education, University of California, Berkeley, 1971, 53.

77. "Report from White House Youth Conference," *Rolling Stone*, 26.

78. Wayne J. Thorburn, "The Unrepresentative Youth," *New Guard*, Summer 1971, 18.

79. "White House Plans for Youth Parley Criticized by Bloc," *New York Times*, March 20, 1971, 22.

80. Neil Boyer to John Richardson Jr., April 30, 1971, White House Youth Conference on the Third Century, PPF, Ford Library.

81. "Report from White House Youth Conference," 25.

82. "Education: Discontent of the Straights," *Time* 97, no. 1 (May 3, 1971): http://www.time.com/time/magazine/article/0,9171,876970,00.html (accessed November 10, 2012).

83. "Report from White House Youth Conference," 24.

84. Nan Robertson, "House Youth Conference Proves to Be Anti-establishment," *New York Times*, April 22, 1971, 28.

85. Bill Brock Press Release, April 25, 1971, Folder 93, Box 15, PWEB.

86. Thorburn, "Unrepresentative Youth," 18.

87. Thorburn, 18.

88. "Delegate Reports on Youth Conference," *Evening Independent*, May 1, 1971, B7.

89. "Youths End 'Fairest' Conference," *Pittsburgh Press*, April 23, 1971, 17.

90. Pat Buchanan to John Ehrlichman, July 23, 1971, White House Conference on Children and Youth [Folder 2 of 2], May 1971–1972, EX MC 3-1, WHCF: Subject Files, NARA II.

91. Nan Robertson, "Youth Proposals Backed by Nixon," *New York Times*, April 16, 1972, 31.

92. *San Francisco Chronicle*, April 14, 1972, White House Conference on Children and Youth [2 of 2, May 1971–1972], EX MC 3-1, Papers of Richard Nixon, NARA II.

93. Leo Tonkin to John Ehrlichman, May 7, 1971, White House Conference

on Children and Youth [1971–1974], GEN MC 3-1, Papers of Richard Nixon, NARA II.

94. Nixon to National 4-H Congress, Chicago, IL, December 1, 1971, White House Conference on Children and Youth [2 of 2, May 1971–1972], EX MC 3-1, Nixon Presidential Materials, NARA II.

95. Nixon to Delegates, March 16, 1972, White House Conference on Children and Youth [2 of 2], May 1971–1972, EX MC 3-1, Papers of Richard Nixon, NARA II.

96. Oval Office, Conversation 473-2, March 25, 1971, White House Tapes.

97. H. R. Haldeman to Finch, February 2, 1971, Folder: Youth Programs 2 of 2, Box 158, WHSF SMOF Haldeman Files, NARA II.

98. YVN Proposal, Folder 20, 3, Box 31, PWEB.

99. *Congressional Record*, Senate, May 9, 1972, Folder 15, Box 11, PWEB.

100. Magruder to Haldeman, "Youth Manifesto," February 15, 1971, Folder: Youth Optional Proposals [2 of 2], Box 43, PRF, NARA II.

101. McLane to Rietz, "Wallace Henley Speech," Folder: (August 1971–January 1972) [8 of 12], Box 55, Papers of James McLane, Nixon Library.

102. Finch to President, Folder: Youth Optional Proposal [2 of 2], Box 43, PRF, NARA II.

103. *First Monday*, November 1, 1971, Folder: White House Youth Initiatives [CFOA 336], Box 43, WHSF SMOF PRF, NARA II.

104. Suri, *Power and Protest*, 244.

105. Jack V. Fox, "Youth Feels Mediation Easy between US, China," *Bangor Daily News*, April 19, 1971, 4.

106. Campus Opinion, August 12, 1971, Folder: Youth Programs [1 of 2], Box 158, PHRH, NARA II.

107. Alan Virta to the President, April 11, 1972, Folder 13, Box 1, UMDCR Presidential Papers, Alan Virta 1971–1972, UMD, College Park, MD.

108. "Pandas and Pucks," June 14, 1972, Folder 14, Box 1, UMDCR Presidential Papers, Alan Virta 1971–1972, College Park, MD.

109. Malek to McLane, October 6, 1971, Folder: Youth Programs [1 of 2], Box 158, PHRH, Nixon Library.

110. Perlstein, *Nixonland*, illustrations, 562.

111. Oval 360-20, September 11, 1972, White House Tapes.

112. McLane to Haldeman, "Youth—Voter Registration and China Initiative." October 6, 1971, Folder: Subject Files, Alphabetical (JSM) Voter Registration [4 of 7], Box 27, PJM, Nixon Library.

Chapter 5. "Acid, Amnesty and Abortion": New Politics and George McGovern's Campaign

1. Crotty, *Decision for the Democrats*, 148.

2. Haldeman, *Haldeman Diaries*, 470.

3. Janet Fraser and Ernest May, eds., *Campaign '72: The Managers Speak* (Cambridge, MA: Harvard University Press, 1973), 146.

4. Ken Rietz to Fred Malek, "McGovern and the Youth Vote," July 5, 1972, Folder: Citizens Youth 2 of 2, Box 22, PFVM, Richard Nixon Library.

5. Rossinow, *Politics of Authenticity*, 235.

6. Andy Soltis, "Muted Politics on Campus," *New York Post*, November 3, 1972, 26. Found in Folder: Youth, 1972, Box 927, PGM, Mudd Library, Princeton University.

7. Terry Ryan, "Youth Vote Impact Shows Up in Elections throughout the US," *Free Lance Star* (Fredericksburg, VA), November 10, 1972, 1.

8. Ripon Society and Clifford Brown Jr., *Jaws of Victory: The Game-Plan Politics of 1972, the Crisis of the Republican Party, and the Future of the Constitution* (Boston: Little, Brown, 1973), 6.

9. *One Bright Shining Moment: The Forgotten Summer of George McGovern*, directed by Stephen Vittoria (2005; Los Angeles, CA: Street Legal Cinema, 2006), DVD.

10. Thurston Clarke, *The Last Campaign: Robert F. Kennedy and the 82 Days That Inspired America* (New York: Holt Paperbacks, 2009), 203.

11. Marjorie Hunter, "M'Govern Opens Presidential Bid with Peace Plea," *New York Times*, August 11, 1968, 1.

12. "Perspectives on Youth: The National Front," Folder: Youth 1971, Box 927, PGM, Mudd Library, Princeton University.

13. Herbert Mitgang, "The New Politics, the Old Casualties," *New York Times*, January 6, 1969, 46.

14. Mitgang, 46.

15. "Tammany Tiger Finds That Its Cubs Can Bite," *New York Times*, July 11, 1969, 42.

16. Lawrence O'Brien, McGovern Commission on Party Structure and Delegate Selection, July 29, 1970, Folder: Youth, 1970, Box 921, PGM, Mudd Library, Princeton University.

17. Testimony of Daniel Wright III, McGovern Commission on Party Structure and Delegate Selection, July 29, 1970, Folder: Youth, 1970, Box 921, PGM, Mudd Library, Princeton University.

18. Frank Mankiewicz and Tom Braden, "Will Young Vote Dump Nixon?," *Palm Beach Post*, April 24, 1971, A19.

19. Letter from Frank Mankiewicz, May 25, 1972, Chronological Files, Box 6, PFFM, JFK Library.

20. Nina Totenberg, "McGovern Staff: Youth and an 'Elder Statesmen,'" Folder: Gary Hart, Box M6, PGM, Mudd Library, Princeton University.

21. *Rolling Stone*, June 8, 1972 (cover).

22. "Political Affiliation by All Age Groups by Region and County, 1967–68," Folder: Youth 1970, Box 107, PFFM, Mudd Library, Princeton University.

23. "Independence Is Valid," *UT Beacon*, November 10, 1972, 8, University of Tennessee Special Collections.

24. "Young People and Their Political Power: A Special Report on the 18 Year Old and the Vote," Folder: Youth Vote, 1972, Box 107, PGM, Mudd Library, Princeton University.

25. Staff Discussion, Cedar Points Farm, McGovern [File 1 of 7], July 25, 1969, Box 38r, PTW, JFK Library.

26. Thompson, *Fear and Loathing: On the Campaign Trail '72* (New York: Warner Books, 1973), 174.

27. Frederick Dutton, *Changing Sources of Power: American Politics in the 1970s* (New York: McGraw Hill, 1971), 55.

28. Dutton, 12.

29. Jack Rosenthal, "Poll Hints Youths May Back Nixon," *New York Times*, July 23, 1972, 40.

30. "Issues '72: The Young; Turning Out," *Time*, September 25, 1972, http://content.time.com/time/magazine/article/0,9171,903573,00.html (accessed November 10, 2013).

31. Steven V. Roberts, "'72 Strategists See the Youth Vote as Vital," *New York Times*, December 26, 1971, 45.

32. Mervin Field, "18 Year-Old Vote Pattern Seen as Liberal," Folder: Youth, 1972, Box 107, PGM, Mudd Library, Princeton University.

33. "Youth and Our Political Process," Folder: Youth 1970, Box 927, PGM, Mudd Library, Princeton University.

34. *Congressional Quarterly*, "Youth Helps Elect 19 Candidates to 92nd Congress," Folder: Youth, 1972, Box 107, PGM, Mudd Library, Princeton University.

35. "Youth and Our Political Process," Folder: Youth 197, Box 927, PGM o, Mudd Library, Princeton University.

36. "Shaping the Future," Folder: Youth 1972, Box 107, PGM, Mudd Library, Princeton University.

37. McGovern Press Release, November 9, 1970, Folder: Youth 1970, Box 921, PGM, Mudd Library, Princeton University.

38. Ed Failor to McGregor, July 12, 1972, Folder: McGovern [Folder 2 of 6], Box 8, PPB, NARA II.

39. UPI, "Freshman of 1970, Older, More Liberal," Folder: Youth, 1972, Box 107, PGM, Mudd Library, Princeton University.

40. Ed Failor to McGregor, July 12, 1972, Folder: McGovern [Folder 2 of 6], Box 8, PPB, NARA II.

41. Jon Wiener, *Gimme Some Truth: The John Lennon FBI Files* (Berkeley: University of California Press, 1999), 114. While the lyrics are on the back jacket of Lennon's next album, *Some Time in New York City*, the FBI marked the report on the rally and the lyrics as confidential.

42. "Thunder in November," from Tim Eckerman, Folder: Youth 1972, Box 107, PGM, Mudd Library, Princeton University.

43. Letter to Frank Mankiewicz, Chronological File: October 3, 1972, Box 14, PFFM, JFK Library.

44. Letter from Frank Mankiewicz to Rick Stearns, Chronological Files: August 1972, Box 9, PFFM, JFK Library.

45. "McGovern Marshalls Youth," *Palm Beach Post*, February 22, 1971, A2.

46. Edward O'Donnell to McGovern, "Suggested Student Youth Movement for the Fall," June 9, 1972, Folder: Youth 1972, Box 107, PGM, Mudd Library, Princeton University.

47. McGovern Speech released October 21, 1971, Folder: Youth 1971, Box 927, PGM, Mudd Library, Princeton University.

48. McGovern Press Release, October 29, 1971, Folder: Youth, 1971, Box 927, PGM, Mudd Library, Princeton University.

49. McGovern Commission, "National One Time, Lifetime, Voter Registration and Universal Voter Enrollment," Folder: Youth 1970, Box 921, PGM, Mudd Library, Princeton University.

50. McGovern Commission.

51. McGovern Commission.

52. "Vote," National Voter Registration Drive, Folder 3, Youth Vote, 1972, Box 1, Thomas Klinkel Collection on George McGovern, MC 166, Mudd Library, Princeton University.

53. From Ann Wexler to Field Organizers, Folder: Anne Wexler, Box 469, PGM, Mudd Library, Princeton University.

54. "McGovern's Togetherness Show," *Newsweek*, Folder: Youth, 1972, Box 107, PGM, Mudd Library, Princeton University.

55. Steven V. Roberts, "If You Are Unregistered, Expect Democrats to Call," *New York Times*, August 7, 1972, 20.

56. Roberts, 20.

57. Memo from Jack Conway to Carroll Ladt, Folder: Youth Citizenship Fund, Box 220, PCC, Mudd Library, Princeton University.

58. Memo from Jack Conway to Carroll Ladt, Folder: Youth Citizenship Fund.

59. Memo from Jack Conway to Carroll Ladt.

60. "Registration Summer—Youth Politics Inc.," August 19, 1971, Chronological File, Box 9, PFFM, JFK Library.

61. Mary McGrory, "McGovern's New Hampshire Campaign Like McCarthy's, But Without Drama," *Toledo Blade*, February 23, 1972, 16.

62. Ed O'Donnell to Students for McGovern Co-coordinators, "Possible Students for McGovern Activities This Spring," Folder: Edward J. O'Donnell, 1972, Box 465, PGM, Mudd Library, Princeton University.

63. "A Full Time Army" Folder: Youth 1972, Box 107, PGM, Mudd Library, Princeton University.

64. Terry Ryan, "Both Sides Aim for New Young Voters," *Tri-city Herald* (Richland, WA), August 15, 1972, 5.

65. Letter to Frank Mankiewicz, October 3, 1972, Chronological File, Box 14, PFM, JFK Library.

66. James Perry, *Us and Them: How the Press Covered the 1972 Election* (New York: Clarkson N. Potter, 1973), 139.

67. Donald Lambro, UPI, "Youth Vote: Workers for Nixon and Students for McGovern?," *Ludington Daily News*, November 6, 1972, 6.

68. "Wisconsin Young Democratic Leader Endorse McGovern," November 11, 1971, Folder: Youth, Box 927, PGM, Mudd Library, Princeton University.

69. Gary Hart, *Right from the Start: A Chronicle of the McGovern Campaign* (New York: Quadrangle, 1973), 85.

70. Hart, 84.

71. Rex Weiner, "Caution on the Left," *New York Times*, July 27, 1972, 31.

72. Terry Ryan, "Edge to Dems in Youth Vote," *Chicago Tribune*, August 17, 1972, 6.

73. Memo from Jack Conway to Carroll Ladt, Folder: Youth Citizenship Fund, Box 220, PCC.

74. Edward O'Donnell to McGovern, "Suggested Student Youth Movement for the Fall," June 9, 1972, Folder: Youth 1972, Box 107, PGM, Mudd Library, Princeton University.

75. Roberts, "If You Are Unregistered, Expect Democrats to Call," 20.

76. Mary McGrory, "McGovern Drive Lacks McCarthy Spark," *Eugene Register-Guard*, February 23, 1972, 12A.

77. Joe Grata, "Crowd Cheers McGovern Here," *Pittsburgh Press*, September 13, 1972, 1.

78. Grata, 1.

79. "McGovern's Togetherness Show," *Newsweek*, Folder: Youth, 1972, PGM.

80. O'Donnell to Hart, Mankiewicz, Folder: Edward O'Donnell, Box 465, PGM, Mudd Library, Princeton University.

81. Thompson, *Fear and Loathing*, 418.

82. Senator's Personal Amendment, Folder: Students, Campuses, Kent State, 1970, Box 569, PGM, Mudd Library, Princeton University.

83. "Four More Hours or Four More Years," pamphlet, Folder: 3, Youth Vote, 1972 Box 1, Thomas Klinkel Collection on George McGovern (MC 166), Mudd Library, Princeton University.

84. Douglas E. Schoen, "Stumping the Airwaves with Candidate McGovern," *Harvard Crimson*, November 3, 1972, http://www.thecrimson.com/article/1972/11/3/stumping-the-airwaves-with-candidate-mcgovern/ (accessed September 10, 2012).

85. Thompson, *Fear and Loathing*, 221.

86. Buchanan Assault Book [Folder 1 of 5], Box 10, Buchanan Papers, NARA II.

87. Thompson, *Fear and Loathing*, 226.

88. Letter from Meyer Field to Lawrence O'Brien, October 13, 1972, Chronological File, Box 144, PSS, JFK Library.

89. Thompson, *Fear and Loathing*, 198.

90. G. Hart, *Right from the Start*, 169.

91. Perry, *Us and Them*, 156–157.

92. *Herald Examiner* (Los Angeles, CA), June 13, 1972, McGovern File, Box 38r, PTW, JFK Library.

93. "Times Survey, Defections in Party Face McGovern," *New York Times*, June 9, 1972, 1.

94. James Wiegart, "Youth and Cold Cash Beat Hubie," *Daily News*, June 7, 1972, Folder: Youth 1972, Box 107, PGM, Mudd Library, Princeton University.

95. Note, February 1972, File: Chronological File, Box 3, PFFM, JFK Library.

96. Letter from Ted Van Dyk to George McGovern, December 8, 1971, Folder: Ted Van Dyk, Box 28, PFM, JFK Library.

97. Joshua M. Glasser, *The Eighteen Day Running Mate* (New Haven, CT: Yale University Press, 2012), 156.

98. R. W. Apple Jr., "O'Brien Reproves McGovern Staff over Lax Effort," *New York Times*, September 1, 1972, 1.

99. Theodore White, *The Making of the President, 1972* (New York: Bantam, 1973), 171.

100. Memo from Ted Van Dyk to George McGovern, August 23, 1972, Folder: McGovern Chronological File, Box 38r, PTW, JFK Library.

101. Gordon Weil to George McGovern, Folder: Gordon Weil, 1970–1972, Box 469, PGM, Mudd Library, Princeton University.

102. "Demo Youth: 'Apple Pie, Moderate,'" *St. Petersburg Times*, July 4, 1972, B2.

103. Patrick Anderson Washington, "Taste of Success," *New York Times*, May 14, 1972, SM13.

104. James Perry, *Us and Them*, 39.

105. Douglas E. Schoen, "Stumping the Airwaves with Candidate McGovern," *Harvard Crimson*, November 3, 1972, http://www.thecrimson.com/article/1972/11/3/stumping-the-airwaves-with-candidate-mcgovern/ (accessed September 2012).

106. Schoen.

107. "McGovern Visit to Portland, Maine," September 15, 1972, Folder: State Press Ops, Maine, Box 8, Papers of Kirby Jones, JFK Library.

108. Jon Nordheimer, "Convention Life: Work, Not Play," *New York Times*, July 15, 1972, 13.

109. In later interviews, Charles Colson claimed that Nixon's campaign directed this demonstration though it is not exactly clear what role, if any, CREEP played given different testimonies from participants.

110. Gordon Weil, *The Long Shot: George McGovern Runs for President* (New York: W. W. Norton, 1973), 147–148.

111. Weil, 147–148.

112. Weil, 147–148.

113. Perry, *Us and Them* (citing Dan Thomasson, *Pittsburg Press*, July 14, 1972, 1), 82.

114. Haynes Johnson, "A Portrait of Democrats New Delegates," *Washington Post*, Folder: The 1972 Election File, The Book [Folder 1 of 3], Box 10, PPB, NARA II.

115. Perry, *Us and Them* (citing Thomasson), 90.

116. James Giglio, "The Eagleton Affair: Thomas Eagleton, George McGovern, and the 1972 Vice-Presidential Nomination," *Presidential Studies Quarterly* 39, no. 4 (December 2009): 51.

117. Perry, *Us and Them* (citing Thomasson), 90.

118. Joseph Califano, *Inside: A Public and Private Life* (New York: Public Affairs, 2005), 263.

119. Jon Herbers, "Democrats Assured of a Platform Fight," *New York Times*, June 28, 1972, 1.

120. Thomas Byrne Edsall and Mary D. Edsall, *Chain Reaction: The Impact of Race, Rights and Taxes on American Politics* (New York: W. W. Norton, 1991), 89.

121. George McGovern, *Grassroots: The Autobiography of George McGovern* (New York: Random House, 1977), 234.

122. Mankiewitz memo, Folder: Labor, Box 20, PFFM, JFK Library.

123. Miroff, *Liberal's Moment*, 187.

124. Victor Riesel, "Labor Works for Youth," Folder: Alphabetical (JSM) Youth No. 3 [1 of 4], Box 29, PJM, Nixon Library.

125. Riesel.

126. Governor Patrick Lucey Speech to the Theatrical Stage Employees and Motion Picture Machine Organization, September 24, 1972, Folder: Labor, Box 20, PFM, JFK Library.

127. Memo from Lester Spielman to Frank Mankiewicz. September 6, 1972, Folder: Labor File, Box 20, PFFM, JFK Library.

128. Letter from John B. Martin to J. K. Galbraith, September 13, 1972, Campaign Correspondence File, Box 531, PJKG, JFK Library.

129. Tom Reynders, "Michigan Voters Seen Giving McGovern Edge," *Toledo Blade*, October 13, 1972, 3.

130. Letter from Frank Mankiewicz to Rick Stearns, August 1972, Chronological File, Box 9 PFFM, JFK Library.

131. Memo from Eli Sagan to Frank Mankiewicz, July 20, 1972, Alphabetical File, Box 28, PFFM, JFK Library.

132. July 28, 1972, Eagleton File, Box 17, PFFM, JFK Library.

133. July 27, 1972, Eagleton File, Box 17, PFFM, JFK Library.

134. Message from Dr. Evelyn Hooker (LA) to Frank Mankiewicz, August 2, 1972, Folder: Chronological File, Box 9, PFFM, JFK Library.

135. Buchanan Assault Book [Folder 1 of 5], Box 10, PPB, NARA II.

136. Kevin Phillips, "How Nixon Will Win," *New York Times*, August 6, 1972, SM8.

137. Khachigian to Buchanan, July 5, 1972, 1972 Election File, The Book [Folder 1 of 3], 1of 8, "Elitist Radical Chic," Box 10, WHSF SF&OF: PRB, NARA II.

138. "Connally Sees More Democrats Supporting Nixon," *New York Times*, September 1, 1972, 41.

139. Oval 217-6, October 6, 1972. White House Tapes.

140. Oval 792-4, October 5, 1972. White House Tapes.

141. Colson to Haldeman, "18 year old vote in 1972," December 9, 1970, Folder: Youth Optional Proposals [2 of 2] [CFOA 336], Box 43, WHSOF, PRF, NARA II.

142. Buchanan to Mitchell, June 6, 1972, Folder Re-election Committee [Folder 1 of 3], Box 8, PPB, 1972 Election File, NARA II.

143. Buchanan to Mitchell.

144. "Marijuana," Folder: Assault Book [1 of 5], Box 10, PPB, NARA II.

145. Pat Buchanan to Mitchell, April 27, 1972, Folder: Subject Files Alphabetical (JSM) McGovern [2 of 3], Box 20, PJM, Nixon Library.

146. Magruder to Mitchell, December 7, 1971, Folder: Alphabetical, Youth, 3 of 4, Box 29, PJM, CRP Collection, Nixon Library.

147. Magruder to Mitchell, December 7, 1971.

148. Rietz to Magruder, December 6, 1971, Folder: Alphabetical, Youth 3 of 4, Box 29, PJM, CPR Collection, Nixon Library.

149. Magruder to Mitchell, December 7, 1971.

150. *Congressional Record*, Representative Louis Frey Jr. (R-Florida), December 9, 1971, Folder: Subject Files, Alphabetical (JSM) Youth No. 3 [1 of 4], Box 29, PJM, Nixon Library.

151. Rietz to Magruder, January 1, 1972, Folder: Subject Files, Alphabetical (JSM) Youth [7 of 8], Box 27, PJM, Nixon Library.

152. See Bob Woodward and Carl Bernstein, *All the President's Men: The Greatest Reporting Story of All Time* (New York: Simon & Schuster, 2014); the Watergate investigation identified only Segretti but identified him as one of Nixon's fifty young provocateurs hired to work with young supporters.

153. Buchanan to Haldeman, Folder: Campaign Strategy Memos from Buchanan [2 of 2], Box 299, PHRH, WSOP, NARA II.

154. Buchanan to Haldeman.

155. Ken Rietz to Fred Malek, "McGovern and the Youth Vote," July 5, 1972. PFVM.

156. Pat Buchanan to Ken Smith, July 23, 1972, Folder: Re-election Committee [Folder 3 of 3], Box 9, PPB, NARA II.

157. Woodward and Bernstein, *All the President's Men*, 262–265.

158. Richard Nixon, Remarks on Accepting the Presidential Nomination of the Republican National Convention, August 23, 1972. Public Papers of the President.

159. Ed O'Donnell Statement, "McGovern Youth Director Calls Nixon 'Unworthy of Youth Support,'" August 31, 1972, Folder Youth 1972, Box 107, PGM, Mudd Library, Princeton University.

160. Patrick Buchanan to Ken Smith, September 13, 1972, Folder: Re-election Committee [Folder 3 of 3], Box 9, PPB, NARA II.

161. Patrick Buchanan to Ken Smith, September 13, 1972; "Why I'm Voting for Nixon," *Chimes* (Calvin College), September 1972, 10.

162. "Issues '72: The Young; Turning Out," http://content.time.com/time/magazine/article/0,9171,903573,00.html (accessed November 10, 2013).

163. Weiner, "Caution on the Left," 31.

164. "Youth for New Politics," October 17, 1972, Folder: Re-election Committee [Folder 3 of 3], Box 9, PPB, 1972 Election File, NARA II.

165. Nick Thimmesch, "McGovern to Try to Straighten Out His Blurred Image," *Observer-Reporter* (Washington, PA), September 28, 1972, A4.

166. Weiner, "Caution on the Left," 31.

167. Ski Helenski, "The Great Bathroom Debate," *UT Beacon*, November 10, 1972, 4. University of Texas Special Collections.

168. "Issues '72," http://content.time.com/time/magazine/article/0,9171,903573,00.html (accessed November 10, 2013).

169. Dutton Memo, Folder: Voter Analysis, 2 of 3, Box 38s, PTW, JFK Library.

170. White, *Making of the President*, 44.

171. Pat Buchanan to Ken Smith, July 23, 1972, Folder: Re-election Committee [Folder 3 of 3], Box 9, PPB, NARA II.
172. Ryan, "Youth Vote Impact Shows Up in Elections throughout the US," 1.
173. Hillary Rodham to Bill Clinton, https://blogs.princeton.edu/mudd/wp-content/uploads/sites/41/mt/docs/Clinton%20Memo.pdf (accessed October, 13, 2010).

Chapter 6. YVP

1. Robert Anthony Podesta to Youth Crew, "4 PM, May 21, 1972," May 22, 1972, Folder: Memo Citizens Youth [1 of 5], Box 43, PFVM, Nixon Library.
2. YVP State Action Plan, Folder: Citizens Youth 1 of 5, Box 43, PFVM, Nixon Library.
3. Novelli to Magruder, March 14, 1972, Subject Files: Alphabetical (JSM) Youth [5 of 8], Box 27, PJM, Nixon Library.
4. Nixon to Haldeman, July 23 1972, Camp David. Nixon Library. https://www.nixonlibrary.gov/virtuallibrary/documents/donated/072372_nixon.pdf (accessed November 11, 2011).
5. Novelli to Magruder, March 14, 1972, PJM.
6. Gareth Smith and Andy Hirst, "Strategic Political Segmentation: A New Approach for a New Era of Political Marketing," *European Journal of Marketing* 35, no. 9/10 (2001): 1058.
7. White, *Making of the President*, 327–229. For more on structure of CRP, see Ripon Society and Brown, *Jaws of Victory*, 6.
8. Rietz interview.
9. Drew Gardner, "Truth: An American Political Anachronism," *Cavalier Daily* (University of Virginia), October 20, 1972, 3.
10. Brock interview.
11. Brock interview.
12. Jeffrey Bell, "The Ordeal of the President; or, Will Richard Nixon Find True Happiness in 1972," *New Guard*, May 1971, 5.
13. William Brock to Advisory Board, "Action Items and Follow Up," Folder (JSM) Youth No. 4 of 4, Box 29, PJM, Nixon Library.
14. James J. Kilpatrick, "Nixon Group Aims at Youth," *Deseret News*, August 16, 1972, A10.
15. Rietz suggests that only 20 percent of American youth attended a college or university, though over 20 percent also attended junior colleges and vocational institutions.
16. Warren Weaver, "GOP Maps Drive for Young Voters: Team Will Woo 25 Million Newly Eligible for Nixon," *New York Times*, December 5, 1971, 42.
17. Ken Rietz to Jeb Magruder, February 24, 1972, Folder: Budget Youth, Box 43, PFVM, Nixon Library.
18. Strachan to Haldeman, "Youth," September 25, 1971, Folder: Youth Programs [1 of 2], Box 158, PHRH, NARA II.

19. Campaign Strategy Group to Attorney General, October 15, 1971, Folder: Re-election Committee [1 of 3], Box 9, PPB, 1972 Election File, NARA II.

20. Tom Tiede, "Youth Vote, Youth Vote, Who's Got the Youth Vote?," *Oscala-Star Banner*, August 14, 1972, 10A.

21. Ted Garish to Fred Malek, "State Priorities for Young Voter Division," September 26, 1972, Folder Citizens Youth [1 of 2], Box 43, PFVM, Nixon Library.

22. YVP State Action Plan.

23. Rietz interview.

24. Maxwell Calloway to Ken Rietz, July 18, 1972, Folder: Citizens Youth [1 of 2], Box 43, PFVM, Nixon Library.

25. Rietz to Magruder, Folder: Youth Memo Citizens [3 of 5], Box 43, PFVM, Nixon Library.

26. Rietz to Kaupinen, March 14, 1972, Folder: Memo Citizens Youth [3 of 5], Box 43, PFVM, CRP Collection, Nixon Library.

27. Robert Odle interview, July 9, 2014.

28. "Republicans Wooing the Youth Vote," *Time*, July 31, 1972, http://content.time.com/time/magazine/0,9263,7601720731,00.html (accessed October 12, 2011).

29. "Politics: GOP Reach to Youth," *Time*, January 31, 1972, http://content.time.com/time/magazine/0,9263,7601720131,00.html (accessed November 11, 2011).

30. Rietz to Magruder, "Youth Position Survey," Folder: Alphabetical, Youth 3 of 4, Box 20, PJM, CRP Collection, Nixon Library.

31. Dennis Clark, "Drive On for Voter Registration," *UT Beacon*, October 5, 1972, 1, University of Tennessee Special Collections.

32. Rietz interview.

33. Rietz to Magruder, Folder: Youth No. 1 [4 of 4], Subject Files, Alphabetical, Box 29, PJM, CRP.

34. Jane Nunley, "Powell Says, 'Nixon Needs Young,'" *UT Daily Beacon*, September 29, 1972, 1, University of Tennessee Special Collections.

35. McLane to Rietz, January 27, 1972, Folder, Youth—August 1971–January 1972, 9 of 12, Box 55, Papers of James McLane, Nixon Library.

36. Buchanan to Grassmuck, Folder: Attitude Study [CFOA 336], Box 45, PRF, Nixon Library.

37. Keene to Magruder, "YAF Convention," September 8, 1971, Folder: Subject Files, Alphabetical (JSM) Young Americans for Freedom, Box 27, PJM, Nixon Library.

38. David Keane to J. Roy Goodearle, August 25, 1971, Folder: Subject Files, Alphabetical (JSM) Young Americans for Freedom (YAF), Box 27, PJM, Nixon Library.

39. Keene to Magruder, "YAF Convention," September 8, 1971.

40. Wayne Thorburn, *A Generation Awakes: Young Americans for Freedom and the Creation of the Conservative Movement* (Ottawa, IL: Jameson Books, 2010), 351.

41. Letters, *New Guard*, November 1972, 24.

42. Thorburn, *Generation Awakes*, 348.

43. Anthony Ripley, "Conservative Forces Take Almost All Young Republican Offices and Staunchly Back Nixon's Policies," *New York Times*, June 27, 1971, 21.

44. Terry Ryan, "Nixon Forces Confident They'll Win Half Youth Vote," *Sarasota Herald Tribune*, August 16, 1972, A5.

45. McLane to Finch, "Youth Action Plan," Folder: Eighteen Year Old Vote, 1972 [1 of 2], Box 56, Papers of James McLane, Nixon Library.

46. Ryan, "Nixon Forces Confident They'll Win Half Youth Vote," A5.

47. "Nixon Gaining California Youth Support," *Lodi News-Sentinel*, September 14, 1972, 7.

48. Rietz to Magruder, "Youth Position Survey," Papers of JSM, CRP Collection, Box 20, Folder: Alphabetical, Youth [3 of 4].

49. Rietz to Magruder.

50. Odle to Magruder, Brock Strategy (JSM) Youth No. 1 [1 of 3], Box 27, PJM, Nixon Library.

51. Ken Clawson, "GOP Finds Solace in Youth Vote," Folder: Alphabetical (JSM) Voter Registration [4 of 7], Box 27, PJM. Also Rietz to Magruder, September 2, 1971, Folder: Alphabetical Subject Files (JSM) Youth [4 of 4], Box 29, PJM.

52. Clawson.

53. Conversation 31-5, October 5, 1972, White House Tapes.

54. See Allen Matusow, *Nixon's Economy*.

55. Young Republicans National Convention Brochure, Folder 4, Box 2, Papers of UMCR, College Republican National Committee, Campaign Literature 1971–1972, University of Maryland.

56. "The Attorney General and Mrs. Mitchell as Honorary Chairmen of the Young Republican Leadership Conference," Papers of Fred Malek, Box 43, Folder Memo Citizens (Youth 5 of 5), Nixon Library.

57. Young Republicans National Convention Brochure.

58. Rietz to Tom Hayden, "California," Folder Subject Files: Alphabetical (JSM) Youth [3 of 3], Box 27, PJM, Nixon Library.

59. Tom Bell interview, August 8, 2016.

60. Steven V. Roberts, "Role of 'Invisible Youths' in 1972 Politics Reviewed," *Nashua Telegraph*, March 22, 1972, 24.

61. Janet Nunley, "Voting Conquers Apathy," *UT Daily Banner*, August 1, 1972, 6, University of Tennessee Special Collections, 6.

62. Roberts, "Role of 'Invisible Youths,'" 24.

63. McLane to Finch, "Youth Action Plan."

64. Rietz to Magruder, "Voter Registration" October 20, 1971, Subject Files: Alphabetical (JSM) Republican National Convention [8 of 10], Box 26, PJM, Nixon Library.

65. "Politics of a Younger America," *St. Petersburg Time*, February 13, 1970, 18.

66. Brock interview.

67. Odle to Magruder, "Youth for Nixon, 1972," April 20, 1971, Folder: (JSM) Youth No. 1 [1 of 3], Box 27, PJM, Nixon Library.

68. Colson to Haldeman, "18 Year Old Vote in 1972," December 9, 1970, Folder: 18 Year Old Vote—1972 [1 of 2], Box 43, PRF, Nixon Library.

69. David Beasley, "Youth Move In," *Cincinnati Magazine*, October 1972, 80.

70. "Senator Brock Concerned with Youth Vote," 9.

71. Nancy Payne to Magruder, "Youth for Nixon and New Alignment of Youth," Folder: Subject Files, Alphabetical (JSM) Youth No. 1 [1 of 3], Box 27, PJM, Nixon Library.

72. Payne to Magruder, "Youth for Nixon and the New Alignment of Youth."

73. Roberts, "Role of 'Invisible Youths,'" 24.

74. Brock interview.

75. Rietz to Magruder, "The Vocation Education Group and First Family Involvement," Folder: Chronological (August 1971–January 1972) [4 of 12], Box 55, Papers of James McLane, WHCF, Nixon Library.

76. Robert Lucas to the President, January 27, 1972, Folder: Memo Citizens Youth [5 of 5], Box 43, PFVM, Nixon Library.

77. McLane to Chapin, January 4, 1972, Folder: Youth (August 1971–January 1972) [6 of 12], Box 56, Papers of James McLane, Nixon Library.

78. Falk to the President, Folder: Declaration of Independence, Bill of Rights, Constitution January 1, 1971–[December 31, 1972], Box FE 4, Richard Nixon Materials, NARA II.

79. Ken Rietz to Fred Malek, "Vocational Student Leaders Endorsing the President," October 2, 1972, Folder: Citizen Youth [1 of 2], Box 43, PFVM, Nixon Library.

80. "Remarks to Members of Young Labor for Nixon," September 23, 1972, Folder: Chronological Files, Box 317, Nixon Library.

81. "Remarks to Members of Young Labor for Nixon," September 23, 1972.

82. Roberts, "Role of 'Invisible Youths,'" 24.

83. Chamberlain, "Nixon Courting 'Square Power,'" 4.

84. Beasley, "Youth Move In," 80.

85. McLane to Finch, "Youth Action Plan."

86. Paul Allen Beck and M. Kent Jennings, "Parents as 'Middlepersons' in Political Socialization," *Journal of Politics*, February 37, no. 1 (February 1975): 83–107; R. D. Hess and J. V. Torney, *The Development of Political Attitudes in Children* (Chicago: Aldine Press, 1967); Paul Allen Beck and M. Kent Jennings, "Family Traditions, Political Periods, and the Development of Partisan Orientations," *Journal of Politics* 53, no. 3 (August 1991): 742–763.

87. McLane to Finch, "Youth Action Plan."

88. Kevin Phillips, "'Kidlash' a Possibility: Important Changes Could Come from Vote of 18–21 Year Olds," *Post-Crescent*, May 2, 1971, A9.

89. Phillips, A9.

90. David Chew interview, July 7, 2016.

91. Jerry Gilbreath interview, August 20, 2016.

92. Hank Haldeman interview, August 20, 2016.

93. Perry Bacon interview, June 3, 2016.

94. Bell interview.

95. Donald Sundquist interview, June 14, 2016.
96. Gilbreath interview.
97. Bacon interview.
98. Bell interview.
99. Gilbreath interview.
100. Tom Davis interview, June 2, 2016; John David Skrentny, *Ironies of Affirmative Action: Politics, Culture, and Justice in America* (Chicago: University of Chicago Press, 1996), 193; Hugh Davis Graham, "Richard Nixon and Civil Rights: Explaining an Enigma," *Presidential Studies Quarterly* 26 (Winter 1996): 103.
101. Freedman, *Inheritance*, 328.
102. Thomas Sugrue and John Skrentny, "The White Ethnic Strategy," in *Rightward Bound: Making America Conservative in the 1970s*, ed. Bruce Schulman and Julian Zelizer (Cambridge, MA: Harvard University Press, 2008), 191.
103. Bell interview.
104. Dean Kotlowski, "Black Power—Nixon Style: The Nixon Administration and Minority Business Enterprise," *Business History Review* 72, no. 3 (1998): 409–445.
105. Ken Rietz to Jeb Magruder, "Don Johnson," February 14, 1972, Folder: Memo Citizens Youth [5 of 5], Box 43, PFVM, Nixon Library.
106. Rietz to Malek, July 13, 1972. Malek to Rietz, "Black Youth Proposal," July 24, 1972, Folder: Citizens Youth [2 of 2], Box 43, PFVM, Nixon Library.
107. Leah Wright Riguer, *The Loneliness of the Black Republican: Pragmatic Politics and the Pursuit of Power* (Princeton, NJ: Princeton University Press, 2015), 183.
108. Al Donalson, "Black Support for Nixon Predicted," *Pittsburgh Press*, September 14, 1972, 20.
109. Strachan to Rietz, "Campus Opinion Poll," December 10, 1971, Folder: Alphabetical, JSM Youth, Box 29, PJM, Nixon Library.
110. Finch to President, April 1971, Folder: Youth—General [3 of 19], Box 56, Papers of James McLane, Nixon Library.
111. Rietz to McLane, December 2, 1971, Folder: Alphabetical, Youth [3 of 4], Box 29, Papers of James McLane, Nixon Library.
112. Rietz interview.
113. "Politics: GOP Reach to Youth," http://content.time.com/time/magazine/0,9263,7601720131,00.html (accessed November 11, 2011).
114. George Gorton interview, July 29, 2012.
115. McCloskey Flyer, Folder: Subject Files Alphabetical (JSM) Contenders [1 of 7], Box 15, PJM, Nixon Library.
116. Kehrli to Colson, "Iowa State Poll," Folder: Youth General [14 of 19], Box 56, Papers of James McLane, Nixon Library.
117. Gorton interview.
118. Gorton interview.
119. Rietz to Magruder, June 22, 1971, Folder: Alphabetical Files (JSM) Mock Elections, Box 22, PJM, Nixon Library.
120. Rietz to Magruder, June 22, 1971.
121. Rietz to Magruder, June 22, 1971.
122. Gorton interview.

123. Rietz to Magruder, June 22, 1971.

124. Dartmouth Polls, Folder, Alphabetical (JSM) Mock Elections, Box 22, PJM, Nixon Library.

125. Rietz to Mitchell, February 3, 1972, Folder: Alphabetical (JSM) Mock Elections, Box 22, PJM, Nixon Library.

126. Gorton interview.

127. "How to Win a Mock Election," Folder: Subject Files: Alphabetical, Young Voters (JSM), Box 27, PJM, Nixon Library.

128. Rietz to Magruder, Folder: (JSM) Mock Elections, Subject Files: Alphabetical, Box 22, PJM, Nixon Library.

129. Bertini interview.

130. George Gorton to Rietz, "New Hampshire 'Young Voters' Rally," January 26, 1972, Folder: Subject Files, Alphabetical (JSM) Youth [7 of 8], Box 27, PJM, Nixon Library.

131. "Youths Open Nixon Drive," Folder: Subject Files, Alphabetical (JSM) Youth [8 of 8], Box 27, PJM, Nixon Library.

132. "Youths Open Nixon Drive."

133. Girard to Magruder, January 24, 1972, Folder: Subject Files, Alphabetical (JSM) Youth [8 of 8], Box 27, PJM, Nixon Library.

134. McCloskey Flyer, Folder: Subject Files Alphabetical (JSM) Contenders [1 of 7], Box 15, PJM, Nixon Library.

135. Gorton interview.

136. Florida's eighteen-to-twenty-year-old population made up 16 percent of Florida's voters, not including the state's sizeable out-of-state student population. Novelli to Magruder, March 14, 1972.

137. Rietz to Magruder, September 1, 1971, Folder: Alphabetical (JSM) [4 of 4], Box 29, PJM, Nixon Library.

138. George Gorton to Ken Rietz, "College Recruitment since School Opened," September 6, 1972, Folder: Citizens Youth [2 of 2], Box 43, PFVM, Nixon Library.

139. Linda Charlton, "G.O.P. Tries Cheers and Chats on Youth," *New York Times*, October 22, 1972, 50.

140. Magruder to Gordon Strachan, "Program for Campus Polls," January 4, 1971, Folder: Subject Files, Alphabetical (JSM) Polling [3 of 5], Box 24, PJM, Nixon Library.

141. Bertini interview.

142. Gorton interview.

143. Joe Abate, September 30, 1971, Folder 5, Box 2, University of Maryland College Republicans Papers, College Republican National Committee, Correspondence 1971–1972. University of Maryland.

144. "Youth! Tomorrow's Responsible Republicans," Folder 10, Box 1, UM-DCR Papers, Presidential Papers Karel Petraitis, 1967–1969, University of Maryland.

145. Bertini interview.

146. Student Organization Application for Space, Folder 14, Box 1, Papers of UMDCR, Presidential Papers, Alan Virta 1972–1973, University of Maryland.

147. Memo, February 1968, Folder 10, Box 1, Papers of UMDCR, Presidential Papers, Karel Petraitis, 1967–1969, University of Maryland.

148. Joe Abate to Alan Virta, June 15, 1972, Folder 5, Box 2, UMCR Papers, College Republican National Committee, Correspondence 1971–1972, University of Maryland.

149. "Top Notch Orator Wins Dallas Trip," *Deseret News*, May 2, 1969, 2C.

150. Alan Virta, July 1, 1972, Folder 14, Box 1, Papers of UMDCR, Presidential Papers, Alan Virta 1971–1972, University of Maryland.

151. Helen Orndorff, June 28, 1972, Folder 14, Box 1, UMDCR, Alan Virta Presidential Papers, 1972–1973, University of Maryland.

152. Alan Virta, July 1, 1972.

153. *Trunkline*, Folder 13, Box 1, Papers of UMDCR, Presidential Papers, Alan Virta 1971–1972, University of Maryland.

154. Karl Rove, *Courage and Consequences: My Life as a Conservative in the Fight* (New York: Simon & Schuster, 2010), 27–37.

155. Joe Abate to Alan Virta, June 15, 1972.

156. Alan Virta to UMCR Alumnae May 6, 1972, Folder 13, Box 1, UMDCR Papers, Presidential Papers, Alan Virta 1971–1972, University of Maryland.

157. *Elephant's Memory* 1, no. 1 (Spring 1972), Folder 13, Box 1, UMDCR Presidential Papers, Alan Virta 1971–1972, University of Maryland.

158. Alan Virta to John Pope, December 1971, Folder 13, Box 1, Papers of UMDCR, Presidential Papers, 1971–1972. University of Maryland.

159. Alan Virta, April 28, 1972, Folder 13, Box 1, Papers of UMDCR, Presidential Papers, Alan Virta 1971–1972, University of Maryland.

160. Dennis Cusick, "Poll Sees Young Voter Apathy," *UT Beacon*, October 2, 1972, 1. University of Tennessee Special Collections.

161. Ken Rietz to Fred Malek, June 9, 1972, Folder: Memo, Citizens Youth, 1 of 5, Box 43, PFVM, Nixon Library.

162. "Tentative Budget: Youth Division," Folder: Budget Youth, Box 43, PFVM, Nixon Library.

163. George Gallup, "Gallup Shows McGovern Gain," *Anchorage Daily News*, October 1, 1972, 1.

164. "Young Voters for the President" College Organizational Manual, Folder 5, Box 2, Papers of UMCR, College Republican National Committee, Correspondence 1971–1972. University of Maryland.

165. Rietz to Tom Hayden, "California," Folder: Subject Files, Alphabetical (JSM) Youth [3 of 3], Box 27, PJM, Nixon Library.

166. Ryan, "Nixon Forces Confident They'll Win Half Youth Vote," A5.

167. Oval 761-7, August 4, 1972, White House Tapes.

168. Campus Opinion, August 12, 1971, Folder: Youth Programs [1 of 2], Box 158, PHRH, NARA II.

169. Davis interview.

170. Haldeman interview.

171. Perlstein, *Nixonland*, 562.

172. Oval Office Conversation 761-7, August 4, 1972, White House Tapes.

173. For liberal/radical critique of media and PR in politics as corrupting and

illusory, see McGinnis, *Selling of the Presidency*; Thompson, *Fear and Loathing*; Timothy Crouse, *The Boys on the Bus* (New York: Random House, 1973); Norman Mailer, *St. George and the Godfather* (New York: Signet, 1972).

174. Colson to the President, April 7, 1971, "Meeting on Youth with Finch, Colson, Haldeman," Folder, Youth: General [3 of 19], Box 56, Papers of James McLane, Nixon Library.

175. Rietz to MacGregor, "Press Conference with Bill Brock to Discuss Young Voters Convention Program," July 24, 1972, Folder: Citizens Youth [2 of 4], Box 29, PJM, Nixon Library.

176. YVP State Action Plan.

177. Karl Ottosen interview, September 6, 2016.

178. Tim Carey interview, August 10, 2016.

179. Haldeman interview.

180. Bacon interview.

181. Barbara Dietrich interview, June 9, 2016.

182. McLane to Rietz, January 17, 1972, Folder: Chronological, August 1971 to January 1972, Box 55, Papers of James McLane, WHCF, Nixon Library.

183. Wallace Henley to Mississippi State Youth Congress, January 17, 1972, Folder: Youth (August 1971–January 1972) [8 of 12], Box 55, Papers of James McLane, WHCF, Nixon Library.

184. Phillips, "'Kidlash' a Possibility", A9.

185. Rietz to Malek, May 24, 1972, Folder: Memo Citizens Youth [1 of 5], Box 43, PFVM, Nixon Library.

186. Nancy Gibbs and Michael Duffy, *The Preacher and the Presidents: Billy Graham in the White House* (New York: Center Street, 2008), 206.

187. Gibbs and Duffy, 206.

188. Dochuk, *From Bible Belt to Sunbelt*, 293.

189. John G. Turner, *Bill Bright and Campus Crusade for Christ: The Renewal of Evangelicalism in Postwar America* (Chapel Hill: University of North Carolina Press, 2008), 144.

190. Dochuk, *From Bible Belt to Sunbelt*, 336.

191. Rietz to Malek, September 18, 1972, Folder: Citizens Youth [2 of 2], Box 43, PFVM, Nixon Library.

192. Bell to Magruder, "The Youth Vote: Workshop in Voter Registration," Folder: Alphabetical [JSM] Youth 3 of 3, Box 29, PJM, Nixon Library.

193. H. R. Haldeman to Finch, "Youth," July 7, 1971, Folder: Youth Programs [1 of 2], Box 158, WHSF SMOF PHRH, H. R. Haldeman to Magruder, June 17, 1971, Folder: Youth Programs [2 of 2], Box 158, WHSF SMOF PHRH, NARA II.

194. YVP State Action Plan.

195. Malek to Ken Rietz, "Young Voter Registration Drive," June 20, 1972, Folder Memo Citizens Youth 1 of 5, Box 43, PFVM, Nixon Library.

196. Ed Harper to Vice President, "Student versus Non-student Attitudes," August 17, 1971, Folder: Youth Programs [1 of 2], Box 158, WHSF SMOF PHRH, NARA II.

197. Nixon to Haldeman, July 23 1972, Camp David. Nixon Library, https://

www.nixonlibrary.gov/virtuallibrary/documents/donated/072372_nixon.pdf (accessed November 11, 2011).

198. "Politics: GOP Reach to Youth," http://content.time.com/time/maga zine/0,9263,7601720131,00.html (accessed November 11, 2011).

199. Ted Garish to Fred Malek, "State Priorities for Young Voter Division," September 26, 1972, Folder: Citizens Youth [1 of 2], Box 43, PFVM, Nixon Library.

200. Ryan, "Nixon Forces Confident They'll Win Half Youth Vote," A5.

201. Gallup, "Gallup Shows McGovern Gain," 1.

202. "Trend toward Nixon Not Conservatism," *Cavalier Daily* (University of Virginia), October 20, 1972, 6.

203. Ken Rietz to Clark MacGregor, July 24, 1972, Folder: Citizens Youth 2 of 2, Box 43, PFVM, Nixon Library.

204. White, *Making of the President*, 327–329. For more on structure of CRP, see Ripon Society and Brown, *Jaws of Victory*, 6.

205. Bertini interview.

Chapter 7. *"Right On, Mr. President": Young Voters and the Politics of Image*

1. Max Lemer, "Young Don't Form Single Sheep-Like Group," *Eugene Register Guard*, August 29, 1972, A10.

2. Nixon, *RN*, 67.

3. AP photo, "The Coronation of King Richard," *Time* 100, no. 9 (August 28, 1972): 11.

4. Russell Baker, "Hugging Is a Complicated Thing," *Pittsburgh-Post Gazette*, February 23, 1982, 7.

5. Letters, *Life Magazine*, September 22, 1972, 27.

6. Russell Baker, "Observer: The Newest Wrinkle in the Youth Game," 34.

7. Haldeman to Tom Davis, July 2, 1970, Folder: Youth Programs [1 of 2], Box 158, PHRH, NARA II.

8. Brock interview.

9. Kathryn Cramer Brownell, *Showbiz Politics: Hollywood in American Public Life* (Chapel Hill: University of North Carolina Press, 2016), 209.

10. Oval 360-20, September 11, 1972, White House Tapes.

11. Ryan, "Nixon Forces Confident They'll Win Half Youth Vote," A5.

12. Young Voters for the President Convention Plan, Folder: Subject Files, Alphabetical (JSM) Convention [2 of 10], Box 15, PJM, Nixon Library.

13. David Greenberg, *Republic of Spin: An Inside History of the American Presidency* (New York: W. W. Norton, 2016), 400.

14. Mort Allin to George Grassmuck, "Thoughts on the Lincoln Speech," Folder: Eighteen Year Old Vote [1 of 2], Box 43, PRF, NARA II.

15. Dennis D. Loo and Ruth-Ellen M. Grimes, "Polls, Politics and Crime: The 'Law and Order' Issues of the 1960s," *Western Criminology Review* 5, no. 1 (2004): 50–67, http://wcr.sonoma.edu/v5n1/manuscripts/Loo.pdf. Flamm, *Law and Order Street Crime*, 128.

16. Oval 761-7, August 4, 1972, White House Tapes.

17. Gorton interview.

18. Ted Besesparis, "Candidates Woo Youth Vote," *Beachcomber* (Palm Beach Junior College) 34, no. 1 (September 5, 1972): http://www.archive.org/stream /Beachcomber_402/1972-730cr_djvu.txt (accessed September 20, 2011).

19. Tim Carey interview, August 10, 2016; Dietrich interview.

20. Gary Burhop interview, May 31, 2016.

21. Dietrich interview.

22. Bacon interview.

23. Gilbreath interview.

24. Allin, "Youth for Nixon Final Report," 18.

25. Glen Elsasser, "Political Boss System to Last: Author," *Chicago Tribune*, August 25, 1969, A11.

26. Wicker, "In the Nation," 46.

27. Prior, "Incumbent in the Living Room," 663.

28. Nixon, *RN*, 354.

29. White, *The Making of the President*, 327–329. For more on structure of CRP, see Ripon Society and Brown, *Jaws of Victory*, 6.

30. Gorton interview.

31. Howard Cohen to Ken Rietz, May 16, 1972, Folder: Memo Citizens Youth 2 of 5, Box 43, PFVM, Nixon Library.

32. Magruder to Mitchell, June 16, 1971, Folder: Subject Files, Alphabetical (JSM) Research [2 of 2], Box 25, PJM, Nixon Library.

33. Magruder, *American Life*, 170.

34. White, *Making of the President*, 327–329. For more on structure of CRP, see Ripon Society and Brown, *Jaws of Victory*, 6.

35. Waterman et al., *Image-Is-Everything Presidency*.

36. Mary Beth Merrin and Hugh L. LeBlang, "Parties and Candidates in 1972: Objects of Issue Voting," *Western Political Quarterly* 32, no. 1 (1979): 59–69, 69.

37. "Television: Electronic Politics; The Image Game," *Time*, September 21, 1970, http://content.time.com/time/magazine/article/0,9171,942277,00 .html (accessed November 10, 2012).

38. Rietz to Magruder, February 24, 1972, Folder: Budget—Youth, Box 31, PFVM, Nixon Library.

39. Ken Rietz to Jeb Magruder, "Young Voters for the President," Folder: Youth Programs 2 of 2, Box 158, PHRH, NARA II.

40. Karl Rove to Sunshine Patriots, Folder 5, Box 2, Papers of UMDCR, College Republican National Committee, Correspondence 1971–1972, University of Maryland.

41. Fred Malek to H. R. Haldeman, September 5, 1971, Folder: Citizens, Youth [1 of 2], Box 43, PFVM. Ken Rietz to Fred Malek, August 31, 1972, Folder Citizens, Youth [1 of 2], Box 43, PFVM, Nixon Library.

42. Finch to President, August 19, 1971, Folder: Youth General [3 of 19], Box 56, Papers of James McLane, Nixon Library.

43. Thomas Frank, *The Conquest of Cool* (Chicago: University of Chicago Press, 1997), 177.

44. Frank, 120–121.

45. Karl Rove, "Buttons! Buttons! Buttons!," Folder 5, Box 2, Papers of UMCR, College Republican National Committee, Correspondence 1971–1972, University of Maryland.

46. Alan Virta to Karl Rove, March 23, 1972, Folder 13, Box 1, Papers of UMDCR, Presidential Papers, Alan Virta 1971–1972, University of Maryland.

47. Rietz interview: When asked how the November Group's executives in the campaign taught the YVP about selling a candidate, Rietz responded, "they learned from us."

48. Rietz interview.

49. Finch to President, "Youth," April 8, 1971.

50. Allin, "Youth for Nixon Final Report," 18.

51. Rietz to Magruder, "Proposed Meeting with College Marketing Corporation," Folder: Youth [3 of 4], Box 29. See also Rietz to Barrett, November 16, 1971, Folder: (JSM) Youth [4 of 4], Box 29. Barrett to Rietz, October 25, 1971, Folder: (JSM) Youth [4 of 4], Box 29, PJM, Nixon Library.

52. Fred Malek to Bill Novelli, "Youth Advertising," March 30, 1972, Folder: Citizens Youth Advertising and PR, Box 22, Nixon Library.

53. Malek to Novelli.

54. Bill Novelli to Fred Malek, "Advertising to Voter Groups," March 20, 1972, Folder: Citizens Youth Advertising and PR, Box 22, Nixon Library.

55. Bill Novelli to Fred Malek, "Advertising to Voter Groups."

56. Bill Gavin to H. R. Haldeman, January 12, 1971, Folder: [CFOA 336] Attitude Study, Box 43, Robert Finch, NARA II.

57. Charlton, "G.O.P. Tries Cheers and Chats on Youth," 50.

58. Lisa Holt, "Campaign Posters: The 1972 Presidential Election," *Journal of American Culture* 9, no. 3 (1986): 65–83, 70.

59. Holt, 70.

60. Rietz to Magruder, "Youth Position Survey," Folder: Alphabetical, Youth [3 of 4], Box 20, PJM, CRP Collection, Nixon Library.

61. Caldiero to *Newsweek*, Folder: Alphabetical, Celebrities [1 of 3], Box 15, PJM, Nixon Library.

62. Magruder to Rietz, May 24, 1972, Folder: Alphabetical, Celebrities [1 of 3], Box 15, PJM, Nixon Library.

63. Buchanan to Magruder, August 1, 1972, Folder: Subject Files, Alphabetical (JSM) Celebrities [1 of 4], Box 14, PJM, Nixon Library.

64. See Brownell, *Showbiz Politics*.

65. H. R. Haldeman to Magruder, "Celebrities," March 21, 1971, Folder: Subject Files, Alphabetical (JSM) Celebrities [1 of 4], Box 14, PJM, Nixon Library.

66. Nixonette Uniform Order Form, Folder: Memo Citizens Youth 1 of 5, Box 43, PFVM, Nixon Library.

67. "Rally Man Manual," Folder 11, Box 21, White House Special Files Collection, Nixon Library, https://www.nixonlibrary.gov/virtuallibrary/documents/whsfreturned/WHSF_Box_21/WHSF21-11.pdf.

68. Dietrich interview.

69. "Not Just a Nixonette," *Eugene Register*, September 7, 1972, D3.

70. "Not Just a Nixonette," D3.

71. *Poughkeepsie Journal,* January 20, 1972, 31.

72. Walker Exit Interview, 72, http://nixon.archives.gov/virtuallibrary/documents/exitinterviews/walker-exit.pdf.

73. Scammon and Wattenberg, *Real Majority.*

74. "Campaign Program: Women Voters for the President," Folder: Subject Files, Alphabetical (JSM) The Women's Vote [5 of 5], Box 27, PJM, Nixon Library.

75. Novelli to Dailey, "Women Voters," April 27, 1972, Folder: Subject Files Alphabetical (JSM) Women, Box 27, PJM, Nixon Library.

76. Novelli to Dailey.

77. Herbert E. Alexander, *Financing the 1972 Election* (Lexington, MA: Lexington Books, 1976), 23.

78. Edwin Diamond, "The City Politic: November Song," *New York Magazine,* November 6, 1972, 8.

79. Aniko Bodroghkozy, *Groove Tube: Sixties Television and Youth Rebellion* (Durham, NC: Duke University Press, 2001), 26.

80. Frank, *Conquest of Cool,* 190.

81. Gilbert, *Cycle of Outrage,* 210.

82. Magruder to Mitchell, June 16, 1971.

83. Diamond, "City Politic," 11.

84. Lawrence Graham, *Youthtrends: Capturing the $200 Billion Youth Market* (New York: St. Martin's, 1987), 6.

85. Museum of the Moving Image, *The Living Room Candidate,* Richard Nixon, 1972, http://www.livingroomcandidate.org/commercials/1972 (accessed July 23, 2011).

86. Deborah Carver, "What We See on the TeeVee: The Average American, Godlike Announcers, and Neither Fear nor Loathing in the 1972 Election," *Rethinking History* 11, no. 2 (2007): 203–213, 209.

87. Frank, *Conquest of Cool,* 120–121.

88. Jeb Magruder to William Timmons, "Rep. Blackburn's Concern about a Recent Commercial," October 16, 1972, Folder: Alphabetical, White House Correspondence [4 of 4], Box 27, PJM, Nixon Library.

89. William Timmons to Jeb Magruder, "Political Commercials," October 8, 1972, Folder: Alphabetical, White House Correspondence [4 of 4], Box 27, PJM, Nixon Library.

90. Jeb Magruder to William Timmons, "Rep. Blackburn's Concern about a Recent Commercial," October 16, 1972.

91. Young Voters for the President Convention Plan.

92. Magruder, *American Life,* 121.

93. Marvin Barrett, ed., *The Politics of Broadcasting* (New York: Thomas Crowell, 1973), 131.

94. "Youth: The Cheerleaders," *Time,* September 4, 1972, http://content.time.com/time/magazine/0,9263,7601720904,00.html (accessed October 11, 2013).

95. Young Voters for the President Convention Plan.

96. Young Voters for the President Convention Plan.

97. "Nixon Youth Corps Pitches In," *St. Petersburg Independent*, August 11, 1972, A2.

98. Sedam to Timmons, "Young Voters Legal Assistance Program," Folder: Citizens Youth [2 of 2], Box 43, PFVM, Nixon Library.

99. Sedam to Timmons.

100. Robert Semple Jr., "Miami Beach Tent City a Carnival of Protesters," *New York Times*, August 22, 1972, A1.

101. McLane to Rietz, "Youth Demonstration at the Republican Convention," January 13, 1972, Folder: James W. McLane, Youth File, August 1971–January 1972 [6 of 12], Box 55, Papers of James McLane, Nixon Library.

102. Joe McGinnis, "The Resale of the President," *New York Times*, September 3, 1972, SM8.

103. Barrett, *Politics of Broadcasting*, 41.

104. Barrett, 48.

105. David Lamb, "Delegate, Policeman and Protestor: 3 Young Men in Same City, Different Orbits," *Los Angeles Times*, August 22, 1972, A1.

106. Robert Decherd, "A Republican Road Show Swamps Miami," *Harvard Crimson*, September 1, 1972, https://www.thecrimson.com/article/1972/9/1/a-republican-roadshow-swamps-miami-pmiami/ (accessed May 5, 2018).

107. *Four More Years*, prod. and dir. by Top Value Television (TVTV), 60 min., Subtle Communications, 1972, videocassette.

108. Thompson, *Fear and Loathing*, 357

109. Letters, *Time*, September 25, 1972, http://www.time.com/time/magazine/article/0,9171,903567,00.html (accessed September 19, 2011).

110. "Youth: The Cheerleaders."

111. State Action Plan, Folder: Subject Files: Alphabetical (JSM) Young Voters, Box 27, PJM, Nixon Library.

112. "Young Voters Adding Spice," *Lakeland Ledger* (Lakeland, FL), August 23, 1972, 8A.

113. "Chancellor Tells City He's Sorry," *Chicago Tribune*, August 23, 1972, 2.

114. Gilbreath interview.

115. "Young Voters Adding Spice," A8.

116. Tim Findley, "Outside the Convention: Cops and Confusion," *Rolling Stone*, September 28, 1972, https://www.rollingstone.com/politics/news/outside-the-convention-cops-and-confusion-19720928 (accessed January 10, 2015).

117. David L. Paletz and Martha Elson, "Television Coverage of Presidential Conventions: Now You See It, Now You Don't," *Political Science Quarterly* 91, no. 1 (Spring 1976): 129.

118. *Four More Years*.

119. Robert Semple Jr., "Youths for Nixon Contrast with Protestors in Park," *New York Times*, August 22, 1972, A16, 1.

120. James T. Wooten, "Unexpected 'Preview' Provides a Jolt to a Hitherto Predictable Convention," *New York Times*, August 23, 1972, 26.

121. Sheila Wolfe, "GOP Has Something for All," *Chicago Tribune*, August 22, 1972, 5.

122. Joe Merton, "The Politics of Symbolism: Richard Nixon's Appeal to White Ethnics and the Frustration of Realignment 1969–72," *European Journal of American Culture* 26, no. 3 (2007): 190.

123. Convention Schedule, August 3, 1972, Folder: Subject Files, Alphabetical (JSM) Convention [1 of 10], Box 15, PJM, Nixon Library.

124. Ron Rosenbaum, "I March with the Young Voters for the President," *Village Voice*, August 31, 1972, 8.

125. Findley, "Outside the Convention," https://www.rollingstone.com/politics/news/outside-the-convention-cops-and-confusion-19720928 (accessed January 10, 2015).

126. Eileen Sheehan, "Nixon Appeals to Youthful Voters at Rally Near Miami," *New York Times*, August 23, 1972, 27.

127. Harris Poll, Folder: Citizens Youth [1 of 2], Box 43, PFVM, Nixon Library.

128. Brock interview.

129. Ken Rietz to Clark MacGregor, "Memo of September 25 Discussing Youth Vote," Folder: Citizens Youth [1 of 2], Box 43, PFVM, Nixon Library.

130. MacGregor to Staff, September 29, 1972, Folder 2: Citizens Youth [1 of 2], Box 43, PFVM, Nixon Library.

131. Fred Asbell interview, June 3, 2016.

132. Tom Campbell interview, June 4, 2016.

133. Barbara Abel, "PAC Rocks with Rock and Tricia," *Milwaukee Journal*, October 2, 1972, 1.

134. Davis interview.

135. Ryan, "Youth Vote Impact Shows Up in Elections throughout the US," 1.

136. "The Independents," *Washington Post*, http://www.washingtonpost.com/wp-srv/politics/interactives/independents/data-year-by-year.html (accessed October 20, 2011).

137. "A New Independent Majority," *Spartanburg Herald*, November 14, 1972, A6.

138. *San Francisco Examiner*, October 17, 1972, Folder: Youth Vote, Box 38u, PTW, JFK Library.

139. Ken Rietz to Fred Malek, October 19, 1972, Folder: Citizens Youth [1 of 2], Box 43, PFVM, Nixon Library.

140. Bertini interview.

141. Mark, *Going Dirty*, 11.

142. Brock interview.

Chapter 8. From Watergate to Reagan

1. Daniel Yankelovich, "A Study of American Youth," Youth Survey/Polls, Box 16, PPF, Ford Library, Ann Arbor, MI.

2. "The Mood of American Youth, 1974," Youth Survey/Polls, Box 16, PPF, Ford Library.

3. "Apathy's What's Ahead in Poll on Campus Vote," *Ft. Lauderdale News*, October 17, 1976, B4.

4. *National on Campus Report*, "Student Elections Being Investigated," May 1975, Folder: College Republicans, Box 1, PPF, Ford Library.

5. American Enterprise Institute to Thelma Duggin, August 11, 1981, Young Americans for Freedom Convention 1981, Box 16, Thelma Duggin Files, Reagan Library, Simi Valley, CA.

6. CIRCLE, http://civicyouth.org/quick-facts/youth-voting/.

7. The White House Director for Youth Affairs, Folder: President Ford Committee (1), Box F73, Ford Library.

8. *Changing Youth Values in the 70s*, Folder: Youth Surveys/Polls, Box 11, PPF, Ford Library.

9. "Are Marijuana Laws Anti-Youth?," *Boston Globe*, January 6, 1971, 1.

10. Donald Critchlow, *The Conservative Ascendancy* (Cambridge, MA: Harvard University Press, 2007), 131.

11. Annual Reports of the CRNC from 1980, 1983, 1986, 1991, National Archives College Republican Collection, http://www.crnc.org/admin/editpage/downloads/CRNChistory.pdf (accessed August 2016).

12. American Enterprise Institute to Thelma Duggin, August 11, 1981, Folder: Young Americans for Freedom Convention 1981, Box 16, Thelma Duggin Files, Reagan Library.

13. Thorburn, *Generation Awakes*, 446.

14. Ellen Goodman, "Reagan and the Favorite Grandfather Factor," *Eugene Register Guard*, June 19, 1987, A8.

15. Daron R. Shaw, "The Effect of TV Ads and Candidate Appearances on Statewide Presidential Votes, 1988–96," *American Political Science Review* 93, no. 2 (1999), 345–361.

16. Mike Steere, "Reagan Youths Burst with Energy," *Toledo Blade*, July 17, 1980, 7.

17. Alan Abramowitz and H. Gibbs Knotts, "Ideological Realignment in the American Electorate: A Comparison of Northern and Southern White Voters in the Pre-Reagan, Reagan, and Post-Reagan Eras," *Politics and Policy* 34, no. 1 (2006): 94–108.

18. Ken Rietz, *Winning Campaigns, Losing Sight, Gaining Insight* (Herndon, VA: Mascot Books, 2016), 107.

19. Powell to Armstrong, Youth Programs: Key Scoring Points, May 25, 1973, Folder: Youth Status, Box 16, PPF, Ford Library.

20. John Flynn, "Hollywood Couple's Daughter, Backed Nixon in 1960, Carries Message to Perry GOP," *Courier Journal*, October 7, 1973, 5.

21. Powell to Armstrong, "Goals through the End of the Administration," June 20, 1974, Folder, Youth Status, Box 16, PPF, Ford Library.

22. Stephen H. Chaffee and Lee Becker, "Young Voters' Reactions to Early Watergate Issues," *American Politics Research* 3 (1975): 3, 360, 379.

23. Donald Sundquist interview, June 14, 2016.

24. Burhop interview.

25. Kelly Bennett, "From San Diego to Moscow," *Voice of San Diego*, June 23,

2008, https://www.voiceofsandiego.org/topics/news/from-san-diego-to-mos cow-george-gortons-strange-and-wild-assignments-5/.

26. Bell interview.

27. Youth Talking Points, NGO Speech, Folder: Youth Status, Box 16, PPF, Ford Library.

28. Bicentennial Minute, James Mugford, Folder: Association of Secondary School Principals, Box 4, PPF, Ford Library.

29. Daniel Yankelovich, "A Study of American Youth." Polls, Box 16, PPF, Ford Library.

30. "Student's Politics Unusual in Texas," *Pampa Daily News* (UPI), February 8, 1976, 18.

31. Pat Norman, "Ford's Girl Next Door," *Akron Beacon Journal*, November 7, 1974, B3.

32. Powell to Armstrong, Progress Report, August 2, 1974, Youth Status, Box 16, PPF, Ford Library.

33. *Target*, April 1974, Folder: Teenage Republicans, Box 16, PPF, Ford Library.

34. Jonathan Schoenwald, *A Time for Choosing: The Rise of Modern American Conservatism* (New York: Oxford University Press, 2001), 220; Schulman, *Seventies*, 43–48, 51; Shirley, *Reagan's Revolution;* James T. Patterson, *Restless Giant: The United States from Watergate to Bush v. Gore* (New York: Oxford University Press, 2005), 62.

35. *Target*, March 1975, Folder: Teenage Republicans, Box 16, PPF, Ford Library.

36. Schulman, *Seventies*, 51.

37. M. Stanton Evans, "Young Republicans Solidly Conservative," *Human Events*, May 4, 1974.

38. Manafort to YR Leaders, January 31, 1975, Folder: Young Republicans, Box 7, PPF, Ford Library.

39. *The Right Report*, May 19, 1975, Folder: The Right Report, Box 28, Robert T. Hartmann Files, Ford Library.

40. "Resolution Endorsing Barry Goldwater for Appointment as Vice-President," April 10, 1974, Folder: Young Republicans, Box 7, PPF, Ford Library.

41. Gwen Anderson to Hartmann, "Resolution," February 27, 1975, Folder: Young Republicans, Box 7, Hartmann Files, Ford Library.

42. Anonymous, Folder: Young Republicans, Box 7, PPF, Ford Library.

43. *Forum*, September 1, 1975, Folder: Young Republicans, Box 7, PPF, Ford Library.

44. PFC Youth Campaign proposal, Marik File: Folder: Special Voter Groups (Youth), Box PFC B3, Ford Library.

45. Proposals for Youth Involvement, March 14, 1973, Youth Status, Box 16, PPF, Ford Library.

46. "GOP to Debate Plan," March 5, 1975, Folder: Ethnic (Republicans), Box 9, PPF, Ford Library.

47. Rules for the Republican Convention, March 5, 1975, Folder: Republican Party, Box 42, James Cannon Files, Ford Library.

48. *The Right Report*, February 9, 1976, Folder: Young Republican Leadership Conference, Box F 63, PFC, Ford Library.

49. Booth to DeBolt, January 20, 1976, Folder: Young Republican Leadership Conference, Box F 63, PFC, Ford Library.

50. "College Campuses Lose Activists—Gain Hacks," *Stanford Daily* 170, no. 4, September 30, 1976, 6.

51. Drew Olim to Powell, January 20, 1976, Folder: National Student Association, Box 4, PPF, Ford Library.

52. George Gallup, "Young Voters Tend to Favor Ford—Poll," *Nevada State Journal* (Reno), March 31, 1976, 40.

53. AP, "Ford Gains in Kansas," *Cincinnati Enquirer*, Sunday, May 9, 1976, A2.

54. "Students Politics Unusual in Texas," 18.

55. "Youths Rate Ford 'Good as President,'" *San Bernardino County Sun*, January 24, 1976, 35.

56. "Wednesday Group," September 2, 1976, Meeting, Folder: House and Senate Wednesday Groups," Box 16, Richard B. Cheney Files, Ford Library.

57. Pew Research Center, "Growing Support for Marijuana Legalization," http://www.pewsocialtrends.org/2014/03/07/millennials-in-adulthood/sdt-next-america-03-07-2014-2-02/.

58. "Ohio Political Scene becomes Warmer," *Circleville Herald*, May 21, 1976, 1.

59. Ford to YR, February 28, 1975, Folder: Young Republicans, Box 7, PPF, Ford Library.

60. Jim Brownell to Nessen, Folder PFC (2), Box F73, People for Ford—Youth Desk File, Ford Library.

61. Rove to Thaxton, June 3 1974, Folder: Report for Republican National Committee (Statistics on Youth), Box 11, PPF, Ford Library.

62. Arthur Levine and Keith R. Wilson, "Student Activism in the 1970s: Transformation Not Decline," *Higher Education* 8, no. 6 (1979), 627–640, "Youth Vote Negligible—Census Finds," *Pittsburgh Press*, July 30, 1978, A23.

63. College Recruitment Manual, College Recruitment, Box F 63, PFC Files, Ford Library.

64. "Ivy League Students Pick Carter over Ford," *Naugatuck Daily News UPI*, October 22, 1976, 10.

65. Doug Willis, "Reagan at the Scene Says He Can Win on Initial Ballot," AP, *Schenectady Gazette*, August 14, 1976, 1.

66. Ford to TAR, June 17, 1976, Folder: Teenage Republicans, Box 16, PPF, Ford Library.

67. Ford to Senior Scholastic Magazine, Folder: PFC (2), Box 10, PPF, Ford Library.

68. Convention Plan, PFC (1), Box 10, PPF, Ford Library.

69. PFC Youth Campaign Proposal, Folder: Marik File: Special Voter Groups (Youth 1), Box PFC B3, Ford Library.

70. Ford Youth Program at the National Convention, April 19, 1976, Program at National Convention, Box F73, PFC, Ford Library.

71. Ford Youth Program at the National Convention.

72. Ford Youth Program at the National Convention.

73. Asa Bushnell, "Convention Vignettes," *Tuscon Dailey Citizen*, August 16, 1976, 2. Bertini interview.

74. Georgianne Burlage, "Ford Backers Find Situation Unconventional," *Denton-Record Chronicle*, August 16, 1976, 1.

75. Linda Adler to Ford, August 30, 1976, Folder: Youth Desk—General, Box F57, PFC, Ford Library.

76. Rossinow, *Politics of Authenticity*.

77. Lewis Fader to Ford, September 15, 1976, Folder: Youth Desk—General, Box F57, PFC, Ford Library.

78. Marlee Means, "Foothill Girl's View of GOP Convention," *Tustin News*, August 26, 1976, 2.

79. Laura Kalman, *Right Star Rising: A New Politics, 1974–1980* (New York: W. W. Norton, 2010), 170.

80. Booth to Peterson, September 7, 1976, Folder: Youth Desk—General, F7 Thomas Ruffin Files, Ford Library.

81. Booth to State Youth Chairman, October 11, 1976, Folder: Youth Desk—General, F7 Thomas Ruffin Files, Ford Library.

82. Uma Pemmaraju, "Taking the Pulse of Poll Watchers," *San Antonio Express*, October 31, 1976, 6F.

83. Sullivan to Booth, March 5, 1976, Marik File—Special Voters—Youth (3), Box B3, PFC, Ford Library.

84. John Robinson to Ford, August 25, 1976, Folder: Correspondence (1), Box F63, PFC, Ford Library.

85. Katherine Hutchison to Jack Ford, August 29, 1976, Folder: Correspondence—Tennessee, Box F72, PFC, Ford Library.

86. Michigan Report, October 3, 1976, Folder: Michigan General, Box F68, PFC, Ford Library.

87. Sullivan to Booth, March 5, 1976.

88. Letter to Booth, September 8, 1976, Folder: Alabama—Correspondence, Box F63, PFC, Ford Library.

89. Jesse Pointdexter, "Young Republican Convention," Folder: Young Republicans, Box 7, PPF, Ford Library.

90. Leah Wright Riguer, *Loneliness of the Black Republican*, 261.

91. Elaine Viets, "Political Veteran at 25 Enjoys the Steady Pace," *St. Louis Dispatch*, December 19, 1973, 77.

92. Riguer, *Loneliness of the Black Republican*, 239.

93. Program of GOP Ethnic Youth: Campaign '76, Folder: Ethnic Youth, Box F73, PFC, Ford Library.

94. Yankelovich Poll, Folder: Youth Survey/Poll, Box 16, PPF, Ford Library.

95. Exchange of Comments between Ford and Trivette, July 2, 1975, Folder: Future Farmers of America, Box 1, PPF, Ford Library.

96. Jim Brown to Powell, September 13, 1974, Folder: US Youth Council, Box 6, PPF, Ford Library.

97. On Youth Talking Points, Folder: Youth Status, Box 16, PPF, Ford Library.

98. Program of GOP Ethnic Youth: Campaign '76.

99. Program of GOP Ethnic Youth.

100. Ellen Goodman, "When Politicians Say 'Ethnic' They Mean the Working Class," *Free Lance Star*, October 5, 1976, 4.

101. J. Anthony Lukas, *Common Ground: A Turbulent Decade in the Lives of Three American Families* (New York: Vintage, 1986), 436.

102. "Ethnic Plan for 1976 Campaign," Folder: National Republican Heritage Groups (Nationalities) Council, Box F25, PFC, Ford Library.

103. Robert Moss, *Creating the New Right Ethnic in the 1970s: The Intersection of Anger and Nostalgia* (Madison, NJ: Fairleigh Dickinson University Press, 2017), 91.

104. Goodman, "When Politicians Say 'Ethnic,'" 4.

105. "Integration or Separation? Nationality Groups in the US and the Republican Party's Ethnic Politics, 1960s–1980s," *Nationalities Papers* 38, no. 4 (2010): 469–490.

106. *GOP Nationalities News*, June 1974, Folder: Ethnic (Republicans), Box 9, PPF, Ford Library.

107. Bush to Johnston, August 17, 1973, Folder: Teenage Republicans, Box 6, PPF, Ford Library.

108. Heritage Youth Committee, Folder: Subject File—Youth for Reagan Sourcebook [1 of 2], Box 136, Ed Meese Files, Reagan Library.

109. Elly Peterson, June 17, 1976, Folder: Ethnic Youth, Box F25, PFC, Ford Library.

110. Program of GOP Ethnic Youth.

111. Program of GOP Ethnic Youth; Robert Moss, *Creating the New Right Ethnic in the 1970s*; Laura Kalman, *Right Star Rising*; Samuel Freedman, *The Inheritance*; Jefferson Cowie, *Stayin' Alive: The 1970s and the Last Days of the Working Class* (New York: New Press, 2010).

112. "Salvador Desantis Jr. to President Ford," April 14, 1975, Folder: College Democrats of America, Box 1, PPF, Ford Library.

113. "State G.O.P. Nationality Unit Backs Nomination of Ford," *New York Times*, June 6, 1976, 32.

114. Program of GOP Ethnic Youth.

115. Johnston to Bush, August 29, 1973, Folder: Teenage Republicans, Box 6, PPF, Ford Library.

116. "Around the City . . . Briefly: Caravan to Take 'Ford to the People' Visits Area," *Tallahassee Democrat*, October 10, 1976, C7.

117. James Gannon, "Young Voters Unexcited by Election," *Times Herald Record* (Middletown, NY), October 19, 1976, 28.

118. *Cincinnati Enquirer*, May 9, 1976, 22.

119. "College Campuses Lose Activists—Gain Hacks," 6.

120. "How Groups Voted in 1976," Roper Center, Cornell University, https://ropercenter.cornell.edu/polls/us-elections/how-groups-voted/how-groups-voted-1976/.

121. "Non-College Youth: Voting and Educational Attainment," *CIRCLE*, http://civicyouth.org/quick-facts/non-college-youth/#vote.

122. "Youth and Adult Voter Turnout from 1972–2002," *CIRCLE*, http://civi cyouth.org/PopUps/FactSheets/FS_Youth%20turnout1972_2002.pdf.

123. Eddie N. Williams, "Black Youth's Potential Political Clout," *Minneapolis Star Tribune*, October 16, 1978, A6.

124. "How Groups Voted in 1976," https://ropercenter.cornell.edu/polls /us-elections/how-groups-voted/how-groups-voted-1976/.

125. "Vermont Roundup," *Burlington Free Press*, October 29, 1976, B1.

126. Diane Jacobsen, Target Report No. 3, National Student Lobby, Washington, DC, April 1978, Folder: Teenage Republicans, Box 6, PPF, Ford Library.

127. "Youth and Adult Voter Turnout from 1972–2002," http://civicyouth.org/PopUps/FactSheets/FS_Youth%20turnout1972_2002.pdf.

128. "If You Don't Vote . . . ," *Delaware County Daily Times* (Chester, Pennsylvania), October 26, 1976, 10.

129. "How Groups Voted in 1976," https://ropercenter.cornell.edu/polls /us-elections/how-groups-voted/how-groups-voted-1976/.

130. Nicholas Knezevich, "Voters Split Ticket," *Pittsburgh Press*, November 3, 1976, 3.

131. David E. Anderson, "Prejudice Falls in Carter Vote," *Plano Daily Star-Courier*, November 28, 1976, 7 (section 2).

132. "Rebuilding the GOP," *Green Bay Press-Gazette*, November 9, 1976, A4.

133. Critchlow, *Conservative Ascendancy*, 151.

134. Charles Kenney, "Carter by 49–38%; Reagan Stuns Bush, 50–23%," *Boston Globe*, February 27, 1980, 1.

135. Adam Clymer, "Late Surge for the Underdogs," *New York Times*, April 23, 1980, A1.

136. Morton Blackwell to William J. Casey, April 3, 1980, Folder: Political Ops (Timmons)—Voter Groups-Youth [2 of 2], Box 285, 1980 Campaign Papers, Reagan Library.

137. E. J. Dionne Jr., "Political Memo: GOP Makes Reagan Lure of Young a Long Term Asset," *New York Times*, October 31, 1988, B4. Eleven percent of youth voted for the Independent John Anderson.

138. Youth Plan, Folder: Campaign Planning—Youth for Reagan, Box 136, Ed Meese Files, Reagan Library.

139. "Bill Brock: Architect of the Republican Victory, 1980," *College Republican*, Winter 1981, 2.

140. Craig Shirley, *Rendezvous with Destiny: Ronald Reagan and the Campaign the Changed America* (Wilmington, DE: Intercollegiate Studies Institute, 2014), 18; Jack Bass, "Southern Republicans: Their Plight is Getting Worse." *Washington Post* (1974–Current File), July 12, 1977, 1.

141. Cliff White, YAF rep. to Youth for Reagan Steering Committee, worked for Heckman. Smith to Antosh, "Position of YAF in YR," Folder: Voter Groups—Youth—General [3 of 4], Box 305, Max Hugel Files, Reagan Library.

142. AEI to Duggin, YAF, Young Americans for Freedom Convention 1981, Box 16, Thelma Duggin Files, Reagan Library.

143. Youth for Reagan Plan, May 15, 1980, Folder: Campaign Planning, Youth for Reagan, Box 104, 1980 Campaign, Ed Meese Files, Reagan Library.

144. Morton Blackwell to William J. Casey, April 3, 1980, Folder: Political Ops (Timmons)—Voter Groups—Youth [2 of 2], Box 285, 1980 Campaign Papers, Reagan Library.

145. Blackwell to Youth Organization Leaders who personally support Reagan for President, April 29, 1980, Folder: Voter Groups—Youth—General [1 of 4], Box 104, 1980 Campaign, Ed Meese Files, Reagan Library.

146. Heritage Program, Folder: Voter Groups—Youth—Training Seminar [2 of 2], Box 311, 1980 Campaign Papers, Reagan Library.

147. Antosh Resume, Folder: Campaign Planning, Youth for Reagan, Box 104, 1980 Campaign, Ed Meese Files, Reagan Library.

148. Antosh Resume.

149. Blackwell to Casey.

150. "Youth Vote Negligible," A23.

151. Youth for Reagan Plan, May 15, 1980.

152. Blackwell to Casey, "1980 Reagan Youth Effort," April 3, 1980, Timmons [2 of 2].

153. Youth for Reagan Proposal, Folder: Voter Groups—Youth General [1 of 4], Box 136, Ed Meese Files, Reagan Library.

154. Rowland Evans and Robert Novak, "Young Republicans to Elect Trickster," *Eugene Register Guard*, April 27, 1977, A15.

155. Youth for Reagan Staff Training, Folder: Subject File—Youth for Reagan Sourcebook [1 of 2], Box 136, Ed Meese Files, Reagan Library.

156. Youth for Reagan Plan, 20, Folder: Campaign Planning—Youth for Reagan, Box 136, Ed Meese Files, Reagan Library.

157. Russell Kirk, "Straws in the Wind," *Oscala Star-Banner*, December 29, 1966, 4.

158. James Naughton, "McCarthy Set to Lean toward Entering Several Democratic Primaries," *New York Times*, July 23, 1971, 12.

159. "Reagan Backed at YAF Parley," *San Diego Union*, August 19, 1979, A-22.

160. Robert W. Kaufman, "Ronald Reagan: A Republican Messiah?," *North American Review* 253, no. 2 (1968): 8–14.

161. Lacy to Casey, May 28, 1980, Folder: Groups—Youth General [2 of 4], Box 311, Max Hugel Files, Reagan Library.

162. Joseph Kraft, "Can Reagan Control His Own Right?," Folder: Campaign Planning Tactics [2 of 4], Box 104, Ed Meese Files, Reagan Library

163. Kraft, "Can Reagan Control His Own Right?"

164. Edwards to Meese, Campaign Planning—Tactics [2 of 4], Box 104, Ed Meese Files, Reagan Library.

165. CR, 1981, College Republican National Committee (1), Box 4, Blackwell Files, Reagan Library.

166. Shirley, *Reagan's Revolution*, 308.

167. Lacy to Casey, May 28, 1980, Folder: Groups—Youth General [2 of 4], Box 311, Max Hugel Files, Reagan Library.

168. YAF Proposal, May 16, 1980, Folder: Youth Subject File, Box 136, Ed Meese Files, Reagan Library.

169. Youth Plan.

170. Blackwell to Hugel, July 23, 1980, Folder: Voter Groups—Youth—General [3 of 4], Box 314, Max Hugel Files, Reagan Library.

171. Thorburn, *Generation Awakes*, 446.

172. Gibble to Casey, May 21, 1980, Folder: Voter Groups—Youth—General [2 of 4], Box 311, Max Hugel Files, Reagan Library.

173. Antosh to Cliff White, September 4, 1980, Folder: Voter Groups—Youth—General [3 of 4], Box 305, Max Hugel Files, Reagan Library.

174. Youth for Reagan Proposal, April 15, 1980, Folder: Campaign Planning, Youth for Reagan, Box 104, 1980 Campaign Paper, Series III, Ed Meese Files, Reagan Library.

175. Diane Jacobsen, Target Report No. 3, April 1978, Folder: Teenage Republicans, Box 6, Ford Library.

176. Tom Jackman, "Young Republicans Stream into Detroit," *Observer* (Notre Dame) 15, no. 5 (August 29, 1980): 8.

177. Youth for Reagan Staff Training, I-10.

178. Progress Report, June 30, Folder: Political Ops (Timmons)—Voter Groups—Youth [2 of 2], Box 257, 1980 Campaign Papers, 1965–1980, Series VIII, William Timmons: Voter Groups, Reagan Library.

179. Youth for Reagan Plan, May 20, 1980, Campaign Planning, Youth for Reagan, Box 104, 1980 Campaign, Ed Meese Files, Reagan Library.

180. Cowie, *Stayin' Alive*; Robert Self, *All in the Family: The Realignment of American Democracy since the 1960s* (New York: Hill and Wang, 2013).

181. Kathy Sawyer and Barry Sussman, "Candidates Don't Arouse the Young Non-voters," *Morning News*, September 21, 1980, 1.

182. Brock interview.

183. Heritage Program.

184. Heritage Program.

185. Godfrey Sperling Jr., "Strategy: How Reagan Plans to Beat President in November," *Lewiston Daily*, July 18, 1980, 5.

186. Sperling, 5.

187. Heritage manual, Voter Groups—Youth—Training Seminar [2 of 2], Box 311, 1980 Campaign Papers, Reagan Library.

188. Flyer, Heritage Youth Committee, Voter Groups—Youth—Training Seminar [2 of 2], Box 311, 1980 Campaign Papers, Reagan Library.

189. Flyer, Heritage Youth Committee.

190. Heritage Youth Committee, Folder: Subject File—Youth for Reagan Sourcebook [1 of 2], Box 136, Ed Meese Files, Reagan Library.

191. Youth Plan.

192. Youth Plan.

193. Mike Steere, "Reagan Youths Burst with Energy," *Toledo Blade*, July 17, 1980, 7.

194. Editorial, "Hyped Up Politics," *St. Petersburg Times*, July 16, 1980, 16A.

195. Blackwell to Casey, April 3, 1980, Political Ops—Voter Groups—Youth [2 of 2], Box 257, Timmons Files, Reagan Library.

196. Kalman, *Right Star Rising*, 350.

197. Osmonds Script, July 16, 1980, Folder: Scheduling Reagan Youth [Donnie and Marie Osmond], Box 257, Timmons Files, Reagan Library.

198. Donnie to Andrews, July 15, 1980, Folder: Scheduling Reagan Youth [Donnie and Marie Osmond], Box 257, Timmons Files, Reagan Library.

199. Osmonds Script, July 16, 1980.

200. "GOP Convention Book: A Young Republican Pillow Fight," *Michigan Daily*, July 15, 1980, 3.

201. Steere, "Reagan Youths Burst with Energy," 7.

202. Tuttle to Reagan State Chairmen, Convention Youth Activities, June 11, 1980, Voter Groups—Youth—General [2 of 4], Box 311, Max Hugel Files, Reagan Library.

203. Tuttle to Reagan State Chairmen, June 11, 1980.

204. Sara Anspach, "Republican Youth Highly Visible at Convention," *Michigan Daily*, July 15, 1980, 3.

205. "Youth Vote Negligible," A23.

206. "Youth Vote Negligible," A23.

207. Robert J. Wagman, "Can Republicans Woo Young Voters?" *Gadsden Times*, August 1, 1980, 4.

208. Blackwell to Bulen, April 24, 1980, Folder: Voter Groups—Youth—General [1 of 4], Box 311, Max Hugel Files, Reagan Library.

209. Youth Plan, 40.

210. Wagman, "Can Republicans Woo Young Voters?," 4.

211. Joyce Frieden, "Republican Leaders Address Meeting of 'Youth for Reagan,'" *Michigan Daily*, July 16, 1980, 5.

212. Blackwell to Hugel, Folder: Voter Groups—Youth—Budget, Box 311, Max Hugel Files, Reagan Library.

213. Antosh to Hugel ("RNC Funds"), Folder: Voter Groups—Youth—Budget, Box 311, Max Hugel Files, Reagan Library.

214. David Wilson to Reagan Bush Leadership, October 29, 1980, Voter Groups—Youth—General [4 of 4], Box 311, Max Hugel Files, Reagan Library.

215. Antosh to Hugel, Student Issues, Folder: Voter Groups—Youth—Budget, Box 311, Max Hugel Files, Reagan Library.

216. Antosh to Hugel, Student Issues.

217. "Young Voters Unattached," *Tuscaloosa News*, September 21, 1980, 15A.

218. Bernard Winraub, "Poor TV Strategy Can Leave Candidates Programmed for Defeat," *Lakeland Ledger*, February 10, 1980, A14.

219. Youth for Reagan Staff Training, I-32.

220. Youth for Reagan Staff Training, I-33.

221. Youth for Reagan Staff Training, I-35.

222. Youth for Reagan Staff Training, I-35.

223. "Peace": http://www.livingroomcandidate.org/commercials/1980/streetgov.

224. Youth for Reagan Staff Training, I-35.

225. Youth Plan, 15.

226. Youth for Reagan, Budget and Structure, 24, Folder: Youth General [2 of 4], Box 311, Max Hugel Files, Reagan Library.

227. October 29 News Release, Folder: Voter Groups—Youth—General [4 of 4], Box 311, Max Hugel Files, Reagan Library.

228. Antosh to Brock, October 11, 1980, Folder: Voter Groups—Youth—General [4 of 4], Box 311, Max Hugel Files, Reagan Library.

229. "Reagan Sweeps Mock Election at the Mount," *Gettysburg Times*, October 1, 1980, 2.

230. Watson to Hugel, October 10, 1980, Folder: Voter Groups—Youth—General [4 of 4], Box 311, Max Hugel Files, Reagan Library.

231. Hawkins to Hugel, October 31, 1980, Folder: Voter Groups—Youth—General [4 of 4], Box 311, Max Hugel Files, Reagan Library.

232. CR, 1981, College Republican National Committee (1), Box 4, Blackwell Files, Reagan Library.

233. CR, 1981.

234. Peggy Polk, "A Resplendent Reagan at Inaugural Balls," *Ukiah Daily Journal,* January 21, 1981, 2.

235. Sandra Webb, "Beach Boys, New Beginning, Young Voters Ball," *CR Magazine,* Winter 1981, 8–9. Found in College Republican National Committee (1), Box 4, PMB, Reagan Library.

Epilogue

1. Michele Reeves, "'Obey the Rules or Get Out': Ronald Reagan's 1966 Gubernatorial Campaign and the 'Trouble in Berkeley,'" *Southern California Quarterly* 92, no. 3 (2010): 275–305, 289.

2. Peter M. Nichols, "'Family Ties' Was a Sitcom for Its Time—the 1980s," *Deseret News,* July 7, 1998, C9. While Reagan's campaign invited Fox to join the 1984 reelection effort, Fox declined, claiming his Canadian citizenship made his involvement inappropriate.

3. Mary McGory, "Youth for Reagan," *Day* (New London, CT), September 24, 1984, "Youth for Reagan," 8.

4. Robert J. Wagman, "Can Republicans Woo Young Voters?," *Gadsden Times,* August 1, 1980, 4.

5. Paul Johnson, "The 80's Generation: The Lost Ideals of Youth," *New York Times,* March 25, 1984, SM90.

6. McGory, "Youth for Reagan," 8.

7. George F. Will, "Our Attire Shows Reagan Influence," *Eugene-Register Guard,* February 5, 1984, A15.

8. Rebecca Nappi, "Youth Makes Swing to Conservatism," *Statesmen Journal,* September 10, 1984, 1.

9. Robert Furlow, "Mondale Warns of Court Packing; Reagan Seeks Youth Vote," *Spartanburg Herald Journal,* October 28, 1984, A6.

10. Margot Hornblower, "Youth: Advertisers Find Sucker Isn't Born Every Minute," *Bulletin,* June 12, 1986, A5.

11. Zachary Cook, "How Impressionable Were the Younger Reagan Cohorts?," *Forum* 12, no. 3 (2014): 481–497.

12. David Shribman, ". . . and Recruit for the Government," *New York Times,* October 12, 1983, B6.

13. Shribman, B6.

14. Alan Pell Crawford, "YAF's Slow Suicide on Washington's Fast Track," *Wall Street Journal,* Eastern ed., August 9, 1984, 1.

15. Crawford, 1.

16. Abramoff to Nofziger, April 25, 1981, Folder: College Republican National Committee (1), Box 4, Papers of Mort Blackwell, Series 1, Reagan Library.

17. AP, "Reagan Won Backing of Youth," *Spokesmen Review,* November 7, 1984, A3.

18. William A. Rusher, "Youth for Reagan Surprising," *Southeast Missourian,* October 16, 1984, 4.

19. "The College Republicans: A Brief History," July 22, 2004, http://www.crnc.org/admin/editpage/downloads/CRNChistory.pdf (accessed November 12, 2013).

20. AP, "Reagan Won Backing of Youth," A3.

21. Asbell interview.

22. See list of interviews in the bibliography.

23. Haldeman interview.

24. Bacon interview.

25. Burhop interview.

26. C-span, https://www.c-span.org/video/?125821-1/committee-responsible-youth-politics (accessed November 12, 2014).

Bibliography

Archival

BAKER CENTER FOR PUBLIC POLICY
University of Tennessee, Knoxville, TN
    PWEB: William Emerson Brock III Collection

GERALD FORD PRESIDENTIAL LIBRARY
Ann Arbor, MI
    PPF: Pamela Powell Files
    James Cannon Files
    PFC: President Ford Committee Files

ALBERT GORE RESEARCH CENTER
Middle Tennessee State University, Murfreesboro, TN
    Papers of Albert Gore Sr.

JOHN C. HODGES LIBRARY
University of Tennessee Library Special Collections and Manuscripts,
    Knoxville, TN
    University of Tennessee Special Collections: Student Unrest
    Daily Beacon, University of Tennessee, Knoxville, TN
    Volunteer, University of Tennessee Yearbook, http://www.lib.utk.edu
    /digitalcollections/ut.html

HORNBAKE LIBRARY, SPECIAL COLLECTIONS
University of Maryland, College Park
    UMDCR: Papers of University of Maryland College Republicans,
    1948–1976.

JOHN F. KENNEDY LIBRARY
Boston, MA
    PFFM: Papers of Frank Fabian Mankiewicz, 1962–1978
    PKJ: Papers of Kirby Jones, 1963–1974
    Robert Kennedy, 1968 Campaign Papers
    PTW: Papers of Theodore White: The Making of the President
        Walter Sheridan, recorded interview by Roberta Greene, August 5,
        1969, 18–21, John F. Kennedy Library Oral History Program
    PJKG: Papers of John Kenneth Galbraith
    PSS: Papers of Sargent Shriver

324 | BIBLIOGRAPHY

SEELEY G. MUDD LIBRARY, SPECIAL COLLECTIONS
Princeton University, Princeton, NJ
Thomas Klinkel Collection on George McGovern
PGM: PGM
PCC: Papers of Common Cause
Papers of Ed O'Donnell

NATIONAL ARCHIVES AND RECORDS ADMINISTRATION (NARA), II
NIXON PRESIDENTIAL MATERIALS, THE WHITE HOUSE TAPES,
College Park, MD
PRF: Papers of Robert Finch
PHRH: Papers of H. R. Haldeman include White House SMOF H. R.
Haldeman
EX FE 4: Declaration of Independence, Bill of Rights
PPB: Include WHSF SM&OF and Papers of Patrick J. Buchanan
FG 308: White House Central Files, Marijuana
FG 288: Campus Unrest, Commission
GEN FG 216-3: Selective Service

RICHARD NIXON PRESIDENTIAL LIBRARY
Yorba Linda, CA
SMOF: Papers of Len Garment
PJM: Papers of Jeb Magruder: Committee for the Re-election of the
President Collection
Papers of James McLane
PFVM: Papers of Fred V. Malek, Committee for the Re-election of the
President Collection
Papers of Len Garment

RONALD REAGAN PRESIDENTIAL LIBRARY
Simi Valley, CA
PMB: Papers of Morton Blackwell
Thelma Duggin Files
Ronald Reagan 1980 Presidential Campaign Files
William Timmons Files
Max Hugel Files
Ed Meese Files

Interviews

Fred Asbell: June 3, 2016
Perry Bacon: June 3, 2016
Tom Bell: August 8, 2016
Cathy Bertini: July 18, 2012
Bill Brock: December 12, 2012
Sam Brown: http://openvault.wgbh.org/catalog?q+Brown%2C+Sam
%2C+1943-(7/2012)

Gary Burhop: May 31, 2016
Tom Campbell: June 4, 2016
Tim Carey: August 10, 2016
David Chew: July 7, 2016
Tom Davis: June 2, 2016
Barbara Dietrich: June 9, 2016
George Gorton: July 29, 2012
Jerry Gilbreath: August 20, 2016
Hank Haldeman: August 20, 2016
Robert Odle: July 9, 2014
Karl Ottosen: September 6, 2016
Ken Rietz: June 6, 2012
Donald Sundquist: June 14, 2016

Printed Primary Sources

Eisenhower, Dwight D. Republican National Convention, August 23, 1956, http://millercenter.org/president/speeches/detail/3359 (accessed July 1, 2014).
Gallup Election Polls by Groups, 1968–1972, http://www.gallup.com/poll /9457/election-polls-vote-groups-19681972.aspx (accessed October 13, 2011).
"The Independents." *Washington Post,* http://www.washingtonpost.com/wp -srv/politics/interactives/independents/data-year-by-year.html (accessed October 20, 2011).
Kendall, Donald. "The Generation Gap: Economic Illiteracy." Remarks Delivered before the National Food Brokers Association Annual Conference, New York, December 5, 1970, *Vital Speeches of the Day* 37 (1971): 245–246.
Lipscomb Babbler.
National Commission on Marihuana and Drug Abuse. *Shafer Commission.* Washington, DC: Government Printing Office, 1972.
National Commission on the Causes and Prevention of Violence. *To Establish Justice, to Insure Domestic Tranquility: Final Report of the National Commission on the Causes and Prevention of Violence.* Washington, DC: Government Printing Office, December 10, 1969.
New Guard. Young Americans for Freedom, 1965–1972. 1961—Sterling, VA, Serial Publication, Boston Public Library, Boston, MA.
Nixon, Richard. "Letter to Educators and University Officials on Campus Extremists." Public Papers of the President. September 27, 1970.
———. "Nixon's Special Message to Congress." Public Papers of the President. May 13, 1969.
———. Public Papers of the President, *Special Message to the Congress on Control of Narcotics and Dangerous Drugs,* July 14, 1969.
———. "Remarks to a Student-Faculty Convocation at the University of Nebraska," January 14, 1971. John T. Woolley and Gerhard Peters, *The*

American Presidency Project (online). Santa Barbara: University of California (hosted), Gerhard Peters (database): http://www.presidency.ucsb.edu /ws/?pid=2955 (accessed October 12, 2012).

―――. "Remarks on Accepting the Presidential Nomination of the Republican National Convention." Public Papers of the President. August 23, 1972.

―――. "Remark to Members of the Association of Student Governments." Public Papers of the President. September 20, 1969. http://proxychi .baremetal.com/csdp.org/research/shafernixon.pdf.

―――. "Statement on Campus Disorders." Public Papers of the President. March 3, 1969.

―――. "Statement on Establishing Nationwide Youth Advisory Committee to the Selective Service System." Public Papers of the President. June 6, 1969.

―――. "Today's Youth: The Great Generation." NBC Radio, October 16, 1968.

President's Commission on Campus Unrest. *The Report of the President's Commission on Campus Unrest.* Washington, DC: Government Printing Office, 1970.

Underground Newspaper Collection (microform), Wooster, OH: Micro Photo Division, Bell & Howell Co. and the Underground Press Syndicate, 1970–[1986?].

US Congress. CIS 70, Environmental Protection Act Hearings, S-3575, May 12, 1970, 13, and CIS 1972, S-261-59, 131.

―――. Congressional Hearings, CIS 70, Basic Educational Opportunity Grant, 570.

―――. Congressional Hearings on Environmental Education Act. HR-14753, March 24, 1970, 32.

―――. Committee on the Judiciary, House US Congressional Hearings to Provide for the Establishment of a Commission on Marihuana, HRG-1969-HJH-0003, October 15 and 16, 1969.

―――. *Extending Voting Rights Act of 1965,* 91st Cong., 2nd sess., *Congressional Record* 116 (June 17, 1970): 20190.

―――. *L.B.J.: A President Who Understands Young People,* 90th Cong., 2nd sess., *Congressional Record* 114 (June 27, 1968): 19079.

―――. *On Lowering the Voting Age,* Amendments to Senate Joint Resolution 7, 92nd Cong., Judiciary Committee Report, February 17, 1971, 6.

―――. Special Subcommittee on Draft, Committee on Armed Services. House Review of the Administration and Operation of the Draft Law CIS 91-2 70, Committee on Armed Services Serial No. 91-80 Selective Service, 12748, H.R. 18025; 91 H.R. 18578.

US Senate. CIS 70, Environmental Protection Act Hearings, S-3575, May 12, 1970, 13.

―――. Committee on the Judiciary, Subcommittee on Constitutional Amendments. *Committee Print: Lowering the Voting Age to 18: A Fifty State Survey of the Costs and Other Problems of Dual-Age Voting.* 92nd Cong., 1st sess., February 1971.

―――. *On Lowering the Voting Age,* Hearings before the Subcommittee on Constitutional Amendments, US Senate Committee on the Judiciary, 91st Congress, February 16, 1970, 35.

———. US Congressional Hearings to Provide for the Establishment of a Commission on Marihuana, October 15 and 16, 1969.

———. US Department of Commerce. "Characteristics of American Youth." *Current Population Reports—Special Studies*, February 18, 1971.

US Senate Hearings before the Subcommittee to Investigate Juvenile Delinquency, HRG-1969-SJS-0027, Committee on the Judiciary. September 15, 1969.

Walker, Ronald H. Exit interview, 72, http://nixon.archives.gov/virtuallibrary /documents/exitinterviews/walker-exit.pdf.

Audio/Visual

Four More Years, prod. and dir. by Top Value Television (TVTV), 60 min. Subtle Communications, 1972, videocassette.

Nixon Campaign Commercials. Museum of the Moving Image, *The Living Room Candidate*, Richard Nixon, 1972. http://www.livingroomcandidate.org /commercials/1972 (accessed July 23, 2011).

Nixon Tapes. https://www.nixonlibrary.gov/virtuallibrary/tapeexcerpts/index .php.

White House Tapes. http://www.csdp.org/research/nixonpot.txt.

Books and Articles

"1970: A Time of In-Betweenity." *Christian Century*, December 30, 1970, editorial page.

Abel, Barbara. "PAC Rocks with Rock and Tricia." *Milwaukee Journal*, October 2, 1972, 1.

"The Administration: Getting It All Together in the Name of Action." *Time*, June 7, 1971, http://content.time.com/time/magazine/article/0,9171 ,905126,00.html.

Alexander, Herbert E. *Financing the 1972 Election*. Lexington, MA: Lexington Books, 1976.

Alexander, Michelle. *The New Jim Crow: Mass Incarceration in the Age of Colorblindness*. New York: New Press, 2010.

Anderson, Jack. "The Washington Merry-Go-Round: Former Nixon Spy Now with Reagan." *Wilmington Morning Star*, December 19, 1975, 2.

Andrew, John. *The Other Side of the Sixties*. Piscataway, NJ: Rutgers University Press, 1997.

AP. "A Night of Dancing for Exuberant Nixon." *Des Moines Register*, January 21, 1973, 4.

Apple, R. W., Jr. "O'Brien Reproves McGovern Staff over Lax Effort." *New York Times*, September 1, 1972, 1.

———. "Youth Vote Likely to Aid Democrats." *New York Times Magazine*, May 10, 1971, 18.

Asbury, Edith Evans. "More Youths Join McCarthy Forces: Pour into New Hampshire for the Final Push." *New York Times*, March 10, 1968, 48.

Baker, Russell. "Observer: The Newest Wrinkle in the Youth Game." *New York Times*, May 21, 1964, 34.

———. "The Observer: The Pied Piper of Minnesota." *New York Times*, March 21, 1968, 46.

Balko, Radley. *Rise of the Warrior Cop: The Militarization of America's Police Forces.* New York: Public Affairs, 2013.

Barker, Karilyn. "How Will Nixon React? Asks Interested Youth." *Palm Beach Daily News*, April 21, 1969, 1.

Barrett, Marvin, ed. *The Politics of Broadcasting.* New York: Thomas Crowell, 1973.

Batten, James K. "Politics 1968: Obeisance at the Altar of Youth." *St. Petersburg Times*, July 18, 1968, 1.

Bauerlein, Mark. *The Dumbest Generation: How the Digital Age Stupefies Young Americans and Jeopardizes Our Future (or, Don't Trust Anybody under Thirty).* New York: Tarcher, 2009.

Baum, Dan. *Smoke and Mirrors: The War on Drugs and the Politics of Failure.* New York: Little Brown, 1996.

Beasley, David. "Youth Move In." *Cincinnati Magazine*, October 1972, 80.

Beck, Paul Allen, and M. Kent Jennings. "Family Traditions, Political Periods, and the Development of Partisan Orientations." *Journal of Politics* 53, no. 3 (August 1991): 742–763.

Bell, Jeffrey. "The Ordeal of the President; or, Will Richard Nixon Find True Happiness in 1972." *New Guard*, May 1971, 5.

Bennett, Stephen Earl. "Left Behind: Exploring Declining Turnout among Non-college Young Whites, 1964–1988." *Social Science Quarterly* 72, no. 2 (1991): 1.

Bernhard, Gene. "Campus Riots Blamed: College Aid Proposals Stalled." *Dispatch* (Lexington, NC), June 15, 1970, 1.

Besesparis, Ted. "Candidates Woo Youth Vote." *Beachcomber* (Palm Beach Junior College) 34, no. 1 (September 5, 1972): http://www.archive.org/stream /Beachcomber_402/1972–73ocr_djvu.txt.

Blum, John Morton. *Years of Discord: American Politics and Society, 1961–1974.* New York: W. W. Norton, 1991.

Bodroghkozy, Aniko. *Groove Tube: Sixties Television and Youth Rebellion.* Durham, NC: Duke University Press, 2001.

Bowman, James, and Kathryn Hanaford. "Mass Media and the Environment since Earth Day." *Journalism Quarterly* (Spring 1976): 164.

Brailsford, Ian. "'Madison Avenue Takes On the Teenage Hop Heads': The Advertising Council's Campaign against Drugs in the Nixon Era." *Australasian Journal of American Studies* 18, no. 2 (December 1999): 45–53.

Braungart, Richard G., and Margaret M. Braungart. "Family, School, and Personal Political Factors in Student Politics: A Case Study of the 1972 Presidential Election." *Journal of Marriage and the Family* 37, no. 4, special section: "Macrosociology of the Family" (November 1975): 823–839.

Broder, David. *The Party Is Over: The Failure of Politics in America.* New York: Harper & Row, 1972.

Brownell, Kathryn Cramer. *Showbiz Politics: Hollywood in American Public Life.* Chapel Hill: University of North Carolina Press, 2016.

Buckley, William F., Jr. "End the Pot Penalties." *Washington Star News,* November 10, 1974, C4.

———. "Study on Campus Unrest Serves No Purpose." *Kentucky New Era,* September 26, 1970, 4.

———. "A Way Out on Voting Age Pledge." *Washington Star,* February 17, 1970, 17.

Bullock, Paul. "Rabbits and Radicals: Richard Nixon's 1964 Campaign against Jerry Voorhis." *Southern California Quarterly* 55, no. 3 (Fall 1973): 319–359.

Burke, Vincent. "Congress Ponders Costs Assists." *Tuscaloosa News,* August 4, 1971, 7.

Bushnell, Asa. "Convention Vignettes." *Tuscon Dailey Citizen,* August 16, 1976, 2.

Califano, Joseph. *Inside: A Public and Private Life.* New York: Public Affairs, 2005.

"Campus Unrest Panelist Says 'Real' Issues Are Being Ignored." *New York Times* (1923–Current file), November 2, 1970, 38.

Carver, Deborah. "What We See on the TeeVee: The Average American, Godlike Announcers, and Neither Fear nor Loathing in the 1972 Election." *Rethinking History* 11, no. 2 (2007): 203–213.

Cassino, Dan. *Consuming Politics: Jon Stewart, Branding, and the Youth Vote in America.* Hackensack, NJ: Fairleigh Dickinson University Press, 2009.

Chamberlain, John. "Nixon Courting 'Square Power.'" *St. Joseph Gazette* (Missouri), May 12, 1969, 4.

Charlton, Linda. "G.O.P. Tries Cheers and Chats on Youth." *New York Times,* October 22, 1972, 50.

Clark, Dennis. "Drive On for Voter Registration." *UT Beacon,* October 5, 1972, 1. University of Tennessee Special Collections.

Clarke, Thurston. *The Last Campaign: Robert F. Kennedy and the 82 Days That Inspired America.* New York: Holt Paperbacks, 2009.

Clelland, Donald A., Thomas C. Hood, C. M. Lipsey, and Ronald Wimberley. "In the Company of the Converted: Characteristics of a Billy Graham Crusade Audience." *Sociological Analysis* 35, no. 1 (Spring 1974): 45–56.

"Coalition Seeking New Youth Voters." *New York Times,* April 14, 1971, 8.

Cohen, Michael A. *American Maelstrom: The 1968 Election and the Politics of Division.* New York: Oxford University Press, 2016.

"Connally Sees More Democrats Supporting Nixon." *New York Times,* September 1, 1972, 41.

Connery, Michael. *Youth to Power: How Today's Young Voters Are Building Tomorrow's Progressive Majority.* New York: Ig, 2008.

Cowie, Jefferson. *Stayin' Alive: The 1970s and the Last Days of the Working Class.* New York: New Press, 2010.

Cox, Jeff. "A Kind of Magic: Even Young Moderate Conservatives Seem to Flock to Eugene McCarthy." *Victoria Advocate,* April 30, 1968, 4.

Coyne, John R., Jr. *The Impudent Snobs: Agnew vs. the Intellectuals Establishment.* New Rochelle, NY: Arlington House, 1972.

Crawford, Alan. *Thunder on the Right: The "New Right" and the Politics of Resentment.* New York: Pantheon, 1980.

Critchlow, Donald. *The Conservative Ascendancy.* Cambridge, MA: Harvard University Press, 2007.

Crotty, William. *Decision for the Democrats.* Baltimore: Johns Hopkins University Press, 1978.

Crouse, Timothy. *The Boys on the Bus.* New York: Random House, 1973.

Cusick, Dennis. "Poll Sees Young Voter Apathy." *UT Beacon,* October 2, 1972, 1. University of Tennessee Special Collections.

Daum, Andreas W., Lloyd C. Gardner, and Wilfried Mausbach, eds. *America, the Vietnam War, and the World: Comparative and International Perspectives.* New York: Cambridge University Press, 2003.

Davis, Belinda, et al., eds. *Changing the World, Changing Oneself: Political Protest and Collective Identities in 1960s/70s West Germany and the U.S.* New York: Berghahn Books, 2009.

Decherd, Robert. "A Republican Road Show Swamps Miami." *Harvard Crimson,* September 1, 1972, https://www.thecrimson.com/article/1972/9/1/a-republican-roadshow-swamps-miami-pmiami/ (accessed May 5, 2018).

"Delegate Reports on Youth Conference." *Evening Independent,* May 1, 1971, 7B.

Delgado, Richard. *Critical Race Theory: The Cutting Edge.* Philadelphia: Temple University Press, 2013.

"Demo Youth: 'Apple Pie, Moderate.'" *St. Petersburg Times,* July 4, 1972, B2.

de Schweinitz, Rebecca. *If We Could Change the World: Young People and America's Long Struggle for Racial Equality.* Chapel Hill: University of North Carolina Press, 2009.

———. "The Proper Age for Suffrage": Vote 18 and the Politics of Age from World War II to the Age of Aquarius." In *Age in America: The Colonial Era to the Present,* ed. Corinne T. Field and Nicholas L. Syrett, 209–236. New York: New York University Press, 2015.

De Toeledano, Ralph. "Poll Confirms Public Support for Nixon." *Reading Eagle,* December 23, 1969, 23.

Diam, Robert S. "Q & A: The Fortune 500–Yankelovitch Survey: Shaken Faith in Nixon." *Fortune,* June 1970, 60.

Diamond, Edwin. "The City Politic: November Song." *New York Magazine,* November 6, 1972, 8–11.

Diamond, Edwin, and Stephen Bates. *The Spot: The Rise of Political Advertising on Television.* Cambridge, MA: MIT Press, 1992.

Dochuk, Darren. *From Bible Belt to Sunbelt.* New York: W. W. Norton, 2011.

Docksai, Ronald. "Welcome to the Remnant." *New Guard,* October 1971, 4.

Dutton, Frederick G. *Changing Sources of Power: American Politics in the 1970s.* New York: McGraw Hill, 1971.

Editors, *Fortune Magazine,* eds. *The Environment: A National Mission for the Seventies.* New York: Perennial Library, 1970.

Edsall, Thomas Byrne, and Mary D. Edsall. *Chain Reaction: The Impact of Race, Rights and Taxes on American Politics.* New York: W. W. Norton, 1991.

"Education: Discontent of the Straights." *Time* 97, no. 1 (May 3, 1971), http://www.time.com/time/magazine/article/0,9171,876970,00.html (accessed November 10, 2012).

Elsasser, Glen. "Political Boss System to Last: Author." *Chicago Tribune*, August 25, 1969, A11.

Eskridge, Larry. "'One Way': Billy Graham, the Jesus Generation, and the Idea of an Evangelical Youth Culture." *American Society of Church History* 67, no. 1 (March 1998): 84.

Evans, Rowland, and Robert Novak. "Inside Report: Nixon's Youth Movement." *Victoria Advocate*, September 8, 1966, 4A.

———. "Young Republicans to Elect Trickster." *Eugene Register Guard*, April 27, 1977, A15.

"Excerpts from President's Message on Drug Abuse Control." *New York Times*, June 18, 1971, 22.

Feeney, Mark. *Nixon at the Movies: A Book about Belief.* Chicago: University of Chicago Press, 2004.

Field, Corinne T., and Nicholas L. Syrett, eds., *Age in America: The Colonial Era to the Present.* New York: New York University Press, 2015.

Fink, Carole, Philipp Gasser, and Detlef Junker, eds. *1968: The World Transformed.* Cambridge, UK: Cambridge University Press, 1998.

Finney, John W. "Humphrey Visits Discotheque and an Auto Plant." *New York Times*, October 18, 1968, 34.

Fiske, Edward. "The Closest Thing to a White House Chaplain: Billy Graham." *New York Times*, June 8, 1969, SM27.

Flamm, Michael. *Law and Order Street Crime, Civil Unrest and the Crisis of Liberalism in the 1960s.* New York: Columbia University Press, 2005.

Flavin, Genevieve. "Voice of Youth." *Chicago Tribune*, March 15, 1970, G12.

Flint, Jerry. "Michigan Studies Rights of Youth." *New York Times*, March 14, 1971, 24.

Flippen, Brooks, J. "Environmental Protection and the Environmental Movement." In *American Environmental History*, ed. Louis S. Warren Carlton, 271–288. Australia: Blackwell, 2003.

———. *Nixon and the Environment.* Albuquerque: New Mexico University Press, 2012.

Fox, Jack V. "Youth Feels Mediation Easy between US, China." *Bangor Daily News*, April 19, 1971, 4.

Fox, Sylvan. "Scores of Youth Seized in Anti-election Protest across the Nation." *New York Times*, November 6, 1968, 3.

Frank, Thomas. *The Conquest of Cool.* Chicago: University of Chicago Press, 1997.

Fraser, Gerald C. "Easing of Laws on Marijuana Proposed at a Conference Here." *New York Times*, June 21, 1969, 13.

Fraser, Janet, and Ernest May, eds. *Campaign '72: The Managers Speak.* Cambridge, MA: Harvard University Press, 1973.

Fraser, Ronald, et al. *1968: A Student Generation in Revolt.* New York: Pantheon, 1988.

Freedman, Samuel. *The Inheritance: How Three Families and America Moved from Roosevelt to Reagan and Beyond.* New York: Simon & Schuster, 1996.

Frick, Daniel. *Reinventing Richard Nixon: A Cultural History of an American Obsession.* Lawrence: University Press of Kansas, 2008.

Frum, David. *How We Got Here: The 70's, the Decade That Brought You Modern Life (for Better or Worse).* New York: Basic Books, 2000.

———."Why the GOP Lost the Youth Vote." *USA Today,* April 9, 2008, http://www.aei.org/article/politics-and-public-opinion/elections/why-the-gop-lost-the-youth-vote/ (accessed, January 20, 2013).

Frydl, Kathleen. *The Drug Wars in America, 1940–1973.* Cambridge, UK: Cambridge University Press, 2013.

Gallup, George. "Gallup Shows McGovern Gain." *Anchorage Daily News,* October 1, 1972, 1.

Gardner, Drew. "Truth: An American Political Anachronism." *Cavalier Daily* (University of Virginia), October 20, 1972, 3.

Gerstle, Gary, and Steve Fraser. *The Rise and Fall of the New Deal Order, 1930–1980,* Princeton, NJ: Princeton University Press, 1990.

Gibbs, Nancy, and Michael Duffy. *The Preacher and the Presidents: Billy Graham in the White House.* New York: Center Street, 2008.

Giglio, James. "The Eagleton Affair: Thomas Eagleton, George McGovern, and the 1972 Vice-Presidential Nomination." *Presidential Studies Quarterly* 39, no. 4 (December 2009): 51.

Gilbert, James. *A Cycle of Outrage: America's Reaction to the Juvenile Delinquent in the 1950s.* New York: Oxford University Press, 1988.

Giroux, Henry. *Politics after Hope: Obama and the Crisis of Youth, Race and Democracy (the Radical Imagination).* New York: Paradigm, 2010.

———. *Youth in Revolt: Reclaiming a Democratic Future (Critical Interventions: Politics, Culture, and the Promise of Democracy).* New York: Paradigm, 2013.

Glasser, Joshua M. *The Eighteen Day Running Mate.* New Haven, CT: Yale University Press, 2012.

Gollan, Antoni. "The Great Marijuana Problem." *National Review,* January 30, 1968, 74–80.

"GOP Tries Cheers and Chats on Youth." *New York Times,* October 22, 1972, 50.

Graham, Lawrence. *Youthtrends: Capturing the $200 Billion Youth Market.* New York: St. Martin's, 1987.

Grata, Joe. "Crowd Cheers McGovern Here." *Pittsburgh Press,* September 13, 1972, 1.

Greenberg, David. *Nixon's Shadow: The History of an Image.* New York: W. W. Norton, 2003.

———. *Republic of Spin: An Inside History of the American Presidency.* New York: W. W. Norton, 2016.

Greenfeld, Meg. "My Generation Is Missing." *Reporter,* May 4, 1967, 35–37.

Haldeman, H. R. *Haldeman Diaries: Inside the Nixon White House.* New York: G. P. Putnam's Sons, 1994.

"Half of US Youth's Did Not Vote." *Columbia Missourian*, January 4, 1973, 3.

Hart, Gary. *Right from the Start: A Chronicle of the McGovern Campaign*. New York: Quadrangle, 1973.

Hart, Jeffrey. "Marijuana and the Counterculture." *National Review*, December 8, 1972, 1348.

Helenski, Ski. "The Great Bathroom Debate." *UT Beacon*, November 11, 1972, 4. University of Tennessee Special Collections.

Helvarg, David. *The War against the Greens: The "Wise-Use" Movement, the New Right, and the Browning of America*. New York: Johnson Books, 2004.

Herberg, Will. "Conservatives and the Jesus Freaks." *New Guard*, November 1971, 15.

Herbers, John. "Conservatives Laud Choice; Moderates Dismayed." *New York Times*, August 9, 1968, 19.

———. "Democrats Assured of a Platform Fight." *New York Times*, June 28, 1972, 1.

———. "Secretary Finch: Still Something of an Enigma as the Administration's 'Liberal.'" *New York Times*, May 18, 1969, E3.

———. "Thousands in the Capital Express Faith in America." *New York Times*, July 5, 1970, 32.

Hess, R. D., and J. V. Torney. *The Development of Political Attitudes in Children*. Chicago: Aldine Press, 1967.

Hickel, Walter. "America Is Tired of Hate: Walter Hickel on the New Politics." *Sarasota Herald-Tribune*, December 12, 1971, 6.

"Hickel Tells Nixon: Heed Youth Cries." *Modesto Bee*, July 7, 1970, 17.

Hilt, Mary. "Averill Park Girl Thrilled by Inaugural Dance with President." *Times Record*, January 24, 1973, 3.

Himmelstein, Jerome L. *The Strange Career of Marijuana*. Santa Barbara, CA: Greenwood, 1983.

Hixson, Walter L. *The Vietnam Antiwar Movement*. New York: Garland, 2000.

Hodkinson, Harold. *Student Participation in Governance*. Education Task Force Paper, Center for Research and Development in Higher Education. University of California, Berkeley, 1971.

Hoff, Joan. *Nixon Reconsidered*. New York: Basic Books, 1993.

Hoffman, Paul. "Coalition to Seek Candidate for '68." *New York Times*, June 13, 1966, 19.

Holt, Lisa. "Campaign Posters: The 1972 Presidential Election." *Journal of American Culture* 9, no. 3 (Fall 1986): 65–83.

Hope, Paul. "Nations Youth Being Courted for Votes." *Reading Eagle*, July 6, 1971, 22.

———. "Nixon Aide Seeks to Enlist Young People." *Reading Eagle*, August 11, 1969, 18.

Horn, Gerd-Rainer. *The Spirit of '68: Rebellion in Western Europe and North America, 1956–1976*. Oxford: Oxford University Press, 2007.

"How Youth Lobby Pushed Vote Bill for 18-Year Olds." *Christian Science Monitor*, June 22, 1970, 8.

Hunter, Marjorie. "M'Govern Opens Presidential Bid with Peace Plea." *New York Times*, August 11, 1968, 1.

"Hustler's Editorial 'All Wet': Fails to Show 'Provincialism.'" *Lipscomb Babbler*, June 1968, 2.

Inwood, Joshua F. J. "Neoliberal Racism: The 'Southern Strategy' and the Expanding Geographies of White Supremacy." *Social and Cultural Geography* 16, no. 4 (June 2015): 407–423

"Issues '72: The Young; Turning Out." *Time*, September 25, 1972, http://con tent.time.com/time/magazine/article/0,9171,903573,00.html (accessed November 10, 2013).

Jacobs, Lawrence R., and Robert Y. Shapiro. "The Rise of Presidential Polling: The Nixon White House in Historical Perspective." *Public Opinion Quarterly* 59 (1995): 163–195.

Jamieson, Kathleen Hall. *Packaging the Presidency: A History and Criticism of Presidential Campaign Advertising*. Oxford: Oxford University Press, 1996.

Jerkins, Gerald. "Draft Deferments Hard for Graduates, Undergrads." *Babbler*, February 21, 1969, 2.

Jobs, Richard Ivan. "Youth Movements: Travel, Protest and Europe in 1968." *American Historical Review* 114, no. 2 (April 2009): 376–404.

Jones, Boisfeuillet. "The Young Republican Plight." *Harvard Crimson*, July 7, 1967, https://www.thecrimson.com/article/1967/7/11/the-young-repub lican-plight-pthe-overwhelming/ (accessed January 13, 2013).

Kabaservice, Geoffrey. *Rule and Ruin: The Downfall of Moderation and the Destruction of the Republican Party*. New York: Oxford University Press, 2012.

Kalman, Laura. *Right Star Rising: A New Politics, 1974–1980*. New York: W. W. Norton, 2010.

Katsiaficas, George. *The Imagination of the New Left: A Global Analysis of 1968*. Boston: South End, 1987.

Keene, David. "The Conservative Case for Richard Nixon." *New Guard*, Summer 1969, 11.

Keniston, Kenneth. *Young Radicals: Notes on the Committed Youth*. New York: Harcourt, Brace, and World, 1968.

Keniston, Kenneth, and Michael Lerner. "Campus Characteristics and Campus Unrest." *Annals of the American Academy of Political and Social Science* 395 (1971): 39–53.

Kennedy, Robert F. *To Seek a Newer World*. New York: Doubleday, 1975.

Kenworthy, E. W. "M'Carthy Strives to Bolster Staff: Seeks Professional Aides." *New York Times*, March 22, 1968, 1.

Kilpatrick, James J. "Conservative View: The Matter of Marijuana." *Tuscaloosa News*, September 27, 1972, 3.

———. "The Matter of Marijuana." *Tuscaloosa News*, September 27, 1972, 3.

———. "Nixon Group Aims at Youth." *Deseret News*, August 16, 1972, 10A.

Klatch, Rebecca E. *A Generation Divided*. Berkeley: University of California Press, 1999.

Klimke, Martin. *The "Other" Alliance: Global Protest and Student Unrest in West Germany and the U.S., 1962–1972*. Princeton, NJ: Princeton University Press, 2009.

Klimke, Martin, and Joachim Scharloth. *1968 in Europe: A History of Protest and Activism, 1956–1977*. New York: Palgrave Macmillan, 2008.

Kling, Bill. "Senate OK's Nixon's Drug Control." *Chicago Tribune*, January 29, 1970, C56.

Kneelands, Douglas E. "Politics Hollow for Missouri Students." *New York Times*, October 14, 1968, 40.

Kraft, Joseph. "Foes of War Can Help to Rally Voters." *Youngstown Vindicator*, May 11, 1970, B2.

Krogh interview. PBS. 2000. http://www.pbs.org/wgbh/pages/frontline/shows /drugs/interviews/krogh.html.

Kuzmarov, Jeremy. *The Myth of the Addicted Army: Vietnam and the Modern War on Drugs*. Amherst: University of Massachusetts Press, 2009.

Lamare, James. "Inter-or-Intragenerational Cleavage? The Political Orientations of American Youth in 1968."*American Journal of Political Science* 19, no. 1 (February 1975): 81–89.

Lamb, David. "Delegate, Policeman and Protestor: 3 Young Men in Same City, Different Orbits." *Los Angeles Times*, August 22, 1972, A1.

Lambro, Donald, UPI. "Youth Vote: Workers for Nixon and Students for McGovern?" *Ludington Daily News*, November 6, 1972, 6.

Lassiter, Matthew D. "Impossible Criminals: The Suburban Imperatives of America's War on Drugs." *Journal of American History* 102, no. 1 (2015): 126–140.

———. *The Silent Majority: Suburban Politics in the Sunbelt South*. Princeton, NJ: Princeton University Press, 2007.

Lawrence, David. "Campus Unrest Linked to Drugs." *Palm Beach Post*, May 28, 1970, A14.

Letter from the People. "Must Learn Cause." *Modesto Bee*, July 29, 1970, 49.

Letters. *New Guard*, November 1972, 24.

Letters. *Time*, September 25, 1972, http://www.time.com/time/magazine /article/0,9171,903567,00.html#ixzz1YPxfBGII (accessed September 19, 2011).

Letters from Readers. *Spokane Daily Chronicle*, November 22, 1971, 4.

Levine, Arthur, and Keith R. Wilson. "Student Activism in the 1970s: Transformation Not Decline." *Higher Education* 8, no. 6 ("Student Activism," November 1979): 627–640.

Logan, Rebecca. "Project 18." http://hin.nea.org/home/48614.htm (accessed October 29, 2011).

Longley, Kyle. *Senator Albert Gore, Sr.: Tennessee Maverick*. Baton Rouge: Louisiana State University Press, 2004.

Loo, Dennis D., and Ruth-Ellen M. Grimes. "Polls, Politics and Crime: The 'Law and Order' Issues of the 1960s." *Western Criminology Review* 5, no. 1 (2004): 50–67.

Ludington Daily News, November 6, 1972, 6.

Lukas, J. Anthony. *Common Ground: A Turbulent Decade in the Lives of Three American Families*. New York: Vintage, 1986.

Lydon, Christopher. "Crowd Loves America, Not War." *New York Times*, July 5, 1970, 32.

Lytle, Mark Hamilton. *America's Uncivil Wars: The Sixties Era from Elvis to the Fall of Richard Nixon*. Oxford: Oxford University Press, 2006.

Magruder, Jeb. *An American Life.* New York: Atheneum, 1974.

Mailer, Norman. *St. George and the Godfather.* New York: Signet, 1972.

Mankiewicz, Frank, and Tom Braden. "What Youth Want to Know." *Modesto Bee,* July 29, 1970, 49.

———. "Will Young Vote Dump Nixon?" *Palm Beach Post,* April 24, 1971, A19.

Mannheim, Karl. "The Problem of Generations." In *Essays on the Sociology of Knowledge by Karl Mannheim,* ed. P. Kecskemetied, 287–319. New York: Routledge & Kegan Paul, 1952.

Marcus, Greil. "Books." *Rolling Stone,* December 7, 1968, 24.

Mark, David. *Going Dirty: The Art of Negative Campaigning.* New York: Rowman & Littlefield, 2006.

Marwick, Arthur. *The Sixties: Cultural Revolution in Britain, France, Italy, and the United States, c. 1958–c. 1974.* New York: Bloomsbury Reader, 1998.

Mason, Robert. *Richard Nixon and the Quest for a New Majority.* Chapel Hill: University of North Carolina Press, 2004.

Matusow, Allen. *Nixon's Economy: Booms, Bust, Dollars and Votes.* Lawrence: University Press of Kansas, 1998.

———. *Unraveling of America: A History of Liberalism in the 1960s.* Athens: University of Georgia Press, 2009.

"McCarthy Outlines His 'New Politics.'" *Chicago Tribune,* April 30, 1968, 18.

McGee, Henry W., III. "The GOP Strategy: Organizing Nixon Youth from the Top Down, Rietz Now Has 200,000 Student Volunteers." *Harvard Crimson,* October 24, 1972, https://www.thecrimson.com/article/1972/10/24/the-gop-strategy-organizing-nixon-youth/ (accessed November 11, 2014).

McGinnis, Joe. "The Resale of the President." *New York Times,* September 3, 1972, SM8, 41.

———. *The Selling of the Presidency: The Classical Account of the Packaging of a Candidate.* New York: Simon & Schuster, 1969.

McGirr, Lisa. *Suburban Warriors: The Origins of the New American Right.* Princeton, NJ: Princeton University Press, 2002.

McGovern, George. *Grassroots: The Autobiography of George McGovern.* New York: Random House, 1977.

"McGovern Marshalls Youth." *Palm Beach Post,* February 22, 1971, A2.

McGrory, Mary. "McGovern Drive Lacks McCarthy Spark." *Eugene Register-Guard,* February 23, 1972, A12.

Mears, Walter R. "President on the Stump: Hecklers' Taunts, Jeers Give Weapons to Nixon." *Freelance Star,* October 20, 1970, 1.

Merrin, Mary Beth, and Hugh L. LeBlang. "Parties and Candidates in 1972: Objects of Issue Voting." *Western Political Quarterly* 32, no. 1 (March 1979): 59–69.

Merton, Joe. "The Politics of Symbolism: Richard Nixon's Appeal to White Ethnics and the Frustration of Realignment 1969–72." *European Journal of American Culture* 26, no. 3 (2007): 190.

Miller, Arthur H., and Warren E. Miller. "Issues, Candidates and Partisan Divisions in the 1972 American Presidential Election." *British Journal of*

Political Science 5, no. 4 (October 1975): 393–434, http://www.jstor.org /stable/193436.

Miller, Steven P. *Billy Graham and the Rise of the Republican South.* Philadelphia: University of Pennsylvania Press, 2009.

Miroff, Bruce. *The Liberal's Moment: The McGovern Insurgency and the Identity Crisis of the Democratic Party.* Lawrence: University Press of Kansas, 2007.

"Mitchell Assails 'Stupid' Students." *New York Times,* September 19, 1970, 10.

Mitgang, Herbert. "The New Politics, the Old Casualties." *New York Times,* January 6, 1969, 46.

Montgomery, Ruth. "Bobby's Charm Fades." *Mid Cities News,* July 23, 1967, 4.

Morgan, J. E. "Old Enough to Fight: Old Enough to Vote." *National Education Association* 32 (February 1943): 34.

Moss, Robert. *Creating the New Right Ethnic in the 1970s: The Intersection of Anger and Nostalgia.* Madison, NJ: Fairleigh Dickinson University Press, 2017.

Mount, Ferdinand. "The Wild Grass Chase." *National Review,* January 30, 1968, 82.

"Much Ado about Nothing." *Lipscomb Babbler,* October 3, 1969, 2.

Muhammad, Khalil Gilbran. *The Condemnation of Blackness: Race, Crime and the Urbanization of America.* Cambridge, MA: Harvard University Press, 2011.

Murray, David. "Payoff for Loyalty: Watch Lindsay in 1972." *Youngstown Vindicator,* August 12, 1968, 11.

Musto, David F., and Pamela Korsemeyer. *The Quest for Drug Control.* New Haven, CT: Yale University Press, 2002.

Nash, George H. *The Conservative Intellectual Movement in America since 1945.* Wilmington, DE: Intercollegiate Studies Institute, 1996.

"National Student Lobby Alerts Students to Issues." *Daily Titan* (University of California–Fullerton), October 25, 1972, 5.

Nations Business, September 1972, BOS.

Naughton, James M. "Nelson (Zap) Rockefeller and Richard (Cool) Nixon." *New York Times,* July 28, 1968, 176.

———. "Nixon Is Seeking to Limit His Role as Conciliator." *New York Times,* January 19, 1971, 31.

———. "Nixon, on TV, Attributes Youth Unrest to Loss of 'Old' Values." *New York Times,* March 16, 1971, 20.

———. "Nixon Picks Panel to Find Causes of Campus Unrest." *New York Times,* June 14, 1970, 1.

"A New Independent Majority." *Spartanburg Herald,* November 14, 1972, A6.

Nixon, Richard. *RN: The Memoirs of Richard Nixon.* New York: Simon & Schuster, 1990.

"Nixon Calls for a War on Drugs." *Palm Beach Post,* March 21, 1972, A4.

"Nixon Gaining California Youth Support." *Lodi News-Sentinel,* September 14, 1972, 7.

"Nixon Plans New Image in Campaign." *Spokesman Review,* May 31, 1968, 14.

"Nixon Popularity Is Found High, Especially among Young Voters." *New York Times,* June 5, 1969, 24.

"Nixon Youth Corps Pitches In." *St. Petersburg Independent,* August 11, 1972, A2.

Nordheimer, Jon. "Convention Life: Work, Not Play." *New York Times,* July 15, 1972, 13.

"Not Just a Nixonette." *Eugene Register,* September 7 1972, D3.

Novak, Michael. *The Rise of the Unmeltable Ethnics: Politics and Culture in American Life.* New York: MacMillan, 1972.

Nunley, Janet. "Powell Says, 'Nixon Needs Young.'" *UT Daily Beacon,* September 29, 1972, 1. University of Tennessee Special Collections.

———. "Voting Conquers Apathy." *UT Daily Beacon,* August 1, 1972, 6. University of Tennessee Special Collections.

Oakley, Don. "New Appraisals of Marihuana: Harsh 'Pot' Laws under Fire." *Prescott Evening Courier,* November 3, 1969, 6.

Packer, George. "The Decade Nobody Knows." *New York Times,* June 10, 2001, http://www.nytimes.com/books/01/06/10/reviews/010610.10packert.html (accessed October 15, 2014).

Paletz, David L., and Martha Elson. "Television Coverage of Presidential Conventions: Now You See It, Now You Don't." *Political Science Quarterly* 91, no. 1 (Spring 1976): 129.

Patterson, James T. *Restless Giant: The United States from Watergate to Bush v. Gore.* New York: Oxford University Press, 2005.

"People Want Safety on the Streets: Nixon Says Law and Order Concerns Americans Most." *Reading Eagle* (Reading, PA), October 27, 1968, 21.

Perlstein, Rick. *Before the Storm: Barry Goldwater and the Unmaking of the American Consensus.* New York: Hill & Wang, 2001.

———. *Nixonland: The Rise of a President and the Fracturing of America.* New York: Scribner, 2008.

Perry, James. *Us and Them: How the Press Covered the 1972 Election.* New York: Clarkson N. Potter, 1973.

Phillips, Kevin. *The Emerging Republican Majority.* New Rochelle, NY: Arlington House, 1969.

———. "How Nixon Will Win." *New York Times,* August 6, 1972, SM8.

"Politics: GOP Reach to Youth." *Time,* January 31, 1972, http://content.time.com/time/magazine/0,9263,7601720131,00.html (accessed November 11, 2011).

Ponte, Powell. "Split in the New Right." *Los Angeles Image,* September 19–October 2, 1969, 7.

"Pot Penalty Recommendations Called 'Sane,' 'Frightening.'" *Sarasota Journal,* March 22, 1972, B9.

"President's Youth Advisor Is Quitting, Nixon 'Image' with Young Dissenters Said Bad." *Florence Times-Daily,* May 5, 1970, 15.

Prior, Markus. "The Incumbent in the Living Room: The Rise of Television and the Incumbency Advantage in U.S. House Elections." *Journal of Politics* 68, no. 3 (August 2006): 657–673.

"Redundant Commission" (editorial). *New York Times,* June 16, 1970, 46.

Reeves, Richard. *President Nixon: Alone in the White House.* New York: Simon & Schuster, 2001.

Reich, Charles. *The Greening of America: How the Youth Revolution Is Trying to Make America Livable.* New York: Random House, 1970.

"The Religious Heritage–Reader's Digest–Bob Hope–Billy Graham–Walt Disney Productions Complex." *Christian Century,* July 1, 1971, editorial page.

"Replies to the Yammies." *Cornell Daily Sun,* October 4, 1972, 4.

"Report from White House Youth Conference." *Rolling Stone,* May 21, 1971, 19.

"Republicans Wooing the Youth Vote." *Time,* July 31, 1972, http://content.time.com/time/magazine/0,9263,7601720731,00.html (accessed October 12, 2011).

Rietz, Ken. *Winning Campaigns, Losing Sight, Gaining Insight.* Herndon, VA: Mascot Books, 2016.

"Rights of Youth Questioned." *Lipscomb Babbler,* May 21, 1971, 2.

Riguer, Leah Wright. *The Loneliness of the Black Republican: Pragmatic Politics and the Pursuit of Power.* Princeton, NJ: Princeton University Press, 2015.

Ripley, Anthony. "Conservative Forces Take Almost All Young Republican Offices and Staunchly Back Nixon's Policies." *New York Times,* June 27, 1971, 21.

———. "National Students Parley Finds Unity Only in Dissatisfaction." *New York Times,* August 20, 1968, 23.

Ripon Society and Clifford Brown Jr. *Jaws of Victory: The Game-Plan Politics of 1972, the Crisis of the Republican Party, and the Future of the Constitution.* Boston: Little, Brown, 1973.

Robbins, William J. "Congress Gets Nixon's Bill to Curb Drug Abuses." *New York Times,* July 16, 1969, 51.

Roberts, Steven V. "72 Strategists See the Youth Vote as Vital." *New York Times,* December 26, 1971, 45.

———. "If You Are Unregistered, Expect Democrats to Call." *New York Times,* August 7, 1972, 20.

———. "A New Trend Seen in Berkeley Vote: Radical Victories Foreseen in Other College Towns." *New York Times,* April 8, 1971, 26.

———. "Role of 'Invisible Youths' in 1972 Politics Reviewed." *Nashua Telegraph,* March 22, 1972, 24.

———. "Youths Meet on 1972 Drive, and Politicians Pay Heed." *New York Times,* December 5, 1971, 65.

Robertson, Nan. "House Youth Conference Proves to Be Anti-establishment." *New York Times,* April 22, 1971, 28.

———. "Youth Proposals Backed by Nixon." *New York Times,* April 16, 1972, 31.

Rome, Adam. "'Give Earth a Chance': The Environmental Movement in the Sixties." *Journal of American History,* September 2003, 525.

Rosen, Sanford Jay. "The Greening of the Scranton Commission." *AAUP Bulletin* 57, no. 4 (December 1971): 506–510.

Rosenbaum, Ron. "I March with the Young Voters for the President." *Village Voice,* August 31, 1972, 8.

Rosenthal, Jack. "Poll Hints Youths May Back Nixon." *New York Times,* July 23, 1972, 40.

Rossinow, Doug. *The Politics of Authenticity: Liberalism, Christianity and the New Left in America.* New York: Columbia University Press, 1998.

"Ross Is Named to DECA Post." *Boca Raton News,* April 16, 1972, A3.

Rossman, Michael. "The Sound of Marching, Charging Feet." *Rolling Stone* 30 (April 5, 1969): 6.

Roszak, Theodore. *The Making of a Counter Culture: Reflections on the Technocratic Society and Its Youthful Opposition.* Berkeley: University of California Press, 1995.

Rove, Karl. *Courage and Consequences: My Life as a Conservative in the Fight.* New York: Simon & Schuster, 2010.

Rowan, Carl. "Nixon's Coronation Need Not Be Boring." *Eugene Register Guard,* August 21, 1972, A12.

"Rules a Result of Immaturity." *Lipscomb Babbler,* December 5, 1969, 2.

Rusher, William A. *The Rise of the Right.* New York: National Review Books, 1993.

Ryan, Terry. "Both Sides Aim for New Young Voters." *Tri-city Herald* (Richland, WA), August 15, 1972, 5.

———. "Edge to Dems in Youth Vote." *Chicago Tribune,* August 17, 1972, 6.

———. "Nixon Forces Confident They'll Win Half Youth Vote." *Sarasota Herald Tribune,* August 16, 1972, A5.

———. "Youth Vote Impact Shows Up in Elections throughout the US." *Free Lance Star* (Fredericksburg, VA), November 10, 1972, 1.

Scammon, Richard M., and Ben J. Wattenberg. *The Real Majority: An Extraordinary Examination of the American Electorate.* New York: Coward-McCann, 1970.

Schmidt, Dana Adams. "President Orders Wider Drug Fight; Asks $155-Million." *New York Times,* June 18, 1971, 1.

Schneider, Gregory L. *Cadres for Conservatism: Young Americans for Freedom and the Rise of the Contemporary Right.* New York: New York University Press, 1999.

Schoen, Douglas E. "Stumping the Airwaves with Candidate McGovern." *Harvard Crimson,* November 3, 1972, http://www.thecrimson.com/article /1972/11/3/stumping-the-airwaves-with-candidate-mcgovern/ (accessed September 2012).

Schoenwald, Jonathan. *A Time for Choosing: The Rise of Modern American Conservatism.* New York: Oxford University Press, 2001.

Schrag, Peter. *The End of the American Future.* New York: Simon & Schuster, 1973.

Schulman, Bruce. *The Seventies: The Great Shift in American Culture, Society, and Politics.* Cambridge, MA: Da Capo, 2002.

Schulman, Bruce, and Julian Zelizer. *Rightward Bound: Making America Conservative in the 1970s.* Cambridge, MA: Harvard University Press, 2008.

Seagull, Louis M. "The Youth Vote and Change in American Politics." *Annals of the American Academy of Political and Social Science* 397 ("Seven Polarizing Issues in America Today," September 1971): 88–96.

Self, Robert. *All in the Family: The Realignment of American Democracy since the 1960s.* New York: Hill and Wang, 2013.

Semple, Robert, Jr. "Miami Beach Tent City a Carnival of Protesters." *New York Times,* August 22, 1972, A1, 1.

———. "Nixon Aides Plan Policy for Youth." *New York Times,* December 8, 1969, 54.

———. "Nixon to Form Youth Panels in All 50 States to Advise on Draft." *New York Times,* June 7, 1969, 2.

———. "Youths for Nixon Contrast with Protestors in Park." *New York Times*, August 22, 1972, A16, 1.

"Senate Bill Includes Complex School Aid." *Miami News*, June 14, 1972, A4.

"Senator Brock Concerned with Youth Vote." *Times-News* (Hendersonville, NC), May 3, 1971, 9.

Shamberg, Michael. *Guerrilla Television*. New York: Holt, Rinehart, & Winston, 1971.

Shaw, Bernard. "20th Century Brings Changes to the American Voter." December 28, 1999, http://archives.cnn.com/1999/ALLPOLITICS/stories/12/28/millenium.voter/index.html (accessed October 20, 2012).

Sheehan, Eileen. "Nixon Appeals to Youthful Voters at Rally Near Miami." *New York Times*, August 23, 1972, 27.

Shiel, Mark. "Banal and Magnificent Space in *Electra Glide Blue* (1973): An Allegory of the Nixon Era." *Cinema Journal* 46, no. 2 (Winter 2007): 91–116.

Shirley, Craig. *Reagan's Revolution: The Untold Story of the Campaign That Started It All*. Nashville, TN: Thomas Nelson, 2005.

Shirley, Craig. *Rendezvous with Destiny: Ronald Reagan and the Campaign that Changed America*. Wilmington, DE: Intercollegiate Studies Institute, 2014.

Sica, Alan, and Stephen Turner, eds. *The Disobedient Generation: Social Theorists in the Sixties*. Chicago: University of Chicago Press, 2005.

Skrentny, John David. *Ironies of Affirmative Action: Politics, Culture, and Justice in America*. Chicago: University of Chicago Press, 1996.

Small, Melvin. *Covering Dissent: The Media and the Anti–Vietnam War Movement*. New Brunswick, NJ: Rutgers University Press, 1994.

Smith, Richard, *On His Own Terms: A Life of Nelson Rockefeller*. New York: Random House, 2014.

Southwick, Thomas P. "Campus Unrest: Which Tack for President's Commission?" *Science*, n.s., 169, no. 3950 (September 11, 1970): 1061–1063.

"Speech from California's Survival Fair." *Rag* 4, no. 21 (April 13, 1970): 13.

"State Attorney Says War on Drugs Succeeding." *Sarasota Herald-Tribune*, October 7, 1968, 2.

Stenberg, Arnold. "The Creative Society: Where the Action Is." *New Guard*, Campus Issue, March 1967, 12.

Stone, Harvey. "The G.O.P. Follies." *Rag* 2, no. 36 (August 15, 1968): 1.

"Student Leaders Becoming Stereotyped; Moderation Often Fails to Be Considered." *Lipscomb Babbler*, November 1, 1968, 2.

"Student NEA Beefs Up Political Image." Guest column: National Education Association. *Florence Times Daily*, August 29, 1970, 4.

"Student Radicalism Changes Faces." *Lipscomb Babbler*, January 14, 1972, 2.

"Student Rebellions Spread as Revolts Achieve Success." *Lipscomb Babbler*, February 21, 1969, 2.

"Students of America!" *Esquire Magazine* 78, no. 3 (September 1972): 75.

"Student Violence—a Means to What End?" *Lipscomb Babbler*, May 22, 1970, 2.

Sugrue, Thomas, and John Skrentny. "The White Ethnic Strategy." In *Rightward Bound: Making America Conservative in the 1970s*, ed. Bruce Schulman and Julian Zelizer, 191. Cambridge, MA: Harvard University Press, 2008.

Suri, Jeremi. *Power and Protest: Global Revolution and the Power of Détente.* Cambridge, MA: Harvard University Press, 2002.

"Talk of the Nation: Kent State Shooting Divided Campus and Country." National Public Radio. May 3, 2010, https://www.npr.org/templates/story/story.php?storyId=126480349 (accessed May 5, 2010).

"Tammany Tiger Finds That Its Cubs Can Bite." *New York Times,* July 11, 1969, 42.

Teague, Randal Cornell. "Environmental Pollution and YAF." *New Guard,* April 1970, 10.

"Television: Electronic Politics; The Image Game." *Time,* September 21, 1970, http://content.time.com/time/magazine/article/0,9171,942277,00.html (accessed November 10, 2012).

"Tennessee's Senator Gore Faces Toughest Race of Political Life." *Sarasota Journal,* October 6, 1970, A8.

"Texas Political Trail: Absentee Record Set." *Victoria Advocate,* May 3, 1972, B12.

"Textual Highlights of Republican Platform." *Gettysburg Times,* August 5, 1968, 3.

Thimmesch. Nick. "Hold Back the Pigeons!" *Telegraph-Herald* (Dubuque, IA), January 17, 1973, 6.

———. "McGovern to Try to Straighten Out His Blurred Image." *Observer-Reporter* (Washington, PA), September 28, 1972, A4.

Thomas, Charles. "The Scales Overturned: Kent State and American Business." http://speccoll.library.kent.edu/4May70/scales.html#_ftnref92.

Thompson, Hunter S. *Fear and Loathing: On the Campaign Trail, '72.* New York: Warner Books, 1973.

Thorburn, Wayne. *A Generation Awakes: Young Americans for Freedom and the Creation of the Conservative Movement.* Ottawa, IL: Jameson Books, 2010.

Thorburn, Wayne J. "Agenda for New Politics." *New Guard,* October 1971, 12.

———. "The Unrepresentative Youth." *New Guard,* Summer 1971, 18.

Tiede, Tom. "Youth Vote, Youth Vote, Who's Got the Youth Vote?" *Oscala-Star Banner,* August 14, 1972, A10.

"Times Survey, Defections in Party Face McGovern." *New York Times,* June 9, 1972, 1.

"Top Notch Orator Wins Dallas Trip." *Deseret News,* May 2, 1969, C2.

Touscher, DeMar. "Student Polls Come On Strong for Bobby." *Deseret News,* May 16, 1968, A11.

"Trend toward Nixon Not Conservatism." *Cavalier Daily* (University of Virginia), October 20, 1972, 6.

Troy, Gill. *Morning in America: How Ronald Reagan Invented the 1980's.* Princeton, NJ: Princeton University Press, 2005.

Tucson Dailey Citizen, August 16, 1976.

Tully, Andrew. "Student Aid Bill Opens Door to Cheating, Fraud." *Beaver County Times,* June 29, 1972, A6.

Turner, John G. *Bill Bright and Campus Crusade for Christ: The Renewal of Evangelicalism in Postwar America.* Chapel Hill: University of North Carolina Press, 2008.

Turner, Wallace. "Humphrey Aides Assail McGovern: Coast Managers Try to Tarnish Dakotans Image." *New York Times,* May 14, 1972, 37.

"Use of LSD Wanes on College Campuses but Price of Education Is Much Too High." *Lipscomb Babbler*, February 28, 1969, 5.

Van Gelder, Lawrence. "Survey Shows College Students Back McCarthy over Kennedy." *New York Times*, March 17, 1968, 1.

Vittoria, Stephen, dir. *One Bright Shining Moment: The Forgotten Summer of George McGovern*. 2005. Los Angeles, CA: Street Legal Cinema, 2006, DVD.

"Volpe to Give Initial Seconding Speech as Nixon Is Proposed for Candidate." *Lewiston Evening Journal* (Lewiston-Auburn, ME), August 7, 1968, 21.

"Vote at 18 and Draft Reforms Backed by Violence Commission." *New York Times*, November 26, 1969, 29.

"Vote at 18 Described as Danger to Nixon." *Milwaukee Journal*, June 29, 1971, 8.

Vote by Groups, 1952–1956. http://www.gallup.com/poll/9451/election-polls-vote-groups-19521956.aspx (accessed July 1, 2014).

Wainwright, Loudon. "One More Try for the Heights." *Life Magazine*, March 1, 1968, 60–68.

Waldron, Martin. "Chicago Police, 'Best in World,' Reject Criticism." *New York Times*, August 30, 1968, 15.

Warren, J. Louis S., ed. *American Environmental History*. Carlton, AU: Blackwell, 2003.

Washington, Patrick Anderson. "Taste of Success." *New York Times*, May 14, 1972, SM13, 39.

Waterman, Richard W., Robert Wright, and Gilbert St. Clair, eds. *The Image-Is-Everything Presidency: Dilemmas in American Leadership*. Boulder, CO: Westview, 1999.

Weems, Robert E., and Lewis A. Randolph. "The Ideological Origins of Nixon's 'Black Capitalism' Initiative." *Review of Black Political Economy*, Summer 2001, 58.

Weil, Gordon. *The Long Shot: George McGovern Runs for President*. New York: W. W. Norton, 1973.

Weiner, Rex. "Caution on the Left." *New York Times*, July 27, 1972, 31.

Wenner, Jann. "Musicians Reject New Political Exploiters." *Rolling Stone* 1, no. 10 (May 11, 1968): 1.

Whitaker, John C. *Striking a Balance: Environment and Natural Resources Policy in the Nixon-Ford Years*. Washington, DC: American Enterprise Institute Press, 1987.

White, Theodore. *The Making of the President, 1972*. New York: Bantam, 1973.

"White House Plans for Youth Parley Criticized by Bloc." *New York Times*, March 20, 1971, 22.

"Why I'm Voting for Nixon." *Chimes* (Calvin College), September 1972, 10.

Wicker, Tom. "The Bitter Senate Struggle in Tennessee." *St. Petersburg Times*, October 21, 1970, A14.

———. "In the Nation: The New Politics." *New York Times*, March 21, 1968, 46.

Wiener, Jon. *Gimme' Some Truth: The John Lennon FBI Files*. Berkeley: University of California Press, 1999.

Willis, Henry. "Nixon Aide's Job: Debate with the Demos." *Eugene Register Guard*, October 22, 1972, A13.

Wills, Gary. "The Forgotten Promises to Youth." *St. Petersburg Times*, January 25, 1971, A14.

————. How Nixon Used the Media, Billy Graham and the Good Lord to Rap with Students at Tennessee U." *Esquire*, September 1970, 119–122, 179–180.

Willworth, James. *Clive: Inside the Record Business.* New York: William Morrow, 1975.

Windt, Theodore. *Presidents and Protesters: Political Rhetoric in the 1960s.* Tuscaloosa: University of Alabama Press, 1990.

Witcover, Jules. *Very Strange Bed Fellows: The Short and Unhappy Marriage of Richard Nixon and Spiro Agnew.* New York: Public Affairs, 2007.

Wittner, Dale. "Young Voters Surge to Enroll in the System." *Life Magazine*, October 15, 1971, 28.

Wolfe, Sheila. "GOP Has Something for All." *Chicago Tribune*, August 22, 1972, 5.

Woodward, Bob, and Carl Bernstein. *All the President's Men: The Greatest Reporting Story of All Time.* New York: Simon & Schuster, 2014.

Wooten, James T. "Unexpected 'Preview' Provides a Jolt to a Hitherto Predictable Convention." *New York Times*, August 23, 1972, 26.

"Young Voters Adding Spice." *Lakeland Ledger* (Lakeland, FL), August 23, 1972, A8.

"Youths End 'Fairest' Conference." *Pittsburgh Press*, April 23, 1971, 17.

"Youths Say G.O.P. Convention Was Irrelevant to Their World." *New York Times*, August 19, 1968, 30.

"Youth: The Cheerleaders." *Time*, September 4, 1972, http://content.time.com /time/magazine/0,9263,7601720904,00.html (accessed October 11, 2013).

Zelizer, Julian. *Arsenal of Democracy: The Politics of National Security—from World War II to the War on Terrorism.* New York: Basic Books, 2010.

Zoller, John. "On Student Unrest." *Triton Times* (UCSD) 11, no. 8 (October 23, 1970): 1.

Index

Young Voters for the President (cont.)
of, 178, 179 (photo), 180, 184, 192,
206, 213; legal assistance program
of, 206; loyalty of, 146; McGovern
and, 190; members of, 184, 187
(photo), 207, 215; Nixon and, 152;
Nixonettes and, 199; office, 153
(photo); photo of, 200; politics and,
166, 184–185; protests and, 190;
rallies and, 211, 214; research by,
195; RNC and, 188, 205, 208; square
chic and, 235; steering committee
of, 206; strategy of, 148–154, 160,
220; structure of, 148–154; student
politics and, 168; successes for, 172;
support from, 208–209; voter registration and, 183; women's role in,
213; workers and, 150; youth organizations and, 158; youth politics and,
174, 267–268; YR and, 158, 159
youth: image and, 214–217; influence
of, 11; media and, 202–205;
religious, 101; selling with, 202
Youth Advisory Boards, 79
Youth Advisory Commission, 78, 79, 80
Youth Advisory Groups, 79
Youth and Media Services, 105
Youth Appreciation Luau, 209
Youth Ball, 1
youth campaign, 6, 9, 10, 32, 68, 214,
221, 231, 245, 249; appeal of, 36;
benefits of, 254
Youth Citizenship Fund (YCF), 119,
120, 140; poster for, 67 (fig.)
Youth Conference, 100
Youth Council, 97, 235, 238
Youth Council Act, 97
youth culture, 47, 205, 263–264;
permissive, 7; radical-liberal, 38
Youth Disco, 262
Youth Division, CRP, 26, 150, 238
Youth for Brock, 8
Youth for Ford, 227, 230, 233, 239,
245, 266
Youth for Goldwater for Vice-President,
20

Youth for Ike-Nixon campaign, 19
Youth for New Politics, 143
Youth for Nixon, 26, 27, 28, 175, 191
Youth for Reagan, 221, 233, 242, 244,
246, 247, 253, 254, 260, 261, 262,
264; benefits of, 248; budget crisis
and, 258; Burma-Shave and, 259;
controlling, 256; coordinators for,
250–251, 257; described, 256–257;
meeting with, 230; members of, 5;
movement conservatives and, 230;
news bureau, 256; plan by, 249;
public relations and, 259; resources
for, 243; square style of, 221; training
schools for, 250; vandalism by,
255–256
Youth for Reagan Canvass Manual, 247
Youth Franchise Coalition, 63, 65, 66
Youth Gala, 262
"Youth Manifesto," 103
youth politics, 3, 11, 19–25, 31–36,
48, 62, 70, 110–120, 122–126, 128,
189, 215, 217, 245–248, 251, 258;
anti-Nixon, 64; antiwar, 38; apathy
for, 241; centrality of, 6; as electoral
concern, 106; GOP and, 4, 263, 265;
history of, 185, 268; independents
and, 154–168; marijuana and, 48,
51; media and, 137; mobilization
of, 83, 268; political elites and,
95; potential of, 86; radical, 141;
scholarship on, 146; stressing,
188; voter registration and, 182;
Watergate and, 218, 219, 221–226
"youth problem," 7, 36, 38, 40, 43, 61,
77, 79, 80, 88, 91, 97, 100, 142, 185,
219; acquiescence on, 64; efforts
on, 82, 84, 103; emergence of, 31;
environment/industry and, 72–76;
stance on, 66; structural causes for,
68
Youth Rally, 42, 43, 83
youth revolt, 2, 36, 40, 75, 124, 145,
263
Youth Services Agency, 25
Youth Speakers Bureau, 105